FACILITATING GROUP COMMUNICATION IN CONTEXT:
INNOVATIONS AND APPLICATIONS WITH NATURAL GROUPS

VOLUME ONE: FACILITATING GROUP
CREATION, CONFLICT, AND CONVERSATION

FACILITATING GROUP COMMUNICATION IN CONTEXT:
INNOVATIONS AND APPLICATIONS WITH NATURAL GROUPS

VOLUME ONE: FACILITATING GROUP
CREATION, CONFLICT, AND CONVERSATION

Edited by

Lawrence R. Frey
University of Colorado at Boulder

 HAMPTON PRESS, INC.
CRESSKILL, NEW JERSEY

Printed in the United States of America

Library of Congress Cataloging-in-Publication Data

Facilitating group communication in context : innovations and applications
   with natural groups / edited by Lawrence R. Frey.
       p. cm.
   Includes bibliographic references and index.
   ISBN 1-57273-652-6 (v. 1) -- ISBN 1-57273-653-4 (v. 1) -- ISBN
   1-57273-614-3 (v. 2) -- ISBN 1-57273-615-1 (v. 2)
     1. Small groups. 2. Communication in small groups. 3. Group
   decision making. I. Frey, Lawrence R.

   HM736..F33 2005
   302.3,4--dc22
                                                    2005050348

Hampton Press, Inc.
23 Broadway
Cresskill, NJ 07626

CONTENTS
VOLUME ONE

INTRODUCTION

FACILITATING GROUP COMMUNICATION IN CONTEXT: INNOVATIONS AND APPLICATIONS WITH NATURAL GROUPS

Lawrence R. Frey
University of Colorado at Boulder

The role of groups in our lives has never been more apparent and important. Every segment of society—from families to classrooms, workplaces, community organizations, governments, and international collaborations—relies on groups. As Frey (1994a) explained:

> The small group is clearly the tie that binds, the nucleus that holds society together. Groups of workers dispose of garbage, fly airplanes, fight fires, and grow most of the food that feeds the nation. Parties in dispute often seek to resolve their differences through mediation and arbitration, while a group of peers decides the legal fate in many criminal and civil trials. Government committees decide what policy proposals will reach the floor of the Senate and House of Representatives, while political action groups (PACs) work furiously behind the scenes to influence these decisions, and the Supreme Court interprets the constitutionality of the laws passed. The army, navy, air force, and marines train men and women in combat teams, while representatives from nations at war negotiate peace settlements in group meetings. (pp. ix-x)

1

Given the pervasiveness and significance of groups to society, it is no wonder that Poole (1998) and many others have claimed that people essentially are group animals and that the small group is *the* fundamental unit of social organization.

As just one example of the importance of groups, consider the business world, where Doyle and Strauss (1976) estimated (some time ago, it should be noted) that 11 million group meetings take place every day in the United States, with studies showing that managers spend about 60% of their time in those group meetings (Mintzberg, 1973; Mosvick & Nelson, 1987) and that organizations with 500 or more people spend approximately 75% of their time preparing, executing, and concluding meetings (van Vree, 1999; for histories of meetings from the early Middle Ages to the present, see Tracy & Dimock, 2004; van Vree, 1999). In a rather scary prediction, Seibold (1979) pointed out that "if we attend just four hours of work or civic meetings per week, we will have spent over 9,000 hours in meetings during an average life-time—more than one year of our life in meetings!" (p. 4).

The general reason for living, learning, and working in groups is because groups potentially are more effective than individuals. Group decision making, for instance, can result in 40%-50% increases in productivity over individual decision making ("The Payoff from Teamwork," 1989), especially when "performance requires multiple skills, judgments, and experiences" (Katzenbach & Smith, 1993, p. 9). The specific reasons for why groups can be more effective than individuals are well documented (see, e.g., Hare, 1994; Maier, 1967; Poole, 1991; Shaw, 1981) and include, according to Seibold and Krikorian (1997), the ability of groups to:

1. Search out and pool greater amounts of information.
2. Bring to bear on the problem a greater number of approaches and greater (collective) knowledge.
3. Critically examine presumptions and correct errors that individuals might make if they were working alone.
4. Combine individual contributions, producing more in the aggregate than individuals could working alone.
5. Anticipate the consequences of their decisions and to adjust them accordingly or to facilitate their acceptance outside the group.
6. Stimulate and motivate members through their social dimension.
7. Increase members' commitment to the decision they help make.
   (p. 274)

Unfortunately, however, as most of us know only too well from personal experience, when left on their own to engage in naturally occurring ("free") discussion, groups often flounder and perform less effectively than they should. The problems with and the disadvantages of working in groups have been well documented. Some of these problems, such as group work often taking longer and costing more than individual work, probably are unavoidable and acceptable. Other problems, however, result because individual members of groups engage in dysfunctional behaviors, such as "social loafing," where individuals reduce their effort when working in a group compared to the amount they would exert working alone (see Harkins, Latané, & Williams, 1980; Harkins & Petty, 1982; Jackson & Williams, 1985; Latané, Williams, & Harkins, 1979a, 1979b), or "free riding," where individuals obtain the benefits of being in a group but do not put in their fair share of the effort (Albanese & Van Feet, 1985; Issac, Walker, & Thomas, 1984; Oliver & Walker, 1984; Olson, 1965), which often leads to the "sucker effect" of other members reducing their efforts (Kerr, 1983). Still other problems occur because of dysfunctional collective processes in which an entire group engages, such as group members *not* (a) using their time efficiently (Holsti, 1971; Langer, Wapner, & Werner, 1961; Poole, 1991); (b) sharing relevant information (Collaros & Anderson, 1969; Propp, 1999; Stasser, 1992; Stasser & Titus, 1985; for a recent review of collective information sharing, or lack thereof, in groups, see Wittenbaum, Hollingshead, & Botero, 2004); (c) encouraging minority and alternative viewpoints (Alderton & Frey, 1983, 1986; Schacter, 1968); (d) managing conflict effectively (Folger, Poole, & Stutman, 2001); (e) developing high-quality relationships (Keyton, 1999); (f) balancing social and task needs (Hewes, 1986); and (g) engaging in planning (Hackman & Kaplan, 1974; Shure, Rogers, Larsen, & Tassone, 1962) and functional decision making (Hirokawa, 1982, 1983, 1985, 1987, 1988; for recent overviews of the functional perspective, see Hollingshead et al., 2005; Wittenbaum et al., 2004; for a recent meta-analysis of the research literature from this perspective, see Orlitzky & Hirokawa, 2001). Too often, groups demonstrate, instead, tendencies such as premature idea evaluation (Collaros & Anderson, 1969), solution orientation (J. Hall & Watson, 1970; Shure et al., 1962), and decision making (Maier, 1970); groupthink ("a mode of thinking that people engage in when they are deeply involved in a cohesive in-group, when the members' strivings for unanimity override their motivation to realistically appraise alternative courses of action," Janis, 1972, p. 9; see also Janis, 1982; Janis & Mann, 1977); and choice shifts/group polarization (individuals' average post-discussion positions being more extreme than, but in the same direction as, their average prediscussion positions; see Bernstein & Vinokur, 1975, 1977; Myers & Lamm, 1975, 1976).

Groups, thus, often do not live up to their potential, a tendency that is the basis for an entire genre of jokes about the inefficiency of groups and group meetings (see Peter, 1989), including: "To kill time, a meeting is the perfect weapon," "A committee is a group that keeps minutes and wastes hours," "A committee is a group of the unfit, appointed by the unwilling, that meets to do the unnecessary," "A committee is a group of individuals that can do nothing alone except meet as a group to decide that nothing can be done," and "A camel is a horse designed by a group." As Seibold and Krikorian (1997) pointed out:

> These jokes reflect what our own experiences sometimes tell us. Meetings can be slow ("kill time"), inefficient ("keep minutes and wastes hours"), and frustrating ("to do the unnecessary"). Meetings also can make us feel powerless individually ("a group of individuals that can do nothing alone") and collectively ("meet as a group to decide that nothing can be done"). And meetings can produce unpredictable and flawed outcomes ("a camel is a horse"). (p. 274)

Given all of these problems with groups and group meetings, it is no wonder that someone humorously said that "on judgment day, the Lord will divide people by telling those on His/Her right hand to enter the kingdom of heaven and those on His/Her left to break into small groups."

The costs of dysfunctional and ineffective groups, however, are no laughing matter. The costs of simply preparing for and conducting groups meetings often are high, with the 3M Corporation, for instance, estimating that group meetings cost the company $78.8 million annually (The 3M Meeting Management Team & Drew, 1994), but the costs of dysfunctional and ineffective groups are staggering, with Smith's (1991) survey of organizations finding that ineffective group meetings resulted in $37 billion being wasted annually.

There also are costs associated with problematic groups at the individual level, with people demonstrating significant dissatisfaction with groups (see Schwartzman, 1989). Monge, McSween, and Wyer (1989), for instance, found that:

> One third of meeting participants feel they have little or no influence on the outcome of decision . . . feel mild, strong or great pressure to publicly express opinions in meeting with which they privately disagree . . . and a quarter of meeting participants say they discuss irrelevant issues 11% to 25% of the time, or more often. (p. iii)

Such feelings and experiences have led many people to develop negative attitudes toward groups, or what Sorensen (1981) called "grouphate" (see also Frey, 1997; Keyton & Frey, 2002; Keyton, Harmon, & Frey, 1996).

Although many people might prefer to work alone because of the problems associated with groups, the fact is, as previously discussed, that working in groups is unavoidable. Lumsden and Lumsden (1993) responded to the oft-heard "I'd really rather work alone." with "Forget it, the twenty-first century works in groups" (p. 3). Given that people cannot live without groups, they need to learn how to live effectively within them. This means doing something about the problems that lead groups not to live up to their potential benefits, which means offering groups help and guidance, especially in terms of group members communicating better. In short, people need "group communication facilitation."

GROUP COMMUNICATION FACILITATION

The term *facilitation* is defined in the *Merriam-Webster Dictionary* as "to make easier"; hence, *group facilitation* can be defined as any meeting procedure, technique, or practice that makes group life easier. *Meeting procedures* are "sets of rules or guidelines which specify how a group should organize its process to achieve a particular goal" (Poole, 1991, p. 55).

Over the years, there has been a tremendous growth in the creation of group facilitation meeting procedures. Indeed, the sheer number of texts devoted to offering advice about and procedures for facilitating groups just since the start of the new millennium is overwhelming (see, e.g., Abernathy & Reardon, 2002; Adams & Means, 2005; Arnold, 2003; Bendaly, 2000; Bens, 2005a, 2005b; Booth, 2000; Bulik, 2000; Cameron, 2001; Chambers, 2002; Christian & Tubesing, 2004; Dale & Conant, 2004; Eller, 2004; Ghais, 2005; Gottlieb, 2003; Griffen-Wesiner, 2005; Havergal & Edmonstone, 2003; Hayden, Frederick, & Smith, 2002; Hogan, 2002, 2003; Howick, Daily, & Sprik, 2002; Iacofano, 2001; Kausen, 2003; Lambert & Meyers, 2004; Landale & Douglas, 2002; Matricardi & McLarty, 2006; McCain & Tobey, 2004; Micale, 2003; Miller, 2004; Priest, Gass, & Gillis, 2000; Putz, 2002; Rees, 2001, 2004, 2005; Rohnke, 2002, Schuman, 2005; Schwarz, 2002, 2005; Weaver & Farrell, 2003; Wilkinson, 2004). Some of these procedures—such as assigning a devil's advocate, brainstorming, and Robert's Rules of Order—have become part of group members' everyday lexicon and facilitation toolkit, whereas others—such as the Delphi method, Interactive Management, and the nominal group technique—are understood and implemented primarily by experts who consult with groups.

There is general agreement about why these group facilitation procedures, in theory, work. By focusing and guiding group members' practices in structured ways, facilitation procedures reduce the chances of engaging in faulty processes and harness the strengths of groups in at least nine ways:

1. Procedures coordinate members' thinking.
2. Procedures provide a set of objective ground rules.
3. Procedures protect groups against their own bad habits.
4. Procedures capitalize on the strengths of groups.
5. Procedures balance member participation.
6. Procedures surface and help manage conflicts.
7. Procedures give groups a sense of closure in their work.
8. Procedures make groups reflect on their meeting process.
9. Procedures empower groups. (Poole, 1991, pp. 75-80)

One important reason why such benefits accrue is because virtually all of these facilitation procedures, in one way or another, structure the *communication* that takes place in groups—that is, "the processes by which verbal and nonverbal messages are used to create and share meaning" (Frey, Botan, & Kreps, 2000, p. 28). The reason for focusing on communication in groups, as Frey (1994a) pointed out, is because "although many factors certainly affect groups, including members' personality traits, the nature of the tasks groups confront, the resources available to them, and so on, communication is the lifeblood that flows through the veins of groups" (p. x). Unfortunately, however, as already discussed, all too often, "when groups are left on their own, those veins become clogged, communication ceases to flow, and the result is that groups flounder and perform less effectively than possible (Frey, 1995a)" (Sunwolf & Frey, 2005). *Group communication facilitation*, therefore, involves using meeting procedures to make it easier for groups to interact and exchange messages for the purposes of creating and sharing meaning. By structuring group communication in particular ways, facilitation unclogs blocked arteries and creates new veins for communication to flow smoothly among members.

However, although many group communication facilitation procedures have been developed, and theoretical rationales for their success have been articulated, there has not been a corresponding increase in research about the use and effects of these procedures (see, e.g., Frey, 1995a; Niederman, 1996; Pavitt, 1993). Research simply has lagged behind practical developments and advice giving.

What research does exist about group communication facilitation was divided by Frey (1995a) into three historical time periods (see also Sunwolf & Frey, 2005). The first period, from about 1890-1945, focused on whether the presence of others in a group had facilitative or inhibitive effects on individuals (e.g., Allport, 1920; Pessin & Husband, 1993; Travis, 1925, 1928; Triplett, 1897; Weston & English, 1926) and whether group discussion was superior to individual problem solving (e.g., Barton, 1926; Dashiell, 1935; Gurnee, 1937; Jenness, 1932; Marston, 1924; Shaw, 1932;

Thorndike, 1938; Timmons, 1939; Watson, 1928). The second historical period, from 1945-1970, focused on the facilitative and inhibitive effects of (a) group meeting procedures, such as Dewey's (1910) "reflective thinking pattern" (e.g., Pyron, 1964; Pyron & Sharp, 1963; Sharp & Millikin, 1964) and Osborn's (1957) "brainstorming" technique (for a review, see Lamm & Trommsdorff, 1973); (b) imposing on groups various "communication networks," "the arrangement or pattern of communication channels among the members of a group" (Shaw, 1981, p. 453), such as the wheel, circle, chair, or "Y," that restricted how group members could communicate with one another; (c) group leadership communication styles and behaviors (e.g., Blake & Mouton, 1968; Lewin & Lippitt, 1938; Lewin, Lippitt, & White, 1939; Lippitt, 1939, 1940; Lippitt & White, 1952); and (d) whole-group formats for facilitating group communication, such as "focus groups" (Merton, 1946; Merton, Fiske, & Kendall, 1956) and "T-groups" (training groups), "sensitivity groups," and "encounter groups" (for reviews, see, e.g., Benne, 1964; Cooper & Mangham, 1971; Golembiewski & Blumberg, 1977; Lieberman, Yalom, & Miles, 1973; Rogers, 1970). Group communication facilitation research during the third historical period, from about 1970-1990, focused on (a) directly comparing group discussion procedures, such as reflective thinking, brainstorming, ideal-solution, and single-question, especially for generating ideas and making decisions (for a review, see Frey, 1995a); (b) training and educating members about group communication meeting procedures (e.g., Firestien, 1990), as well as providing feedback to groups about their interaction and performance (for a review, see Nadler, 1979); and (c) assessing the facilitative effects of new group communication technologies, such as teleconferencing, computer conferencing, and electronic meeting systems (for a review, see Scott, 1999). The end of the 1990s (1999) even saw the establishment of *Group Facilitation: A Research & Applications Journal*, sponsored by the International Association of Facilitators.

This body of research has yielded mixed results with regard to the effects of group communication facilitation (see Pavitt, 1993). One reason for the mixed results is because the bulk of this research has been conducted in laboratory settings with zero-history student groups meeting once to solve artificial problems created by the researcher and not with real-life groups confronting everyday problems (although some of that research involves classroom groups studied over a semester, and there have been some notable studies conducted on real-world groups, such as the previously noted research on leadership by Lewin and his colleagues). The problems with such laboratory research on groups are well documented (see Frey, 1994a, 1994c, 1995a, 1996), with Frey (1994c) pointing out that:

The ability to generalize from student, zero-history laboratory/class-room groups to real-life, bona fide groups is limited, primarily because students, unlike their real-world counterparts, have little investment in these groups and the tasks they are asked to solve, and because the laboratory/classroom setting hardly mirrors the significant contextual factors that impinge on groups in the real world. (p. 554)

Given the lack of generalizability from studies of laboratory and classroom groups, Pavitt (1993) concluded that:

Until more definite research findings exist there is no firm basis for recommendations to practitioners concerning the use of formal discussion procedures for guiding real-world groups in their decision making. Thus those of us who continue to teach and recommend the use of formal procedures must do so on faith rather than on solid ground. (p. 231)

In response to the problems plaguing research on laboratory and classroom groups, researchers during the 1990s started to study communication in naturally occurring groups (see, e.g., Adelman & Frey, 1994, 1997; Adelman & Schultz, 1991; Barker, 1993; Barker, Melville, & Pacanowsky, 1993; L. A. Baxter & Clark, 1996; Bird, 1999; Cawyer & Smith-Dupré, 1995; Conquergood, 1991, 1992; Conquergood & Siegel, 1990; Croft, 1999; Glaser, 1994; Gouran, 1993; Hirokawa & Rost, 1992; Lammers & Krikorian, 1997; Propp & Nelson, 1996; Ruud, 1995; Sunwolf & Seibold, 1998; Weitzel & Geist, 1998; Wright, 1997; Zimmerman & Applegate, 1992; see also the studies in Frey, 1994b), and that work continues today (see, e.g., the studies in Frey, 2003). As researchers moved into the field, they started to study a wider array of groups than the traditional laboratory focus on problem-solving and decision-making task groups. In addition to studying problem-solving and decision-making groups and teams in organizations (for a review of such research, see H. H. Greenbaum & Query, 1999), researchers studied children's and adolescents' groups (Socha & Socha, 1994; Sunwolf & Leets, 2003, 2004), community groups (e.g., Brock & Howell, 1994; Howell, Brock, & Hauser, 2003; Kramer, 2002), computer-mediated groups (e.g., Bird, 1999; Krikorian & Kiyomiya, 2003; Meier, 2003), families (e.g., L. A. Baxter & Clark, 1996; Petronio, Jones, & Morr, 2003; for a review, see Socha, 1999), gangs (Conquergood, 1991, 1992, 1994), health-care teams (Berteotti & Seibold, 1994; Ellingson, 2003), mountain-climbing groups (e.g., Houston, 2003), school boards (e.g., Tracy & Standerfer, 2003), social support groups (e.g., Cawyer & Smith-Dupré, 1995; Yep, Reece, & Negrón, 2003; for a review, see Cline, 1999), and many more. This research often employed ethnographic methods (e.g., participant observation and in-depth interviews; see Dollar & Merrigan, 2002; Frey 1994c), included the production of documentary films/videotapes (e.g., Adelman & Schultz, 1991; Conquergood & Siegel, 1990) in addition to written work, and were informed by and contributed to the development of specific theories that explained communication in natural groups, such as the bona fide group perspective (see Putnam & Stohl, 1990, 1996; Stohl & Holmes, 1993; Stohl & Putnam, 1994, 2003), the naturalistic paradigm as applied to groups (see Frey, 1994c), and, most recently, the symbolic-interpretive perspective (Frey & Sunwolf, 2004, 2005).

Most of these studies, however, have been descriptive, with little attention directed toward facilitating communication in real-world groups, with the exception of some focus group research conducted, for instance, with gang members and at-risk youth (Chapel, Peterson, & Joseph, 1999) and women mediators (Cooks & Hale, 1992). Moreover, when facilitation work was reported, it often took the form of personal "success" stories from consultants, with little empirical evidence provided for the claims made (see Gouran, 1995). One exception was an edited text by Frey (1995b) that featured original research studies documenting how communication in natural groups had been facilitated. The chapters in that text examined a wide variety of group communication facilitation procedures—including Interactive Management (Warfield, 1976, 1994), intergroup dialogue forums, SYMLOG (System for the Multiple Level Observation of Groups; Bales & Cohen, 1979), focus groups, team-building techniques, and group decision support systems (electronic meeting systems)—employed with diverse natural groups to, for instance, (a) engage in effective group problem solving and decision making (e.g., creating an action plan to promote greater participation in Comanche Tribal governance; Broome, 1995); (b) encourage constructive dialogue to resolve conflict and differences in groups (e.g., increasing awareness, identifying issues, promoting constructive dialogue, and identifying solutions to gender issues in an international professional service firm concerned about the dearth of women in its upper management; Murphy, 1995); (c) empower groups by providing members with feedback (e.g., easing tensions within a functional work group comprised of physicians, medical residents, and nursing staff; Keyton, 1995); (d) generate information about respondents through the use of focus groups for the purposes of planning, conducting, and evaluating communication campaigns (e.g., evaluating the performance of an urban residential adolescent substance abuse rehabilitation center to meet the needs of community members; Kreps, 1995); and (e) building teams (e.g., facilitating team process within a self-regulating group of employees managing a new-design plant; Seibold, 1995). Those studies provided empirical evidence regarding the facilitation of group communication and demonstrated some of the promises and challenges of facilitating natural groups of people confronting real problems (see Frey, 1995a). This 2-volume text is a follow up to that text.

OVERVIEW OF THE TEXTS

These two texts continue the work started by Frey (1995a) to respond to the gap that exists between advice-giving about and empirical documentation of the facilitation of natural group communication by showcasing how scholars have employed various innovative procedures to facilitate communication in natural groups. To select the chapters, an open call was issued through appropriate print and online sources seeking proposals for original research studies to be commissioned that explored and documented researchers' facilitation of communication in real-life groups. All theoretical perspectives, methodological approaches, facilitation procedures, and natural contexts were welcome, as long as the proposed chapter focused on the facilitation of communication in natural (not laboratory or classroom) groups. Chapter proposals explained the (a) type of natural group studied and its specific goals, problems, and/or issues faced; (b) group communication facilitation employed; (c) methods used to study the facilitation; and (d) possible results and conclusions, including ways the chapter potentially contributed to understanding group communication facilitation.

This call resulted in a large number of chapter proposals being submitted. Indeed, I was so impressed with the number and high quality of the proposals submitted that I asked Barbara Bernstein of Hampton Press, who had published my 1995 edited group communication facilitation text and had contracted with me for this text, whether it might be possible to produce a 2-volume set, and she immediately saw the advantages of doing so. I am grateful to Barbara for her enthusiastic support of this project and the other projects with which I have been and am involved with Hampton Press (Frey, 1995b; Frey & Carragee, in press). She is a good personal friend of mine and a supportive professional friend of the communication field and the group communication area, in particular. I also want to thank the contributors to this text, not only for the excellent chapters they wrote but also for their receptivity to my never-ending editorial comments and requests, and their patience with the production of this 2-volume set.

As explained below, Volume 1 showcases original research studies of how group communication facilitation procedures have been employed to help create groups, manage group conflict, and promote group conversation and discussion; Volume 2 presents original studies documenting how such procedures have been used to promote effective task group communication (planning, making decisions, evaluating actions, and promoting change) and team communication. Together, these texts provide needed empirical research regarding the significant effects that group communication facilitation can have on group life, and offer important insights about facilitating communication in natural groups.

Volume 1, Part I: Facilitating Group Creation

One popular conception, and focal point for research, is that groups grow and develop over time. Although scholars differ on whether group development follows a linear, sequential stage model—such as Tuckman's (1965) and Tuckman and Jensen's (1977) stage model of forming (developing a shared sense of the group), storming (managing conflict), norming (agreeing on rules of behavior), performing (working on the task), and adjourning (ending the group)—a cyclical model—such as the multiple sequence model of group development (Poole, 1981, 1983a, 1983b; Poole & Roth, 1989a, 1989b), in which groups are viewed as cycling repeatedly through any number of different stages in a variety of orders as members work on three interlocking "activity tracks" of task-process activities (to manage tasks), relational activities (to manage interpersonal relationships), and topical focus (to address issues of concern to a group), with "breakpoints" marking the shift to a new track—or some other model (for recent reviews of group development theory and research, see Arrow, Poole, Henry, Wheelan, & Moreland, 2004; Arrow, Henry, Poole, Wheelan, & Moreland, 2005; Wheelan, 2005b), scholars generally agree that the initial formation of a group, especially its first few meetings, is a time of anxiety and uncertainty for members (see, e.g., Bion, 1961; Slater, 1966; Stock & Thelen, 1958) as they seek to be included, become motivated to participate, and try to identify with the group (see Barge & Frey, 1997; see also Wheelan & Furbur, Volume 2). It is not surprising, therefore, that practitioners have created facilitation procedures for making people feel comfortable during the first group meeting, primarily through the use of "icebreakers" exercises designed to help members get to know one another; indeed, the number of recent group facilitation texts cited earlier that are devoted to icebreakers is substantial. However, these icebreakers typically do not go beyond the "name, rank, and serial number" introduction of members, and little is known empirically about the effects of using them; some group communication textbooks (e.g., Beebe & Masterson, 1997; Galanes & Adams, 2004) actually suggest that traditional icebreakers may cause potential problems, such as perceived differences emerging from the information shared as members engage in self-comparison (one-upping or one-downing themselves) and compete for status in a newly formed group, thereby creating further tension during this initial stage. The two chapters in this section offer new and innovative procedures for facilitating communication during the initial meeting(s) of a group for the purpose of promoting group creation and development.

In Chapter 1, Sunwolf abandons traditional icebreaker activities and offers, instead, an original facilitation procedure—empathic attunement facilitation—designed for the initial meeting of small, zero-history training groups of professional helpers. In the study described, training groups of trial lawyers are offered as an exemplar of the more general challenges of facilitating the first moments of a group's life. Sunwolf developed empathic attunement facilitation to help groups of defense attorneys who represent indigent incarcerated defendants learn to listen to their clients in new ways, draw on under-accessed information about their clients' worlds, and stimulate problem-solving group processes involving the creation of new case strategies their clients would accept and support. The primary facilitation method relied on to accomplish these goals operates by changing the type of communication that occurs when these helpers meet for the first time (zero history) as a task group. Influenced by two group communication theories (symbolic convergence theory and structuration theory), Sunwolf describes how empathic attunement facilitation was used with several small-sized groups of capital defense lawyers who attended week-long trial advocacy training programs designed to prevent their clients from receiving the death penalty, and the outcomes that resulted for group members, and she suggests future applications of this group communication facilitation procedure for other training groups of helping professionals.

In Chapter 2, Holly Siebert Kawakami starts by explaining how groups have become increasingly diverse and multicultural as a result of recent U.S. demographic changes and globalization trends. Although diversity in groups, compared to homogeneity, can have significant positive effects (e.g., surfacing multiple perspectives and producing higher quality decisions), diversity also presents communication challenges for members that can be difficult to overcome, leading to the need to facilitate the creation of high-quality interpersonal relationships early on in group development. In particular, cultures differ in the extent to which they privilege verbal versus nonverbal communication, with those from "high-context" cultures (also called "collectivist" or "interdependent self-construal" cultures) emphasizing nonverbal behavior over verbal behavior (and relationships over tasks) and those from "low-context" cultures (also called "individualistic" or "independent self-construal" cultures) emphasizing verbal over nonverbal behavior (and tasks over relationships) (E. T. Hall, 1976, 1983). Given that the United States is a low-context culture, it is not surprising that group communication facilitation procedures focus on verbal communication, with little attention directed toward nonverbal communication in groups (see Ketrow, 1999; for an exception, see Kalani, 2004). This almost-exclusive focus on verbal communication is unfortunate, for relational communication in groups, in general, largely is accomplished through nonverbal interaction among members, and in diverse groups, specifically, some members may come from cultures that privilege nonverbal communication, leading individuals who rely on verbal communication to potentially misinterpret the meanings of the nonverbal behaviors displayed. Karakami seeks to fill this gap by documenting how nonverbal group communication facilitation procedures—specifically, kinetic exercises that focus on body movement—were employed using a 4-stage process (introduction to the theme, engagement in the kinetic exercise, individual reflection, and facilitated group reflection and debriefing) during the early stage of formation with three diverse groups comprised of members from high- and low-context cultures (two U.S. domestic groups and one international group) to help those who come from different cultural backgrounds to know and better understand one another for the purposes of promoting better member relationships and group task outcomes.

Volume 1, Part II: Facilitating Group Conflict Communication

The experience of conflict among members is an inevitable feature of group life; in fact, a certain amount of conflict in groups is healthy (e.g., for promoting creativity and effective decision making; see Nicotera, 1997), and some scholars believe that groups first must work through a stage of conflict before members fully are ready to engage the task (see, e.g., Braaten, 1974/1975; Dunphy, 1968; R. D. Mann, Gibbard, & Hartman, 1967; Mills, 1964; Tuckman & Jensen, 1977; Wheelan & Furbur, Volume 2). History, however, is replete with the devastating effects of not managing conflict effectively within, but especially between, groups. Moreover, given the significant conflict that currently exists between groups, especially in this post-September 11, 2001 world, and the devastating effects such conflict can have (e.g., war and genocide), and given that facilitation directed toward managing conflict within groups, such as problem-solving and decision-making task groups (see, e.g., Folger et al., 2001; Nicotera, 1997), and within organizations (see, e.g., O'Rourke & Collins, 2005; Rahim, 2001; Sorenson, 1999) has received considerable attention, the chapters in this section focus on facilitating conflict management between groups (see, e.g., T. S. Jones, 2005; Tindale, Dykema-Engblade, & Wittkowski, 2005). The first three chapters follow up on work done with regard to understanding cross-cultural group communication, in general (for a review, see Shutter, 2002), and managing interethnic and intercultural conflict, in particular (see, e.g., Comas-Díaz, 2002; Eliasson, 2002; Ting-Toomey & Oetzel, 2001); the last two chapters examine conflict management between groups embedded within the same culture (the United States). All of these facilitations involve whole-group formats, with specific meeting procedures embedded within those formats, that primarily are designed to address affective conflict (relationally based conflict) and secondarily to manage procedural conflict (process-based conflict about how to work on a task) or task conflict (see Nicotera, 1997).

Chapter 3 by Benjamin J. Broome describes efforts to facilitate citizen peace-building groups on the divided Mediterranean island of Cyprus. Broome's facilitation makes extensive use of Interactive Management (IM), an approach to complex group problem solving based on Warfield's (1994) science of generic design that utilizes a carefully selected set of methodologies—most commonly, the nominal group technique and/or ideawriting first employed to generate ideas that then are organized and evaluated using interpretive structural modeling and/or field and profile representations—matched to the phase of group interaction and the requirements of the situation. Broome describes in detail three stages of IM applications to the situation in Cyprus. First, IM was used over a 9-month period with a core group of Greek Cypriots and Turkish Cypriots to design an agenda for peace-building activities on the island. Second, additional IM projects were conducted with a variety of targeted groups of young business leaders, young political leaders, and leaders of groups focused on women's issues. Third, a group of local facilitators were trained in IM methodologies and facilitation practices, and these facilitators applied the IM process with a variety of groups on the island. Broome concludes the chapter by examining some specific contributions of group facilitation to building peace in Cyprus and some cultural considerations and cautions related to the facilitation of communication in citizen groups involved in protracted conflict situations.

In Chapter 4, Joseph H. Albeck, Sami Adwan, and Dan Bar-On suggest that telling one's personal and family story in encounter groups that include members from all sides of communities engaged in intractable conflict can help to "work through" some of the intergenerational consequences of such conflict. This unique storytelling approach to cross-cultural group communication was first developed in To Reflect and Trust (TRT) encounters that brought together descendants of Holocaust survivors and descendants of Nazi perpetrators in the early and mid 1990s, and later was adopted for use with activists involved in peace-building efforts in Northern Ireland, Palestine and Israel, and South Africa. Albeck et al. first discuss the rationale for using this group communication facilitation procedure to work through intractable conflict, comparing it to two other, commonly used procedures: human relations groups and confrontational groups. They then explain how this procedure was used to work through the Holocaust in the original TRT group and how it was adapted for the Northern Ireland and Palestinian-Israeli contexts. Emerging from those encounters is a set of guidelines for structuring intergroup and intragroup dialogue that is organized into three categories—(a) principle guidelines (e.g., goals and facilitation); (b) process considerations (e.g., focusing on personal experiences and stories and improving participants' skills); and (c) technical aspects (e.g., time and space requirements)—with specific examples from the encounters used to illustrate each category. Albeck et al. conclude that this group communication facilitation procedure can help participants to "complete the historical circle" by working through important aspects of large-scale historical conflicts to integrate the various perspectives represented for the purpose of developing a new, shared narrative for living and working together in the future.

In Chapter 5, Ifat Maoz and Donald G. Ellis explore the use of dialogue groups to promote transformation in interactions between Israeli-Jews and Palestinians. After a brief history of this deep-seeded, and seemingly intractable, conflict, they explain group processes designed to ameliorate the conflict between these two groups. They argue that traditional conflict-resolution methods, which typically use third-party power mediation to achieve political settlements, often are ill suited to groups experiencing power asymmetries, strong emotions, and distrust. Instead, Maoz and Ellis employ reconciliation-aimed dialogue groups, whose goals include transforming relationships between conflicting parties, redressing inequality, and accentuating the co-creation of agreement through in-depth interaction between members that produces a nuanced understanding of one another. They first describe the nature, structure, and content of Palestinian-Israeli-Jews youth dialogue group workshops with which they have been involved, and then evaluate those workshops using both qualitative (interview) and quantitative (questionnaire) methods to investigate whether participants changed their attitudes toward the other group members following participation in these dialogue groups. The qualitative data indicate that although participants arrived at the workshops feeling threatened by the other side and traumatized as a result of the continuing violent encounters between the sides, the dialogic group encounters enabled the youth to interact on a personal level that created more favorable perceptions of the other side. This positive attitude change was verified by the quantitative data, which show that both Palestinians and Israeli-Jews rated each other significantly more favorably after the workshop than before it on attributes—such as being "tolerant," "considerate of others," and "good hearted"—that are directly relevant to promoting reconciliation and cooperative relations between the two sides. Maoz and Ellis conclude that effectively facilitated transformative dialogue group meetings can help to establish the ground for members of groups involved in acute conflict to understand each other and cooperate.

Turning to conflict management between groups embedded within the same society, Gregg B. Walker, Steven E. Daniels, and Anthony S. Cheng, in Chapter 6, focus on the role that facilitated group communication can play in the conflict that characterizes many environmental and natural resource decision-making situations in the United States. Walker et al. first define the complex and controversial nature of environmental conflict, and then propose that Collaborative Learning (CL)—a group-based methodology that integrates systems thinking, conflict management, and adult learning ideas—is ideal for working through environmental and natural resource management conflict and decision-making situations. They explain the foundations of CL, its three levels (philosophy, framework, and tactics/techniques), and the facilitation of CL workshops, including the use of small and large group interaction, and then describe three applications of CL to environmental conflict management that have been particularly comprehensive and that include quantitative data collected from participants to evaluate the facilitated CL group processes and activities. Together, the three cases demonstrate how the CL group communication facilitation procedure offers stakeholders opportunities to understand more fully and contribute meaningfully to the substance of natural resource management decision situations and, thereby, participate in collaborative environmental decision-making and conflict-resolution projects. Walker et al. conclude the chapter by sharing five tentative lessons they have learned from this work about group communication facilitation processes, in general, and the CL approach, in particular.

Chapter 7, the final chapter in this section, by Richard W. Sline, describes an intervention designed and facilitated to manage an intergroup conflict over control of the highly successful Park City (Utah) International Jazz Festival. The "ownership" of the event (and its significant budget residue) was in dispute between the Park City Jazz Foundation, a nonprofit organization that originally had conceived the Festival, and the Park City Chamber-Bureau, a combined chamber of commerce and convention/visitor/tourism bureau that had provided the organizational infrastructure to run the event since its inception. Embedded within this substantive intergroup conflict was significant affective conflict between Foundation and Chamber-Bureau representatives that was beginning to interfere with the functioning of staff and volunteers who produced the Festival. Sline explains the group communication facilitation he used to help these two groups manage this conflict, beginning with a description of the process (Schein, 1969) or collaborative (Block, 1981) consulting approach he adopts, in general (see also Milburn, Kenefick, & Lambert, Volume 2), and the action research intervention model (French & Bell, 1984) he employs, in particular. He then describes the case in detail, beginning with the discovery process used to gather information, followed by the findings, including the two Festival ownership perspectives that emerged, advantages and disadvantages of each perspective, and the recommendations that were made. He then explains the group communication facilitation procedures he used (employing, for instance, a group call-out procedure and buzz groups) to help participants "peel away" the results and recommendations from his research report in a "confrontation meeting" (Beckhard, 1967) involving key Festival stakeholders that deviated in important, innovative ways from standard group meeting planning guidelines (e.g., distributing the report section by section at the meeting rather than giving participants the full report prior to the meeting). Sline examines the outcomes of this facilitation, drawing on relevant literature from intergroup conflict meeting facilitation to explain why it was effective, and concludes that this procedure helped the decision makers to reflect on, discuss, and collectively make sense of the data generated during the discovery process and, ultimately, to accept and implement many of the recommendations that Sline offered.

Volume 1, Part III: Facilitating Group Conversation and Discussion

One of the initial reasons for studying and teaching group communication was because group discussion was seen as promoting democracy (especially over totalitarianism) and the involvement of citizens in public life (see Barge, 2002; Frey, 1996; Gouran, 1999). Pedagogical texts (e.g., Baird, 1928; B. Baxter, 1943; Coyle, 1947; Crowell, 1963; Gastil, 1993a; Haiman, 1951; Kilpatrick, 1940) and scholarly essays (e.g., Gastil, 1992, 1993b) have stressed this relationship, for, as Johnson (1939) contended, group discussion is "the fundamental and essential factor in democracy" and, therefore, "its technique must be mastered by the average citizen and its philosophy must be inculcated in the habits and attitudes of all people" (p. 400). However, according to Barge (2002), in studying and teaching people how to engage in group deliberation, scholars and educators have focused primarily on two forms of communication: *problem talk*, which "disposes group members toward viewing situations and issues as problems to be solved and propels them along a conversational trajectory that involves identifying the problem, analyzing its causes, proposing possible solutions, and planning actions," and *debate*, "involving (a) breaking issues/problems into parts; (b) seeing distinctions between the parts; (c) justifying/defending assumptions; (d) persuading, selling, and telling; and (e) gaining agreement on one meaning" (p. 162). A number of scholars have taken exception with problem talk and debate as being the only or even primary forms of group deliberation that best promote democracy. Instead of problem talk, they advocate *appreciative inquiry*, "identifying positive resources—what works best in the community—and [using] these results . . . as a frame for creating some future course of action" (Spano, 2001, p. 40; see also Cooperrider & Srivastva, 1987; Cooperrider & Whitney, 1999); instead of debate, they privilege *dialogue*, "a collective and collaborative communication process whereby people explore together their individual and collective assumptions and predispositions" (Barge, p. 168) by adopting a position of "both/and" (instead of "either/or," as in debate), "suspending" their assumptions, and balancing advocacy and inquiry (see Barge; Pearce & Littlejohn, 1997). These forms of communication are believed to be especially helpful for enabling people with very disparate views about controversial public issues (e.g., immigration) to enhance their understanding of one another and to coordinate their actions (see Pearce & Littlejohn). The chapters in this final section of Volume 1 focus on facilitating these types of group conversations and discussions.

In Chapter 8, Shawn Spano explores public dialogue as a form of communication that can enhance and strengthen relationships between and among local government officials and community members. As such, public dialogue can be employed to address a variety of public problems and can help to produce a number of important civic outcomes, including community building, conflict resolution, decision making, and long-range planning. Spano describes the methodology for facilitating public dialogue that was developed by the Public Dialogue Consortium (PDC), a nonprofit organization involved in a multiyear, citywide, collaborative project in Cupertino, California. The methodology is characterized by the integration of communicative practices and action research principles with well-established theoretical perspectives derived from social constructionism and the coordinated management of meaning (CMM) to produce a "practical theory" that situates specific group communication facilitation skills and techniques (neutrality, curiosity and wonder, dialogic listening, appreciative questioning, systemic questioning, and reflecting and reframing) within the context of larger event and strategic process designs. The application of this approach to facilitating public dialogue is examined in light of the 2-day facilitation training event and subsequent daylong community forum that were part of the PDC's Cupertino project. Spano shows how the success of the PDC methodology depends, in part, on responding to the challenges and opportunities that result from linking communication theory and practice together, and he discusses four implications of this group communication facilitation approach: (a) dealing with *praxis* and methodological openness; (b) connecting facilitation to academic research; (c) engaging nondialogic forms of communication; and (d) focusing on dialogue and ideologically neutral group facilitation.

In Chapter 9, Sharon Howell, Bernard Brock, and Kenneth Brown explain their facilitation of a diverse group that assisted a school board in developing a safe and respectful high school environment that involved creating a community consensus for the group's recommendations to change the name of a local high school mascot—Redskins. They examine how their group communication facilitation, informed by their work in social action, feminist, and antiracist organizations, explicitly brought the social context into the group's communication and decision-making processes and helped group members to move from a focus on individual identity to one of group identification, using three interrelated theoretical approaches: (a) the bona fide group perspective to explain the relationship between social context and the development and functioning of the group; (b) structuration theory to understand group functioning, emphasizing the emergence of rules within the group that encouraged open, democratic processes and the use of resources to expand the range of options available to achieve the group's goals; and (c) a dramatistic perspective to explore contrasting rhetorical visions of the community posed by the group in public deliberations designed to develop the community consensus for the name change. The facilitation strategies employed involved (a) expanding group members' shared social context and problem identification through the use of focus groups; (b) developing group identification through a balance of engaging conflict to surface differences and sharing stories to create connection; and (c) enhancing the group's commitment to democratic, transparent processes in the public campaign to create community consensus. Howell et al. conclude the chapter by discussing how group communication facilitators can use as a source of strength the differences that exist in groups comprised of individuals representing differing ethnic, social, and cultural experiences.

Chapter 10, by Beatrice Schultz and Patricia Kushlis, concludes this section and this volume by examining a training program conducted for moderators/facilitators of self-selected discussion groups talking about controversial international issues over monthly working lunch meetings. These group discussions follow a presentation by an invited speaker and are designed to educate members and guests about current international issues and their implications for U.S. foreign policy; as such, these groups encourage participants to express divergent views to better understand the complex dynamics of a particular foreign affairs issue or set of issues. As the people responsible for the luncheon discussion programs, Schultz and Kushlis designed a special training program for moderators of the group discussions that involved a review of some group facilitation techniques and their theoretical foundations. They describe the selection of the moderators, background information moderators received, training techniques they employed, and the subsequent group communication procedures (specifically, participant introductions and forecasting rules; procedural and content interventions; reframing, reminding, and summarizing; and dealing with obstacles) these moderators used to facilitate the participation of members of these discussion groups at the next monthly meeting, including, based on the moderators' verbatim written and oral reports, followed by the authors/facilitators' analysis, how well those techniques worked. Schultz and Krushlis conclude the chapter by examining some lessons learned from this process about facilitating group discussions.

Volume 2, Part I: Facilitating Group Task Communication: Planning, Decision Making, Evaluating, and Promoting Change

Although, as previously explained, many researchers who moved from the laboratory to the field to study and facilitate groups have focused on groups that traditionally would not be classified as problem-solving and decision-making task groups and on group processes that are related more to the social dimension than the task dimension of group life, as pointed out at the beginning of this chapter, the sheer number of task groups and their significance to society makes them incredibly important to group communication scholars, practitioners, and group members. Accordingly, a number of scholars and practitioners facilitate communication in naturally occurring problem-solving and decision-making task groups, most often groups embedded within organizational contexts. The chapters in this first section of Volume 2 examine how group communication facilitation techniques have been employed to help natural task groups plan, make decisions, evaluate their processes and outcomes, and promote change.

In Chapter 1, Trudy Milburn, James V. Kenefick, and Alethia Lambert examine a half-day facilitated retreat planning session held by the board of directors of an organization that offers a site for daily drop-ins by parents and caregivers of young children, support groups for new parents, monthly educational workshops for parents, and classes for children in art, music, science, computers, Spanish, and French. As the recording secretary for the board and a group communication scholar who recognized problems that were plaguing the group meetings, Milburn suggested the retreat and recommended Kenefick as the outside facilitator. Milburn et al. first review the process consultation framework (Schein, 1988; see also Sline, Volume 1) that Kenefick used to design and facilitate the meeting, provide background on the group's problems and the initiation of the facilitation, and then analyze the interactions that occurred at that retreat meeting from the dual perspectives of ethnography of communication and conversation analysis (see, e.g., Moerman, 1988; Philipsen 1990/1991). Their close analysis of the group's discourse, using many examples of verbatim conversation, reveals the ways in which Kenefick—from the initiating phase to the facilitative interventions (especially those related to creating and maintaining an agenda and to managing meetings)—and the group participants co-constructed through interaction a collaborative working relationship and the effects of this relationship on group members simultaneously learning about and blending together the typical discourse of their group's meetings with the discourse of facilitation. Milburn et al., thus, show how group communication facilitation constitutes a jointly constructed process rather than a persuasive role that a designated person ("the facilitator") plays during a group meeting, concluding that the goal of facilitation is to help group members come to a collective understanding of how communication can be used effectively to manage their group processes and problems.

In Chapter 2, Timothy G. Plax, Patricia Kearney, Terre H. Allen, and Ted Ross explain their use of focus group facilitation to research and develop a nationwide educational program, called *USA Fund's® Life Skills*, designed to teach college students financial literacy by assisting them with debt management in college and beyond. Focus groups have become a popular form of group communication facilitation used in social research (see, e.g., Bloor, Frankland, Thomas, & Robson, 2001; Fern, 2001; T. L. Greenbaum, 1998, 2000; Krueger & Casey, 2001; Litosseliti, 2003; Morgan, 1997), and Plax et al. begin by explaining how this facilitation technique can yield reliable and valid data when it is used effectively to meet a number of scientific criteria with respect to focus group design, implementation, and facilitation. They then describe their use of focus groups to develop this educational program, explaining the objectives of the focus groups, sampling design employed, facilitation of the groups, and the results of the facilitation with regard to the financial literacy curriculum created (consisting of five instructional modules, each designed as a 1-hour workshop to be delivered to student borrowers by financial aid professionals). They conclude the chapter by identifying some critical issues that can affect the successful facilitation of large-scale focus group research and development projects and offering practical advice for planning and facilitating focus groups, especially with respect to situating focus group facilitation in the larger organizational context in which it typically is embedded.

Chapter 3 by Satish Kedia presents a case study examining how an evaluation system to assess the effectiveness of substance-abuse treatment programs in Tennessee was facilitated in a group setting. *Evaluation research*, which has become a central concern in U.S. organizational culture (especially in the human services sector), is a form of policy research that involves the collection and analysis of information about a program, product, or service to determine its efficiency and effectiveness. Evaluation commonly is a group effort involving many stakeholders, including program administrators, policy makers, service providers, consultants, and client advocates, with diverse agendas and interests who, nonetheless, must work together to evaluate a program, product, or service. Thus, engaging in effective group communication is key to developing a successful evaluation system. Kedia first provides an overview of various approaches to evaluation, followed by an explanation of the specific evaluation approach he employed to facilitate this initiative: a modified version of empowerment evaluation, proposed by Fetterman, Kaftarian, and Wandersman (1996), which is a non-hierarchical, participatory, and collaborative approach that seeks to establish a group environment in which participants feel that they have ownership of and control over the evaluation process. After reviewing the public health problem of substance abuse, funding for combating this problem, and the central role of evaluation in such funding, Kedia walks through the case study, explaining his role as a group facilitator in developing the evaluation system and in applying the steps involved in empowerment evaluation to the group deliberations, showing how encouraging supportive engagement, as well as balanced contributions derived from the communal setting in which the exchanges take place, from all stakeholders, not just the facilitator, can assist in realizing the emergent and negotiated goals for an evaluation process.

Chapter 4 by Marya L. Doerfel and Julie L. Toshach is a case study of a women's investment club that was suffering from various problems, including frequent delays on key decisions that needed to be made, unequal participation by members, and member attrition. In line with the tenets of the functional theory of group communication and decision making (see, e.g., Hollingshead et al., 2005; Wittenbaum et al., 2004), especially with regard to its identification of cognitive, affiliative, and egocentric constraints impinging on group work (see, e.g., Gouran, 1982; Gouran & Hirokawa, 1996), the authors intervened with this group using the round robin component of the nominal group technique (NGT), a form of brainstorming in which ideas first are generated privately by individual group members and then are shared publicly in the group with each member taking a turn. After explaining functional theory and the group communication facilitation techniques of brainstorming and the NGT, Doerfel and Toshach provide an overview of the investment club activities and members (which included Toshach, Doerfel's sister, as the president), as well as the communication problems that plagued this group prior to the intervention. They then walk through the intervention, showing how the identified constraints were managed effectively via the training of Toshach in using the round robin component of the NGT with this group. They demonstrate how, over the course of the next six months, this group communication facilitation technique helped members to develop emergent norms of equal participation, open communication, and consensual decision making that resulted in progress with regard to members' attendance, participation, and decision making. They conclude the chapter by explaining how this facilitation effort both verifies tenets of functional theory and extends that theory in an important way by recognizing the need to facilitate effective relational communicative behaviors (in addition to task communicative behaviors) to help groups move forward toward completion of their tasks.

Volume 2, Part II: Facilitating Team Communication

In many ways, the concepts examined in the previous section of this volume on task group communication (planning, decision making, evaluating, and promoting change), as well as those examined in the three sections of Volume 1 (group creation, group conflict communication management, and group conversation and discussion), all come together in this section devoted to facilitating team communication, for the concept of a "team" implies a high-performing, cohesive group that can engage effectively in all of the group communication processes and practices examined thus far. It is no wonder, then, that many contemporary organizations have instituted team-based structures as their way of operating (and many other groups, such as families, recreational groups, and sports groups, routinely refer to themselves as "teams"), and the scholarly and popular literatures are replete with texts offering research on and lots of advice about teams (see, e.g., recent texts by Adams & Means, 2005; Beatty & Barker Scott, 2005; Blanchard, Randolph, & Grazier, 2005; Bowers, Salas, & Jentsch, 2005; Boynton & Fischer, 2006; DuFrene & Lehman, 2005; Duke Corporation Education, 2005; Ellingson, 2005; Ghaye, 2005; Gignac, 2005; Gold, 2005; Gordon, 2005; Harris & Sherblom, 2005; Humphrey, 2005; L. B. Jones, 2005; R. Jones, Oyung, & Pace, 2005; Lenicioni, 2005; Longman & Mullins, 2005; Macchia, 2005; L. Mann, 2005; Martin, 2005; Massey, 2005; Midura & Glover, 2005; Neider & Schriesheim, 2005; Rothwell, 2004; Salemi, 2005; Snell & Janney, 2005; Thompson & Choi, 2005; West, Tjosvold, & Smith, 2005; Wheelan, 2005a). It is worth pointing out, however, that some scholars have raised serious questions about whether teams are just another mechanism of organizational control and surveillance, and they have identified some particular problems and paradoxes of trying to enact what is supposed to be an egalitarian form in what still are hierarchically structured organizations (see, e.g., Barker, 1993, 1999; Ezzamel & Willmott, 1998; Frey, 1995c; Sewell, 1998; Stohl, 1995b) situated in the larger culture of the United States that privileges individualism and personal responsibility (see Schein, 1995). With this important understanding foregrounded, the chapters in this section explore the facilitation of team communication.

In Chapter 5, Susan A. Wheelan and Sharon Furbur begin by pointing out that the extant research literature reveals little to no effects of facilitation on team performance and productivity, a problem they attribute to a lack of consideration regarding group developmental stages by those who design and facilitate interventions. To address this problem, they describe an intervention employed with 10 organizational work teams to facilitate group development, communication, and productivity that takes group development into account. They first review theory and research on group development, showing that groups progress through stages and that a group's stage of development is related to that group's effectiveness; consequently, interventions need to help teams reach the higher stages of group development. They then describe their intervention, explaining the teams and recent changes in the structure of the organization in which the teams are embedded, goals of the facilitation, and the initial consultation process with the teams, which included team members completing the Group Development Questionnaire (GDQ; Wheelan & Hochberger, 1996), which assesses the developmental stage achieved by work groups. The teams then participated in four days of training over the next eight months that included information about, among other things, team development, communication, and productivity, with team members completing the GDQ again between days 2 and 3, and between days 3 and 4. The GDQ team profile results were fed back to members, along with the profiles of teams in similar organizations and the strategies those teams employed to become more effective. Team members then participated in a goal-setting process based on their GDQ results, identified team strengths and weaknesses, and offered suggestions for how to move to the higher stages of group development. To illustrate how this facilitation process worked, Wheelan and Furbur discuss in detail the facilitation strategies used with two of the teams. They then evaluate the facilitation of all 10 teams, documenting how the teams' level of development increased significantly, based on the GDQ results over time, and how their performance improved in the year following the facilitation, based on company records. They conclude the chapter by discussing how the successful facilitation of team communication and performance must take into account the developmental stage of a group and focus on the team as a system rather than on individual members.

In Chapter 6, John Gribas and Judy Sims demonstrate how a group communication facilitation approach that focuses on the facilitator as "sense-maker," capitalizes on the power of metaphor, and stresses the ambiguity of symbols helped staff members of a university student support service office to gain a more flexible understanding of "teamness." They first provide theoretical background regarding the team concept as a symbolically ambiguous metaphor that affects individual and collective action and outline a set of group facilitation guidelines focused on metaphoric illumination and strategic symbolic reorientation of the team concept. They then present the case study, demonstrating how office document analysis (specifically, a recent annual report written by the office director) and in-depth interviews conducted with the staff members revealed a variety of relational, group-level problems stemming from members' problematic assumptions about teams. Their intervention relied on the final report they wrote, first presented to each staff member individually and then discussed by all members as a group, to expose staff members' problematic conceptions and to suggest options for symbolic reorientation of the team metaphor. Using extended excerpts from the recommendations section of that report to illustrate the facilitation goals of metaphoric illumination and symbolic reorientation through strategic ambiguity, Gribas and Sims demonstrate how they focused on the team metaphor to help staff members make sense of their collective past and present and how they employed symbolic ambiguity to encourage members to develop new perspectives that could move the group forward. To assess the longitudinal impact of the facilitation, follow-up interviews were conducted with staff members one year later. Although some of the specific action steps recommended had not been enacted, staff members continued to view the facilitation as a positive and beneficial experience and saw the value of maintaining symbolic ambiguity regarding the team metaphor. Gribas and Sims conclude the chapter by discussing the utility of employing metaphoric illumination as a group communication facilitation procedure.

Chapter 7, by John Parrish-Sprowl, explores the efficacy of a structure predicated on team facilitation for engaging in organizational change. Using the bona fide group perspective as a theoretical foundation—which argues that groups have permeable boundaries, shifting borders, and are interdependent with their relevant contexts—and an action research methodology, Parrish-Sprowl demonstrates how he assisted a unionized manufacturing company in shifting from a traditional line manufacturer to a team-based structure. He first describes the organizational context, including the previous failed change attempt and the resulting conversations among employees that any change effort was doomed to fail. He then explains how he facilitated the change process, first gathering information about people, processes, and products through observation and interviews, and forming a working relationship with the union president (who had been pivotal in the demise of the previous change program), and then offering employee training that addressed team structures and functions, trained team leaders, and placed participants into functional teams. To support the training program, and to stress the interdependence of groups with their contexts, workers visited other organizations associated or in competition with the company. Despite these efforts, however, the teams demonstrated process problems because of shifting members or low team loyalty due to competing group loyalties (especially to the union), as well as organizational barriers to performance (such as other departments not fulfilling the teams' requests). Parrish-Sprowl, thus, developed a facilitation program that involved (a) training to improve the team leaders' facilitation skills; (b) creating a team of facilitators to support team leaders; and (c) using senior management to facilitate team interface with other organizational units. This multifaceted approach to team facilitation resulted in improved team performance. Parrish-Sprowl concludes the chapter by discussing how the bona fide group perspective, coupled with an action research methodology, produced a facilitation effort that shifted the "discourse of failure" that characterized change efforts in this company to a team environment in which both individual groups and systemically connected groups worked together to achieve collective goals.

In Chapter 8, Joachim Stempfle describes a computer-simulation method he designed for facilitating cooperative problem solving in multidisciplinary project teams—typically entrusted with highly complex tasks and characterized by multiple team membership, remote cooperation, and the use of modern communication technology—in the pharmaceutical industry. Stempfle starts by explaining the challenges that project teams face in the pharmaceutical industry, particularly in the company that requested the facilitation, and the goals addressed via the facilitation. He then explicates the theoretical bases—including complex decision making, intergroup relations, and the role of communication in team problem solving—of the facilitation, which employed an action-learning, computer-simulated business scenario that models important conditions under which these multidisciplinary project teams operate, such as superordinate goals, task complexity and interdependence, and physical separation of team members. The simulation divides participants into subteams assigned to three departments of a company, with each department located in a separate room, operating a computer terminal that is network linked with the other computers. Action stages, during which participants made decisions, alternate with reflection stages, where participants reflect on and discuss their performance in the action stages. Experiences shared by the participants of four workshops conducted thus far demonstrate the capability of this group communication facilitation procedure to promote profound learning about the task, self, teamwork, and cross-departmental cooperation. Stempfle concludes the chapter by discussing how computer simulations provide a unique learning environment that combines the advantages of on-the-job training and classroom learning, and how improvement in team performance in these simulations largely is attributable to changes in the ways teams communicate, especially with regard to members' ability to metacommunicate about their thinking and acting as a team.

In Chapter 9, the final chapter in this section and volume, Edward A. Mabry and Fay Sudweeks discuss the use of a team-based, collaborative model of facilitation, predicated on the mediational action theory of leadership, in a computer-supported collaborative work (CSCW) project environment. Mediational leadership focuses on facilitating group decision making and relationship management, and Mabry and Sudweeks examine how mediational action can be practiced collaboratively in a multigroup project environment for the express purpose of providing expert leadership on a critical task. After examining the CSCW group context and relationships among leadership, facilitation, and virtual collaboration, they explain the virtual field ethnographic methods they employed to study the use of a functionally relevant expert team—dubbed the "Oracles"— as a collaborative facilitation structure to provide leadership on a specific task (content-analytic coding) integral to the work of a virtual project group, a research group studying online group communication, with the group itself constituted and completing its work entirely through computer-mediated interaction. The data analyzed include e-mail archives, questionnaires completed by group members involved in coding activities, and the authors' participant-observation standpoints. Using extended e-mail message sequences, Mabry and Sudweeks show how Oracles were approached for assistance directly and by looping inquiries through the group's designated nominal leader (Mabry, called the "Commish"), with both types of collaborative leadership patterns effective in providing facilitation. The communication environment of the Oracles group also indicated that it functioned effectively as a site of mediational action. Mabry and Sudweeks conclude the chapter by discussing the efficacy of using mediational leadership practices as a facilitation technique in a virtual group context and the benefits of team-based collaborative facilitation both in CSCW and, potentially, in other groups as well.

FACILITATING COMMUNICATION IN NATURAL GROUPS

The chapters in these two volumes, as a set, shed important light on significant issues and practices relevant to facilitating communication in natural groups. To help reveal these issues and practices, authors were sent a questionnaire that asked them to respond to a number of questions regarding the group communication facilitation study described in their chapter. This section explores some of the most salient issues and practices identified, using some of the researchers' experiences to explicate and explain them.

The first issue concerns the shared impetus that drives this group communication facilitation work: the desire to make a difference in the lives of groups and their members. Although these scholars certainly are interested in contributing to the body of knowledge about group communication theory, research, and practice, their efforts are driven first and foremost by their commitment to bringing their resources—group communication facilitation knowledge and skills—to bear to help groups solve the problems that plague them. The important problems that are confronted include (in the order they appear in the texts):

- Helping capital defense lawyers to prevent the death penalty from being imposed on their indigent incarcerated defendants (Sunwolf)
- Assisting multicultural groups to overcome the communication challenges posed by and achieve the benefits of diversity (Kawakami)
- Promoting peace between groups that have experienced war and bloodshed (Broome, Albeck et al., and Maoz & Ellis)
- Working through environmental and natural resource management conflict and decision-making situations (Walker et al.)
- Managing group conflict over the control and operation of a successful music festival (Sline)
- Sponsoring public dialogue about salient civic problems (Spano)
- Developing a safe and respectful high school environment that does not practice discrimination (Howell et al.)
- Guiding discussion groups talking about controversial international issues (Schultz & Kushlis)
- Aiding the development of a neighborhood center that serves as a resource for parents and their children (Milburn et al.)
- Teaching college students financial literacy that assists them with debt management in college and beyond (Plax et al.).
- Evaluating and increasing the effectiveness of substance-abuse treatment programs (Kedia)
- Making the meeting practices of a financial investment club more effective (Doerfel & Toshach)
- Improving the development, communication, and productivity of teams in a large insurance company (Wheelan & Furbur)

- Encouraging staff members of a university student support service office to gain a more flexible understanding of the concept of "teams" (Gribas & Sims)
- Facilitating the shift in a manufacturing company from a traditional hierarchical structure to a team-based structure (Parrish-Sprowl)
- Showing multidisciplinary pharmaceutical project teams how to engage in cooperative problem solving (Stempfle)
- Supporting the work of a virtual research project group (Mabry & Sudweeks)

Second, although these scholars primarily are interested in helping groups to solve these problems, they also *are* concerned with advancing group communication (facilitation) theory, research, and practice. Accordingly, they use their research skills to document their group communication facilitation efforts so that other scholars, practitioners, and group members can learn from those efforts. These studies, thus, constitute "applied communication research." As Cissna (1982) explained:

> Applied research sets out to contribute to knowledge by answering a real, pragmatic social question or by solving a real pragmatic, social problem. Applied *communication* research involves such a question or problem of human communication or examines human communication in order to provide an answer or solution to the question or problem. (editorial statement)

Moreover, these research studies represent a particular form of applied communication scholarship that involves scholars intervening into group discourse, helping group members to understand and, when necessary, change their communication processes and practices, as opposed to simply describing the communication problems faced by these groups or studying someone else's group communication facilitation efforts. In that sense, they meet Frey's (2000) more narrow definition of applied communication scholarship as "the study of researchers putting their communication knowledge and skills into practice" (p. 179; see also Frey, in press).

Third, although the central purpose of these studies (in line with applied communication research) is not to advance group communication (facilitation) theory, per se, virtually all of the facilitation practices reported on in these two volumes are informed by theoretical perspectives. Sunwolf, for instance, used symbolic convergence theory and narrative theory to create her empathic attunement facilitation procedure; Kawakami's facilitations

are based on high- versus low-context theory; Spano's public dialogue practices are grounded in social constructionism and CMM theory; Howell et al.
used the bona fide group perspective (as did Parrish-Sprowl), structuration
theory, and a dramatistic perspective; Doerfel and Toshach's facilitation
practices are based on the functional perspective of group decision making;
Wheelan and Furbur's facilitation emerges from group development theory;
Gribas and Sims's work employs metaphor theory; and Stempfle's facilitation workshops are based on theories of complex problem solving and intergroup relations. By being theoretically grounded, these studies provide support for the explanatory power of these theories in practice, demonstrating,
as Lewin (1951) claimed, that "there is nothing so practical as a good theory" (p. 169). Moreover, in some cases, such as Albeck et al.'s facilitation of
storytelling in intercultural dialogue groups, these scholars are building
grounded theory through the group communication facilitation practices
they employ and analyze. Hence, these studies further show, as Levy-
Leboyer (1988) claimed, that "there is nothing so theoretical as a good
application" (p. 785). These applied communication research studies, thus,
show the interrelationship of theory and application, demonstrating, as
Wood (1995) contended, that "applied communication research is practicing
theory and theorizing practice" (p. 157).

Fourth, these studies demonstrate the wealth and breadth of group communication facilitation procedures that are available. As the sections of the
two volumes show, the facilitation procedures range from those designed to
create groups, to those that manage group conflict communication, encourage group conversation and discussion, advance group task communication
(specifically, planning, decision making, evaluating, and promoting change),
and produce team communication. Although these group communication
facilitation procedures primarily emphasize verbal communication, as
Kawakami's chapter shows, there also are nonverbal communication procedures. Some of these facilitation procedures, such as Interactive
Management, Collaborative Learning, empowerment evaluation, the nominal group technique, and focus groups, are well known and have been
employed by many others; consequently, these studies add to our growing
knowledge about these procedures. Other procedures employed, however,
such as empathic attunement, kinetic exercises, To Reflect and Trust
encounters, the Group Development Questionnaire, and team metaphoric
illumination, were created (or substantially reworked) by these scholars and
offer new and important group communication facilitation procedures to add
to the facilitator's toolkit.

Fifth, these studies show that virtually any research method can be
employed to document group communication facilitation efforts. The methods used include quantitative questionnaires (e.g., Walker et al. and

Wheelan & Furbur), close textual analysis of group discourse (e.g., Milburn et al.), in-depth individual interviews (Maoz & Ellis), focus group interviews (e.g., Plax et al.), and participant observation (e.g., Mabry & Sudweeks), with a number of studies employing multimethodological procedures (e.g., Maoz & Ellis's use of quantitative questionnaires and qualitative interviews). These studies, thus, deconstruct the traditional divide that often has been drawn between quantitative and qualitative research methods. Moreover, a number of these studies are based on action research, in which researchers collaborate with groups to decide which facilitation procedures and research methods work best. A good example of such collaboration regarding facilitation procedures is Spano's public dialogue work with the City of Cupertino, which involved collaboration between the consortium of which Spano is a member, the city manager, and the city council member who served as mayor at the time. Spano and his colleagues, following their usual procedure, came to the planning of the public dialogue event with a draft idea and negotiated the specifics with the key stakeholders to make sure that facilitation met the needs of the city. Perhaps this interactive approach to group facilitation is one reason why virtually all of these research studies incorporate, in one way or another, the voices of the group members studied.

Sixth, the studies demonstrate various ways in which scholars become involved in facilitating groups. In many cases, the researchers served as consultants who were invited to facilitate the groups. Wheelan, for instance, had done some previous consulting work for the company reported on in her chapter; Plax, Kearney, and Allen have worked together many times over the last 20 years and were selected as consultants for this project based on the submission of a written project proposal, followed by oral interviews with and presentations to the company's debt-management team; Parrish-Sprowl was chosen from several consultants under consideration to assist the manufacturing company; Spano had to go through several gatekeepers, including the mayor and the city council, before being given a contract to host the public dialogue; and Stempfle owns a consulting company and was asked to do the workshops by a company representative responsible for human resources development who had heard a speech that Stempfle gave.

Coming in as an outsider to facilitate a group has both disadvantages and advantages. On the negative side, consultants hired by management may be seen by group members as being a pawn of management. Spano claims that city residents who participate in the public dialogues his group facilitate often initially see the consortium as being aligned either with the city or with some political cause or agenda. Stempfle reports that the participants in his computer-simulation workshops often state that they resent being sent there by their superiors.

In such cases, consultants must work hard to overcome the perception that their facilitation is designed to promote management's interest. In his chapter, Parrish-Sprowl talks about the problems he encountered convincing the union president to sign onto the team-based structure he was trying to facilitate in the company, and the lengths to which he went to form a working relationship with this person and to convince employees that he was not there to subvert the union and trample the rights of workers in favor of management, even as he tried simultaneously to maintain the confidence of management. Howell et al. found that the most important aspect of the culture of the community with which they worked was members' desire not to have "outsiders" make decisions for them or make judgments about them. To counteract this concern, Howell et al. acknowledged their position as outsiders and used that as a way to make clear that the decisions being discussed rested with the group—not with them as the facilitators. Gribas and Sims argue that one reason the staff of the university student support service office they studied could not conclude that they were the director's "hired guns" was because the final report they wrote offered pretty candid assessments of the director's role in the ongoing problems and suggested some specific guidelines for the director's improvement.

Being an outside, neutral facilitator, however, sometimes can be advantageous. Gribas and Sims, for instance, were selected as facilitators, in part, because they did not have personal relationships with any of the team members. In Sline's case, participants involved in the intergroup conflict knew that some negative issues had to come to light for positive change to occur, and they wanted a neutral outsider who could do this "dirty work." For Broome, being a neutral facilitator proved very beneficial for working with Greek and Turkish Cypriots, although he constantly grapples with the degree to which his intervention as a third party could produce too much dependency on outsiders and whether he should be involved in activities that might be perceived as an external influence on internal affairs.

In some cases, the researchers were either members or leaders of the groups being facilitated or the organizations that sponsored the groups. Milburn, for instance, was a member of the board that engaged in the facilitated retreat and suggested Kenefick as the facilitator; Toshach was president of the investment club during the time the facilitation took place, and Doerfel, a professor, is her sister; Schultz was the chair of the facilitated luncheon discussions; and Kedia, as the director of a substance abuse prevention project, was appointed to the Evaluation Advisory Committee to serve as the evaluator. With respect to organizational membership, Sunwolf is an ongoing faculty member of the capital defense college attended by attorneys who are looking for better ways to defend their capital cases. As a faculty member, Sunwolf serves as both a lecturer in the program and as a co-leader of the small breakout groups of 7-8 attorneys. Support for using and studying the empathic attunement technique described in her chapter was given by the director of the program. Moreover, because of her association with the capital defense college, membership as a capital defense lawyer, 15 years of serving as a public defender and as a Training Director for Colorado's Public Defender Office, and her experiences as a national trial consultant, she was viewed by the program's organizers and by the group members as an "insider," which proved invaluable for engaging in her facilitation efforts.

Most of the groups facilitated, regardless of whether from an outsider or insider perspective, were located in or near the area where the researchers live. Kawakami, for instance, was living in Japan and the opportunity to facilitate arose when she was invited to do so by a decision maker for the group; Maoz, a professor at The Hebrew University of Jerusalem, was invited by a local organization conducting workshops between Israeli-Jews and Palestinians to be the workshop evaluator; and Howell et al. were invited into a local school district by school administrators who knew of their work in a nearby community. In at least two cases, however, the facilitation took place in a very different locale, requiring both a substantial amount of time and funding. Plax et al.'s facilitation, which took place all over the United States, only was possible because it was sponsored by a very large corporation. Broome's facilitation was a result of a Fulbright grant that allowed him to live in Cyprus for two years. The grant was initiated by Greek and Turkish Cypriots who met each other during various visits abroad to participate in conflict resolution training seminars; because of the difficulties they had meeting face-to-face on the island, they requested a Fulbright scholar in conflict resolution who could act as a third-party facilitator for their peace-building activities. It also is important to note, however, that before arriving in Cyprus to take up his Fulbright residency, Broome had visited Cyprus several times as part of the facilitation team for a U.S.-based consortium conducting conflict resolution training on the island; consequently, before he facilitated the particular peace-building group discussed in his chapter, he already had established working relationships with the members.

In all cases, regardless of the way the researchers came to facilitate the groups, their facilitation of the groups as an outsider or insider, or where the facilitation took place, they became involved with the groups because their values resonated with the work the groups were trying to accomplish. For instance, Sunwolf's desire to see the death penalty abolished drives her participation with the capital defense college and her work with capital defense lawyers; Adwan, Bar-On, and Maoz live and work in Israel and are committed to facilitating peace between Israelis-Jews and Palestinians; Kushlis's interest in facilitating the luncheon group discussions of foreign policy issues stems directly from her foreign affairs career in public diplomacy; Milburn's involvement with the neighborhood center started when her 6-month-old child took a movement class there, and two years later, she responded to a call in the newsletter for new board members and became a board member; Plax, Kearney, and Allen's interest in teaching college students financial literacy arose from mentoring college students who ultimately accumulated vast amounts of student loan debt, and these faculty members have found it increasingly difficult to attract new faculty members to their university, located in a geographic region of the United States that is more expensive than the norm, if they have a high debt load; and Howell, as a lesbian, has firsthand knowledge of discrimination and seeks to prevent it from affecting others.

Seventh, facilitating groups in the natural setting, as opposed to the laboratory, where conditions can be carefully controlled, often affects the design and conduct of the facilitation, creating challenges and constraints. For instance, many of the facilitation efforts reported in these volumes were affected by physical considerations, such as time, space, and travel. In Milburn et al.'s facilitation of a retreat group, the time limit imposed some restrictions, because the group was not able to extend beyond the time allotted and did not complete the tasks initially agreed on. In Sline's case, he had to wait to begin the assessment and design phases of the facilitation project until after the dust had settled from the jazz festival. Kawakami explains to the groups she facilitates the need for a space where participants can physically move about easily as they engage in the kinetic exercises, but she often finds herself working in a tight, unusable space. She often has to improvise, moving into a hall space, which is workable but not ideal, or an outdoor space. Conducting focus groups across the United States posed considerable challenges for Plax et al., with travel delays, for instance, proving difficult to manage when using professional facilities that have recruited participants in advance and provided incentives for them to attend; in such cases, rescheduling the focus groups was not an option. During some particularly bad weather, Plax et al.'s team did a "planes, trains, and automobiles" marathon to make it on time to the scheduled focus group.

Group facilitation efforts also are affected by organizational needs, resources, and constraints. In some cases, organizational resources can be quite helpful. In Plax et al.'s case, they were provided with professional, state-of-the-art focus group facilities, and the facilities did all of the recruiting of the focus group participants, including providing incentives for them to attend.

In other cases, organizations impose significant constraints on group facilitation efforts. The program in which Sunwolf works, for instance, insisted on a co-leader for each group; consequently, one challenge Sunwolf faces is motivating her various co-leaders, some of whom she has worked with before but others she is meeting for the first time, before the group facilitation to try something new, and she has to balance respecting their ideas about how to accomplish the first group meeting with her desire to perform the empathic attunement facilitation the same way each time. Sponsors of applied communication research also often expect to participate in how communication problems are addressed by researchers (see Frey, O'Hair, & Kreps, 1990). Sline, for instance, was given an initial list of people the organization wanted him to interview in the data-gathering phase of this project, but with the approval of the organizational leaders, he expanded the list as interviewees suggested that he talk with additional stakeholders. In Plax et al.'s case, the company's involvement in the development of the protocol questions and the pressure of formulating questions that the company saw as "fitting its image," yet able to obtain the type of information necessary to meet the goals of the project, affected the way the focus groups were facilitated; essentially, the company said, "Find out what we are doing wrong and how we can do it better, but don't say anything negative about us."

There also are institutional constraints imposed by universities on the conduct of research. In particular, university researchers must get approval from their Institutional Review Board (IRB) to conduct research. In Doerfel and Toshach's case, the IRB required each individual in the group to sign a consent form that indicated her rights as a research participant. If any one member disagreed and refused to sign the form, Doerfel and Toshach would not have been able to use any of that person's participation in the case report. Given that the group was small, any member who did not consent would have canceled the writing of the case; fortunately, that did not occur. As another example, Kedia was concerned with increasing client participation in the outcomes research being conducted about substance abuse prevention programs, but needed to do so in a manner that adhered to the Federal Policy for the Protection of Human Subjects for informed consent.

There also are broader societal and cultural issues and constraints that affect group facilitation efforts. Kedia had to make sure that certain features of the facilitation met government regulations; for example, the survey questionnaires used had to meet the specifications of the Government Performance and Results Act and the Substance Abuse Prevention and Treatment Block Grant Performance Indicators. In Broome's work with peace-building groups in Cyprus, nearly everything in the natural setting—the changing political situation, restrictions on meeting together across community lines, official and unofficial propaganda that painted a negative image of the peace-building groups, and threats (some carried out) against individuals in the group because of their willingness to "meet with the enemy"—affected the facilitation, including not even being able to meet at times as a group.

Eighth, assuming all of these problems can be successfully managed, groups sometimes demonstrate resistance to facilitation efforts. Many groups simply do not use effective meeting procedures in their daily interactions—which is why the facilitation is called for in the first place—and they resist attempts to incorporate them in their work habits, even during the facilitation process. Poole and DeSanctis (1990) reported that 50% of the groups in their studies on procedure use did not follow the procedures faithfully.

In most of the studies reported in these volumes, groups readily accepted the facilitation effort, perhaps because of the credibility of these facilitators/researchers, the ways in which the facilitation procedures employed resonated with the groups' processes and values (such as by encouraging open discussion and democratic decision making; see Stohl, 1995a), or because these procedures were designed or adapted based on interaction with group and organizational members to meet their specific needs. Stempfle's entire facilitation, including the software program involved, was completely custom-designed to meet the needs of the contracting company; the company told Stempfle about the specific problems to be addressed and Stempfle created the facilitation to address those problems.

In some cases, however, group members did demonstrate some resistance. For instance, in their chapter, Doerfel and Toshach discuss the investment club members' skepticism about spending time on communication problems, as members did not see the challenges their group faced as being related to communication and, consequently, thought that a focus on communication procedures would detract them from their goal of learning about and making investments. As one member exclaimed, "We don't want to waste time with any of that touchy-feely stuff." Parrish-Sprowl, in his chapter, talks about how he had to overcome the "discourse of failure" conversations in which employees engaged in response to a previous failed organizational change effort, which raises the issue of whether resistance to facilitation efforts sometimes is due to a history of mediocre facilitation. Spano points out that residents and city officials often favor an argumentative or debate model of communication over the dialogue model that Spano's group promotes, seeing dialogue as "too soft" and "inconclusive." Interestingly, Spano notes that because the facilitation event chronicled in his chapter took place in October 2001, shortly after the September 11, 2001 terrorist attacks, participants were more open, friendly, and receptive to the public dialogue than usual, showing, again, the effects of the larger culture on group facilitation efforts.

Resistance sometimes occurs on the part of specific subgroup members or even a single group member. Kawakami routinely has experienced group members from low-context cultures that privilege verbal communication as being leery of engaging in nonverbal exercises. Sline had full support and cooperation from one of the groups involved in the conflict but experienced resistance from some people associated with the other group. Milburn et al.'s facilitation of the retreat group was going very well, but the makeup of the group changed halfway through the meeting with the addition of a new member, who was in a leadership role, but had not been involved in any of the initial meetings between the client and consultant, and who expressed much resistance to Kenefick's facilitation of the group.

Although resistance to group facilitation procedures certainly makes facilitation more difficult, some resistance probably is a healthy sign that the facilitation is, in fact, working. As Poole (1991) explained:

> In a nutshell, procedures improve group performance because they make groups uncomfortable. Procedures counteract sloppy thinking and ineffective work habits which are part and parcel of everyday group interaction. Because they go against the grain, procedures are "unnatural" and, hence, uncomfortable for groups. The central question, then, is how to get groups to take this bad-tasting medicine. (p. 66)

Ninth, in addition to constraints, there are important ethical decisions that must be made in facilitating natural groups. Although ethical decisions inform all types of research (see, e.g., recent texts by Barbaum & Byron, 2001; Fisher, 2003; Gregory, 2003; Iltis, 2005; Loue, 2000; Sales & Folkman, 2000; Shamoo & Resnik, 2002), they are particularly important in applied research with natural groups, especially group facilitation research, because researchers are intervening into and changing people's lives (see, e.g., Kimmel, 1988).

One important consideration in all research, but especially in the type of research reported in these volumes, is the need for confidentiality, as violations can have serious consequences. For instance, in Albeck et al.'s case, some of the TRT group members were convicted of crimes or had been wanted by police for political activities, and leaks to the media would put some members at risk for physical harm or retaliation by people outside the group. Because of the importance of maintaining confidentiality, confidentiality agreements often are tested by group members. Wheelan and Furbur, for instance, let team members know in advance that they, as consultants, would not talk about individuals or teams with anyone; nevertheless, some managers did ask about a few individuals and teams, and Wheelan and Furbur reminded them of their agreement to respect confidentiality.

Confidentiality also applies to the reporting of findings from such research, both to the members of the group studied and to others (e.g., members of the scholarly community). Maoz and Ellis, for instance, are very careful in all that they write not to break the trust that they have established with the organization sponsoring the Palestinian-Israeli-Jews dialogue groups and not to hurt the people who participate in those groups.

Sometimes, however, confidentiality cannot be fully maintained. Gribas and Sims report that the most difficult ethical issue they faced was determining how to deal honestly and openly with what was being suggested by team members about the limitations of the director of the office staff; they believed that it was important to include this information in the final report that everyone received, but also felt the need to be highly sensitive, particularly since the director was the one who invited the facilitation in the first place. Sline's approach to working with groups and organizations (indeed, the contract he signs with them) calls for full disclosure of issues, problems, and conflicts. Sline's report about the intergroup conflict, which the entire group "unpealed" section by section during the facilitation, had some very strong and potentially hurtful comments about three people involved in the conflict. Given his approach, he was compelled to include these comments in the report (without attribution to who said them), but in fairness to the three individuals who had been singled out, he spoke with them in private before the meeting to forewarn them of what the report contained, and he paid close attention to their emotional needs throughout the day of the facilitation. Although each of them felt hurt, they subsequently thanked Sline for the professional way in which he handled this delicate situation.

In addition to confidentiality related directly to the group facilitation, researchers sometimes learn things along the way that they had not anticipated. Spano reports that the more his group establishes relationships with city staff, the more the staff confides in the group about "behind the scenes" conflicts and dramas, putting Spano and his colleagues in a delicate position.

Facilitators and researchers also must decide how much to disclose about themselves to group members. For Howell et al., the main ethical issue they faced in trying to prevent discrimination from occurring in the school environment was how to let the group know that Howell is a lesbian. Given the current political climate in Michigan, gay and lesbian speakers have been barred from classes, there are suspicions about the so-called "homosexual agenda," and Howell et al. themselves had some concern that if this information became known, efforts in the community to undercut the development of the group could use the "gay issue" as a way to attack the group. They decided to let this information come out naturally, in the choice of language that Howell used and in the type of examples or personal references she introduced. At the same time, however, they decided that Brown would take the lead on issues related to public policy and the gay community; in this way, they tried to create some distinction between policy concerns and personal identity, but this continues to be a troublesome issue in their facilitation work on fighting discrimination.

Facilitators also must decide when and when not to intervene into a group's discourse. In Mabry and Sudweek's facilitation of a virtual research project group, they needed to avoid being overly directive with their advice when issues pertained to questions of what should constitute interpretive discretion on the part of content coders. They struggled with how to be helpful to group members without necessarily conveying conclusions to researchers who needed to exercise independent judgment. This dilemma resulted in the leadership group (the Oracles) having to maintain some "in-group" confidentiality regarding the substance of their deliberations vis-à-vis other group project members.

In cases in which the facilitators either know members of the group or are working together, ethical concerns arise about how to handle that relationship. The established relationship between Milburn and Kenefick, for instance, meant that Kenefick was able to gain more information about the group from Milburn's perspective that may have biased or influenced his facilitation work with the group than had he not known Milburn well at all. During the facilitation, however, Kenefick "bracketed" his relationship with Milburn and tried to interact with her in the same way that he did with other members.

Facilitators also must decide how to handle any problems that occur as a result of their facilitation. In one of Stempfle's workshops, for instance, a problem occurred in which a project leader was not able to cope well with the challenges arising from the dynamics of the simulation. Although this was a painful experience for this participant, it also probably was a necessary experience, as it pointed out problems that occurred during the daily work of the project team. Following the facilitation workshop, based on Stempfle's suggestion, the internal human resource development expert of the company had an extensive talk with this project leader about how to develop herself to be better able to handle such situations. This situation showed that by simulating a realistic and challenging work environment, a central goal of Stepmfle's facilitation, the possibility is created for people to fail to meet the demands of the situation and to fall short of their expectations. In such cases, it is very important to debrief those individuals thoroughly and to offer further facilitation after the official facilitation has ended.

This last point raises a final important ethical issue of how committed facilitators and researchers are to the groups they facilitate and study. Too often, group facilitations are treated as a one-shot medicine to solve long-term, systemic problems. Perhaps this is why many people fear facilitators who come in, diagnose problems, engage in a facilitation, and then depart, leaving the group to cope with what has been stirred up from the facilitation. Deep-seated, problematic group communication issues, however, do not disappear over night; changes in behavior require time and multiple opportunities to continue to discuss and work on desired behaviors. That is why, for instance, Gribas and Sims returned a year later to conduct follow-up interviews to evaluate the effects of the facilitation and the current needs of the office staff. Although group facilitation is not, of course, a lifelong commitment to the group being facilitated, all of the authors talked about the significance of the relationship they established with the individual group members, the group, and the organization as a result of the facilitation—a relationship that, for many, continues to this day.

CONCLUSION

In an article titled "Humans Would Do Better without Groups," Buys (1978) identified many of the problems that groups cause and concluded that people would do better without most groups. In response, Anderson (1978) wrote an essay, titled "Groups Would Do Better without Humans," in which he humorously argued that he looked forward to the day when computers would replace humans in groups because "humans seldom work at maximum ability levels, seldom communicate with any degree of accuracy or logic and are constantly in need of social-emotional satisfaction for their simpering insecurities about affection, esteem, love, etc." (p. 557).

It perhaps is possible for groups to do better without humans, but not for humans to do without groups. There is, however, an alternative to getting rid of groups or replacing humans in groups: Offer people the facilitation needed to engage in effective group communication, and document those efforts so that others may learn from them. Although group communication facilitation procedures certainly are not magical elixirs that will solve all of the problems that plague groups, and facilitating and studying real people solving real problems is difficult to do well, demanding lots of skill (and luck) on the part of facilitators and researchers to meet the challenges posed, as the research evidence from the chapters in these two volumes shows, when done well, such work yields valuable results that can make a significant difference in group life.

REFERENCES

Abernathy, R., & Reardon, M. (2002). *HotTips for facilitators: Strategies to make life easier for anyone who leads, guides, teaches, or trains groups.* Tucson, AZ: Zephry Press.

Adams, T., & Means, J. A. (2005). *Facilitating the project lifecycle: The skills & tools to accelerate progress for six sigma and project teams.* San Francisco: Jossey-Bass.

Adelman, M. B., & Frey, L. R. (1994). The pilgrim must embark: Creating and sustaining community in a residential facility for people with AIDS. In L. R. Frey (Ed.), *Group communication in context: Studies of natural groups* (pp. 3-22). Hillsdale, NJ: Erlbaum.

Adelman, M. B., & Frey, L. R. (1997). *The fragile community: Living together with AIDS.* Mahwah, NJ: Erlbaum.

Adelman, M. B. (Producer), & Schultz, P. (Director). (1991). *The pilgrim must embark: Living in community* [Videotape]. Chicago: Terra Nova Films.

Albanese, R., & Van Fleet, D. D. (1985). Rational behavior in groups: The free-riding tendency. *Academy of Management Review, 10,* 244-255.

Alderton, S. M., & Frey, L. R. (1983). Effects of reactions to arguments on group outcome: The case of group polarization. *Central States Speech Journal, 34,* 88-95.

Alderton, S. M., & Frey, L. R. (1986). Argumentation in small group decision-making. In R. Y. Hirokawa & M. S. Poole (Eds.), *Communication and group decision-making* (pp. 157-173). Beverly Hills, CA: Sage.

Allport, F. H. (1920). The influence of the group upon association and thought. *Journal of Experimental Psychology, 3,* 159-182.

Anderson, L. R. (1978). Groups would do better without humans. *Personality and Social Psychology Bulletin, 4,* 557-558.

Arnold, K. J. (2003). *Team energizers: Fifty practical team activities.* Fairfax, VA: QPC Press.

Arrow, H., Henry, K. B., Poole, M. S., Wheelan, S., & Moreland, R. (2005). Traces, trajectories, and timing: The temporal perspective on groups. In M. S. Poole & A. B. Hollingshead (Eds.), *Theories of small groups: An interdisciplinary perspective* (pp. 313-367). Thousand Oaks, CA: Sage.

Arrow, H., Poole, M. S., Henry, K. B., Wheelan, S., & Moreland, R. (2004). Time, change, and development: The temporal perspective on groups. *Small Group Research, 35,* 73-105.

Baird, A. C. (1928). *Public discussion and debate.* Boston: Ginn.

Bales, R. F., & Cohen, S. P. (1979). *SYMLOG: A system for the multiple level observation of groups.* New York: Free Press.

Barge, J. K. (2002). Enlarging the meaning of group deliberation: From discussion to dialogue. In L. R. Frey (Ed.), *New directions in group communication* (pp. 159-177). Thousand Oaks, CA: Sage.

Barge, J. K., & Frey, L. R. (1997). Life in a task group. In L. R. Frey & J. K. Barge (Eds.), *Managing group life: Communicating in decision-making groups* (pp. 29-51). Boston: Houghton Mifflin.

Barker, J. R. (1993). Tightening the iron cage: Concertive control in self-managing teams. *Administrative Science Quarterly, 38,* 408-437.

Barker, J. R. (1999). *The discipline of teamwork: Participation and concertive control.* Thousand Oaks, CA: Sage.

Barker, J. R., Melville, C. W., & Pacanowsky, M. E. (1993). Self-directed teams at Xel: Changes in communication practices during a program of cultural transformation. *Journal of Applied Communication Research, 21,* 297-312.

Barbaum, D. R., & Byron, M. (2001). *Research ethics: Text and readings.* Upper Saddle River, NJ: Prentice Hall.

Barton, W. A., Jr. (1926). The effect of group activity and individual effort in developing ability to solve problems in first-year algebra. *Educational Administration and Supervision, 12,* 412-518.

Baxter, B. (1943). *Group experience, the democratic way.* New York: Harper & Brothers.

Baxter, L. A., & Clark, C. L. (1996). Perceptions of family communication patterns and the enactment of family rituals. *Western Journal of Communication, 60,* 254-268.

Beatty, C. A., & Barker Scott, B. A. (2005). *Building smart teams: A roadmap to high performance.* Thousand Oaks, CA: Sage.

Beckhard, R. (1967). The confrontation meeting. *Harvard Business Review, 45,* 149-155.

Beebe, S. A., & Masterson, J. T. (1997). *Communicating in small groups: Principles and practices* (5th ed.). New York: Longman.

Bendaly, L. (2000). *Brain teasers for team leaders: Hundreds of word puzzles and number games to energize your meetings.* Toronto: McGraw-Hill Ryerson.

Benne, K. D. (1964). History of the play group in the laboratory setting. In L. P. Bradford, J. R. Gibb, & K. D. Benne (Eds.), *T-group theory and laboratory method: Innovation in re-education* (pp. 80-135). New York: John Wiley.

Bens, I. (2005a). *Advanced facilitation strategies: Tools and techniques to master difficult situations.* San Francisco: Jossey-Bass.

Bens, I. (2005b). *Facilitating with ease!: Core skills for facilitators, team leaders and members, managers, consultants, and trainers* (2nd ed.). San Francisco: Jossey-Bass.

Bernstein, E., & Vinokur, A. (1975). What a person thinks upon learning he has chosen differently from others: Nice evidence for the persuasive-arguments explanation of choice shifts. *Journal of Experimental Social Psychology, 11,* 412-426.

Bernstein, E., & Vinokur, A. (1977). Persuasive argumentation and social comparison as determinants of attitude polarization. *Journal of Experimental Social Psychology, 13,* 315-332.

Berteotti, C. R., & Seibold, D. R. (1994). Coordination and role-definition problems in health-care teams: A hospice case study. In L. R. Frey (Ed.), *Group communication in context: Studies of natural groups* (pp. 107-131). Hillsdale, NJ: Erlbaum.

Bion, W. R. (1961). *Experiences in groups and other papers.* New York. Basic Books.

Bird, S. E. (1999). Chatting on Cynthia's porch: Creating community in an e-mail fan group. *Southern Communication Journal, 65*, 49-65.

Blake, R. R., & Mouton, J. S. (1968). *Corporate excellence through grid organization development.* Houston: Gulf.

Blanchard, K., Randolph, A., & Grazier, P. (2005). *Go team! Take your team to the next level.* San Francisco: Berrett-Koehler.

Block, P. (1981). *Flawless consulting: A guide to getting your expertise used.* San Diego, CA: University Associates.

Bloor, M., Frankland, J., Thomas, M., & Robson, K. (2001). *Focus groups in social research.* Thousand Oaks, CA: Sage.

Booth, N. (2000). *75 icebreakers for great gatherings: Everything you need to bring people together.* St. Paul, MN: Brighton.

Bowers, C., Salas, E., & Jentsch, F. (Eds.). (2005). *Creating high-tech teams: Practical guidance on work performance and technology.* Washington, DC: American Psychological Association.

Boynton, A., & Fischer, B. (2006). *Virtuoso teams: Lessons from great teams that changed the world.* New York: Prentice Hall Professional Business.

Braatan, L. J. (1974/1975). Developmental phases of encounter groups: A critical review of models and a new proposal. *Interpersonal Development, 75*, 1144-1150.

Brock, B. L., & Howell, S. (1994). Leadership in the evolution of a community-based political action group. In L. R. Frey (Ed.), *Group communication in context: Studies of natural groups* (pp. 135-152). Hillsdale, NJ: Erlbaum.

Broome, B. J. (1995). The role of facilitated group process in community-based planning and design: Promoting greater participation in Comanche tribal governance. In L. R. Frey (Ed.), *Innovations in group facilitation: Applications in natural settings* (pp. 27-52). Cresskill, NJ: Hampton Press.

Bulik, K. J. (2000). *Group games & activity leadership.* State College, PA: Venture.

Buys, C. J. (1978). Humans would do better without groups. *Personality and Social Psychology Bulletin, 4*, 123-125.

Cameron, E. (2001). *Facilitation made easy: Practical tips to improve meetings and workshops* (2nd ed.). London: Kogan Page.

Cawyer, C. S., & Smith-Dupré, A. (1995). Communicating social support: Identifying supportive episodes in an HIV/AIDS support group. *Communication Quarterly, 43*, 243-258.

Chambers, R. (2002). *Participatory workshops: A sourcebook of 21 sets of ideas and activities.* Sterling, VA: Earthscan.

Chapel, G., Peterson K. M., & Joseph, R. (1999). Exploring anti-gang advertisements: Focus group discussions with gang members and at-risk youth. *Journal of Applied Communication Research, 27*, 237-247.

Christian, S., & Tubesing, N. L. (2004). *Icebreakers a la carte.* Duluth, MN: Whole Person Associates.

Cissna, K. N. (1982). Editor's note: What is applied communication research? *Journal of Applied Communication Research, 10*, Editorial Statement.

Cline, R. J. W. (1999). Communication in social support groups. In L. R. Frey (Ed.), D. S. Gouran, & M. S. Poole (Assoc. Eds.), *The handbook of group communication theory and research* (pp. 516-538). Thousand Oaks, CA: Sage.

Collaros, P. A., & Anderson, L. R. (1969). The effect of perceived expertness upon creativity of members of brainstorming groups. *Journal of Applied Psychology, 53,* 159-163.

Comas-Díaz, L. (2002). Managing ethnic conflicts. *Peace and Conflict: Journal of Peace Psychology, 8,* 165-166.

Conquergood, D. (1991). "For the nation!" How street gangs problematize patriotism. In R. Troester & C. Kelley (Eds.), *Peacemaking through communication* (pp. 8-21). Annandale, VA: Speech Communication Association.

Conquergood, D. (1992). Life in Big Red: Struggles and accommodations in a Chicago polyethnic tenement. In L. Lamphere (Ed.), *Structuring diversity: Ethnographic perspectives on the new immigration* (pp. 95-144). Chicago: University of Chicago Press.

Conquergood, D. (1994). Homeboys and hoods: Gangs and cultural space. In L. R. Frey (Ed.), *Group communication in context: Studies of natural groups* (pp. 23-55). Hillsdale, NJ: Erlbaum.

Conquergood, D. (Producer), & Siegel, T. (Producer & Director). (1990). *The heart broken in half* [Videotape]. New York: Filmmakers Library.

Cooks, L. M., & Hale, C. L. (1992). A feminist approach to the empowerment of women mediators. *Discourse & Society, 3,* 277-300.

Cooper, C. L., & Mangham, I. L. (1971). *T-groups: A survey of research.* London: Wiley-Interscience.

Cooperrider, D. L., & Srivastra, S. (1987). Appreciative inquiry in organizational life. In R. W. Woodman & W. A Pasmore (Eds.), *Research in organizational change and development* (Vol. 1, pp. 129-169). Greenwich, CT: JAI Press.

Cooperrider, D. L., & Whitney, D. (1999). *Appreciative inquiry.* San Francisco: Berrett Koehler Communications,

Coyle, G. L. (1947). *Group experience and democratic values.* New York: Woman's Press.

Croft, S. E. (1999). Creating locales through storytelling: An ethnography of a group home for men with mental retardation. *Western Journal of Communication, 63,* 329-347.

Crowell, L. (1963). *Discussion, methods of democracy.* Chicago: Scott, Foresman.

Dale, F., & Conant, S. (2004). *101 teambuilding activities: Ideas every coach can use to enhance teamwork, communication and trust.* Durham, NC: Excellence in Performance.

Dashiell, J. F. (1935). Experimental studies of the influence of social situations on the behavior of individual human adults. In C. Murchison (Ed.), *Handbook of social psychology* (pp. 1097-1158). Worchester, MA: Clark University Press.

Dewey, J. (1910). *How we think.* Boston: D.C. Heath.

Dollar, N. J., & Merrigan, G. M. (2002). Ethnographic practices in group communication research. In L. R. Frey (Ed.), *New directions in group communication* (pp. 59-78). Thousand Oaks, CA: Sage.

Doyle, M., & Strauss, D. (1976). *How to make meetings work: The new interaction method*. New York: Wyden Books.

DuFrene, D. D., & Lehman, C. M. (2005). *Building high-performance teams* (2nd ed.). Mason, OH: South-Western.

Duke Corporation Education. (2005). *Building effective teams*. Chicago: Dearborn.

Dunphy, D. C. (1968). Phases, roles, and myths in self-analytical groups. *Journal of Applied Behavioral Science, 12*, 523-542.

Eliasson, J. (2002). Perspectives on managing intractable conflict. *Negotiation Journal, 18*, 371-374.

Eller, J. (2004). *Effective group facilitation in education: How to energize meetings and manage difficult groups*. Thousand Oaks, CA: Corwin Press.

Ellingson, L. L. (2003). Interdisciplinary health care teamwork in the clinic backstage. *Journal of Applied Communication Research, 31*, 93-117.

Ellingson, L. L. (2005). *Communicating in the clinic: Negotiating frontstage and backstage teamwork*. Cresskill, NJ: Hampton Press.

Ezzamel, M., & Willmott, H. (1998). Accounting for teamwork: A critical study of group-based systems of organizational control. *Administrative Science Quarterly, 43*, 358-396.

Fern, F. (2001). *Advanced focus group research*. Thousand Oaks, CA: Sage.

Fetterman, D. M., Kaftarian, A. J., & Wandersman, A. (Eds.). (1996). *Empowerment evaluation: Knowledge and tools for self-assessment and accountability*. Thousand Oaks, CA: Sage.

Firestien, R. L. (1990). Effects of creative problem-solving training on communication behaviors in small groups. *Small Group Research, 21*, 507-521.

Fisher, C. B. (2003). *Decoding the ethics code: A practical guide for psychologists*. Thousand Oaks, CA: Sage.

Folger, J. P., Poole, M. S., & Stutman, R. K. (2001). *Working through conflict: Strategies for relationships, groups, and organizations* (4th ed.). New York: Longman.

French, W. L., & Bell, C. H., Jr. (1984). *Organizational development: Behavioral science interventions for organization improvement* (3rd ed.). Englewood Cliffs, NJ: Prentice-Hall.

Frey, L. R. (1994a). The call of the field: Studying communication in natural groups. In L. R. Frey (Ed.), *Group communication in context: Studies of natural groups* (pp. ix-xiv). Hillsdale, NJ: Erlbaum.

Frey, L. R. (Ed.). (1994b). *Group communication in context: Studies of natural groups*. Hillsdale, NJ: Erlbaum.

Frey, L. R. (1994c). The naturalistic paradigm: Studying small groups in the postmodern era. *Small Group Research, 25*, 551-577.

Frey, L. R. (1995a). Applied communication research on group facilitation in natural settings. In L. R. Frey (Ed.), *Innovations in group facilitation: Applications in natural settings* (pp. 1-23). Cresskill, NJ: Hampton Press.

Frey, L. R. (Ed.). (1995b). *Innovations in group facilitation: Applications in natural settings*. Cresskill, NJ: Hampton Press.

Frey, L. R. (1995c). Magical elixir or what the top tells the middle to do to the bottom?: The paradoxes and promises of facilitating work teams for promoting organizational change and development. In R. Cesaria & P. Shockley-Zalabak (Eds.), *Organization means communication: Making the organizational communication concept relevant to practice* (pp. 173-188). Rome, Italy: Sipi Editore.

Frey, L. R. (1996). Remembering and "re-membering": A history of theory and research on communication and group decision making. In R. Y. Hirokawa & M. S. Poole (Eds.), *Communication and group decision making* (2nd ed., pp. 19-51). Thousand Oaks, CA: Sage.

Frey, L. R. (1997, November). *Grouphate: Implications for research, facilitation, and pedagogy.* Paper presented at the meeting of the National Communication Association, Chicago, IL.

Frey, L. R. (2000). To be applied or not to be applied, that isn't even the question; but wherefore art thou, applied communication researcher? Reclaiming applied communication research and redefining the role of the researcher. *Journal of Applied Communication Research, 28*, 178-182.

Frey, L. R. (Ed.). (2003). *Group communication in context: Studies of bona fide groups* (2nd ed.). Mahwah, NJ: Erlbaum.

Frey, L. R. (in press). Across the great applied divides: Problems, purposes, and practices of applied communication scholarship. In L. R. Frey & K. N. Cissna (Eds.), *Handbook of applied communication.* Mahwah, NJ: Erlbaum.

Frey, L. R., Botan, C. H., & Kreps, G. L. (2000). *Investigating communication: An introduction to research methods* (2nd ed.). Boston: Allyn and Bacon.

Frey, L. R., & Carragee, K. M. (in press). *Communication activism* (2 Vols.). Cresskill, NJ: Hampton Press.

Frey, L. R., O'Hair, D., & Kreps, G. L. (1990). Applied communication methodology. In D. O'Hair & G. L. Kreps (Eds.), *Applied communication theory and research* (pp. 23-56). Hillsdale, NJ: Erlbaum.

Frey, L. R., & Sunwolf. (2004). The symbolic-interpretive perspective on group dynamics. *Small Group Research, 35*, 277-306.

Frey, L. R., & Sunwolf. (2005). The symbolic-interpretive perspective of group life. In M. S. Poole & A. B. Hollingshead (Eds.), *Theories of small groups: An interdisciplinary perspective* (pp. 185-239). Thousand Oaks, CA: Sage.

Galanes, G. J., & Adams, K. (with Brilhart, J. K.). (2004). *Effective group discussion: Theory and practice* (11th ed.). Boston: McGraw-Hill.

Gastil, J. (1992). A definition of small group democracy. *Small Group Research, 23*, 278-301.

Gastil, J. (1993a). *Democracy in small groups: Participation, decision making and communication.* Philadelphia: New Society.

Gastil, J. (1993b). Identifying obstacles to small group democracy. *Small Group Research, 24*, 5-27.

Ghais, S. (2005). *Extreme facilitation: Guiding groups through controversy and complexity.* San Francisco: Jossey-Bass.

Ghaye. T. (2005). *Developing the reflective healthcare team.* Malden, MA: Blackwell.

Gignac, F. (2005). *Building successful virtual teams.* Boston: Artech House.

Glaser, S. R. (1994). Teamwork and communication: A 3-year case study of change. *Management Communication Quarterly, 7,* 282-296.

Gold, N. (Ed.). (2005). *Teamwork: An interdisciplinary perspective.* New York: Palgrave Macmillan.

Golembiewski, R., & Blumberg, A. (Eds.). (1977). *Sensitivity training and the laboratory approach: Readings about concepts and applications* (3rd ed.). Itasca, IL: F. E. Peacock.

Gordon, S. (2005). *We are a team.* New York: Marshall Cavendish Benchmark Books.

Gottlieb, M. R. (2003). *Managing group process.* Westport, CT: Praeger.

Gouran, D. S. (1982). *Making decisions in groups: Choices and consequences.* Glenview, IL: Scott, Foresman.

Gouran, D. S. (1993). Factors affecting the decision-making process in the Attorney General's Commission on Pornography: A case study of unwarranted collective judgment. In C. M. Miller & B. C. McKinney (Eds.), *Government commission communication* (pp. 123-144). Westport, CT: Praeger.

Gouran, D. S. (1995). Foreword. In L. R. Frey (Ed.), *Innovations in group facilitation: Applications in natural settings* (pp. vii-x). Cresskill, NJ: Hampton Press.

Gouran, D. S. (1999). Communication in groups: The emergence and evolution of a field of study. In L. R. Frey (Ed.), D. S. Gouran, & M. S. Poole (Assoc. Eds.), *The handbook of group communication theory and research* (pp. 3-36). Thousand Oaks, CA: Sage.

Gouran, D. S., & Hirokawa, R. Y. (1996). Functional theory and communication in decision-making and problem-solving groups: An expanded view. In R. Y. Hirokawa & M. S. Poole (Eds.), *Communication and group decision making* (2nd ed., pp. 55-80). Thousand Oaks, CA: Sage.

Greenbaum, H. H., & Query, J. L., Jr. (1999). Communication in organizational work groups: A review and analysis of natural work group studies. In L. R. Frey (Ed.), D. S. Gouran, & M. S. Poole (Assoc. Eds.), *The handbook of group communication theory and research* (pp. 539-564). Thousand Oaks, CA: Sage.

Greenbaum, T. L. (1998). *The handbook for focus group research* (2nd rev. ed.). Thousand Oaks, CA: Sage.

Greenbaum, T. L. (2000). *Moderating focus groups: A practical guide for group facilitation.* Thousand Oaks, CA: Sage.

Gregory, I. (2003). *Ethics in research.* New York: Continuum.

Griffin-Wiesner, J. (2005). *Generators: 20 activities to recharge your intergenerational group.* Minneapolis, MN: Search Institute.

Gurnee, H. (1937). Maze learning in the collective situation. *Journal of Experimental Psychology, 11,* 348-368, 437-464.

Hackman, J. R., & Kaplan, R. E. (1974). Interventions into group process: An approach to improving the effectiveness of groups. *Decision Processes, 5,* 459-480.

Haiman, F. (1951). *Group leadership and democratic action.* Boston: Houghton Mifflin.

Hall, E. T. (1976). *Beyond culture*. Garden City, NY: Anchor Press.

Hall, E. T. (1983). *The dance of life: The other dimension of time*. Garden City, NY: Anchor Press/Doubleday.

Hall, J., & Watson, W. H. (1970). The effects of a normative intervention on group decision making performance. *Human Relations, 23*, 299-317.

Hare, A. P. (1994). Individual versus group. In A. P. Hare, H. H. Blumberg, M. F. Davies, & M. V. Kent (Eds.), *Small group research: A handbook* (pp. 261-70). Norwood, NJ: Ablex.

Harris, T. E., & Sherblom, J. C. (2005). *Small group and team communication* (3rd ed.). Boston: Pearson/Allyn and Bacon.

Harkins, S. G., Latané, B., & Williams, K. (1980). Social loafing: Allocating effort or taking it easy? *Journal of Experimental Social Psychology, 16*, 457-465.

Harkins, S. G., & Petty, R. E. (1982). Effects of task difficulty and task uniqueness on social loafing. *Journal of Personality and Social Psychology, 43*, 1214-1229.

Havergal, M., & Edmonstone, J. (2003). *The facilitator's toolkit* (2nd ed.). Burlington, VT: Gower.

Hayden, P., Frederick, L., & Smith, B. J. (2002). *A road map for facilitating collaborative teams*. Longmont, CO: Sopris West.

Hewes, D. E. (1986). A socio-egocentric model of group decision-making: An amplification of socio-egocentric theory. In R. Y. Hirokawa & M. S. Poole (Eds.), *Communication and group decision-making* (pp. 265-291). Beverly Hills, CA: Sage.

Hirokawa, R. Y. (1982). Group communication and problem-solving effectiveness I: A critical review of inconsistent findings. *Communication Quarterly, 30*, 134-141.

Hirokawa, R. Y. (1983). Group communication and problem-solving effectiveness II: An exploratory investigation of procedural functions. *Western Journal of Speech Communication, 47*, 54-74.

Hirokawa, R. Y. (1985). Discussion procedures and decision-making performance; A test of a functional perspective. *Human Communication Research, 12*, 203-224.

Hirokawa, R. Y. (1987). Why informed groups make faulty decisions: An investigation of possible interaction-based explanations. *Small Group Behavior, 18*, 3-29.

Hirokawa, R. Y. (1988). Group communication and decision-making performance: A continued test of the functional perspective. *Human Communication Research, 14*, 487-515.

Hirokawa, R. Y., & Rost, K. M. (1992). Effective group decision making in organizations: Field test of the vigilant interaction theory. *Management Communication Quarterly, 5*, 267-288.

Hogan, C. (2002). *Understanding facilitation: Theory and principle*. London: Kogan Paul.

Hogan, C. (2003). *Practical facilitation: A toolkit of techniques*. Sterling, VA: Kogan Page.

Hollinghead, A. B., Wittenbaum, G. W., Paulus, P. B., Hirokawa, R. Y., Ancona, D. G., Peterson, R. S., et al. (2005). A look at groups from the functional perspective. In M. S. Poole & A. B. Hollingshead (Eds.), *Theories of small groups: Interdisciplinary perspectives* (pp. 21-62). Thousand Oaks, CA: Sage.

Holsti, O. (1971). Crises, stress, and decision-making. *Interactional Social Science Journal, 23,* 53-67.

Houston, R. (2003). In the mask of thin air: Intragroup and intergroup communication during the Mt. Everest disaster. In L. R. Frey (Ed.), *Group communication in context: Studies of bona fide groups* (2nd ed., pp. 137-156). Mahwah, NJ: Erlbaum.

Howell, S., Brock, B., & Hauser, E. (2003). A multicultural, intergenerational youth program: Creating and sustaining a youth community group. In L. R. Frey (Ed.), *Group communication in context: Studies of bona fide groups* (2nd ed., pp. 85-108). Mahwah, NJ: Erlbaum.

Howick, D., Daily, S., & Sprik, A. (2002). *The new compleat facilitator: A handbook for facilitators.* Madison, WI: Howick Associates.

Humphrey, W. S. (2005). *TSP—leading a development team.* Upper Saddle River, NJ: Addison-Wesley.

Iacofano, D. S. (2001). *Meeting of the minds: A guide to successful meeting facilitation.* Berkeley, CA: MIG Communications.

Iltis, A. S. (Ed.). (2005). *Research ethics.* New York: Routledge.

Issac, R. M., Walker, J. M., & Thomas, S. H. (1984). Divergent evidence on free riding: An experimental examination of possible explanations. *Public Choice, 43,* 113-149.

Jackson, J. M., & Williams, K. D. (1985). Social loafing on difficult tasks: Working collectively can improve performance. *Journal of Personality and Social Psychology, 49,* 937-942.

Janis, I. L. (1972). *Victims of groupthink: A psychological study of policy decisions and fiascoes.* Boston: Houghton Mifflin.

Janis, I. L. (1982). *Groupthink: Psychological studies of policy decisions and fiascoes* (2nd ed.). Boston: Houghton Mifflin.

Janis, I. L., & Mann, L. (1977). *Decision making: A psychological analysis of conflict, choice, and commitment.* New York: Free Press.

Jenness, A. (1932). The role of discussion in changing opinion regarding a matter of fact. *Journal of Abnormal and Social Psychology, 27,* 29-34.

Johnson, A. (1939). Teaching the fundamentals of speech through group discussion. *Quarterly Journal of Speech, 25,* 440-447.

Jones, L. B. (2005). *The four elements of success: A simple personality profile that will transform your team.* Nashville, TN: Thomas Nelson.

Jones, R., Oyung, R., & Pace, L. (2005). *Working virtually: Challenges of virtual teams.* Hershey, PA: IRM Press.

Jones, T. S. (2005). Mediating intragroup and intergroup conflict. In S. A. Wheelan (Ed.), *The handbook of group research and practice* (pp. 463-483). Thousand Oaks, CA: Sage.

Kalani. (2004). *Together in rhythm: A facilitator's guide to drum circle music.* Los Angeles: Alfred.

Katzenbach, J. R., & Smith, D. K. (1993). *The wisdom of teams: Creating the high-performance organization*. New York: Harper Business School Press.

Kausen, R. C. (2003). *We've got to start meeting like this!: How to get better results with fewer meetings*. Coffee Creek, CA: Life Education.

Kerr, N. L. (1983). Motivation losses in small groups: A social dilemma analysis. *Journal of Personality and Social Psychology, 48*, 349-363.

Ketrow, S. (1999). Nonverbal aspects of group communication. In L. R. Frey (Ed.), D. S. Gouran, & M. S. Poole (Assoc. Eds.), *The handbook of group communication theory and research* (pp. 251-287). Thousand Oaks, CA: Sage.

Keyton, J. (1995). Using SYMLOG as a self-analytical group facilitation technique. In L. R. Frey (Ed.), *Innovations in group facilitation: Applications in natural settings* (pp. 148-174). Cresskill, NJ: Hampton Press.

Keyton, J. (1999). Relational communication in groups. In L. R. Frey (Ed.), D. S. Gouran, & M. S. Poole (Assoc. Eds.), *The handbook of group communication theory and research* (pp. 192-222). Thousand Oaks, CA: Sage.

Keyton, J., & Frey, L. R. (2002). The state of traits: Predispositions and group communication. In L. R. Frey (Ed.), *New directions in group communication* (pp. 99-120). Thousand Oaks, CA: Sage.

Keyton, J., Harmon, N., & Frey, L. R. (1996, November). *Grouphate: Implications for teaching group communication*. Paper presented at the meeting of the Speech Communication Association, San Diego, CA.

Kilpatrick, W. H. (1940). *Group education for a democracy*. New York: Association Press.

Kimmel, A. J. (1988). *Ethics and values in applied social research*. Newbury Park, CA: Sage.

Kramer, M. W. (2002). Communication in a community theatre group: Managing multiple group roles. *Communication Studies, 53*, 151-170.

Kreps, G. L. (1995). Using focus group discussions to promote organizational reflexivity: Two applied communication field studies. In L. R. Frey (Ed.), *Innovations in group facilitation: Applications in natural settings* (pp. 177-199). Cresskill, NJ: Hampton Press.

Krueger, R. A., & Casey, M. A. (2000). *Focus groups: A practical guide for applied research* (3rd ed.). Thousand Oaks, CA: Sage.

Krikorian, D., & Kiyomiya, T. (2003). Bona fide groups as self-organizing systems: Applications to electronic newsgroups. In L. R. Frey (Ed.), *Group communication in context: Studies of bona fide groups* (2nd ed., pp. 335-366). Thousand Oaks, CA: Sage.

Lambert, J., & Meyers, S. (2004). *Trainer's diversity source book: 50 ready-to-use activities, from icebreakers through wrap ups*. Alexandria, VA: Society for Human Resource Management.

Lamm, H., & Trommsdorff, G. (1973). Group versus individual performance on tasks requiring ideational proficiency (brainstorming): A review. *European Journal of Social Psychology, 3*, 361-388.

Lammers, J. C., & Krikorian, D. H. (1997). Theoretical extension and operationalization of the bona fide group construct with an application to surgical teams. *Journal of Applied Communication Research, 25*, 17-38.

Landale, A., & Douglas, M. (2002). *The fast facilitator: 76 facilitator activities and interventions covering essential skills, group processes and creative techniques*. Aldershot, Hampshire, England: Gower.

Langer, J., Wapner, S., & Werner, H. (1961). The effects of danger upon the experiences of time. *American Journal of Psychology, 74*, 94-97.

Latané, B., Williams, K., & Harkins, S. (1979a). Many hands make light the work: The causes and consequences of social loafing. *Journal of Personality and Social Psychology, 37*, 822-832.

Latané, B., Williams, K., & Harkins, S. (1979b). Social loafing. *Psychology Today, 13*(3), 104-110.

Lenicioni, P. M. (2005). *Overcoming the five dysfunctions of a team: A field guide for leaders, managers, and facilitators*. San Francisco: Jossey-Bass.

Levy-Leboyer, C. (1988). Success and failure in applying psychology. *American Psychologist, 43*, 779-785.

Lewin, K. (1951). *Field theory in social science: Selected theoretical papers* (D. Cartwright, Ed.). New York: Harper & Row.

Lewin, K., & Lippitt, R. (1938). An experimental approach to the study of autocracy and democracy: A preliminary note. *Sociometry, 1*, 292-300.

Lewin, K., Lippitt, R., & White, R. K. (1939). Patterns of aggressive behavior in experimentally created "social climates." *Journal of Social Psychology, 10*, 271-299.

Lieberman, M. A., Yalom, I. D., & Miles, M. B. (1973). *Encounter groups: First facts*. New York: Basic Books.

Lippitt, R. (1939). Field theory and experiment in social psychology: Autocratic and democratic group atmosphere. *American Journal of Sociology, 45*, 26-49.

Lippitt, R. (1940). An experimental study of the effect of democratic and authoritarian group atmospheres. *University of Iowa Studies in Child Welfare, 16*, 43-195.

Lippitt, R., & White, R. K. (1952). An experimental study of leadership and group life. In G. E. Swanson, T. M. Newcomb, & E. L. Hartley (Eds.), *Readings in social psychology* (pp. 340-355). New York: Holt.

Litosseliti, L. (2003). *Using focus groups in research*. New York: Continuum.

Longman, A., & Mullins, J. (2005). *The rational project manager: A thinking team's guide to getting work done*. Hoboken, NJ: John Wiley & Sons.

Loue, S. (2000). *Textbook of research ethics: Theory and practice*. New York: Kluwer Academic/Plenum Press.

Lumsden, G., & Lumsden, D. (1993). *Communicating in groups and teams: Shared leadership*. Belmont, CA: Wadsworth.

Macchia, S. A. (2005). *Becoming a healthy team: Five traits of vital leadership*. Grand Rapids, MI: Baker Books.

Maier, N. R. F. (1967). Assets and liabilities in group problem-solving: The need for an integrative function. *Psychological Review, 74*, 239-249.

Maier, N. R. F. (1970). *Problem solving and creativity in individuals and groups*. Belmont, CA: Brooks/Cole.

Mann, L. (2005). *Leadership, management, and innovation in R & D project teams*. Westport, CT: Praeger.

Mann, R. D., Gibbard, G. S., & Hartman, J. J. (1967). *Interpersonal styles and group development: An analysis of the member-leader relationship*. New York: John Wiley.

Marston, W. M. (1924). Studies in testimony. *Journal of Criminal Law & Criminology, 15*, 5-31.

Martin, N. R. M. (2005). *A guide to collaboration for IEP teams*. Baltimore: Paul H. Brookes.

Massey, T. (2005). *Ten commitments for building high performance teams*. Bandon, OR: Robert D. Reed.

Matricardi, J., & McLarty, J. (2006). *Group time activities A to Z*. Clifton Park, NY: Thomson Delmar Learning.

McCain, D. V., & Tobey, D. D. (2004). *Facilitation basics*. Alexandria, VA: ASTD Press.

Meier, C. (2003). Doing "groupness" in a spatially distributed work group: The case of videoconferences at Technics. In L. R. Frey (Ed.), *Group communication in context: Studies of bona fide groups* (2nd ed., pp. 367-397). Thousand Oaks, CA: Sage.

Merton, R. K. (1946). The focused interview. *American Journal of Sociology, 51*, 541-557.

Merton, R. K., Fiske, M., & Kendall, P. L. (1956). *The focused interview*. Glencoe, IL: Free Press.

Micale, F. A. (2003). *Power meetings: Mastering the art of planning, running, and leading meetings*. Irvine, CA: Entrepreneur Media.

Midura, D. W., & Glover, D. R. (2005). *Essentials of team building: Principles and practices*. Champaign, IL: Human Kinetics.

Miller, B. C. (2004). *Quick teambuilding activities for busy managers: 50 exercises that get results in just 15 minutes*. New York: American Management Association.

Mills, T. M. (1964). *Group transformation: An analysis of a learning group*. Englewood Cliffs, NJ: Prentice-Hall.

Mintzberg, H. (1973). *The nature of managerial work*. New York: Harper and Row.

Moerman, M. (1988). *Talking culture: Ethnography and conversation analysis*. Philadelphia: University of Pennsylvania Press.

Monge, P. R., McSween, C., & Wyer, J. (1989). *A profile of meetings in corporate America: Results of the 3M meeting effectiveness study*. Los Angeles: University of Southern California, Annenberg School of Communication.

Morgan, D. L. (1997). *Focus groups as qualitative research* (2nd ed.). Thousand Oaks, CA: Sage.

Mosvick, R. K., & Nelson, R. B. (1987). *We've got to start meeting like this: A guide to successful business meeting management*. Glenview, IL: Scott, Foresman.

Murphy, B. O. (1995). Promoting dialogue in culturally diverse workplace environments. In L. R. Frey (Ed.), *Innovations in group facilitation: Applications in natural settings* (pp. 77-93). Cresskill, NJ: Hampton Press.

Myers, D. G., & Lamm, H. (1975). The polarizing effect of group discussion. *American Scientist, 63,* 297-303.

Myers, D. G., & Lamm, H. (1976). The group polarization phenomenon. *Psychological Bulletin, 83,* 602-627.

Nadler, D. (1979). The effects of feedback on task group behavior: A review of the experimental literature. *Organizational Behavior and Human Performance, 23,* 309-338.

Neider, L. L., & Schriesheim, C. A. (Eds.). (2005). *Understanding teams.* Greenwich, CT: Information Age.

Nicotera, A. M. (1997). Managing conflict in groups. In L. R. Frey & J. K. Barge (Eds.), *Managing group life: Communicating in decision-making groups* (pp. 104-130). Boston: Houghton Mifflin.

Niederman, F. (1996). Acquiring knowledge about group facilitation: Research propositions. In *Proceedings of the 1996 ACM SIGCPR/SIGMIS Conference on Computer Personnel Research* (pp. 58-67). New York: ACM Press.

O'Rourke, J., & Collins, S. D. (2005). *Managing conflict and workplace relationships.* Mason, OH : South-Western.

Oliver, K., & Walker, M. (1984). The free rider problem: Experimental evidence. *Public Choice, 43,* 3-24.

Olson, M., Jr. (1965). *The logic of collective action: Public goods and the theory of groups.* Cambridge, MA: Harvard University Press.

Orlitzky, M., & Hirokawa, R. Y. (2001). To err is human, to correct for it divine: A meta-analysis of research testing the functional theory of group decision-making effectiveness. *Small Group Research, 32,* 313-341.

Osborn, A. (1957). *Applied imagination: Principles and procedures of creative thinking* (Rev. ed.). New York: Scribner.

Pavitt, C. (1993). What (little) we know about formal group discussion procedures: A review of relevant research. *Small Group Research, 24,* 217-235.

Pearce, W. B., & Littlejohn, S. W. (1997). *Moral conflict: When social worlds collide.* Thousand Oaks, CA: Sage.

Pessin, J., & Husband, R. W. (1933). Effects of social stimulation on human maze learning. *Journal of Abnormal and Social Psychology, 28,* 148-154.

Peter, L. J. (1989). *Peter's quotations: Ideas for our times.* New York: Bantam Books.

Petronio, S., Jones, S., & Morr, M. C. (2003). Family privacy dilemmas: Managing communication boundaries within family groups. In L. R. Frey (Ed.), *Group communication in context: Studies of bona fide groups* (2nd ed., pp. 23-56). Mahwah, NJ: Erlbaum.

Philipsen, G. (1990/1991). Situated meaning, ethnography, and conversation analysis. *Research on Language and Social Interaction, 24,* 225-238.

Poole, M. S. (1981). Decision development in small groups I: A comparison of two models. *Communication Monographs, 48,* 1-24.

Poole, M. S. (1983a). Decision development in small groups II: A study of multiple sequences in decision making. *Communication Monographs, 50,* 206-232.

Poole, M. S. (1983b). Decision development in small groups III: A multiple sequence model of group decision development. *Communication Monographs, 50*, 321-341.

Poole, M. S. (1991). Procedures for managing meetings: Social and technological innovation. In R. A. Swenson & B. O. Knapp (Eds.), *Innovative meeting management* (pp. 53-109). Austin, TX: 3M Meeting Management Institute.

Poole, M. S. (1998). The small group should be the fundamental unit of communication research. In J. S. Trent (Ed.), *Communication: Views from the helm for the 21st century* (pp. 94-97). Boston: Allyn and Bacon.

Poole, M. S., & DeSanctis, G. (1990). Understanding the use of group decision support systems: The theory of adaptive structuration. In J. Fulk & C. Steinfield (Eds.), *Organizations and communication technology* (pp. 175-195). Newbury Park, CA: Sage.

Poole, M. S., & Roth, J. (1989a). Decision development in small groups IV: A typology of group decision paths. *Human Communication Research, 15*, 323-356.

Poole, M. S., & Roth, J. (1989). Decision development in small groups V: A test of a contingency model. *Human Communication Research, 15*, 549-589.

Priest, S., Gass, M. A., & Gillis, L. (2000). *The essential elements of facilitation.* Dubuque, IA: Kendall/Hunt.

Propp, K. M. (1999). Collective information processing in groups. In L. R. Frey (Ed.), D. S. Gouran, & M. S. Poole (Assoc. Eds.), *The handbook of group communication theory and research* (pp. 225-250). Thousand Oaks, CA: Sage.

Propp, K. M., & Nelson, D. (1996). Problem-solving performance in naturalistic groups: A test of the ecological validity of the functional perspective. *Communication Studies, 47*, 33-45.

Putnam, L. L., & Stohl, C. (1990). Bona fide groups: A reconceptualization of groups in context. *Communication Studies, 41*, 248-265.

Putnam, L. L., & Stohl, C. (1996). Bona fide groups: An alternative perspective for communication and group decision making. In R. Y. Hirokawa & M. S. Poole (Eds.), *Communication and group decision making* (2nd ed., pp. 147-178). Thousand Oaks, CA: Sage.

Putz, G. B. (2002). *Facilitation skills: Helping groups make decisions* (2nd ed.). Bountiful, UT: Deep Space Technology.

Pyron, H. C. (1964). An experimental study of the role of reflective thinking in business and professional conferences and discussions. *Speech Monographs, 31*, 157-161.

Pyron, H. C., & Sharp, H., Jr. (1963). A quantitative study of reflective thinking and professional conferences and discussions. *Speech Monographs, 31*, 157-161.

Rahim, M. A. (2001). *Managing conflict in organizations* (3rd ed.). Westport, CT: Quorum Books.

Rees, F. (2001). *How to lead work teams: Facilitation skills* (2nd ed.). San Francisco: Pfeiffer.

Rees, F. (2004). *25 activities for developing team leaders.* San Francisco: Pfeiffer.

Rees, F. (2005). *The facilitator excellence handbook* (2nd ed.). San Francisco: Pfeiffer.

Rogers, C. (1970). *Carl Rogers on encounter groups*. New York: Harper and Row.

Rohnke, K. E. (2002). *A small book about large group games*. Dubuque, IA: Kendall/Hunt.

Rothwell, J. D. (2004). *In mixed company: Communicating in small groups and teams* (6th ed.). Belmont, CA: Wadsworth.

Ruud, G. (1995). The symbolic construction of organizational identities and community in a regional symphony. *Communication Studies, 46,* 201-221.

Salemi, R. (2005). *Leading after a layoff: Five proven steps to quickly reignite your team's productivity*. Avon, MA: Adams Media.

Sales, B. D., & Folkman, S. (Eds.). (2002). *Ethics in research with human participants*. Washington, DC: American Psychological Association.

Schacter, S. (1968). Deviation, rejection, and communication. In D. Cartwright & A. Zander (Eds.), *Group dynamics: Theory and research* (3rd ed., pp. 165-181). Beverly Hills, CA: Sage.

Schein, E. H. (1969). *Process consultation*. Reading, MA: Addison-Wesley.

Schein, E. H. (1988). *Process consultation: Its role in organizational development* (Vol. 1, 2nd ed.). Reading, MA: Addison-Wesley.

Schein, E. H. (1995). Kurt Lewin in the classroom, in the field, and in change theory: Toward a theory of managed learning. *Systems Practice, 9,* 71-93.

Schuman, S. P. (Ed.). (2005). *The IAF handbook of group facilitation: Best practices from the leading organization in facilitation*. San Francisco: Jossey-Bass.

Schwartzman, H. B. (1989). *The meeting: Gatherings in organizations and communities*. New York: Plenum Press.

Schwarz, R. M. (2002). *The skilled facilitator: A comprehensive resource for consultants, facilitators, managers, and coaches* (Rev. ed.). San Francisco: Jossey-Bass.

Schwarz, R. M. (2005). *The skilled facilitator fieldbook: Tips, tools, and tested methods for consultants, facilitators, managers, trainers, and coaches*. San Francisco: Jossey-Bass.

Scott, C. R. (1999). Communication technology and group communication. In L. R. Frey (Ed.), D. S. Gouran, & M. S. Poole (Assoc. Eds.), *The handbook of group communication theory and research* (pp. 432-472). Thousand Oaks, CA: Sage.

Seibold, D. R. (1979). Making meetings more successful: Plans, formats and procedures for group problem-solving. *Journal of Business Communication, 16,* 3-20.

Seibold, D. R. (1995). Developing the "team" in a team-managed organization: Group facilitation in a new-design plant. In L. R. Frey (Ed.), *Innovations in group facilitation: Applications in natural settings* (pp. 282-298). Cresskill, NJ: Hampton Press.

Seibold, D. R., & Krikorian, D. H. (1997). Planning and facilitating group meetings. In L. R. Frey & J. K. Barge (Eds.), *Managing group life: Communicating in decision-making groups* (pp. 270-305). Boston: Houghton Mifflin.

Sewell, G. (1998). The discipline of teams: The control of team-based industrial work through electronic and peer surveillance. *Administrative Science Quarterly, 43*, 397-428.

Shamoo, A. E., & Resnik, D. B. (2002). *Responsible conduct of research*. New York: Oxford University Press.

Sharp, J., Jr., & Millikin, J. (1964). Reflective thinking ability and the product of problem-solving discussion. *Speech Monographs, 31*, 124-127.

Shaw, M. E. (1932). Comparison of individuals and small groups in the rational solution of complex problems. *American Journal of Psychology, 44*, 491-504.

Shaw, M. E. (1981). *Group dynamics: The psychology of small group behavior* (3rd ed.). New York: McGraw-Hill.

Shure, G. H., Rogers, M. S., Larsen, I. M., & Tassone, J. (1962). Group planning and task effectiveness. *Sociometry, 25*, 263-282.

Shutter, R. (2002). Cross-national group communication research: Prospect and promise. In L. R. Frey (Ed.), *New directions in group communication* (pp. 273-283). Thousand Oaks, CA: Sage.

Slater, P. (1966). *Microcosm*. New York: John Wiley and Sons.

Smith, S. M. (1991). Managing your meeting for a "bottom line payoff." In R. A. Swanson & B. O. Knapp (Eds.), *Innovating meeting management* (pp. 19-34). Austin, TX: 3M Meeting Management Institute.

Snell, M. E., & Janney, R. (2005). *Collaborative teaming: Teachers' guide to inclusive pratices* (2nd ed.). Baltimore: Paul H. Brookes.

Socha, T. J. (1999). Communication in family units: Studying the first "group." In L. R. Frey (Ed.), D. S. Gouran, & M. S. Poole (Assoc. Eds.), *The handbook of group communication theory and research* (pp. 475-492). Thousand Oaks, CA: Sage.

Socha, T. J., & Socha, D. M. (1994). Children's task-group communication: Did we learn it all in kindergarten? In L. R. Frey (Ed.), *Group communication in context: Studies of natural groups* (pp. 227-246). Hillsdale, NJ: Erlbaum.

Sorenson, R. L. (1999). Conflict management strategies used in successful family businesses. *Family Business Review, 12*, 133-146.

Spano, S. (2001). *Public dialogue and participatory democracy: The Cupertino community project*. Cresskill, NJ: Hampton Press.

Stasser, G. (1992). Information salience and the discovery of hidden profiles by decision making groups: A "thought experiment." *Organizational Behavior and Human Decision Processes, 52*, 156-181.

Stasser, G., & Titus, W. (1985). Pooling of unshared information in group decision making: Biased information sampling during discussion. *Journal of Personality and Social Psychology, 48*, 1467-1478.

Stock, D., & Thelen, H. A. (1958). *Emotional dynamics and group culture: Experimental studies of individual and group behavior*. New York: New York University Press.

Stohl, C. (1995a). Facilitating bona fide groups: Practice and paradox. In L. R. Frey (Ed.), *Innovations in group facilitation: Applications in natural settings* (pp. 325-332). Cresskill, NJ: Hampton Press.

Stohl, C. (1995b). Paradoxes of participation. In R. Cesaria & P. Shockley-Zalabak (Eds.), *Organization means communication: Making the organizational communication concept relevant to practice* (pp. 199-215). Rome, Italy: Sipi Editore.

Stohl, C., & Holmes, M. E. (1993). A functional perspective for bona fide groups. In S. A. Deetz (Ed.), *Communication yearbook* (Vol. 16, pp. 601-614). Newbury Park, CA: Sage.

Stohl, C., & Putnam, L. L. (1994). Group communication in context: Implications for the study of bona fide groups. In L. R. Frey (Ed.), *Group communication in context: Studies of natural groups* (pp. 284-292). Hillsdale, NJ: Erlbaum.

Stohl, C., & Putnam, L. L. (2003). Communication in bona fide groups: A retrospective and prospective account. In L. R. Frey (Ed.), *Group communication in context: Studies of bona fide groups* (2nd ed., pp. 399-414). Mahwah, NJ: Erlbaum.

Sunwolf, & Frey, L. R. (2005). Facilitating group communication. In S. A. Wheelan (Ed.), *The handbook of group research and practice* (pp. 485-509). Thousand Oaks, CA: Sage.

Sunwolf, & Leets, L. (2003). Communication paralysis during peer group exclusion: Social dynamics that prevent children and adolescents from expressing disagreement. *Journal of Language and Social Psychology, 22*, 355-384.

Sunwolf, & Leets, L. (2004). Being left out: Rejecting outsiders and communicating group boundaries in childhood and adolescent peer groups. *Journal of Applied Communication Research, 32*, 195-223.

Sunwolf, & Seibold, D. R. (1998). Jurors' intuitive rules for deliberations: A structurational approach to jury decision making. *Communication Monographs, 65*, 282-307.

The payoff from teams. (1989, July 10), *Business Week*, p. 57.

The 3M Meeting Management Team, & Drew, J. (1994). *Mastering meetings: Discovering the hidden potential of effective business meetings.* New York: McGraw-Hill.

Thompson, L. L., & Choi, H-S. (Eds.). (2005). *Creativity and innovation in organizational teams.* Mahwah, NJ : Erlbaum.

Thorndike, R. L. (1938). The effect of discussion upon the correctness of group decisions, when the factor of majority influence is allowed for. *Journal of Social Psychology, 9*, 343-464.

Timmons, W. M. (1939). *Decisions and attitudes as outcomes of the discussion of a social problem* [Contributions to Education, No. 777]. New York: Columbia University, Teachers College, Bureau of Publications.

Tindale, R. S., Dykema-Engblade, A., & Wittkowski, E. (2005). Conflict within and between groups. In S. A. Wheelan (Ed.), *The handbook of group research and practice* (pp. 313-328). Thousand Oaks, CA: Sage.

Ting-Toomey, S., & Oetzel, J. G. (2001). *Managing intercultural conflict effectively.* Thousand Oaks, CA: Sage.

Tracy, K., & Dimmock, A. (2004). Meetings: Discursive sites for building and fragmenting community. In P. J. Kalbfleisch (Ed.), *Communication yearbook* (Vol. 28, pp. 127-165). Mahwah, NJ: Erlbaum.

Tracy, K., & Standerfer, C. (2003). Selecting a school superintendent: Sensitivities in group deliberation. In L. R. Frey (Ed.), *Group communication in context: Studies of bona fide groups* (2nd ed., pp. 109-134). Mahwah, NJ: Erlbaum.

Travis, L. E. (1925). The effect of a small audience upon eye-hand coordination. *Journal of Abnormal and Social Psychology, 20,* 142-146.

Travis, L. E. (1928). The influence of the group upon the stutter's speed in free association. *Journal of Abnormal and Social Psychology, 23,* 45-51.

Triplett, N. (1897). The dynamogenic factors in peacemaking and competition. *American Journal of Psychology, 9,* 507-533.

Tuckman, B. W. (1965). Developmental sequences in small groups. *Psychological Bulletin, 63,* 384-399.

Tuckman, B. W., & Jensen, M. A. C. (1977). Stages in small group development revisited. *Group and Organizational Studies, 2,* 419-427.

van Vree, W. (1999). *Meetings, manners, and civilization: The development of modern meeting behaviour* (K. Bell, Trans.). New York: Leicester University Press.

Warfield, J. N. (1976). *Social systems: Planning, policy, and complexity.* New York: Wiley.

Warfield, J. N. (1994). *A science of generic design: Managing complexity through systems design* (2nd ed.). Salinas, CA: Intersystems.

Watson, G. B. (1928). Do groups think more efficiently than individuals? *Journal of Abnormal and Social Psychology, 23,* 328-336.

Weaver, R. G., & Farrell, D. (2003). *Crisis at Santa's workshop: Using facilitation to get more done in less time.* San Francisco: Berrett-Koehler.

Weitzel, A., & Geist, P. (12998). Parliamentary procedure in a community group: Communication and vigilant decision making. *Communication Monographs, 65,* 244-259.

West, M. A., Tjosvold, D., & Smith, K. G. (Eds.). (2005). *The essentials of teamworking: International perspectives.* Hoboken, NJ: Wiley.

Weston, S. B., & English, H. B. (1926). The influence of the group on psychological test scores. *American Journal of Psychology, 37,* 600-601.

Wheelan, S. A. (2005a). *Creating effective teams: A guide for members and leaders* (2nd ed.). Thousand Oaks, CA: Sage.

Wheelan, S. A. 2005b). The developmental perspective. In S. A. Wheelan (Ed.), *The handbook of group research and practice* (pp. 119-132). Thousand Oaks, CA: Sage.

Wheelan, S., & Hochberger, J. (1996). Validation studies of the Group Development Questionnaire. *Small Group Research, 27,* 43-170.

Wilkinson, M. (2004). *The secrets of facilitation: The S.M.A.R.T. guide to getting results with groups.* San Francisco: Jossey-Bass.

Wittenbaum, G. M., Hollingshead, A. B., & Botero, I. C. (2004). From cooperative to motivated information sharing in groups: Moving beyond the hidden profile paradigm. *Communication Monographs, 71,* 286-310.

Wittenbaum, G. M., Hollingshead, A. B., Paulus, P. B., Hirokawa, R. Y., Ancona, D. C., Peterson, R. S., et al. (2004). The functional perspective as a lens for understanding groups. *Small Group Research, 35,* 17-43.

Wood, J. T. (1995). Theorizing practice, practicing theory. In K. N. Cissna (Ed.), *Applied communication in the 21st century* (pp. 181-192). Mahwah, NJ: Erlbaum.

Wright, K. B. (1997). Shared ideology in Alcoholics Anonymous: A grounded theory approach. *Journal of Health Communication, 2*, 83-99.

Yep, G. A., Reece, S. T., & Negrón, E. L. (2003). Culture and stigma in a bona fide group: Boundaries and context in a "closed" support group for "Asian Americans" living with HIV infection. In L. R. Frey (Ed.), *Group communication in context: Studies of bona fide groups* (2nd ed., pp. 157-180). Mahwah, NJ: Erlbaum.

Zimmerman, S., & Applegate, J. L. (1992). Person-centered comforting in the hospice interdisciplinary team. *Communication Research, 19*, 240-263.

I

FACILITATING GROUP CREATION

1

EMPATHIC ATTUNEMENT FACILITATION

STIMULATING IMMEDIATE TASK ENGAGEMENT

IN ZERO-HISTORY TRAINING GROUPS OF

HELPING PROFESSIONALS*

Sunwolf

Santa Clara University

> The physical labor is minimal . . . but what gets you is the agitation
> of dealing with people. I don't think this is a unique reaction.
> Doctors, lawyers, psychiatrists, waiters, cab drivers, and shoe clerks
> suffer from the same syndrome. Anyone who deals with the public.
> People exert a pressure, deliberately or unconsciously. They force
> their wills. Their passions, wants, angers, lies, and fears come on
> like strong winds. Deal with people, and inevitably you feel you're
> being buffeted. No, that's no good. You feel like you're in a blender,
> being sliced, chopped, ground, and pureed.
> —Sanders (1978, p. 98)

Professional helpers are challenged by the dialectical tension they experience between wanting to establish healthy connection with and healthy disengagement from the clients they serve. What is the nature of mindful service to others and how might group communication facilitators strengthen

---

*I would like to thank Ellen Kreitzberg, founder and Director of the Bryan R. Shechmeister Death Penalty College at Santa Clara University, who inspires and nourishes capital defense lawyers across the country, and who allowed me the freedom to explore this novel facilitation in that program's small group workshops.

the professional development of those whose careers are committed to serving distressed clients? Given that career helpers regularly attend small group training sessions (required annually for professional development and certification), group facilitation is a powerful tool for assisting them to manage the inevitable tension between connection and disengagement with their distressed clients. The facilitation intervention described in this chapter is grounded in these two reflections and offers a new technique ("empathic attunement") for facilitating the initial meeting of zero-history groups of helping professionals.

Although the first developmental stage of decision-making/problem-solving task groups has been the focus of study by group scholars, attention to facilitating this stage has been largely neglected (with the exception of some traditional ice-breaker exercises that generally are not designed to connect with a group's particular task). This chapter seeks to fill that gap, offering an alternative to the limitations of traditional techniques used to facilitate the beginning stages of group life, with small training groups of professional "helpers" as the focal point. Helpers represent an especially appropriate group of people to examine, for as a result of professional licensing requirements, many career helpers who regularly serve populations in distress receive annual professional education in small groups of similar others they have not previously met or worked with but with whom they now share a common group task of learning new ways to serve their clients. Professional service providers bring with them to these zero-history training groups frustrating stories of their most challenging or problematic clients. These stories contain vivid examples of how helpers frequently dance on the sharp edges of burnout, even at the outset of their careers, as service careers involve complex tasks, driven by multiple motives, which require managing a healthy balance between the dialectical tension involving connection and disengagement. Within such a context, group facilitation techniques can offer helpers communication tools that can help them to reconnect with their distressed clients, as well as to connect with one another during group training.

In the study described in this chapter, training groups of helpers (in this case, trial lawyers) are offered as an exemplar of the more general notion of the challenges of facilitating the first moments of a group's life. In this particular case, empathic attunement facilitation was used to help groups of defense attorneys (known as "capital defense" lawyers when they are appointed to represent a defendant facing the death penalty) who represent indigent incarcerated defendants (e.g., without funds to hire a lawyer) learn to listen to their clients in new ways, draw on underaccessed information about their clients' worlds, and stimulate problem-solving group processes involving the creation of new case strategies their clients would both accept and support. In particular, the facilitation was designed to help group member-attorneys advocate more successfully their clients' life stories to jurors on the issue of whether to impose a life or death sentence. The primary method relied on to accomplish these goals operates by changing the type of communication that occurs when these helpers meet for the first time in a small (zero-history) group.

Influenced by two group communication theories (symbolic convergence theory and structuration theory), as well as by concepts from social cognition (e.g., attribution making, social impression management, and cognitive distortions), this original facilitation technique is designed for the *initial* stage of small, zero-history training groups. Zero-history groups have been significant sources of data for group communication scholars; Frey's (1994) review of group scholarship published in communication journals from 1980-1988, for instance, showed that 64 percent of the studies involved such groups, yet little attention has been paid to developing specific techniques to assist these groups in accomplishing this phase in novel ways.

This chapter begins by describing relevant task challenges faced by all professional helpers who serve distressed clients, followed by an explanation of the task issues that are specific to capital defense attorneys. After reviewing the theoretical foundations, cognitive concepts, and group process functions of the empathic attunement facilitation technique, I describe how the technique was used with several small-sized groups of capital defense lawyers who attended week-long trial advocacy programs. Finally, I discuss the outcomes of empathic attunement facilitation for these group members, along with suggested future applications of the facilitation for other training groups of helping professionals.

THE HELPER'S PIT: CHALLENGES FACING PROFESSIONAL SERVICE PROVIDERS

> The very worst times are the ones when I have felt so much and hurt so long for a family that finally I can't feel anything at all.
> —Anonymous helper (cited in Larson, 1993, p. 58)

Caring helpers experience an exhausting struggle with professional burnout, with high empathy and helper stress being positively correlated (e.g., Stotland, Mathews, Sherman, Hansson, & Richardson, 1978, found that high-empathy nurses were the first to leave the rooms of dying patients). As Dass and Gorman (1985) explained:

> There are times when service is effortless. Other days, burnout. With
> one person, I'm totally open and present. With the next, I might as
> well be on Mars. Sometimes the chance to care for another human
> being feels like such grace. But later on, I'll hear myself thinking,
> "Hey, what about me?" (p. 10)

Larson (1993), a nationally recognized expert on hospice care, first described and coined the concept, "the helper's pit." Larson's metaphor describes someone needing help as standing at the bottom of a deep pit, with a helper standing on the edge of that pit. Larson explained the task of the helper-on-the-pit's-edge as one of attempting to provide caring service without falling into the pit *with* the distressed client. If the helper slides into the pit, useful empathy for the client transforms into personal distress for the helper. Facilitating new perspectives for helpers through group work can make a difference by enlarging helpers' capacities for understanding the complex emotional states of their clients and avoiding the disabling burnout that results from falling into the helper's pit. In particular, capital defense attorneys need to understand the motivational differences between effective empathy-driven helping and potentially disabling distress-driven helping.

EMPATHY-DRIVEN VERSUS DISTRESS-DRIVEN ADVOCACY: CONTEXTUAL CHALLENGES FACING CAPITAL DEFENSE ATTORNEYS

> Death is different, not just in the nature of the penalty and in the
> preparation and presentation of a penalty phase of a trial. Death is
> different in the emotional toll it takes on everyone involved in capi-
> tal litigation.
> —Bryan R. Shechmeister Death Penalty College (2000)

Scholars who study natural groups share the viewpoint that understanding group processes requires acknowledgement of the environmental, cultural, and other real-world constraints within which these groups perform their tasks (Frey, 1994, 2003). At the same time, it is clear that other variables affect group processes and outcomes, including individual members' experiences and motivations, unique task characteristics (including the degree to which the task is salient to group members), and group climate (Sunwolf & Seibold, 1999). Hence, given that effective facilitation involves consideration of the ways groups are embedded in social systems (Stohl, 1995), as well as the individual experiences and emotions of each group member, multiple internal and external factors challenge group facilitators.

Attorneys appointed to death penalty cases are often poorly resourced, given unmanageable caseloads, and must cope with clients who have no voice in who represents them. These attorneys have received no training in *empathy-driven advocacy* (advocacy motivated by a helper's affective connection with a client's experiences and values) versus *distress-driven advocacy* (advocacy motivated by a helper's personal distress while attempting to cope with a client's problem-solving issues). Capital defense lawyers are problem solvers, trained to strategically solve their clients' legal dilemmas using the tools of the justice system. Many attorneys, consequently, arrive at death penalty training seminars in understandable personal distress, with a tendency to be self-focused (expressing much self-doubt), distant from their clients (leading them to reduce or delegate personal visits with clients), and blame their clients (for lack of cooperation). Specific challenges that affect such lawyers' expectations and motivations for small group work include concern about executing the innocent, representing clients while inadequately resourced, and dealing with disabled, vulnerable, or non-cooperating clients.

Executing the Innocent

Capital defense attorneys realize that their clients may be executed, whether or not they are innocent. On January 11, 2003, Illinois Governor George Ryan pardoned four men and granted clemency to all remaining 167 inmates on death row. It was an extraordinary reversal of policy for a law-and-order Republican and staunch supporter of capital punishment. As Ryan explained in his public clemency speech, "I had to ask myself, could I send another man's son to death under the deeply flawed system of capital punishment that we have in Illinois?" (Wilgoren, 2003, p. 13).

The motivation for the governor's unexpected emptying of death row in Illinois was the same motivation that explains the extraordinary stresses experienced by capital defense attorneys. Governor Ryan had been aware that a convicted killer named Anthony Porter had been released from prison and death row, just 48 hours before his execution was scheduled, after it was discovered that another man had actually committed the crime. That state's investigation exonerated 13 more death row inmates, reporting that, in all probability, some innocent men had, in fact, already been executed. Capital defense attorneys, thus, are burdened by the knowledge that innocent people are convicted, their appeals are denied, and they are then wrongfully executed by the State.

These attorneys struggle, in particular, with the fact that defense attorney error can be responsible for both lost trials and lost lives. As Governor Ryan said in his commutation speech:

If the system was making so many errors in determining whether someone was guilty in the first place, how fairly and accurately was it determining which guilty defendants deserved to live and which deserved to die? What effect was race having? What effect was poverty having? And in almost every one of the exonerated 17, we not only have breakdowns in the system with police, prosecutors and judges, we have terrible cases of *shabby defense lawyers* [italics added]. There is just no way to sugar coat it. *There are defense attorneys that did not consult with their clients, did not investigate the case, and were completely unqualified to handle complex death penalty cases* [italics added]. They often didn't put much effort into fighting a death sentence. If your life is on the line, your lawyer ought to be fighting for you. (Wilgoren, 2003, p. 13)

In the case of Illinois, 33 of the death row inmates had been represented by an attorney who had later been disbarred and suspended from practicing law. There is, consequently, professional consensus among trial lawyers that the greatest challenge a criminal defense attorney may one day face is the representation of a person charged in a capital case.

Representing While Inadequately Resourced

If drunk drivers are a hazard to the road because they have made a *choice* to drive while ability impaired, many capital defense lawyers admit they become *involuntary* hazards to their clients, impaired because they must advocate while being inadequately resourced. Attorneys who represent clients facing the death penalty undertake a sacred interpersonal task, yet are challenged by: (a) a lack of resources to adequately investigate and prepare their cases for trial; (b) prosecutors who are well resourced, have access to multiple avenues of expertise and investigation, and who are frequently politically motivated to file death charges to gain popular appeal in their communities; (c) a negative community climate, including an adverse press, angry feelings from the victim's family and friends, and distrust of criminal defense attorneys in general; (d) judges who attempt to streamline and hasten proceedings; and (e) citizen jurors who generally believe in the death penalty and, during the complex jury selection process in capital cases, are excused from serving if they state they are opposed to the death penalty.

Dealing With Disabled, Vulnerable, or Non-cooperating Clients

> The most glaring weakness is that no matter how efficient and fair
> the death penalty may seem in theory, in actual practice it is primari-
> ly inflicted upon the weak, the poor, the ignorant, and against racial
> minorities.
>
> —Former California Governor Pat Brown (Death Penalty
> Information Center, 2003a, ¶16)

Clients facing the death penalty are frequently mentally retarded, psychologically disabled, or victims of physical and sexual abuse during childhood.
Mental health experts have testified that mentally retarded persons' characteristic suggestibility and willingness to please, for example, leads them to
falsely confess to capital crimes (Death Penalty Information Center, 2003b).
At the same time, as of July, 2003, there were 82 juveniles nationally await-
ing execution on death row (Streib, 2003). In addition to issues of mental
impairment and young age, clients who come from traditionally marginalized racial groups are executed in disproportionate numbers to their representation in the population in the United States, and when the race of the
victim is factored into the equation, the disparity is remarkable: As of July
9, 2003, the number of White defendants executed nationally for an interra-
cial murder was 12, whereas the number of black defendants executed for
killing a White victim was 179 (Death Penalty Information Center, 2003d).
Another critical factor affecting who receives the death penalty is early
physical, sexual, and emotional child abuse. Childhood abuse is ignored not
only by jurors but by the "helpers," the lawyers appointed to represent
clients facing the death penalty: In June 2003, the U.S. Supreme Court
reversed the death sentence of a man because his attorneys failed to inform
the jury that their client had been repeatedly raped, beaten, and denied food
as a child, and that his mother burned his hands on the stove as punishment
(Death Penalty Information Center, 2003c). These clients often have important stories to tell juries, but are extraordinarily challenging clients when it
comes to developing successful relationships with their attorneys.

Notwithstanding the challenges discussed above, the toughest part of the
journey a capital defense lawyer faces may be the *unexpected* unwillingness
of a client to join in the lawyer's life-saving efforts. Lawyer after lawyer
shares frustrated tales of clients who refuse to discuss their psychological
backgrounds, will not give permission for their family members to be contacted, and, most painful of all, angrily refuse an offer to plead to a life sentence, even when such an offer is proposed by the prosecution.

These attorneys arrive at advocacy training programs with a wide range
of general trial experiences, dissimilar experiences on handling death penal-

ty cases in particular (some with no previous death penalty trials), and a variety of ethnicities, ages, value systems, and personalities represented, as well as many anxieties about their task. All of these capital defense attorneys, however, share one overwhelming fear: that the human being they represent will, due to some mistake or lack of attention on their part, be executed by the government. In such a context, these helpers need enhanced empathic attunement with their clients and greater distance from their own distress to engage in and maintain empathy-driven advocacy.

THEORETICAL AND CONCEPTUAL FRAMEWORK FOR EMPATHIC ATTUNEMENT FACILITATION

Symbolic convergence and structuration theories provide a foundation for the empathic attunement facilitation intervention for zero-history groups of helping professionals. This form of facilitation is further shaped by specific concepts from developmental models of group processes, techniques for provoking creativity in task groups, perceptual distortion processes associated with social cognition, and empathic techniques from counseling psychology. Each of these influences is explained below.

Symbolic Convergence Theory

One of the most powerful ways in which a group's unique culture, task identity, and cohesiveness may be created is through shared fantasy. Symbolic convergence theory (Bormann, 1986, 1990) explains how certain types of communication, especially shared fantasies, function to shape a group's identity, which, in turn, influence task and relational group processes. A *fantasy* is defined by Bormann (1986) as the creative and imaginative shared interpretation of events that fulfills a group psychological or rhetorical need; *group fantasy themes* consist of the common content of the stories that group members tell. Furthermore, the fantasy of one group member may lead to a *fantasy chain*, a string of connected stories that revolve around a common theme. *Convergence* refers to the fact that during interaction, private symbolic worlds of members intersect and overlap, coming together. Communicated fantasies perform important functions for small groups in that they (a) help to create a unique group identity, (b) allow difficult information to be dealt with indirectly, (c) direct a group's task by endorsing or condemning particular behaviors, and (d) provide entertainment and fun for group members (Brilhart, Galanes, & Adams, 2001). Shared fantasy, thus, helps group members to make sense of their group experiences and to anticipate task demands. Although fantasies and fantasy chains occur spontaneously in groups, they can also be provoked by facilitators using the empathic attunement facilitation, as described below.

Structuration Theory

A structurational approach to the study of groups focuses on how a group uses various structures and rules to create and recreate itself. According to structuration theory (see, e.g., Poole, Seibold, & McPhee, 1996), group processes constrain and are constrained by the rules and resources members bring to their group experiences. Both internal and external factors influence the types of structures groups create or appropriate, and these structures may represent conflicting values of group members (Sunwolf & Seibold, 1998). Structures in a group might include, for example, methods of voting, how meetings begin and end, and organizational agendas. Rules might include who speaks, how speaking turns are gained, and what type of talk is considered appropriate or inappropriate.

Especially relevant to zero-history groups is that members enter such groups with salient beliefs about the interactions that should take place (Anderson, Riddle, & Martin, 1999). Trial attorneys, when entering training groups, bring with them a variety of experiences and judgments about what constitutes an "effective" capital defense and what a talented lawyer should do for a client when the death penalty is involved. When placed into small training groups, attorneys are immediately constrained by their professional socialization. Criminal defense attorneys typically hold strong positive or negative evaluative judgments about their colleagues (and realize that they are likewise the subject of peer judgment), which are, in part, a result of the fact that it is mandatory that every death penalty trial is appealed (necessitating a micro review of effective assistance of counsel, which becomes a matter of public record and well known within legal communities). The logical, nonemotional training of criminal defense lawyers also predisposes them to communicate with one another in linear, evaluative language. Empathic attunement facilitation, as explained below, helps these group members to confront this tendency and to derail their normal way of interacting.

Group Processes

The structure of the empathic attunement facilitation is grounded in an understanding of the phases communication scholars have found that small groups typically go through developmentally. Empathic attunement takes into account the primary tension that frequently emerges during initial stages in task groups, as well as the unique challenges that creative tasks pose to members of small groups with no prior history of working together.

Group development. Groups go through stages of development, beginning with their first meeting (zero-history moment), in which members begin the process of defining their tasks and determining the type of relationships they will have with one another. During the formation stage, the most important task confronting members is to orient themselves to the group (Tuckman, 1965). Fisher (1970) described this stage as an "orientation" phase in which members get acquainted with one another, as well as with the agreed-on task. Frequently, during this phase, members are hesitant to express strong opinions, because they are uncertain about how other members think (see also Wheelan's, 1994, integrative five-stage group development model, in which the first stage of dependency and inclusion is characterized by group interaction that tends to be tentative and polite). Anderson et al. (1999) suggested that it is during this first stage, which they called the "encounter" phase, when a group culture is effectively created, including norms about both behavior and *thinking*. Facilitation interventions, such as empathic attunement, during this initial stage can help problem-solving groups of helping professionals, in particular, to adopt novel norms that members can draw on throughout the group's life.

Primary tension. Most people enter a new group with caution, uncertain about what their role will be. Bormann (1990) described *primary tension* as the social unease and inhibitions that members feel during the initial stage of a new group. Group members are often anxious to create a good first impression (Engleberg & Wynn, 2000), particularly with professional peers. Although primary tension normally dissipates over time, groups that are time constrained can potentially benefit from interventions that help to relieve primary tension. Group facilitators frequently attempt to minimize this tension by helping members to know more about one another before focusing on the task (e.g., through the use of ice-breaking activities) and, thereby, create connections among members. However, perceived status differences among group members can create further tensions during this initial stage (Beebe & Masterson, 1997); for example, one source of primary tension is a self-centered competition for status in newly formed groups (Brilhart et al., 2001). One unwanted outcome of traditional ice-breakers that focus on demographic introductions among professional peers is that people engage in self-comparison (one-upping or one-downing themselves). As described below, the empathic attunement facilitation, in contrast, operates during the first moments of a newly formed group to stimulate healthy social connections among members and to decrease people's self-centered focus and resulting tension.

Creative tasks. The first assigned task of small training groups of attorneys in advocacy programs is to brainstorm new trial-and-sentencing strategies. Unfortunately, the necessary shift a task group must accomplish from critical/logical thinking to creative thinking (and back again) may not occur at the time and in the manner that is most needed by a particular group (Sunwolf, 2002). Johnson and Hackman (1995) pointed out that groups without special training in creative problem-solving techniques frequently make mistakes that derail the creative problem-solving process, especially when members are experiencing perceptual problems (e.g., prejudging the feasibility of potential solutions) or emotional blocks (e.g., fear of being negatively judged by other members). Social conditions (e.g., anticipated criticism, uncertainty, and perceived status differentials) confronting task groups also discourage effective creative communication processes. VanGundy (1984) found that group members must allow one another to move beyond their original perceptions of problems and solutions to successfully engage in creative problem solving. Although group work is a dynamic, cyclical process, employing formal procedures can enhance a group's ability to successfully engage in structuring, creating, analyzing, and agreeing tasks (see, e.g., Sunwolf & Seibold's, 1999, function impact model, which describes how formal group procedures affect individual members, group processes, and task outcomes). In particular, facilitators can help task groups to engage in upside-down thinking, communicating in ways that provoke novel approaches to thinking about tasks. Although most facilitators are familiar with brainstorming techniques, few group scholars and trainers are aware of the wide variety of techniques that have been developed to provoke group creativity (for a description of 36 under-applied facilitation techniques that can provoke creative processes in task groups, see Sunwolf, 2002). As one example, "role-storming" is a facilitation technique in which each group member is asked to assume the role of someone who may be affected by or who may affect the problem, and then the group brainstorms the problem from this person's point of view. An adaptation of role-storming is the major tool of the empathic attunement technique described below.

Social Cognition

Group communication facilitators can be usefully informed by the research on social cognition—the way people make sense of and think about the behaviors of other people. Social cognition affects the complex reactions group members have to one another, particularly when they have no prior history together. The empathic attunement facilitation takes into account social perception processes—specifically, impression management, attribution making, cognitive distortions, and the development of interpersonal empathy.

Impression management. People typically engage in positive self-presentation strategies in social situations, especially new situations. Individuals derive intrinsic satisfaction from projecting a positive image of themselves in others' eyes and, at the same time, people are highly motivated to avoid social disapproval and pejorative impressions made by others (Fiske & Taylor, 1991). These motivations and the need to present a positive self-image are particularly salient for members of professional peer groups.

Attribution making. When interpersonal conflicts occur, people create attributions about who caused the problem or who should be held accountable for an unwanted outcome. It is common, for instance, to attribute more responsibility to others for actions that produce severe as opposed to mild consequences (Shaver, 1970). When clients refuse the advice of their advocates, appear ungrateful for the efforts of helpers, or seem to place themselves in unnecessary jeopardy (e.g., defendant-clients refusing to cooperate with their lawyers in their own defense), attorneys may blame the client and seek confirmation from attorney-peers that they have been relatively blameless in their client relationships. Capital defense attorneys, as helpers, have considerably more social power than their incarcerated clients and, thus, would benefit from a group facilitation technique that immediately creates an opportunity to connect with a client's worldview without blaming that client for resisting the attorney's advice.

Cognitive distortions. People systematically distort (overuse or underuse) social perceptual data (Fiske & Taylor, 1991). Criminal defense attorneys with clients facing a death penalty are under extreme stress and need coaching on how to become aware of the typical distortions they have developed about their clients and the facts of the case (e.g., clients being perceived as "stubborn" rather than "fearful" and a client's childhood being perceived as excellent "factual" mitigation evidence rather than as "painful" re-lived abuse). As a result of perceptual distortion and biased points of view, helpers can both know and not know something at the same time, through the process of selective attention. Facilitation can assist professionals in re-selecting and foregrounding social data that they have previously deselected.

Developing empathy. Psychotherapists who orient toward the "self"-psychology school of counseling privilege clients' views of their worlds and, thus, object to the "experience-distant" questioning of clients by helpers, arguing that such questioning fails to provide meaningful information from a client's perspective (Rowe & MacIsaac, 1995). Self-psychology was heavily influenced by Kohut (1959), who argued that "empathy" was the major tool used by psychiatrists for helping clients to heal and that questioning clients should be engaged in with the goal of creating understanding (a collaborative orientation) rather than solely for the purpose of gathering data (a traditional helper orientation).

This is a particularly useful perspective for capital defense attorneys, as they are trained (and rewarded) in law school to engage in data-driven questioning of witnesses and clients. Furthermore, self-psychology offers a useful perspective for understanding clients' resistance to such questioning, as people are defensive when they feel threatened and self-protective when they feel vulnerable (Rowe & MacIsaac, 1995). Rather than seeing a client's defenses and resistances as obstacles that need to be overcome, self-psychology suggests that helpers need to understand the *adaptive* function clients have developed. This is exemplified in capital cases for clients facing execution, who may experience the greatest need to create and recreate protective ways of interacting with their helper-attorneys. As a result, capital defense attorneys can benefit from a group facilitation technique that helps them to value, experience, and more accurately perceive the world in which a client facing the death penalty lives every day. Without this critical empathic bridge, a collaborative attorney-client relationship cannot develop, placing the client's life in even greater jeopardy.

THE ZERO-HISTORY GROUP EMPATHIC ATTUNEMENT FACILITATION

em•path•ic *adj.* the experiencing as one's own the emotions of another.
at•tune•ment *n.* the process of bringing things that are separate into harmony.

Empathy involves both cognitive role taking and an other-oriented emotional responsiveness that allows helpers to imagine what it would be like to be in another person's predicament (Larson, 1993). Helpers may feel compassion or concern for a client (e.g., sympathy), but they typically do not experience a state that matches that of the other person. Facilitators can employ group work to help professional helpers understand differences between compassion and empathy, so that helpers can make informed choices about what they are offering clients.

It is generally agreed that group facilitation procedures theoretically work by focusing and guiding group members' communication, decision-making, conflict-resolving, and creative processes in a structured manner, while drawing on group strengths (see Frey, 1995, introduction to this volume; Poole, 1991). Facilitating *emotional* change for group members necessitates approaches that produce shifts in the way in which they make meaning and that help them to gain access to underlying dysfunctional schemas they have created about other people (Greenberg, Rice, & Elliott, 1993). The empathic attunement group technique structures five group processes for zero-history training groups of helping professionals by: (a) creating a supportive group culture for talking about difficult professional challenges, (b) relieving primary tension among group members who have not previously met, (c) redirecting problem-solving task goals by inviting a cognitive shift in how helpers perceive their clients' worlds, (d) prestimulating individual members' creativity for problem-solving brainstorming tasks, and (e) establishing participation norms for speaking, listening, and offering feedback. Poole (1991) listed nine ways that facilitation procedures enhance group processes, five of which are relevant to the empathic attunement facilitation: (a) coordinating members' thinking, (b) protecting groups against their own bad habits, (c) capitalizing on the strengths of groups, (d) balancing member participation, and (e) empowering groups.

Method

The groups described here were comprised of lawyers who came from around the United States to attend an intensive, week-long annual trial advocacy program at the Santa Clara University Law School (Bryan R. Shechmeister Death Penalty College, jointly sponsored by Santa Clara University, California Attorneys for Criminal Justice, California Public Defenders Association, and the American Bar Association's Death Penalty Representation Project). The goals of this program are to teach attorneys the skills, knowledge, and insights (into both themselves and other people) that are needed to successfully defend a capital (death penalty) case. More importantly, perhaps, this advocacy program seeks to foster and maintain a spirit of cooperation and community among attendee-lawyers and faculty-lawyers, united in the common goal of saving the lives of marginalized, underresourced human beings. The program takes one further significant approach by focusing the entire 7-day training session on the *aggravation/mitigation* portion of a capital defense trial (evidence and arguments supporting either a sentence of life or death, after considering the entire life of the defendant, as well as circumstances of the crime) rather than on the *guilt/innocence* portion (evidence and arguments supporting either a verdict of guilty or not guilty of the crimes charged). This approach has the effect of forcing capital defense attorneys to consider the real possibility that a jury might *convict* their client. Hence, the only question (hypothetically) remaining to be faced is whether the jury will vote to execute a defendant.

Participants. Enrollment in this program is limited to 64 criminal defense attorneys, generally selected by the program administrator on either a first-come-first-served or a greatest-urgency-for-an-upcoming-trial basis, along with the qualifier that each has a pending trial for which the death penalty is being sought against a client.

Gaining access. One of the problems scholars studying and practicing group facilitation have experienced is not only gaining access to natural groups but getting groups to accept their expertise and facilitation efforts (see Frey, 1995, introduction to this volume; Poole, 1991). In this particular case, I was viewed by the program's organizers and by group members as a valued "insider," recognized professionally in three ways as (a) a former capital defense attorney and training director for a large public defender office, (b) an experienced national trial consultant and faculty member of trial advocacy programs, and (c) a university scholar who conducts research on the dynamics of jury deliberations and courtroom persuasion. Prior to developing the empathic attunement intervention, I had been an ongoing faculty member at this capital defense college. Support for using this technique was given by the director of the program. I was an active participant-observer in the group facilitations described, serving as one of approximately 15 faculty members from around the country. I served as both a lecturer in the program and as a small group coleader (together with another coleader) in small breakout groups of 7-8 attorneys. In addition to observations made during the group training, I conducted interviews with cofacilitators and kept notes of the reactions expressed by participants. Although most attendee-attorneys and cofacilitator faculty members had attended other trial advocacy programs, this was their first exposure to this particular technique.

Use of group work in the program. These attorneys, who have never met one another, are assigned to work in the same group of eight members for seven days, with one to two facilitators (who rotate among groups daily); occasionally, two attorneys on the same trial are admitted to the program, but are assigned to different small groups for training. The training is intense, lasting daily from dawn to dark (7:30 a.m. to 9:00 p.m.), and includes lectures and demonstrations, but with a primary focus on small group workshops. Each day, attorney-participants meet in their small groups, performing, receiving feedback, and brainstorming various aspects of the mitigation portion of a death penalty trial (e.g., that portion of the trial that follows a conviction on the substantive charges of murder, including exercises on opening statements, closing argument, and conversations with jurors). Meals are spent together, in an atmosphere of a compassionate, supportive community. Most small group members continue to sit together during lunch, still discussing the work of the morning and anticipating the tasks of the afternoon and evening.

Issues challenging participants' problem-solving task. This facilitation was designed to circumvent dysfunctional dynamics observed during many years of facilitating similar groups of attorneys. Attorneys are educated and trained in rationality, but capital defense attorneys also need skills that are grounded in affect (e.g., ability to establish rapport, feel empathy, and express compassion). Although lawyers are adept at logic, analysis, and abstract thinking (left-hemisphere brain functions), to connect with clients and jurors on the issue of death, they benefit by more frequent engagement in whole-brained activities, as the two hemispheres seem to be functionally specialized for processing different emotions, as well as for thought. When people talk, brain scans show that the blood-flow pattern changes in their brains, with more activity in the left side, but when people are asked to "imagine," this pattern reverses (Ornstein, 1997). A left-brain advocate argues the merits of one side of a case over another side, but to persuade a juror to vote for life rather than death, the values and emotions of each juror must be engaged (Sunwolf, 2000). Hence, these training groups can benefit from techniques that help participants to engage their right-brain spheres (e.g., imagination, emotion, creativity, sensation, and images) at the outset of the group's problem-solving task. Adding to these benefits, recent research suggests that the right-brain hemisphere is not just the container for positive emotions but is, in fact, the center for processing "negative" emotions, such as anger (Ornstein, 1997). Hence, a criminal defense attorney's own fears and anger cannot be adequately accessed with facilitation techniques that stimulate only left-brain hemisphere processing (e.g., facts, lists, or numbers). Intriguingly, a facilitator has the opportunity of coaching attorney members in novel group processes, who, in turn, can use these skills to *facilitate* new group processes for the members of another decision-making group—the jury (Sunwolf, 1997). In fact, if trial attorneys ignore the potential effects that group deliberation processes have on verdicts, jurors may create group processes that are both unexpected and unwelcome by trial attorneys and their clients (Sunwolf & Seibold, 1998).

The traditional introductory facilitation technique used regularly with trial attorneys (indeed, with most facilitated zero-history groups) at a first small group session focuses on helping them to get acquainted with other group members; specifically, faculty leaders ask group members to sequentially introduce themselves (e.g., enumerating prior experience, type of practice, number of trials, and reasons that brought them to this program), although some leaders prefer to have lawyers "interview" one another in pairs and then "introduce" their partner to the group (an assignment that still focuses on traditional demographics of group members rather than on clients). Most typically, 1-2 hours are devoted to this introductory group phase, followed by an opportunity for each lawyer to describe the facts of his or her "problem" case. The group's task is to offer new strategies for each member's death penalty case, as well as to give feedback to each member during a variety of small group trial exercises (e.g., opening statements and closing arguments).

The facilitation technique. Empathic attunement facilitation dispenses with this traditional introductory exercise and, instead, turns the attentional energy of a group of helpers toward understanding more about their clients' subjective worlds. As previously described, capital defense attorneys have typically developed a view of their death penalty clients as "problems" (e.g., stubborn, narcissistic, angry, or manipulative) and, consequently, the role that helpers assume in this technique is of their most "difficult" client; for professional helpers who come for training with multiple challenging clients, the empathic attunement facilitation technique challenges them (step 6 described below) to take on the role of the client they find most challenging (or difficult).

The technique involves the following steps (see Table 1.1): (1) at zero history, during the first assembly of the small group, no one initially introduces him or herself, either by name, caseload, or experience; (2) the facilitator explains to the group that a specific technique will be offered, and requests their support; (3) an empty chair is placed in the center of the group's circle of chairs; (4) group members are told that they will be asked, one at a time, to sit in the chair and to respond to two specific prompts from the facilitator; (5) they are reminded that they have a lot of knowledge about their clients, both biographical and experiential, based on their professional

Table 1.1. Facilitation Procedure for the Empathic Attunement Technique

Activity Summary	This technique allows participants to briefly role play one of their clients in response to two stimulus questions
Group Phase	Zero-history facilitation, appropriate in the first moments of the initial meeting of the group, before members have introduced themselves
Time	15-20 minutes for the initial role play by each group member, followed by 15-20 minutes for the group discussion
Group Size	5-8 members
Application Group	Professionals seeking development and training, whose careers involve them in helping others in distress
Requirements	A room with no outside distractions or interruptions, moveable chairs to arrange in a U-shape, and a moveable chair for the performance of the "client"
Cofacilitator	Recommended (primary responsibilities are to monitor reactions of individual group members during the exercise and to initiate group discussion)
Facilitation of empathic attunement exercise [experiencing empathic attunement to the client]	1. Arrange chairs in a U-shaped (not circle), with the facilitator sitting at either end of the U-shaped formation of chairs. 2. Greet group members as they enter the room for their first session and invite them to have a seat. 3. Acknowledge that there have been no formal introductions (yet) but, instead, that participants are being invited to experience a different way of beginning this training session, and request their support. 4. Place an empty chair in the center of the U-shaped formation of chairs on which members are seated. 5. Remind participants that the goal of the training group is to gain new insights into how to be helpers for distressed clients. Suggest that they know a lot about their clients of which they may not be aware. 6. Explain that each person will be asked, one at a time, to sit in the chair and answer two, and only two, questions. 7. Tell participants that when they sit in the central chair, they should use all the information they have from experiencing their client to become that client, adopting the client's voice, behaviors, and attitudes. 8. Encourage the group to listen in silence, helping the attorney who is role switching to remain in that role. 9. Ask for a volunteer ("Would someone be willing to help us begin?").

Table 1.1. Facilitation Procedure for the Empathic Attunement Technique (con't)

	10. Tell the volunteer participant to close his/her eyes and think about all the experiences he/she has had with that client. Invite the participant's best job of imagining, for a moment, that he/she is that client. Ask the participant to consciously abandon his/her own personality and perspective.
	11. Create a moment of silence and then ask the participant in the chair, "Tell me, who are you and what are you most afraid of in your life right now?"
	12. When the participant has stopped answering the question, use a simple prompt: "Say some more about that."
	13. After the participant answers, pose the second question: "Tell me about the lawyer (doctor, minister, counselor, etc.) on your case. What's she(he) like?"
	14. Demonstrate nonverbal active listening behaviors to the role player/participant.
	15. Thank the role player and immediately request another volunteer ("Who is willing to help us next?").
Facilitation of Group Discussion [creating empathic attunement to the group]	1. Address the group members with a nondirective question ("What was that like for you?" "What did you notice?" or "What surprised you?"), and then call on individual members. Follow with these questions: a. What made this exercise challenging to perform? b. What happened for you when you were role playing your client? c. What did you connect with when you were listening to others role play? d. How might this experience affect your goals at this program? e. What connections did you become aware of with others?

relationship with that client; (6) they are told that when they sit in the chair, they should become the client, adopting the behavior of that client as they have experienced it, but adopting as well the client's voice, behaviors, and attitudes; (7) as each attorney sits in the central chair, the group remains silent, allowing the attorney to adjust to the new role; (8) the facilitator poses the first prompt, "Who are you and what are you most afraid of?"; (9) the attorney, as client, answers the question, as the group listens; (10) the facilitator poses a second prompt to the attorney (who is now responding in the role of client), "Tell me about the lawyer you have on your case"; (11)

the attorney, as client, provides an answer; (12) after a moment of silence has passed, the facilitator (without commenting on what has taken place) requests another volunteer; (13) after all group members have participated, group discussion of the experience, both as a role player and as an audience listening to each role play, is facilitated ("What was that like for you?").

Facilitating the physical environment. Chairs are arranged in a U-shape, so that the member who is role playing, in the center, will not have his or her back to any group member.

Facilitating group primacy: The latent value of first moments. When the first moments of a group session are not cluttered with administrative small talk, members not only calm and settle themselves in the initial silence as the group gathers but become aware that something "different" than what normally happens may occur. Novelty and anticipation can themselves facilitate openness to new points of view.

Facilitating role switching and dramatic performance of problematic clients. The ability to role switch is a valuable tool for helpers. One of the outcomes of a technique that facilitates role switching is that the dramatizing of clients (who helpers may have experienced as difficult or challenging) necessitates that the helper successfully gain access to information about the client's subjective world. By engaging in such role switching, "problem" clients are, in effect, "re-personned" by their helpers.

Facilitating small group feedback and discussion. All group members react and connect to the dramatic "performance of client" engaged in by every other member and, as a result, have an experiential basis for discussing the role they played or the role playing they watched. As discussion of the role plays begins, the facilitator has an opportunity to model for group members "confirming feedback" (e.g., mirroring a response, extending a response, or clarifying a response rather than disagreeing with it), which can be challenging for attorneys who are trained to verbally defend or attack, and for most helpers who have professional positions of social power. Typically, attorneys are primed to disagree, argue against, or point out discrepancies in what another person says. Subsequent group discussion benefits from this modeling of connective-confirming feedback, in that such listening-focused feedback enhances group cohesion, develops a safe climate, and creates a compassionate group culture.

Working with cofacilitators. My facilitation of groups of capital defense attorneys using this technique has consistently been in partnership with a coleader; on several occasions in group work with newer trial attorneys, I have facilitated the empathic attunement technique alone. Although this facilitation can be performed by a single facilitator, it is advantageous to have two facilitators. Not only can a second person mindfully monitor how group members are experiencing the exercise but cofacilitation allows the person leading the exercise to have the option of beginning the feedback phase not with the group but with the cofacilitator (e.g., by posing the question to him or her, "How was that for you as the fears of these clients were shared?" or "What did you notice about how we were reacting to these clients?"). If the cofacilitator knows that the partner facilitator will initiate group discussion following the exercise, he or she can model constructive feedback, as well as mirror other appropriate reactions for the group.

Outcomes and Discussion

At the outset, one of the strengths of the group work described here relates to its ecological validity. Not only were real people attending real training sessions (as opposed to students involved in a laboratory facilitation) but this particular advocacy program does not use hypothetical fact patterns for the training sessions. Attorney-participants were required to bring a real case they were handling, currently set for trial (within weeks or months of the training); consequently, they were using the group work to help solve problems for a client whose life is their professional responsibility. Everything that happened in these training groups, thus, had high saliency for participants. Using the empathic attunement facilitation encouraged attorneys to abandon their familiar personae and step, instead, into their client's experience of the case, the upcoming trial, and, from their client's perspective, their court-appointed lawyer. From the outset of these groups, the facilitation technique helped members to bond with one another based on values, frustrations, and the human frailties of their respective clients in ways that occur less frequently using resume-style ice-breaker introductions. To document these bonds, the results are discussed below as observed by several cofacilitators, participants, and by me.

Individual member outcomes. Role switching with a client can successfully penetrate attorneys' familiar egotism at the outset of group work and enable them to become "attuned" and brought into harmony with their most problematic clients. Subsequent group discussion during the training week about troublesome facts of the case was seen, according to participants, through the perspective of their clients; lawyers realized they had re-encountered their clients through dramatization. In addition, group members appeared to be listening with greater intensity to one another, in physical stillness. As one cofacilitator who observed the technique for the first time said afterwards, "Each attorney was mesmerized!" (J. D. Delgado, personal communication, January 23, 2003).

When the first attorney began the role switch, each group member watching had the opportunity of observing, in effect, four people: the performing attorney and that attorney's client, as well as the listening attorney and the listener's client. The dramatic performances triggered relevant reflection about distressed clients at the outset of group work. Several attorneys shared the immediate experience of having felt that the tuition, travel, and stresses of a full week of training suddenly seemed worth it because they were "getting their money's worth" in new thinking and imagining. One cofacilitator made the observation, "My impression was that they're immediately thinking to themselves, 'Buckle your seatbelts, this is going to be a wild ride!'" (J. D. Delgado, personal communication, January 23, 2003). Another faculty cofacilitator had the same, independent reaction. He described his observation of individual member effects as the exercise was beginning:

> I looked at the four nearest me, and they were *stunned*! I think they were speechless for awhile. In those moments, they appeared to be making a mental shift from "the-world-revolves-around-me" to "let-me-see-what-my-client's-world-might-be." (S. Harmon, personal communication, January 21, 2003)

Facilitators also suggested, however, that some group members might have felt momentarily inadequate, even ashamed about how little they had thought about their clients, even though they saw themselves as extraordinarily people oriented. As a cofacilitator explained, "It's an epiphany moment for them. For the first time, they realize there's a gap here, and they have been invited into a paradigm shift" (S. Harmon, personal communication, January 21, 2003).

Compared to similar groups of attorneys I have facilitated using traditional get-acquainted introductions during the group's first session, where complaints about clients are humorously shared, complaints about clients are dramatically reduced using the empathic attunement technique, with attorneys rechanneling their "client"-focused frustrations into complaints about judges, prosecutors, or lack of resources. Empathic attunement, thus, transforms old perspectives that function to position capital defense attorneys *in opposition* to their clients ("Why won't he take this amazing deal I managed to get him?!") into connecting perspectives ("He's afraid."). One cofacilitator compared the process that emerges from using empathic attunement at the outset of group work to a medical model: When an unsuspecting patient has just been told she has cancer, she will eventually want a competent doctor, but initially, the patient wants a doctor who understands her deep fear (S. Harmon, personal communication, January 21, 2003). Clients facing the death penalty may also need some demonstration of interpersonal connection that precedes a demonstration of legal competency.

Evidence that group members experienced this different initial facilitation in a positive way is the fact that members immediately shared what happened with the other members of the program who had not been members in that group. For the next several days, participants told me that they had heard about the exercise and wished they had been there. In addition, the nature of the individual comments made during the discussion that followed the role play suggested immediate facilitated changes for group members; representative comments included: "I know they were doing *their* client, but I wanted to stop them and say, 'I've represented that guy!'"; "I was embarrassed to think I'd never asked him what he was scared of. It's such a 'duh' on a death penalty case, you just never talk about it. Then I realized in my role play that it wasn't dying he was afraid of!"; "I wanted to cry"; "I felt so afraid, even when it was just my client that was talking about being afraid"; "That's the first time I really *got* why he'd rather die than spend the rest of his life in prison"; "I thought that if I could talk that way in closing argument, to the jury, they'd never be able to kill him. Is there a way I could do that?"; "I started liking my client again"; and "I remembered how long it had been since I visited him, and even longer since I looked him in the eyes. I'm so afraid I'll lose his case."

Group process outcomes. The primary tension phases of getting acquainted and easing into the task are collapsed using the empathic attunement facilitation technique, dramatizing the ultimate goal for group members, which is to spend the entire week with their clients first in mind for every exercise. All of the cofacilitators observed that the usual get-acquainted icebreaker activities took longer, were attended to more sporadically by group members, and resulted in less group cohesion; the consensus among cofacilitators about this traditional technique was that after such "personal" introductions, a group was a nominal one only. In contrast, one experienced faculty member's description as a cofacilitator of empathic attunement was particularly vivid: "The group took on a completely different personality out-of-the-box than any group of attorneys I have worked with, seeming *captivated* with the stories of one another's clients rather than distracted by their own cases" (J. D. Delgado, personal communication, February 22, 2002). For the next several days, because faculty leaders rotate to different small groups each day and I was no longer with my original group, I checked with

the new leaders to see how they would describe the group member relationships and processes in the first group I facilitated. Consistently, they reported that group members were fully engaged in subsequent case brainstorming, offered compassionate rather than aggressive feedback to one another,
and that they seemed to honestly "enjoy" one another. Many factors may
have contributed to those processes, but the facilitation appears to show that
when aggressive trial attorneys perform compassionate portrayals of their
clients in a small group setting, they experience an emotional connection
with one another that positively affects subsequent group work.

Client-relational outcomes. Frequently, when lecturing at other continuing legal education programs, I run into former attorneys who participated
in the empathic attunement facilitated group session. They often describe
the change that the facilitation helped them to make in the relationships with
their capital defense clients. One participant typifies the insights that seem
to endure after the program. Nine months after attending the death penalty
advocacy program, this participant sent an email about the outcome of his
trial to the program director (copied to the faculty) that included the following comment:

> I do want to mention the value of one of the exercises my group did
> per the instructions of Sunwolf and Steve Harmon. It was a role-
> playing exercise where we had to play the role of our client and talk
> about the attorney. Not only has that exercise made me think about
> my relationship with clients and the growth I need to strive for, but
> in T.'s [the client] case, I think it did help me better recognize some
> of the issues T. was wrestling with that weren't really related to the
> normal prep[aration] of the case, such as the incredible sense of guilt
> he was feeling over the pain his actions caused the victim's family
> and his struggle to maintain some sort of self-worth while trying to
> answer the question of how he could have done what he did. (per-
> sonal communication, April 17, 2002)

I subsequently contacted this attorney by email to ask him to share what he
remembered about the empathic attunement exercise I facilitated with his
small group on the first day of the program. The lawyer replied that the first
question in the empathic attunement facilitation posed to him when he was
role playing his client ("Who are you and what are you most afraid of?")
seemed to help the most. Experiencing his client's worst fear led him to
attempt new attorney-client conversations when he returned from the program. For the first time, he was able to help a client facing the death penalty
for killing someone to re-vision his prior life and to see that no one should
be defined by the worst thing that person has ever done. As he explained:

Thinking about it now, this doesn't seem to be something that should have been epiphany-like for me. However, I have to face the fact that over the almost 9 years I've been doing public defender work, I've become a bit jaded. So your exercise was a shot in the arm in some ways and has reminded me of a few things. While the whole idea of not defining a person as the worst thing he/she has ever done is something we sometimes build an argument *to a jury* on, I needed to be reminded that sometimes such a discussion needs to be had with the very real human client sitting across the table from me. I think I've run into the (bad) habit of focusing so much on evidentiary matters and more of a business-like approach to this work (after all, that helps keep emotional involvement to a minimum, right?) that I had forgotten that in many cases, it's basic human interaction that can be the difference-maker in the case. I tend to assume that what clients are scared of is the worst-case scenario from a sentencing perspective. . . . Once I got on the same page with him and we talked a little more about who he was, some of his attitude changed a bit. (personal communication, May 30, 2002)

Moreover, after sharing more about his client in a self-described stream-of-consciousness style, this lawyer offered a new thought:

I also have to mention that question #2 ["Tell me about the lawyer you have on your case"] gets involved with the above discussion, too. In fact, after writing that I'm concerned mostly with question #1, and then considering what's spilled out of me in this memo, I'm now thinking that it's very hard to consider one question without the other. The whole notion of being too business-like and focused on development of "the case" is probably how T. saw me (though he was so polite and respectful toward me and the other members of his team, he never would have said this to us). This part of the exercise makes me take a look at how I'm dealing with my clients and whether I'm meeting a need they might have to deal with me on a more human level versus dealing with me only as their advocate. (personal communication, May 30, 2002)

Limitations of These Observations

Facilitating real-world groups in natural settings is tricky business, demanding far more maneuvering and tightrope-walking skills than is required for facilitating laboratory groups (see Frey, 1995, and his introduction to this text). Although this intervention changed many of the subsequent discussions within these groups, as well as helped members to reconceptualize those problems they were seeking group assistance to solve, there is clearly a need for additional verification of the effects of this facilitation (both for similar groups and dissimilar ones). At the same time, there are adaptations of this technique to particular groups that need to be considered and cautions that need to be documented for group members that may involve unanticipated negative reactions to the client role-play task.

Facilitators should be sensitive to the moment-by-moment effects the empathic process is having on *each* group member. By its very nature, facilitation at the point of zero history is always functioning as an ice-breaker, yet ice-breakers affect members differently. Facilitators must keep in mind that any intense structured activity designed to reduce members' inhibitions and increase their awareness can be misused (Forbess-Greene, 1980). As a result, the following three guidelines are recommended: (a) Group members should never be forced to participate and should be told at the outset that they have the right to refrain from revealing anything that feels too uncomfortable, (b) group members should agree that specific information generated in this exercise should be kept confidential from those not attending the training college (because real clients are being portrayed), and (c) facilitators should debrief the group immediately after the intervention and monitor individual members for signs that follow-up debriefing with them may be necessary.

RECOMMENDATIONS FOR FURTHER APPLICATIONS

Helping relationships are always *personal* relationships. To be successful as caregivers or service providers, people must have the ability to enter into meaningful emotional relationships with the people they assist and to make room for them in their own emotional worlds (Larson, 1993). There is an old adage that reminds us: "People don't care what you know until they know that you care."

In this chapter, I have offered a new method of facilitating zero-history training groups of helping professionals: physicians, nurses, hospice workers, home-care providers, teachers, probation officers, social service workers, group home specialists, legal aid specialists, therapists, counselors, victim-assistance workers, community trauma specialists, missionaries, and ministers or priests, among others. These are people who frequently find themselves standing at the edge of the helper's pit, attempting to help someone in distress at the bottom. Empathic attunement facilitation redirects the thinking such helpers bring to group training about their (a) relational task with one another (What type of communication support is useful to other peer-members with challenging clients?); (b) problem-solving task (How do our distressed clients see their situations and us as their helpers? How can group problem solving offer novel solutions for helpers and clients?); and (c) current and future relationships with clients they serve (How can I use my client's traumatized perspective to revitalize our relationship, as well as to create new ways to help with the client's problem?).

Empathic attunement facilitation offers two critical outcomes for helpers: (a) reducing the professional, ego-involved self-comparisons that typically occur between members in training group work; and (b) heightening group members' awareness of dysfunctional distances they may have created between themselves and their clients. First, empathic attunement facilitation avoids the natural tendency of helping professionals to begin small group work by engaging in status-laden self-comparisons, encouraging, instead, more connective empathy identification through role switching. The first knowledge group members had about one another, using the empathic facilitation technique, did not concern number of trials or length of experience but their ability to dramatically humanize their clients. Group members observing the role switch were pulled into the facilitation technique, drawn to the painful drama, and began to care about a dramatized human they had never met. By doing so, the clients virtually joined the small group and were "present." Second, empathic attunement facilitation leads helpers to become aware of ineffective helping that is created because of feelings of anger, sadness, or frustration with difficult clients. Such feelings cause professionals to distance themselves from their clients and to engage in avoiding behaviors, behaviors that may be unconscious for helpers (Larson, 1993). This facilitation tool immediately refocuses group members onto the thoughts and fears of their clients rather than on their own personal, distress-driven concerns. When a helper's anxiety increases, he or she is trapped in a separate pit from the helpee; helping others, consequently, becomes more difficult.

Extending the empathic attunement facilitation further, group communication scholars need to examine the unique communication challenges that other small groups face during the initial formation stage and the role that facilitation might play during that stage in meeting relational and task issues. The larger theme this chapter touches on is the formation of group life and the role of facilitation in enriching the communication that occurs during that formative period, by connecting opening activities to individual and collective goals of group members. Role switching offers a dynamic way of performing empathy, giving both the role player and observers a valuable text for communication during their subsequent problem-solving stages. Further investigation, in fact, may demonstrate that the performance of empathy in small groups is socially "contagious," such that when one group member struggles to empathically attune to another human being, other group members "catch" that attunement, enriching their immediate capacities for interpersonal connection within the new group.

CONCLUSION

Group work is particularly valuable for helpers who interact with distressed clients, students, patients, or parishioners. There exists a need for the development, application, and in-depth study of facilitation interventions that assist helpers in peer-group training to develop new perspectives from which to view both the behaviors and emotions of those they serve. As a result, I suggest that initial, facilitated ice-breaker activities (which are traditionally unconnected to a group's subsequent task) can be re-envisioned through an empathic facilitation technique that simultaneously creates community and stimulates group task outcomes. Facilitated group work is a valuable resource for professional helpers, in particular, who frequently struggle alone and are vulnerable to career burnout. Successful helping must be a "we" thing rather than a "me" thing, for success is always greatest when it is the product of many heads, hands, and hearts.

REFERENCES

Anderson, C. M., Riddle, B. L., & Martin, M. W. (1999). Socialization processes in groups. In L. R. Frey (Ed.), D. S. Gouran, & M. S. Poole (Assoc. Eds.), *The handbook of group communication theory and research* (pp. 139-163). Thousand Oaks, CA: Sage.

Beebe, S. A., & Masterson, J. T. (1997). *Communicating in small groups: Principles and practices* (5th ed.). New York: Longman.

Bormann, E. G. (1986). Symbolic convergence theory and communication in group decision-making. In R. Y. Hirokawa & M. S. Poole (Eds.), *Communication and group decision-making* (pp. 219-236). Beverly Hills, CA: Sage.

Bormann, E. G. (1990). *Small group communication: Theory and practice* (3rd ed.). New York: Harper & Row.

Brilhart, J. K., Galanes, G. J., & Adams, K. (2001). *Effective group discussion: Theory and practice* (10th ed.). Boston: McGraw-Hill.

Bryan R. Shechmeister Death Penalty College. (2000). *The Bryan R. Shechmeister Death Penalty College, August 5-10, 2000* [Brochure]. Santa Clara, CA: Santa Clara University.

Dass, R., & Gorman, P. (1985). *How can I help? Stories and reflections on service.* New York: Alfred A. Knopf.

Death Penalty Information Center. (2003a). *In Ryan's words: "I must act."* Retrieved January 13, 2003, from http://www.deathpenaltyinfo.org/article.php?scid=13&did=551

Death Penalty Information Center. (2003b). *Mental retardation and the death penalty.* Retrieved January 13, 2003, from http://www.deathpenaltyinfo.org/article.php?scid=28&did=176

Death Penalty Information Center. (2003c). *News from the U.S. Supreme Court.* Retrieved January 13, 2003, from http://www.deathpenaltyinfo.org/article.php?did=248&scid=38#recent%20decisions

Death Penalty Information Center. (2003d). *Race of death row inmates executed since 1976.* Retrieved January 13, 2003, from http://www.deathpenaltyinfo.org/article.php?scid=5&did=184#inmaterace

Engleberg, I., & Wynn, D. (2000). *Working in groups: Communication principles and strategies* (2nd ed.). Boston: Houghton Mifflin.

Fisher, B. A. (1970). Decision emergence: Phases in group decision making. *Speech Monographs, 37,* 53-66.

Fiske, S. T., & Taylor, S. E. (1991). *Social cognition* (2nd ed.). New York: McGraw-Hill.

Forbess-Greene, S. (1980). *The encyclopedia of icebreakers: Structured activities that warm-up, motivate, challenge, acquaint, and energize.* St. Louis, MO: Applied Skills Press.

Frey, L. R. (1994). The naturalistic paradigm: Studying small groups in the postmodern era. *Small Group Research, 25,* 551-577.

Frey, L. R. (1995). Introduction: Applied communication research on group facilitation in natural settings. In L. R. Frey (Ed.), *Innovations in group facilitation: Applications in natural settings* (pp. 1-23). Cresskill, NJ: Hampton Press.

Frey, L. R. (2003). Introduction: Group communication in context: Studying bona fide groups. In L. R. Frey (Ed.), *Group communication in context: Studies of bona fide groups* (2nd ed., pp. 1-20). Mahwah, NJ: Lawrence Erlbaum.

Greenberg, L. S., Rice, L. N., & Elliott, R. (1993). *Facilitating emotional change: The moment-by-moment process.* New York: Guilford Press.

Johnson, C. E., & Hackman, M. Z. (1995). *Creative communication: Principles & applications.* Prospect Heights, IL: Waveland Press.

Kohut, H. (1959). Introspection, empathy, and psychoanalysis: An examination of the relationship between mode of observation and theory. In. P. H. Ornstein (Ed.), *The search for the self* (Vol. 1, pp. 205-232). New York: International Universities Press.

Larson, D. G. (1993). *The helper's journey: Working with people facing grief, loss, and life-threatening illness.* Champaign, IL: Research Press.

Ornstein, R. (1997). *The right mind: Making sense of the hemispheres.* New York: Harcourt Brace.

Poole, M. S. (1991). Procedures for managing meetings: Social and technological innovations. In R. A. Swanson & B. O. Knapp (Eds.), *Innovative meeting management* (pp. 53-110). Austin, TX: 3M Meeting Management Institute.

Poole, M. S., Seibold, D. R., & McPhee, R. D. (1996). The structuration of group processes. In R. Y. Hirokawa & M. S. Poole (Eds.), *Communication and group decision making* (2nd ed., pp. 114-146). Thousand Oaks, CA: Sage.

Rowe, C. E., & MacIsaac, D. S. (1995). *Empathic attunement: The "technique" of psychoanalytic self psychology.* Northvale, NJ: Jason Aaronson.

Sanders, L. (1978). *The sixth commandment: A novel.* New York: G. P. Putnam.

Shaver, K. G. (1970). Defensive attribution: Effects of severity and relevance on the responsibility assigned for an accident. *Journal of Personality and Social Psychology, 14,* 101-113.

Stohl, C. (1995). Facilitating bona fide groups: Practice and paradox. In L. R. Frey (Ed.), *Innovations in group facilitation: Applications in natural settings* (pp. 325-332). Cresskill, NJ: Hampton Press.

Stotland, E., Mathews, K. E., Sherman, S. E., Hansson, R. O., & Richardson, B. Z. (1978). *Empathy, fantasy, and helping.* Beverly Hills, CA: Sage.

Streib, V. (2003, April 1). *The juvenile death penalty today: Death sentences and executions for juvenile crimes, January 1, 1973-June 30, 2003.* Retrieved July 19, 2003, from http://www.law.onu.edu/faculty/streib/juvdeath.htm

Sunwolf (1997, July). Changing the way jurors deliberate: Reshaping the individual assumptions jurors make about power and conflict. *The Defender,* pp. 15-21.

Sunwolf (2000). Talking story in trial: The power of narrative persuasion. *The Champion, 24,* 26-31.

Sunwolf (2002). Getting to "GroupAha!": Provoking creative processes in task groups. In L. R. Frey (Ed.), *New directions in group communication* (pp. 203-217). Thousand Oaks, CA: Sage.

Sunwolf, & Seibold, D. R. (1998). Jurors' intuitive rules for deliberation: A structurational approach to the study of communication in jury decision making. *Communication Monographs, 65,* 282-307.

Sunwolf, & Seibold, D. R. (1999). The impact of formal procedures on group processes, members, and task outcomes. In L. R. Frey (Ed.), D. S. Gouran, & M. S. Poole (Assoc. Eds.), *The handbook of group communication theory and research* (pp. 395-431). Thousand Oaks, CA: Sage.

Tuckman, B. W. (1965). Developmental sequence in small groups. *Psychological Bulletin, 63,* 384-399.

VanGundy, A. B. (1984). *Managing group creativity: A modular approach to problem solving.* New York: American Management Associations.

Wheelan, S. A. (1994). *Group processes: A developmental perspective.* Boston: Allyn and Bacon.

Wilgoren, J. (2003, January 11). 4 death row inmates are pardoned. *The New York Times,* Sec. A, p. 13.

2

KINETIC FACILITATION TECHNIQUES FOR PROMOTING RELATIONSHIPS AMONG MEMBERS OF DIVERSE GROUPS

Holly Siebert Kawakami
University of New Mexico

Groups are becoming more and more diverse, whether in the organizational workplace, educational setting, or local neighborhood, both as a result of U.S. domestic demographic changes and globalization trends (see, e.g., Earley, 1993; Kirchmeyer & Cohen, 1992; Larkey, 1996; Triandis, 1995). However, research has not kept pace with this rapid change, as the study of cultural diversity in small groups continues to be a relatively underexplored area (see Frey, 2000; Ketrow, 1999; Oetzel, 2003).

Evidence that does exist suggests that heterogeneous groups are more likely than homogeneous groups to produce higher quality decisions (see, e.g., Kirchmeyer & Cohen, 1992; Larkey, 1996; McLeod, Lobel, & Cox, 1996; Watson, Kumar, & Michaelsen, 1993), especially when those groups are confronted with creative, innovative, and rapidly changing tasks (see Eisenhart & Schoonhoven, 1990; Kono, 1988; Nemeth, 1986; Pelz & Andrews, 1976). However, research also shows that diversity is potentially problematic, as some diverse groups demonstrate less successful outcomes compared to homogeneous groups (see, e.g., Ancona & Caldwell, 1992; Wiersema & Bird, 1993).

One of the reasons heterogeneous groups do not always perform to their capacity is because diversity in groups presents challenges in interpersonal relations and communication among members that can be difficult to overcome (see Kirchmeyer, 1993; Kirchmeyer & Cohen, 1992; Ruhe & Eatman, 1977; Triandis, 1960; Triandis, Hall, & Ewen, 1965; Vaid-Raizada, 1985). The more diversity that is present in a group, the more interactional misunderstandings among members are likely to occur (Earley, 1993; Kirchmeyer & Cohen, 1992; Larkey, 1996; Watson et al., 1993), making it more difficult for a group of diverse people, in comparison to a relatively homogeneous group, to achieve cohesion and other positive group outcomes. In summarizing the extant literature on the effects of culture and cultural diversity on communication in work groups, Oetzel (2003) claimed that "culturally diverse groups have more group process difficulty (e.g., more tension and conflict) than do culturally homogeneous groups" and that the promised "benefits occur only if diversity is managed properly" (p. 121).

The research, thus, suggests that attention to the promotion of high-quality relationships among group members may be critical to the success of diverse groups. Perhaps in earlier times, when groups were more homogeneous, it was unnecessary to focus on the relational communication occurring within groups, unless there were significant relational problems among members, but with the acceleration of diversity in groups, more attention early on to relational issues in diverse groups is needed. However, a review of U.S. literature on group communication facilitation reveals that initial relationship building among group members is typically neglected or minimized (Ketrow, 1999; Keyton, 1999).

Moreover, relational communication is accomplished largely through nonverbal interaction among group members, although verbal interaction also certainly plays a part (see Ketrow, 1999). Even though people may be unaware of being influenced, they are greatly influenced by others' nonverbal behaviors, and make decisions and judgments based on those behaviors (see Hall, 1976, 1983). Particularly in diverse groups, some of the members may come from cultures that privilege nonverbal behavior as equal to or more important than verbal behavior in understanding the meaning of people's actions, and individuals with differing cultural backgrounds may misinterpret the meanings of nonverbal behaviors.

Unfortunately, group communication scholars have not generally focused attention on the importance, nature, and effects of nonverbal communication in groups, focusing, instead, on nonverbal communication in dyads (and even then not systematically) and generalizing the results to groups (see Ketrow, 1999). Moreover, little attention has been paid to either the connection of nonverbal behavior to high-quality productive relationships in groups or the facilitation of nonverbal behavior in groups for promotion of high-quality and productive relationships among members (see Ketrow, 1999). This gap in the research is due perhaps to the fact that the majority of studies and group communication facilitation techniques originated with U.S. academics and practitioners.

When small groups are comprised of individuals of diverse cultural backgrounds, however, the significance of nonverbal communication comes to the fore. The emphasis in the extant literature on understanding and facilitating verbal communication for creating successful groups may not, therefore, be the best way to facilitate relationships among members of groups that include individuals who highly value relational communication. Instead, an emphasis on nonverbal communication as a means of promoting relationships may be more appropriate and effective.

In this chapter, I introduce nonverbal interaction exercises as a facilitation method for group members to come to know and better understand one another, and to promote better working relationships and task outcomes, especially during the early stages of a group's formation, when individuals are developing their commitment to the group. A diverse group requires focused attention and facilitation during the early stages of group life to achieve the type of initial relationships among members that can promote effective group problem solving, decision making, and task achievement. Unless all of the members of a diverse group feel committed to the group, their full involvement and contribution may not occur and, consequently, the potential positive effects of diversity in groups may not be achieved; instead, a negative drain on the group can occur that lessens its success in comparison to a homogeneous group.

I begin the chapter by exploring the connections among nonverbal behavior, relational communication, and cultural diversity. I then explicate the steps comprising the specific nonverbal communication facilitation method employed—kinetic exercises—and provide examples of group applications and their outcomes to illustrate this method. Three groups, two U.S. domestic groups with varying degrees of diversity and one international group, were chosen as examples to explain the processes and effects of kinetic exercises in groups.

NONVERBAL BEHAVIOR, RELATIONAL COMMUNICATION, AND CULTURAL DIVERSITY

Studies show and scholars agree that at least 60 percent and as much as 90 percent of interaction is nonverbal (Birdwhistell, 1952; Burgoon, Buller, & Woodall, 1996; Mehrabian & Ferris, 1967). The exact percentage is less important than the fact that nonverbal communication carries significant weight in human interaction. As Burgoon (1980) claimed in summarizing the research literature on nonverbal behavior, "The overwhelming conclusion has been that the nonverbal channels carry more information and are believed more than the verbal band, and that visual cues generally carry more weight than vocal ones" (p. 184).

Nonverbal communication is a complex system with categories common to all cultures but performed differently according to cultural meaning, norms, and customs. Individual expression varies within the range of signals that fit within the categories of nonverbal communication, making the nonverbal code system analogic (Burgoon, 1994) and, therefore, complex. Burgoon and other scholars also stress the multichanneled and simultaneous nature of nonverbal communication in comparison to verbal communication.

Ekman and Friesen's (1972) research on nonverbal communication provides a rationale for the use of nonverbal exercises to promote high-quality interpersonal relationships among group members. As they explained:

> Our aim [in studying nonverbal communication] has been to increase understanding of the individual, his feelings, mood, personality, and attitudes, and to increase understanding of any given interpersonal interaction, the nature of the relationship, the status or quality of communication, what impressions are formed, and what is revealed about interpersonal style or skill. (p. 353)

Communication through nonverbal channels is, therefore, key to forming impressions of other individuals, interpreting their behavior, and establishing *relational communication* with them; that is, "the verbal and nonverbal messages that create the social fabric of a group by promoting relationships between and among group members" (Keyton, 1999, p. 192).

Focusing on relational communication is important because a group of individuals, especially diverse individuals, do not automatically become a working team; team building is a process that develops over time. A period of time devoted to relationship building at the early stages of a group's formation may, thus, be essential to promoting individual members' commitment to the group, minimizing later misunderstandings, and building the group cohesion that will provide the base from which members can work through difficulties and achieve the higher productivity of which diverse groups are capable.

The lack of attention paid by scholars and practitioners to relationship building in groups is unfortunate, especially because more and more working groups are comprised of individuals from diverse cultural backgrounds. In comparison to the dominant U.S. culture, many other cultures emphasize relational communication to the extent that group tasks cannot be attended to unless relational matters have been properly considered and group members reach a certain level of comfort that enables them to feel a part of and to identify with the group and with the other members. In other words, individuals from cultures that emphasize relational communication cannot immerse themselves fully within a group and proceed to engage in group tasks until they establish high-quality relationships with the other members of the group.

Individuals from cultures that emphasize relational communication also tend to privilege meaning communicated through nonverbal behavior over verbal behavior. Hall (1976, 1983) distinguished cultures with regard to whether they were *high-context cultures*, in which people emphasize relationships over tasks and nonverbal behavior over verbal behavior, or *low-context cultures*, in which people emphasize tasks over relationships and value verbal behavior over nonverbal behavior. Individuals from high-context cultures, thus, value relational aspects of completing tasks together, tending to find it difficult to feel part of a group and be a fully contributing member until time has been devoted to developing the roots of personal relationships and a certain level of trust with the other group members (Bantz, 1993; Earley, 1993; Kirchmeyer, 1993; Kirchmeyer & Cohen, 1992; Watson & Kumar, 1992). Hence, for individuals from high-context cultures, initial relationship building is an important antecedent to their ability to work wholeheartedly toward group goals.

The conceptual categorization of high-context versus low-context cultures does not imply a value judgment and is always a comparison of cultures rather than absolute. High-context and low-context orientations are also related to other cultural dimensions, such that a high-context orientation is commonly linked to collectivist and interdependent self-construal cultures (Hofstede, 1980; Kim, Triandis, Kagitsibasi, Choi, & Yoon, 1994), whereas a low-context orientation is commonly linked to individualistic and independent self-construal cultures (Oetzel, 1995; Ting-Toomey, 1993).

U.S. mainstream culture tends to be low-context in its communication style, whereas many other cultures around the world, and many women and minority ethnic groups within the United States, tend to demonstrate a high-context communication style. The low-context orientation of the U.S. dominant culture may explain why scholarship about group interaction, in general, and group formation, in particular, seems to neglect the fundamental role of nonverbal communication in fostering the trust and rapport necessary for establishing strong relationships that motivate people to commit fully to a group (Ketrow, 1999; Keyton, 1999).

Hence, when groups are comprised of individuals of diverse cultural backgrounds, the significance of nonverbal behavior and relational communication becomes apparent. In particular, a major challenge is for low-context-oriented individuals to further their understanding of a high-context communication orientation. Although the reverse is also true, my experience in facilitating groups concurs with Hall's (1983) observations of dominant-culture U.S. Americans that low-context-oriented individuals find it more difficult to achieve the observational and interpretive skills for understanding high-context-oriented communication styles than the opposite case. High-context-oriented individuals generally find it frustrating but possible to follow the thinking of low-context-oriented behavior.

The significance of nonverbal communication to those from high-context cultures and the need for individuals from low-context cultures to understand the importance of nonverbal modes of communication lead to the search for facilitative techniques based largely on nonverbal behavior for members of diverse groups. As shown in the remainder of this chapter, facilitation using nonverbal behavior provides a means of emphasizing relational communication, especially during the early stages of group life, but also across the life span of a group, that fosters the level of trust, honesty, and genuine caring among group members that potentially helps them to manage the issues and concerns produced by group diversity.

KINETIC EXERCISES

There are many forms of nonverbal communication that could potentially be facilitated in groups. I chose to develop facilitation exercises using the *kinesics* category of nonverbal communication, coined by Birdwhistell (1952), which was derived from the Greek word for movement and refers to all forms of body movement, including gestures, facial expressions, posture, and touch (Burgoon et al., 1996). The related word, *kinetics*, which comes from the Greek word for moving, is the term I use to describe the movement exercises I employ with groups.[1]

Birdwhistell's assumptions about kinetic communication are directly connected to the reasons why movement exercises can potentially promote rapport and trust among group members. As Birdwhistell (1970) explained, "Kinesics is concerned with abstracting . . . those groups of movement which are of significance to the communicational process and thus to the interactional systems of particular social groups" (p. 192). Birdwhistell's assumptions included: (a) all body movements have potential meaning in

---

[1]The terms "kinesic" and "kinetic" are virtually interchangeable and, thus, either could be used to describe movement exercises; "kinesthetic" is another similar term. I chose kinetic, as it is referenced in the dictionary and might be more familiar to participants. However, I normally use the term "movement" when actually facilitating groups.

communication contexts; (b) people are influenced, often unconsciously, sometimes negatively, by the bodily activity of others; and (c) an individual's kinesics have idiosyncratic features but are also part of a larger, shared social system or culture. The facilitation process of using kinetic exercises, especially the debriefing of those exercises with participants, emphasizes Birdwhistell's points about how people are influenced and impacted by others' bodily activity.

Kinetics is common to all individuals and cultures, but also differs across cultures and individuals. Body language is generally considered "natural," not learned as is language, which makes body language largely unconscious and taken for granted, even though people receive and interpret essential cues for understanding others and negotiating relationships through body language. Although the way people move is often taken for granted, especially in low-context cultures, Birdwhistell (1970), Condon (1968, 1982), Hall (1983), and other scholars have devoted much scholarship to understanding what kinetics informs us about individuals, including their cultural characteristics and how kinetics influence interaction. They have found that kinesics is similarly structured to language and, therefore, individuals may tell as much about themselves through their body language as they do through their speech acts—perhaps more, as kinesics are also simultaneously multichanneled.

I developed kinetic facilitation based on consideration of differences across ethnic cultures and as a means for bridging language barriers, although that does not preclude consideration of gender, class, sexual orientation, and other diversity characteristics of concern within and between cultures. To bridge differences in communication styles between those from high- and low-context orientations, which are, in turn, linked with differences between collectivist and individualist orientations, interdependent and independent self-construals, and other cultural dimensions that influence communication styles, since 1995, I have developed a repertoire of kinetic exercises that uses movement deliberately to promote a way of knowing and understanding others in a group (see Figure 2.1). These kinetic exercises are particularly useful during the early stages of group activity, before engaging in the task aspects of group work, for establishing relational trust and rapport among group members, and may make a difference in the ability of a diverse group to accomplish both its task and relational goals. However, as at least one of the cases examined in this chapter shows, kinetic exercises are also beneficially used over the course of the ongoing life of a group to maintain, deepen, and reinforce relationships among members. I explain below how kinetic exercises promote interactional synchrony, emotional connections, and group cohesion, as well as some additional reasons for using such exercises.

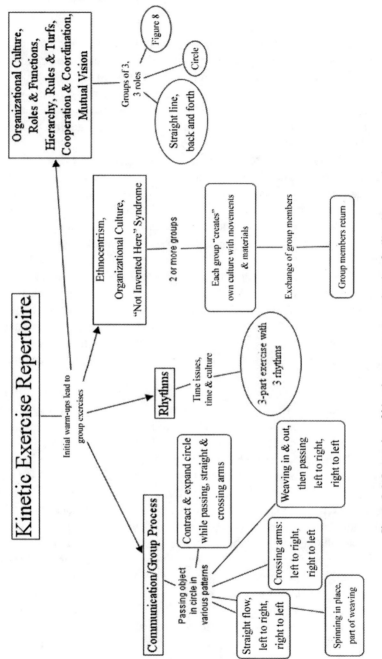

Figure 2.1. Repetoire of kinetic group communication facilitation exercises

Promoting Interactional Synchrony

Interactional synchrony, written about by Condon (1982) and Sheflen (1982), posits that individuals who interact unconsciously attempt to achieve, within a relatively short period of time, a similar rhythm with one another through interconnected verbal and nonverbal behavior. Kinetic exercises draw on this natural inclination by intentionally placing individuals in facilitated group experiences that emphasize nonverbal communication and, thereby, intentionally speed up the process of achieving synchrony. As group members practice the exercises, they experience the satisfaction and enjoyment of achieving synchronous movement with fellow members.

Promoting Emotional Connections within a Group

A variety of research reports that the dynamics within a group, including level of member participation (Kelsey, 1998), the development of a climate of trust and intimacy (Jarboe & Witteman, 1996), and communicative exchange (Larkey, 1996), affect the productivity of a task group. One of the overall objectives of using kinetic exercises with a group is to facilitate a way of knowing other members that fosters emotional connections based on mutual respect so that the conflicts that inevitably occur later between members will be dealt with from within the context of these connections. A purely cognitive, instrumental approach to perceiving others in a group does not necessarily facilitate the bonding, trust, and capacity for collaboration that are necessary for achieving high-quality group outcomes (Kambiz & Benton, 1999; Katzenbach & Smith, 1993; Kawakami, Horspool, Hart, Schoeppner, & Sullivan-Gallegos, 2003), especially in diverse groups. A process, either facilitated or self-directed, that helps members of a group to think of themselves as a collective unit is necessary. To achieve high-quality outcomes, members need to balance the tensions between self and others, such that they respect each other as individuals and also develop a collective consciousness whereby they look out for common interests.

Promoting Group Cohesion

In research about development of group cohesion, scholars have suggested ideas such as group members valuing the personal rather than the social identities of members (Oetzel, 1995), practicing mindfulness (Gudykunst, 1993, 1995; Ting-Toomey, 1999), and taking advantage of the tendency of an open attitude of members at the beginning of group formation before any violation of expectations accumulate and contribute to stereotyping

(Burgoon, 1995). Although all are excellent points, there is no indication in the research literature regarding *how* group members are to practice these objectives and achieve group cohesion. The use of kinetic exercises with group members is one method for developing group cohesion and accomplishing the objectives outlined by other scholars.

Other Reasons for Using Kinetic Exercises

There are at least three other overlapping reasons—inclusivity, creation of common ground while respecting diverse viewpoints, and a short time frame—for choosing kinetics as a nonverbal medium for promoting relationships among group members both early in the development of a group and throughout the course of a group's life to preserve the relationships formed. First, movement exercises are structured so that they are inclusive, involving all members of a group in the same activity at the same time without requiring special skills. By involving all members, kinetic exercises focus on the development of trust and rapport. Engaging in kinetic exercises together as a group enables the individual members to know one another in a relational context rather than solely in a task context, and encourages expression other than verbal and analytical (Gardner, 1993). In addition, the exercises are conducive to promoting the type of group interaction necessary for producing high-quality task outcomes because they are embodied, collective experiences that enable participants to make connections between the exercise and group procedures and tasks.

A second reason for using movement exercises is that the mutually performed activities create a common ground of experience, through members engaging together in an exercise and eliciting their feedback about that exercise. In addition, debriefing the exercise together may reveal and make explicit differing assumptions, values, and worldviews among members that have both cultural and individual idiosyncratic origins, and may lead to greater understanding of and respect for those differences. Periodic use of kinetic exercises over the duration of a group's life can assist in maintaining positive relational communication among members, even when they are confronted with conflict regarding the task.

In particular, use of the nonverbal channel of kinesics respects and values individuals who use high-context and collectivist communication styles, as well as those individuals whose strengths lay in intelligences less recognized by the dominant culture (Gardner, 1993). Members with a high-context communication style who need relational connection before feeling part of a group are often relieved and inspired by the emphasis given to nonverbal means of communication. These members tend to feel they are in familiar territory, which empowers them to more fully express and explain themselves verbally more fully to their fellow group members. The use of kinetics does not prohibit verbal expression but positions it in a secondary, supportive role, in contrast to a low-context orientation, which positions kinetics and other nonverbal behavior in a secondary, supportive role. The use of movement with group members who have a low-context orientation allows them to experience something similar to a high-context orientation, leading them to a new appreciation of how individuals with a high-context orientation communicate, particularly when those individuals are inhibited from full verbal expression due to their limited use of English, or any other dominant language. Low-context and individualistic-oriented members can have the kinetic exercises introduced as part of the overall group task, giving them a reasonable rationale and motivation for spending time on the exercises. Hence, group members from a variety of orientations can be comfortable with the time spent on these kinetic exercises, which also promotes group cohesion.

Individuals coming to the exercise with differing contextual orientation and communication styles can, therefore, find common ground through performance of the movements and also better understand their differences through the debriefing process. Sharing the experience enables greater insight into one's own and other members' assumptions and sense making.

A third reason for using kinetic exercises is that it is possible to compact into a short time frame what usually occurs naturally over a long period of time in a group. The telescoping of the process of group relationship formation into a short period of time deliberately invites members to concentrate on how they interact together. An exercise can be completed in as little time as an hour, although a half day will allow for more variety and discussion during debriefing. The fact that these kinetic exercises can be completed in a short time frame makes them possible to use even when groups have other agendas to complete, and without too much intrusion into members' busy schedules.

Recorded reflections by members of groups about relationships and tasks often demonstrate that by the end of a group's life, or after a long period of time being together, people finally come to understand the meanings of other members' behaviors that would have been helpful to have known long before that time. Not only are the exercises short in duration but they also speed up the time spent on relationship building. Spending focused time in the early stages of group formation using kinetic exercises to build relationships as a base for subsequent discussion and disclosure, instead of sole reliance on verbal exchange, speeds up the process of knowing and understanding other members. As members come to know one another better through these exercises, the group becomes more high-context in communication style, resulting in more empathic understanding of one another, less time taken for backtracking, or long, verbal explanations of behavior.

METHODOLOGY AND PROCESS

My interest in developing kinetics as a method for facilitating communication in groups originally arose from my participation in 1995 in a group of about 60 academicians and practitioners in the intercultural communication field who, after a long, intensive day of seminars and a quick dinner, walked into a room for an evening program. I recall how tired and anxious everyone looked. The leader was a musician, Keith Terry,[2] who began by performing body music and rhythmic movement with found objects and then moved on to conducting group rhythmics and vocalics. Well before the end of the 2-hour session, everyone's fatigue and anxiety had disappeared, replaced with renewed energy, smiles, and laughter.

Already having had 15 years of experience as a trainer of intercultural communication, and 11 years of experience teaching intercultural communication, I knew that the transformation I witnessed was important. I proceeded to develop kinetic exercises and introduced them to groups at academic conferences, in classrooms, and to organizations in both Japan, where I am a permanent resident, and in the United States, where I am from originally. Participants' response, after some initial puzzlement or anxiety, has consistently been positive, with many making a point of telling me months or years later how fresh the experience remains and how clearly they recall the knowledge they obtained from it.

The process of using kinetic exercises emphasizes (a) communication among group members through nonverbal means; (b) individual reflection to connect the somatic, bodily experience with cognitive functions; and (c) self-disclosure and revelation to the level comfortable for each individual in processing an exercise. The exercises themselves are short, movement patterns that involve all members, invite group creativity, and foster trusting relationships and rapport among members. There is a repertoire of exercises (see Figure 2.1) from which to choose and customize for groups depending on their membership, goals, tasks, and the particular contexts within which they are embedded, including corporate, educational, nonprofit, and other types of group settings. To develop the exercises, I borrowed from and was inspired by many other disciplines, including yoga, bioenergetics, eurythmy, Japanese tea ceremony (*chado*), Feldenkrais, and *tai chi chih*.

---

[2]Terry is aware that his seminar inspired me, and I have continued to learn from him. He approaches communication through music and rhythm (see his Web site: www.crosspulse.com), whereas I start from a communication perspective and use movement as a nonverbal means to consider points of interpersonal interaction within a group.

Four-Phase Process

I use a four-phase facilitation process that was adapted, with permission, from the methodology used by Annmarie Ehrlich, a eurythmy practitioner with 40 years of experience who incorporated this facilitation process into management consulting in the Netherlands and Germany. The four phases for facilitating kinetic exercises with groups are:

1. Introduction to the Theme: A theme, chosen either by the facilitator based on knowledge about the group or decided on by the group, is introduced with time spent brainstorming about it. The theme is something the group wants to or needs to focus on, something as broad as communication or as specific as the next meeting facilitation. Introducing the theme focuses members' attention on a particular aspect of the group context. Openly talking about that theme sets the norm that all ideas are invited to be shared and heard.

2. Engagement in the Kinetic Exercise: The facilitator explains, models, and practices the kinetic exercise chosen by introducing a basic movement pattern. Once the group becomes familiar with the pattern, variations are introduced and coached. Group members are then invited to innovate and expand on the basic patterns.

3. Individual Reflection: Members individually engage in stream of consciousness writing or journaling with guidance from the facilitator. Individuals are encouraged to begin with their concrete experience of the kinetic exercise and to then move to more abstract levels that include insights about their own behavior within the group, interpersonal relationships in the group, and implications for the group's interaction.

4. Facilitated Group Reflection and Debriefing: The facilitator asks the individuals to come together as a group to share their concrete experiences of the kinetic exercise. The facilitator encourages members to offer their insights about the implications of the exercise experience for group work and leads a dialogue aimed at promoting better mutual understanding and creating future ways of working and interacting together.

Thus, this four-phase process first introduces participants to the method and focuses their thoughts on the theme for their group. Participants then practice some basic kinetic patterns and are invited to collaborate on variations of those patterns. The individual reflection of phase three facilitates links between the experiential and cognitive domains. After recall of the concrete experience, more abstract levels of thinking are encouraged, with participants making learning connections between behaviors and situations for themselves as individuals and for the group as a collective unit. Phase four is similar to debriefing in any training session, inviting sharing and discussion that builds on and adds to the development of trust and rapport among members.

CASE STUDIES

Having outlined the need for a nonverbal facilitation technique that is appropriate for groups comprised of diverse members and that may be used at the point of group formation and during the duration of the group to focus attention on relational communication, I now introduce three applications that illustrate specific types of kinetic exercises using the methodological steps previously outlined. The three case studies describe how kinetic exercises were facilitated for groups that operated in three different contexts and that were comprised of diverse individuals (diversity being defined in a broad sense to include gender, age, class, and profession, as well as ethnicity and nationality). These three case studies were conducted in natural settings, two domestic and one international. All the groups invited me to facilitate the kinetic exercises, and the participants voluntarily gave me their self-reflection notes to use for research purposes.

Domestic U.S. Case Study

The first case study is of a U.S. domestic group from a nonprofit organization that consisted of 12 people, both male and female, of two generations (youth and adult), and that was ethnically diverse, with the majority being Latino/Latina/Hispanic and the minority being White/Anglo. One of the leaders of this group, a participant in a university class where I conducted two kinetic exercises, invited me to lead kinetic exercises for one of the group's regularly scheduled professional development sessions.

The fact that the majority (10) of the group members were teenagers—middle school and high school students employed as recreation leaders for young children—who participated along with the adult, professional leaders, posed a special challenge, as the teenagers had not appeared interested or involved in another professional development session that I observed. These teenagers were from a working-class, downtown neighborhood. The summer program paid them a nominal amount to be counselors to younger children in a program that provided enrichment, skills development, and healthy recreation for the children for half days, Monday through Friday. Once the young children left after lunch, the teenagers stayed for another hour and a half for feedback, discussion, and weekly professional development.

I followed the four kinetic exercise phases previously outlined, but I decided to cut short the time devoted to brainstorming and discussion of the theme to physically involve the group members as soon as possible. The theme for them was "Being in a Group/Working with a Group," which was arrived at after earlier consultation with the adult educators. As is ideal but not always possible, we were able to go to another place for the actual exercises, an outdoor space that was very pleasant.

I asked the members to stand and form a circle, explained briefly what we would do, and then asked them to move to a basic beat of four to contract and expand the circle (this and the following variations are shown in Figure 2.1 under "Communication/Group Process"). I then asked them to perform various movement patterns, such as contractions and expansions of the circle and weaving in and out of the circle. After they practiced a pattern, I asked them for ideas on variations of that movement, which they enthusiastically shouted out without hesitation. The entire group then tried the new ideas one by one, and practiced them. At times, I removed myself from the circle to watch or to facilitate the activity from the sidelines to let members empower themselves as a group.

Early on, I divided the group into two subgroups, according to alternating persons. I asked them to think of names for their subgroup, as it would be more interesting to call out a name rather than a number or letter. They readily thought of names, one being Pigs and the other being Docs, both of which had some significance to them. They appeared to quickly form identities and take pride in their new subgroups. They supported others in their subgroup, at the same time engaging in good-natured ribbing and teasing of their own members and members of the other subgroup.

After moving through the series of the patterns described for about 20 minutes, we returned to the original room. I asked them to write about their experience of the movements just performed, in any combination of words, diagrams, and illustrations, including writing in Spanish if they wanted to do so. Although the teenagers did not stay totally silent and talked to one another during this third phase of the process, they did produce reflections. Compared to other groups comprised of college age and older adults that I have facilitated, this group of predominately teenage participants produced many drawings, with almost half of them drawing a diagram of one of the kinetic patterns. Almost all identified themselves on paper as a Pig or a Doc, with many using tag lettering for the name and others using a picture. One young man wrote the following prose poem about the movement he had experienced:

We formed a circle
We named the "one" and "two" group
We spun, we weaved
We bumped into each other
We changed places
We remained in a circle
We pulsated like a jellyfish
We dizzied ourselves by going in circles

He also drew a large frontal picture of himself as a sprite-like character and wrote, "This reminds me of chains. The links, the weaving in and out. Of pulsing, like a light—a star—pulses at night in the distance."

Another participant drew a large basketball with the name DOC beneath it in the center of the paper. She then wrote in very small print in the upper right-hand corner, "The twirling reminds me of b[asket]-ball. When I think of b-ball, I think of whom I love." Another young man wrote, "Today I spun around in circles for about 45 minutes. I also weaved in-between. People, it was fun. I also saw a pig in the clouds. I came up with the idea to spin while weaving between people."

I then proceeded to the debriefing of the experience, phase four, by asking members for their thoughts and reflections about the exercise. This produced a spirit of involvement and excitement in the room, with communication readily flowing between the youth and their adult leaders, and a willingness on the part of all participants to listen to one another. There were numerous moments of building on others' thoughts and ideas, and good-natured teasing also occurred. A couple of young people who had expressed reluctance to write anything because of fear of being "wrong," after being reassured, proceeded to share their drawings and written comments with confidence.

I was given 1.5 hours for the entire group facilitation procedure. At the end of that time period, I suggested that having already gone slightly past the time allotted, we would need to end the session. There was, however, no indication that the teenagers were anxious to leave, even though that was the end of the day for them. They behaved differently in this session from a previous session I had observed, where they appeared disinterested, too cool for such goings-on, and, at the same time, unsure of what was expected of them. Moreover, their discussions and demeanor during the facilitated session seemed to me to be confident, energetic, and unselfconscious.

In addition to the comments they wrote, once encouraged to think about working together as a group, members talked about the need to pay attention and listen to each other when working together, the importance of practicing something new together, how the whole group had participated, that a lot of new ideas were generated, that changes are hard and take a while to learn, and that the experience was fun, even cool. The teenagers' reflections revealed that the kinetic exercise helped them to think about and come to conclusions about working with others, the meaning of being in a group, group identities, and thoughts about other groups to which they belonged, including neighborhood gangs. The adults also readily contributed their thoughts and were able to learn more about the teenagers as individuals minus their typical veneer of cool disinterest.

Domestic U.S. Team-Building Case Study

Another U.S. domestic case study involved a graduate-level class of 12 people, including the instructor, who met for four weekends of intensive coursework over a semester. Although I have conducted a variety of kinetic exercises with many college classes to introduce intercultural and communication concepts through movement, in the case of this graduate class, the participants were not only studying team development but were also trying to develop themselves into a team with two subteams. This case study also demonstrates the value of using kinetic exercises after the initial stage in a group's experience, after members have had some time to work together.

The participants were mature adults whose diversity stemmed largely from their professions, which included education, management, military, training, computer systems, and consulting. There were two men in the group of 12, and there appeared to be little ethnic diversity, the majority being white/Anglo, with one Latina/Hispanic female. After consultation with the instructor, I was scheduled to have 1.5 hours midway through the course to introduce the kinetic exercise. As a member of the class, the participants knew me, but unlike all of them, who had taken various classes with one another, I was a newcomer from a different department. All they knew ahead of time was that I would introduce an exercise that was one of a series of exercises for team building.

Starting with phase one, I explained the rationale behind the use of kinetic exercises for team building and asked them to suggest a theme. It was no surprise that they decided on and then brainstormed about the theme of high-performing teams. Their brainstorming produced the key words of trust, communication, common purpose, commitment, enthusiasm, fun, passion, intrinsically motivated, and excellence, plus the drawing of a cartoon figure that encompassed large ears and a big smile. Having spent time focusing on the theme, we then moved outside for phase two—the exercise itself.

After some warm-up movements in a circle, I explained and demonstrated each part of a three-part exercise (shown in Figure 2.1 as "Organizational Culture, Roles, & Functions, Hierarchy, Rules & Turfs, Cooperation & Coordination, Mutual Vision") and then guided them through the practice of each part. Participants then were asked to divide into four groups of three, chosen by them. They proceeded to practice the parts and then the whole exercise in those groups. The three parts of this kinetic exercise were a forward-and-back repetitive movement forming a straight line, a circle going around that straight line, and a figure eight moving around the other two shapes. I periodically called for the participants to switch roles within their groups so that each person tried each of the three parts in succession.

Although each part seems simple, it takes considerable teamwork to build to a harmonious combination, an inclusive rhythm, and smooth transitions. Both the class instructor and I participated. I left my group periodically to guide and encourage the other groups, but mainly let them work out for themselves how to smoothly combine and blend all the parts together. Phase two concluded with each group showing the other groups its routine. It was evident that, in a short period of time, each group had developed pride in its identity, felt somewhat competitive toward the other groups, and felt successful. However, everyone also applauded and encouraged the other groups in turn.

We returned to the classroom, where participants engaged in individual reflection—phase three—as I guided them through writing about their experience of the exercise. In phase four, all participants spoke about the experience and discussed what they had learned about team building. Many commented that they appreciated the change in venue to the outside fresh air on a lovely day with the chance to move, stretch, and re-energize. Many noticed that although everyone received the same instructions, there was considerable uniqueness in how each group worked and practiced together and creativity in each final product. As one participant said, "Such diversity in style! The four groups started with the same steps, but the end result looked much different for each team."

Several people emphasized the overall safety and level of comfort they felt, now midway through the course, but also due to the steps of the exercise and the encouragement and help received from others during it. They noted that there had been a lot of laughter and occasional goofing off that demonstrated enjoyment of the activity, although several participants also stated that some of the laughter might have been frustration, as usually each person was best in one of the roles and switching was difficult or confusing. However, no one gave up. They observed that within each group, they needed to try again, try another way, communicate better, and work together toward the goal that many described as "synchronicity." To achieve synchronicity, or the smooth execution of the movements simultaneously, each person had to understand how all the parts contributed to the whole pattern of the exercise.

Some participants identified the three parts of the exercise in specific ways, such as the line as a straightforward style, the circle as visionary, and the figure eight as a facilitator role; or as being linear, circular, and meandering styles, respectively; or concretely, as the front-line worker, management, and the "creatives" of the organization. One participant observed that her group had produced a satisfactory final product (performance), but felt that it had never achieved synchronicity compared to the other groups. As she explained:

> By chance, we completed the task, getting through the series of steps in our final performance. We never really worked "together" on the performance. We simply kept doing our steps and hoped we would end on the right count.
>
> As I watched the other groups perform, it occurred to me that some of the other groups had achieved synchronicity. They had coordinated their roles. They had problem solved about how to best approach the task. They established their own norms and interpretation of the task. Communication was the key to their work.
>
> As a team, we knew that the objective was to coordinate the steps to fit together and to end on the same beat. We did not have common goals of rhythm or use of space. These could have come out of dialogue and problem solving. . . . We didn't discuss or share our own interpretation of the steps and rules. . . . We were letting unspoken assumptions interpret the rules. Some of the other teams experienced that communication itself builds trust. . . . The groups that experienced synchronicity did so through communication and more specifically through dialogue [defined by Kambiz & Benton, 1999, as the creative exploration of complex issues, a deep sense of listening, and suspending one's views]. . . . Our group's focus was on recalling the initial rules and practicing. Communication through dialogue and the trust that would have been formed through it, would have elicited problem solving, experimentation, creativity, and perhaps even synchronicity.

As we ended the session, two members who had been huddling together for a few minutes announced that they had made a breakthrough for the class project and were listing teamwork-related words all beginning with the letter "c." So far, they had thought of 12 words, such as caucus, colloquy, chat, consensus, conversation, and conference. It appeared that, in addition to reinforcing learning about team development and performance, these group members were able to use the kinetic exercise as a springboard to the future direction of their project, learn more about themselves within groups, and identify key concepts of team development. Lunchtime was delayed due to the extent of time devoted to the topic before my session, but no one seemed to mind and, instead, continued to comment about the fun they had and lessons learned from the exercise.

International Case Study

The third case study was conducted at a university in Japan with an internationally diverse group of six people (men and women) who were full-time or part-time Japanese faculty, and one visiting faculty member from South Korea. Japanese was the common language used. Although I am a U.S. American, I am fluent in Japanese and, thus, was able to facilitate the session in that language.

Both Japanese and Korean cultures have been identified as high context and collectivist (see Hall, 1976, 1983; Hofstede, 1980); therefore, all participants were familiar with the meaning of high-context communication style, although, of course, each culture's high-context orientation is unique. Japanese and Korean cultures have many similarities and are in close geographical proximity, but the two peoples also have a long history of mutual animosity and hostility, a mixture of familiarity and conflict that often makes it difficult for Koreans and Japanese to successfully communicate.

Two faculty, the senior professor whom I had known for about six years and his colleague who had been recently introduced to me, invited me to facilitate a kinetic session because they were seeking ways to help their colleagues develop professionally as an academic unit and also to smooth communication between the standing Japanese faculty and the visiting faculty member from South Korea. The senior professor thought that the Korean female visiting faculty member was feeling the effects of both culture shock and homesickness, and observed that faculty members had little opportunity to know one another on a personal level.

For this group of academics, I spent some time at the beginning of the facilitated session talking about the theory and reasoning behind the use of kinetic exercises to build my credibility, establish rapport, and ease them into the movements that would be required, an unusual request for faculty. Four members of the group had never met me, so it was necessary to take the time to lay such a foundation. Fortunately, the setting was physically comfortable, and even included refreshments, and ample space for movement was available adjacent to the seating area. Although it is better for participants to be dressed comfortably, including wearing comfortable shoes, this group was dressed formally, as is customary at Japanese universities, which meant that the female faculty member wore high-heeled shoes and all of the male faculty members wore suits and ties.

The theme chosen for this group after prior consultation with the senior professor was "Education." During phase one, we brainstormed about the meanings of education and members talked about their individual educational experiences, thereby indirectly opening the door to more personal communication. Two sides of education were expressed: one being the conforming side, with "rules" and "schedules"; the other being cultivation of human resources, looking to the future, and also "fun," "interesting," and "how to live."

I then explained the kinetic exercise and invited the participants to join me in the adjacent space. The kinetic exercise was the same as that used with the second domestic U.S. team-building case described ("Organizational Culture" in Figure 2.1), but I introduced it for this group as corresponding to three roles within the educational system: the administrators moving straight forward and backward, the instructors moving in a circle, and the students moving in a figure eight pattern.

First, we collectively practiced each of the three parts of this particular exercise. I then coached them as they formed two groups of three and blended the three moves together. Every person engaged in each of the three parts in succession. Before long, they were laughing as they practiced the moves with one another. I continued to encourage them, but mainly let them work out the intricacies for themselves and was not a participant myself. Unusual for a group of academics in Japan, they became animated and joked as they engaged in the exercise, and they appeared to be kind and helpful to one another.

After they were able to carry out the exercise to their satisfaction, I asked them to return to their seats and guided them through individual reflection regarding the exercise (phase three), inviting them to write their thoughts in any of three languages (Japanese, Korean, or English) and to express themselves in drawings if they wished. They all chose to write in Japanese and had no difficulty filling up a page or more, although no one made any drawings.

For phase four, group debriefing, we discussed everyone's reflections about the exercise, all expressed with much good humor and collaborative support that elicited a lot of personal disclosure and examples that had been unknown to the other members. They also added more thoughts and key words to the brainstorming list about education and about intercultural communication.

One participant said:[3]

> Well, my first role was as a student, and the student's theme was challenging, and because it was challenging, it was [so] fun for me. And the second role is the teacher. For me it was the most uncomfortable because I become between, and I felt disturbed a lot, so I didn't like it so much there. Finally, I was the administrator. At first I felt very good because I felt like I'm a leader because I'm in front of the [other] people. (Kawakami, 2003, p. 132)

Another participant reflected:

> If we say that education in Japan is now at a crisis, what we usually see in a university setting is, if the assumption is true, we are putting too much burden on the students. The professors do research and do education, but they don't seem to care about the students. And then, the administrators were the bad guys. They make rules and enforce them, but don't tell students how they can achieve their goals exactly. So we hear so often that they just tell students, "If you don't make this class, you won't be able to graduate." And stop there. Thinking about university teaching, we have to put ourselves in the students' shoes. . . . Now universities must be heading toward the world of active learning or teaching. (Kawakami, 2003, p. 136)

Regarding the process of performing the movements together, another participant said:

> Well, there are some moments that are very subtle, when we find out the shape of the three different figures match together somewhere. We have a common rhythm, right? . . . And we draw the shape from the lines, but still we have to focus on the rhythm that we have to share. But once we get out of the line or divert from this fixed pattern of rhythm I get a little annoyed or frustrated because I just couldn't attune myself enough to the thing happening outside my field. So, my keyword today was attunement. The three people have to be aware of what other people are doing. . . . I wouldn't say the word harmony, but it's a spontaneous sharing of the same field. (Kawakami, 2003, p. 136)

---

[3]The quotations are taken from the published proceedings of the university's programs. Although everyone spoke Japanese during the actual program, the publication utilized an English translation of the transcript.

There was then some discussion about the meaning of "field" as a context, vision, and as a specialty, all of which contribute to the difficulties of communication. In summarizing the educational nature of the activity, a participant said:

> What you have got us to think about today through this exercise I think is very important in thinking about what education should be, ought to be. And I think it is very important for educators to be physically together in a face-to-face situation like the one you put us in, so that we can [have] some kind of a common ground to get us started. (Kawakami, 2003, p. 138)

This participant added that distance education is a growing trend and speculated on how it might be possible to attain a similar experience with the use of distance technology.

The Korean visiting faculty member who had been feeling cut off and homesick was able to express her feelings by relating her feelings of confusion and displacement to the exercise. She ended the session in a more positive state of mind, as demonstrated by the smile on her face and her stated plans to get together informally with her colleagues. There was discussion about balancing different aspects of a career, as some had to commute between two universities in different parts of the country; the real experience of intercultural communication compared to theories about it; and points about cooperation and collaboration. I introduced discussion about rhythms in education based on Hall's (1976, 1983) research in New Mexico with three different ethnic groups, and there was further discussion about how one formulates a rhythm for a Japanese classroom. When the time came to conclude the session, no one was eager to leave and everyone lingered to talk a little more.

DISCUSSION OF THE CASE STUDIES

These three examples, from group settings with different types of diversity, demonstrate that the basic model of kinetic exercises focusing on nonverbal expression works successfully with a variety of groups to help members learn more about one another for the purpose of building trust and rapport among them. Although the kinetic exercise was the same for the second and third cases, they were used in different ways, tied to different themes, and evoked some different responses.

Focusing on a theme in phase one enables kinetic exercises to be customized for each group. The method is, thus, flexible and can be accommodated to different groups, cultures, and languages. The exercises all use movement, but nothing that is culturally based, nor do the movements require any athletic or dance ability. Depending on an individual's background and the setting, a request to engage in such movements may be very unusual; however, the introductory phase and the exercise process gradually reduce participants' uncertainty and create a nonthreatening and non-performance-oriented experience. Emphasis is placed on what can be observed and learned through the kinetic exercise and the interaction it engenders among participants rather than on the degree of skill exhibited by members.

This group communication kinetic facilitation method differs from many techniques with shortcomings that prevent a group from becoming fully functioning and highly successful. Such techniques too often (a) focus on content over context; (b) assume the formation of an immediate group mentality without a deliberate process for working towards it; (c) concentrate only on the cognitive aspects of the practical steps necessary for working toward a group task, leaving out the emotional aspects of group membership; and (d) attempt to minimize the initial time devoted to relationship building, although time must often be taken up later to "fix" relational problems that occur.

Expecting a collection of individuals in a natural setting to automatically function as a cohesive, committed, high-performing group is counterproductive. Individuals must go through a process of giving up some autonomy, ego involvement in their personal goals, and turf defensiveness to "buy into" group membership and collaboration, and to make a commitment to the entire group and its goals. Key to the willingness to commit is that individuals must come to feel an emotional connection to other members of the group, be able to put the group first, and believe that the success of one member depends on the success of all members.

Future Research

Two goals for future research are suggested based on numerous experiences using kinetic exercises with various groups. The first goal is to follow at least one group, and preferably more, from its inception to the completion of at least some of its tasks to document the effects of using kinetic exercises, at the time of formation and periodically throughout the period that the group meets, on the group's communication effectiveness, level of cohesion, and ability to resolve conflict. In addition to observation, in-depth interviews conducted with individual members and with the group as a whole (e.g., a focus group) would add to an understanding of the effects of kinetic exercises on members' knowledge about self and others, development of trust among group members, and successful completion of group tasks.

A second goal for future research is to contact group members who formerly participated in kinetic exercises at intervals such as 1, 3, 6, and 12 months after the exercises and ask them through questionnaires and/or interviews about the new learning gained from the kinetic exercises and the effects of those exercises on their comfort level, emotional safety, relationships, participation, and completion of tasks in that group and in subsequent groups.

CONCLUSION

The extant literature on group formation often leaves out or glosses over how group members can and need to develop relationships early on that are based on mutual trust and rapport, concentrating instead on operating procedures, decision making, and other strategies for achieving task results. Without some initial intentional focus on relational communication, groups often compensate later by, for example, frequent backtracking to unravel unproductive behaviors. Once unproductive behaviors are in place, of course, backtracking is never as effective or satisfactory as initially creating positive experiences through emotional attachments and effective working patterns among group members.

Kinetic exercises that involve all group members in a nonthreatening, non-culturally based series of movements that emphasize nonverbal expression is one method that facilitators and/or members can use at the time of initial group formation and periodically throughout a group's existence to promote members' commitment to the group, and emotional attachment and mutual trust among members. By emphasizing nonverbal channels of communication rather than verbal channels, individuals in a group come to learn about and understand other members in a relatively more high-context way, which is very important for productivity.

High-context learning and understanding is effective both from an intracultural and intercultural perspective. In more homogeneous groups, the exercises help members to learn about others' behaviors and personalities and to develop the trust needed to build group cohesion. In groups comprised of members from both low- and high-context cultures, kinetic exercises help individuals with a more high-context orientation to feel confident in their ways of expression, and lead individuals with a more low-context style to understand more about and be able to engage in high-context modes of communication.

Cultural diversity in groups brings with it the challenge of bridging the gaps between the different styles represented. Whereas most of the literature on groups is based on groups comprised of low-context individuals, more groups today are comprised of people from both high- and low-context orientations. A major challenge posed by cultural diversity is how to be inclusive of individuals with high-context communication styles, such that their input is fully recognized, valued, and contributes to promoting high-quality, successful outcomes.

Kinetic exercises emphasize nonverbal means of expression for the purposes of promoting relational communication and emotional connections among group members. These exercises are inclusive, provide a common experience for bonding with appreciation for differences, and are conducted in a short time frame that telescopes experience and accelerates knowledge typically attained over a long period time. Kinetic exercises fill the relational gap in a group's formation by intentionally focusing on the building of mindful relationships among group members, which is especially necessary for individuals with a high-context orientation. As a group communication facilitation tool, kinetic exercises assume that personal relationships are essential for accomplishing group tasks and that these exercises provide a means for individuals to transition into committed group members who value group life.

REFERENCES

Ancona, D. G., & Caldwell, D. F. (1992). Demography and design: Predictors of new product team performance. *Organization Science, 3*, 321-341.

Bantz, C. R. (1993). Cultural diversity and group cross-cultural team research. *Journal of Applied Communication Research, 21*, 1-20.

Birdwhistell, R. (1952). *Introduction to kinesics*. Louisville, KY: University of Louisville Press.

Birdwhistell, R. (1970). *Kinesics and context; essays on body motion communication*. Philadelphia: University of Pennsylvania Press.

Burgoon, J. K. (1980). Nonverbal communication research in the 1970s: An overview. In D. Nimmo (Ed.), *Communication yearbook* (Vol. 4, pp. 179-197). New Brunswick, NJ: Transaction Books.

Burgoon, J. K. (1994). Nonverbal signals. In M. L. Knapp & G. R. Miller (Eds.), *Handbook of interpersonal communication* (pp. 229-285). Thousand Oaks, CA: Sage.

Burgoon, J. K. (1995). Cross-cultural and intercultural applications of expectancy violations theory. In R. L. Wiseman (Ed.), *International and intercultural communication annual: Vol. 19. Intercultural communication theory* (pp. 194-214). Thousand Oaks, CA: Sage.

Burgoon, J. K., Buller, D. B., & Woodall, W. G. (1996). *Nonverbal communication: The unspoken dialogue* (2nd ed.). New York: McGraw-Hill.

Condon, W. A. (1968). Linguistic-kinesic research and dance therapy. In *Combined Proceedings of Third and Fourth Annual Conference on Dance Therapy* (Vol. 3, pp. 21-42). Baltimore: Association for American Dance Therapy.

Condon, W. A. (1982). Cultural microrhythms. In M. Davis (Ed.), *Interaction rhythms: Periodicity in communicative behavior* (pp. 53-77). New York: Human Sciences Press.

Earley, P. C. (1993). East meets West meets Mideast: Further explorations of collectivist and individualist work groups. *Academy of Management Journal, 36,* 319-348.

Eisenhart, K., & Schoonhoven, C. (1990). Organizational growth: Linking founding team, strategy, environment and growth among U.S. semiconductor ventures, 1978-1988. *Administrative Science Quarterly, 35,* 504-529.

Ekman, P., & Friesen, W. (1972). Hand movements. *Journal of Communication, 22,* 353-374.

Frey, L. R. (2000). Diversifying our understanding of diversity and communication in small groups: Dialoguing with Clark, Anand, and Roberson (2000). *Group Dynamics: Theory, Research, and Practice, 4,* 222-229.

Gardner, H. (1993). *Frames of mind: The theory of multiple intelligences.* New York: Basic Books.

Gudykunst, W. B. (1993). Toward a theory of effective interpersonal and intergroup communication: An anxiety/uncertainty management perspective. In R. L. Wiseman & J. Koestler (Eds.), *Intercultural communication competence* (pp. 33-71). Newbury Park, CA: Sage.

Gudykunst, W. B. (1995). Anxiety/uncertainty management (AUM) theory. In R. L. Wiseman (Ed.), *International and intercultural communication annual: Vol. 17. Intercultural communication theory* (pp. 8-58). Thousand Oaks, CA: Sage.

Hall, E. T. (1976). *Beyond culture.* Garden City, NY: Anchor Press.

Hall, E. T. (1983). *The dance of life: The other dimension of time.* Garden City, NY: Anchor Press/Doubleday.

Hofstede, G. (1980). *Culture's consequences: International differences in work-related values.* Beverly Hills, CA: Sage.

Jarboe, S. C., & Witteman, H. R. (1996). Intragroup conflict management in task-oriented groups: The influence of problem sources and problem analyses. *Small Group Research, 27,* 316-338.

Kambiz, M., & Benton, C. (1999). Rapid team learning: Lessons from team New Zealand America's Cup campaign. *Organization Dynamics, 27,* 48-62.

Katzenbach, J. R., & Smith, D. K. (1993). *The wisdom of teams: Creating the high-performance organization.* Boston: Harvard Business School Press.

Kawakami, H. S. (2003). Movement wo yoita ibunka communication training. In H. Yamaji (Ed.), *FD series on English presentation II. Report of seminar discussions* (Vol. 40, pp. 129-140). Chiba, Japan: National Institute of Multimedia Education.

Kawakami, H. S., Horspool, A., Hart, T. L., Schoeppner, J. M., & Sullivan-Gallegos, L. (2003). *The criteria of highly performing teams: A comparison of the literature and interview themes of highly performing teams.* Unpublished manuscript, University of New Mexico, Albuquerque.

Kelsey, B. L. (1998). The dynamics of multicultural groups: Ethnicity as a determinant of leadership. *Small Group Research, 29,* 602-623.

Ketrow, S. M. (1999). Relational communication in groups. In L. R. Frey (Ed.), D. S. Gouran, & M. S. Poole (Assoc. Eds.), *The handbook of group communication theory and research* (pp. 251-287). Thousand Oaks, CA: Sage.

Keyton, J. (1999). Relational communication in groups. In L. R. Frey (Ed.), D. S. Gouran, & M. S. Poole (Assoc. Eds.), *The handbook of group communication theory and research* (pp. 192-222). Thousand Oaks, CA: Sage.

Kim, U., Triandis, H. C., Kagitsibasi, C., Choi, S-C., & Yoon, G. (Eds.). (1994). *Individualism and collectivism: Theory, methods, and applications.* Thousand Oaks, CA: Sage.

Kirchmeyer, C. (1993). Multicultural task groups: An account of the low contribution levels of minorities. *Small Group Research, 24,* 127-148.

Kirchmeyer, C., & Cohen, A. (1992). Multicultural groups: Their performance and reactions with constructive conflict. *Group & Organization Management, 1,* 153-170.

Kono, T. (1988). Factors affecting the creativity of organizations: An approach from the analysis of new product development. In K. Urabe, J. Child, & T. Kagano (Eds.), *Innovation and management: International comparisons* (pp. 105-144). New York: Walter de Gruyter.

Larkey, L. K. (1996). Toward a theory of communicative interactions in culturally diverse work groups. *Academy of Management Review, 21,* 463-491.

McLeod, P. L., Lobel, S. A., & Cox, T. H., Jr. (1996). Ethnic diversity and creativity in small groups. *Small Group Research, 27,* 248-264.

Mehrabian, A., & Ferris, S. R. (1967). Inference of attitudes from nonverbal communication in two channels. *Journal of Consulting Psychology, 31,* 248-252.

Nemeth, C. (1986). Differential contributions of majority vs. minority influence. *Psychological Review, 93,* 23-32.

Oetzel, J. G. (1995). Intercultural small groups: An effective decision-making theory. In R. L. Wiseman (Ed.), *International and intercultural communication annual: Vol. 19. Intercultural communication theory* (pp. 247-270). Thousand Oaks, CA: Sage.

Oetzel, J. G. (2003). The effects of culture and cultural diversity on communication in work groups: Synthesizing vertical and cultural differences with a face-negotiation perspective. In L. R. Frey (Ed.), *New directions in group communication* (pp. 121-137). Thousand Oaks, CA: Sage.

Pelz, D. C., & Andrews, F. M. (1976). *Scientists in organizations: Productive climates for research and development* (Rev. ed.). Ann Arbor: University of Michigan, Institute for Social Research.

Ruhe, J., & Eatman, J. (1977). Effects of racial composition on small work groups. *Small Group Research, 8,* 479-486.

Scheflen, A. E. (1982). Comments on the significance of interaction rhythms. In M. Davis (Ed.), *Interaction rhythms: Periodicity in communication behavior* (pp. 13-28). New York: Human Sciences Press.

Ting-Toomey, S. (1993). Communicative resourcefulness: An identity negotiation perspective. In R. L. Wiseman & J. Koester (Eds.), *International and intercultural communication annual: Vol. 17. Intercultural communication competence* (pp. 72-111). Newbury Park, CA: Sage.

Ting-Toomey, S. (1999). *Communicating across cultures.* New York: Guilford Press.

Triandis, H. C. (1960). Cognitive similarity and communication in a dyad. *Human Relations, 13,* 175-183.

Triandis, H. C. (1995). The importance of contexts in studies of diversity. In S. E. Jackson & M. N. Ruderman (Eds.), *Diversity in work teams: Research paradigms for a changing workplace* (pp. 225-233). Washington, DC: American Psychological Association.

Triandis, H. C., Hall, E. R., & Ewen, R. B. (1965). Member heterogeneity and dyadic creativity. *Human Relations, 18,* 33-35.

Vaid-Raizada, V. K. (1985). Management of interethnic conflict in an Indian manufacturing organization. *Group and Organization Studies, 2,* 419-427.

Watson, W. E., & Kumar, K. (1992). Differences in decision making regarding risk taking: A comparison of culturally diverse and culturally homogeneous task groups. *International Journal of Intercultural Relations, 16,* 53-65.

Watson, W. E., Kumar, K., & Michaelsen, L. K. (1993). Cultural diversity's impact on interaction process and performance: Comparing homogeneous and diverse task groups. *Academy of Management Journal, 36,* 590-602.

Wiersema, M. F., & Bird, A. (1993). Organizational demography in Japanese firms: Group heterogeneity, individual dissimilarity, and top management team turnover. *Academy of Management Journal, 36,* 996-1025.

II

FACILITATING GROUP CONFLICT
COMMUNICATION

3

FACILITATING GROUP COMMUNICATION IN PROTRACTED CONFLICT SITUATIONS
PROMOTING CITIZEN PEACE-BUILDING
EFFORTS IN CYPRUS*

Benjamin J. Broome
Arizona State University

Conflicts that involve ethnic groups fighting for control of physical resources—such as territory, oil, and water—and over identity issues—such as language, religion, and cultural heritage—fill the headlines of today's newspapers, magazines, and television screens. For most ordinary citizens of the United States, reports of these conflicts form the essence of their geopolitical knowledge of world affairs. Even those who have never traveled beyond the boundaries of their own state are familiar with the names of relatively small countries or provinces, such as Bosnia, Chechnya, East Timor, Kashmir, Kosovo, Sri Lanka, and Somalia. Unfortunately, it is violence and war that put these names in our vocabulary.

With such clashes dominating the attention of both the public and the world's diplomats, the time is ripe for those who study and practice group communication facilitation to examine how the methods they use might be applied in protracted international conflicts. I believe that culturally appro-

*This chapter is dedicated to my Greek-Cypriot and Turkish-Cypriot colleagues and friends who work as peace builders in Cyprus. I would like to express special thanks to the Cyprus Fulbright Commission for its leadership in supporting bicommunal, peace-building activities on the island.

priate group facilitation methods can make important contributions to deep-rooted conflicts; at the same time, the application of those methods and the study of such applications have the potential to meet the call of communication scholars such as Craig (1989), Craig and Tracy (1995), and Cronen (1995) to develop more "practical theory" that can inform our response to important, real-world situations. In this chapter, I attempt to take up this challenge by describing my experience with efforts to facilitate citizen peace-building groups on the divided Mediterranean island of Cyprus, where the Greek-Cypriot and Turkish-Cypriot communities have been torn apart by a conflict that first divided the two communities 40 years ago. I hope that this case study will be useful for both group communication practitioners involved in similar conflicts and for those who study and teach in this arena.

My experience in Cyprus started in 1994, when I accepted a position as Senior Fulbright Scholar in residence on the island, with responsibility for offering seminars, workshops, and training in communication, problem solving, intergroup relations, and conflict resolution to members of the Turkish-Cypriot and Greek-Cypriot communities.[1] In the following sections, I first provide a context for my facilitation work by giving a brief overview of the Cyprus conflict. I then describe the methodologies I used and how they were applied in working with peace-building groups on the island. I conclude by examining some of the contributions, cultural considerations, and cautions related to the facilitation of communication in citizen groups involved in protracted conflict situations.

OVERVIEW OF THE CYPRUS CONFLICT

Cyprus, a small island situated in the eastern Mediterranean approximately 40 miles south of the Turkish coast and 60 miles west of Syria, is home to two primary ethnic communities that are distinguished by differences in language, cultural heritage, and religion, and that are divided by views of the past, politics of the present, and visions of the future. The Greek Cypriots, who are primarily Christian Orthodox, with cultural and linguistic ties to Greece, comprise approximately 80 percent of the population, whereas the Turkish Cypriots, who are predominately Muslim, with cultural and linguistic ties to Turkey, make up approximately 20 percent of the population. The island is divided from east to west by a United Nations-patrolled buffer

---

[1]The conflict resolution Fulbright Scholar position in Cyprus was created at the request of Greek-Cypriot and Turkish-Cypriot individuals who recognized the need for outside third-party assistance to make progress in their peace-building efforts on the island.

zone, usually referred to as the "Green Line," which was first created (in the capital city of Nicosia) following hostilities that began in 1963. In 1974, following an overthrow of the elected government of Cyprus by forces acting under the direction of the ruling military junta in Greece, Turkey sent military forces to the island, driving most of the Greek Cypriots living in the north of Cyprus from their homes and businesses, and turning overnight one-third of the Greek-Cypriot population into refugees. The northern 40 percent of the island fell under Turkish control, and nearly all Turkish Cypriots living in the south of Cyprus fled to the Turkish-controlled area; the southern 60 percent of the island remained under administration of Greek Cypriots. As a result of the 1974 war, two ethnically homogeneous zones were created, and after nearly 400 years of living together (not always peacefully) in mixed and adjacent villages scattered throughout the island, Greek Cypriots and Turkish Cypriots were now forcibly divided into two geographic zones, separated by barbed wire and land mines.[2]

Since the cease fire arranged immediately after the war in 1974, there has been little progress in negotiations to reach agreement on the future of the island. Over these past three decades of separation, the two communities have grown further apart. Greek Cypriots, who head the internationally recognized government of the island, view themselves as victims of Turkish aggression, denied by an illegal occupying army access to their homes, lands, and businesses in the north of the island. They envision the future of Cyprus as a unified state consisting of two primary communities (Greek Cypriot and Turkish Cypriot) under a single national identity. Turkish Cypriots, who operate under a self-declared government (recognized only by Turkey), feel isolated and trapped by international embargos and dependence on Turkey that prevent them from developing their economic potential and building fully functioning democratic institutions. They envision the future of Cyprus as a confederation of two sovereign states functioning loosely under a weak bicommunal national governmental structure. Because of past actions by each side toward the other that brought disruption, displacement, loss of life, and other forms of suffering, both sides feel victims of aggression and neither side trusts the other.

---

[2]For more details of the Cyprus conflict, see Attalides (1979), Bahcheli (1990), Bolukbashi (1998), Calotychos (1998), Hitchens (1997), Joseph (1997), Koumoulides (1986), Markides (1977), Mirbagheri (1998), O'Malley and Craig (1999), Richmond (1998), Savvides (2002), Stearns (1992), Theophanous (1996), and Volkan (1979). For updates on the Cyprus conflict from a Turkish perspective, see The Turkish Economic and Social Studies Foundation's (TESEV) Web site (http://www.tesev.org.tr/eng/); for a view of the conflict from a Greek perspective, see the Hellenic Foundation for European and Foreign Policy's (ELIAMEP) Web site (http://www.eliamep.gr).

For more than 25 years, the Greek-Cypriot and Turkish-Cypriot communities have been almost completely cut off from communication with one another. This physical divide has affected nearly every aspect of their lives—limiting economic growth (particularly in the north), social development, advancement of the education system, integration into the international community, and protection of irreplaceable environmental resources, and resulting in the waste of billions of dollars in military expenditures. The Cyprus conflict is also an important source of tension between the countries of Greece and Turkey, and it is a major roadblock to Turkey's hopes of joining the European Union.

The failure to resolve the Cyprus conflict has also negatively affected the psychological condition of residents, who carry a sense of injustice about the past and anxiety about the future. Finally, the lack of progress toward peace has prevented the creation of a multicultural society that could be a model for the Middle East and for the world. Instead of a place where individuals of different faiths, languages, and cultural identities live together in peace, Cyprus has become one of the world's purest examples of a divided society. Historically, only the Berlin Wall and the Korean demilitarized zone managed to stand longer, and with the former now gone, Nicosia is left as the only divided capital in Europe.

Although there has not been a great deal of progress at the political level during the past three decades, a number of initiatives have taken place at the citizen level to try to improve relations between the two communities. Periodic conflict resolution workshops sponsored by third parties were held with representatives of the two communities during the 1970s and early 1980s (see Burton, 1969; Doob, 1987; Mitchell, 1981; Stoddard, 1986; Talbot, 1977), leading to more frequent interventions in the late 1980s and early 1990s (see Diamond & Fisher, 1995; Fisher 1992, 1997; Hadjipavlou-Trigeorgis, 1993, 1998).[3] Since the mid-1990s, numerous third parties have worked with peace-building groups in Cyprus, helping to support citizen-based activities aimed at bridging the divide between the two communities (for an overview of conflict resolution activities in Cyprus, see Broome, 1998). The work of these citizen groups has fostered greater contact between individuals and groups from the two sides of the conflict.

---

[3]The most important third-party role in the early 1990s was filled by the Institute for Multi-Track Diplomacy (IMTD), based in Washington, DC. The efforts of IMTD and the Cyprus Consortium (see Diamond & Fisher, 1995), which included IMTD, the Conflict Management Group (CMG) at Harvard University, and members of the National Training Laboratories (NTL), made it possible for the work that is the focus of this chapter to take place.

FACILITATION PROCESS

The work in which I was engaged in Cyprus involved extensive use of interactive design methodologies—in particular, a process known as "Interactive Management" (IM). Based on Warfield's (1994) science of generic design, the IM process is a system of facilitation and problem solving that helps groups to develop outcomes that integrate contributions from individuals with diverse views, backgrounds, and perspectives. Established as a formal system of facilitation in 1980 after a developmental phase that started in 1974, IM was designed to assist groups in dealing with complex issues (see Ackoff, 1981; Argyris, 1982; Cleveland, 1973; Deal & Kennedy, 1982; Kemeny, 1980; Rittel & Webber, 1974; Simon, 1960). The theoretical constructs that inform IM, developed over the course of more than two decades of practice, draw from both behavioral and cognitive sciences, with a strong basis in general systems thinking.[4]

The IM approach carefully delineates content and process roles, assigning to participants responsibility for contributing ideas and to the facilitator responsibility for choosing and implementing selected methodologies for generating, clarifying, structuring, interpreting, and amending ideas. Emphasis is given to balancing behavioral and technical demands of group work (Broome & Chen, 1992) while honoring design laws concerning variety, parsimony, and saliency (Ashby, 1958; Boulding, 1966; Miller, 1956). IM has been applied in a variety of situations to accomplish many different goals, including assisting city councils in making budget cuts (Coke & Moore, 1981), developing instructional units (Sato, 1979), designing a national agenda for pediatric nursing (Feeg, 1988), creating computer-based information systems for organizations (Keever, 1989), improving the U.S. Department of Defense's acquisition process (Alberts, 1992), promoting world peace (Christakis, 1987), improving Tribal governance process in Native American communities (Broome, 1995a, 1995b; Broome & Christakis, 1988; Broome & Cromer, 1991), and training facilitators (Broome & Fulbright, 1995).

---

[4]The formal practice of IM exists in several locations around the world, including Instituto Tecnologico y de Estudios Superiores de Monterrey, Mexico; Center for Interactive Management, New Delhi, India; City University, London, England; University of São Paulo, Brazil; Southwest Fisheries Science Center, La Jolla, California; Christakis, Whitehouse, and Associates (CWA), Berwyn, Pennsylvania; Defense Systems Management College (DSMC), Fort Belvoir, Virginia; Ford Motor Company, Dearborn, Michigan; Arizona State University, Tempe; and Americans for Indian Opportunity (AIO), Albuquerque, New Mexico.

In a typical IM session, a group of participants who are knowledgeable about a particular situation engage in (a) developing an understanding of the situation they face, (b) establishing a collective basis for thinking about their future, and (c) producing a framework for effective action. In the process of moving through these phases, group members can develop a greater sense of teamwork and gain new communication and information-processing skills.

IM utilizes a carefully selected set of methodologies, matched to the phase of group interaction and the requirements of the situation. The most common methodologies are the nominal group technique, ideawriting, interpretive structural modeling, and field and profile representations. The first two methodologies are primarily employed for the purpose of generating ideas that are then structured using one or more of the latter three methodologies.

The *nominal group technique* (NGT; Delbeq, Van De Ven, & Gustafson, 1975) is a method that allows individual ideas to be pooled, and is best used in situations in which uncertainty and disagreements exist about the nature of possible ideas. NGT involves five steps: (a) presentation of a stimulus question to participants; (b) silent generation of ideas in writing by each participant working alone; (c) "round-robin" presentation of ideas by participants, with recording on flipchart by the facilitator of these ideas and posting of the flipchart paper on walls surrounding the group; (d) serial discussion of the listed ideas by participants for the sole purpose of clarifying their meaning (i.e., no evaluation of ideas is allowed at this point); and (e) implementation of a closed voting process in which each participant is asked to select and rank five ideas from the list, with the results compiled and displayed for review by the group.

Ideawriting (Warfield, 1994) is a method that utilizes relatively small groups of 4-6 persons each, formed by dividing a larger group into several working teams, for the purpose of developing ideas and exploring the meaning of those ideas through open discussion. Ideawriting involves five steps: (a) presentation of a stimulus question to participants; (b) silent generation of ideas in writing by each participant working alone; (c) exchange of written sheets of ideas among all group members, with opportunity for individuals to add ideas as they read others' papers; (e) discussion and clarification of unique ideas; and (f) an oral report of the ideas generated by each working group in a plenary session. In this plenary session, duplicate ideas across the working groups are eliminated from the set and new ideas (if any) are added; the resulting set of ideas is then ready for use in the next stage of the group's work, which might involve one or more of the following methodologies.

Interpretive structural modeling (ISM; Warfield, 1994) is a computer-assisted methodology that helps a group to identify relationships among ideas and to impose structure on those ideas to help mange the complexity of the issue. Specifically, the ISM software utilizes mathematical algorithms that minimize the number of queries necessary for exploring relationships among a set of ideas (see Warfield, 1976). ISM can be used to develop several types of structures depicting the relationships among a set of ideas, including influence structures (e.g., "supports" or "aggravates"), priority structures (e.g., "is more important than" or "should be learned before"), and categorizations of ideas (e.g., "belongs in the same category with"). The five steps of ISM are: (a) identification and clarification of a list of ideas (using a method such as NGT or ideawriting); (b) identification and clarification of a "relational question" for exploring relationships among ideas (e.g., "Does idea A support idea B?," "Is idea A of higher priority than B?," or "Does idea A belong in the same category with idea B?"); (c) development of a structural map by using the relational question to explore connections between pairs of ideas (see below); (d) display and discussion of the map by the group; and (e) amendment to the map by the group, if needed.

In the third step of developing a structural map, questions are generated by the ISM software and are projected onto a screen located in front of the group. The questions take the following form:

"Does idea A relate in X manner to idea B?"

"A" and "B" are pairs of ideas from the list developed by participants in the first step of ISM and the question of whether they "relate in X manner" is the statement identified in the second step.

For example, if a group is developing an influence structure with problem statements, the question might read:

"Does problem A significantly aggravate problem B?"

Using the ISM methodology, the group engages in discussion about this relational question and a vote is taken to determine the group's judgment about the relationship. A "yes" vote is entered in the ISM software by the computer operator if a majority of the participants see a significant relationship between the pair of ideas; otherwise, a "no" vote is entered. Another pair of ideas is then projected on the screen in front of participants, another discussion is held, and a vote is taken. This process is continued until the relationships between all necessary pairs of ideas have been explored. The ISM software then provides to the facilitator the information from which a structural map can be constructed, showing the result of the group's series of judgments about pairs of ideas. The length of time required to complete discussion of all necessary pairs of ideas depends on the total number of ideas in the set, but, generally, the process requires 3-5 hours of group deliberation. The number of necessary queries also depends on the total number of ideas in the set, but the ISM software is able to infer during the structuring process an average of approximately 70-80 percent of the judgments involved in relating the complete set of ideas.

The influence structuring work conducted with ISM can be considered an activity in "mapping perceptions" of the group members. Participants are given the opportunity to explore connections and links between ideas in ways that probably would have gone undetected without such structuring work. ISM can, thus, provide participants with useful insights into the relationships between ideas, and it generates a product, a structural map of those relationships that can guide their thinking as they design potential solutions.

Field representation (Warfield & Cardenas, 1995) organizes ideas in a way that allows a large amount of information to be worked with effectively. There are different types of field representations that are useful for different types of applications, but, typically, a field representation portrays a significant amount of information organized in a form that (a) is appropriate for use in making decisions and (b) maintains an ongoing, visible record of intermediate decision making en route to a final portrayal of the total set of choices that has been made. A field representation shows a set of categories and the members of each of those categories. When appropriate, the group might engage in a structuring process (using ISM) to sequence the categories according to agreed-on criteria.

The portrayal of choices in the field representation technique constitutes a *profile representation*. In constructing a profile, a group examines the first category of the field and chooses elements from that category. Each choice is represented graphically by drawing a line from the bullet in front of a selected element down to a "tie line," a continuous line drawn at the base of the graphic, beneath the full category set. After all choices are made, the selected elements are connected to the tie line; all elements that have not been selected remain unconnected. In this way, the viewer is presented with a graphical portrayal of both selected items and the full set of items considered for inclusion in the final product.

Taken as a set, the methodologies used in IM possess several characteristics that are particularly useful in working with groups involved in conflict situations such as the one in Cyprus. First, they promote the development of a dynamic set of ideas that constantly change as needed. The initial idea set proposed by a group can grow larger as new situations are encountered and as new individuals are brought into the planning process. This process, thus, promotes openness to new perspectives and opinions. Second, the methodologies help to turn the initial list of ideas into an organized, meaningful set of categories that reflect the uniqueness of the situation. Rather than relying on pre-established categories that may not apply to the current situation, participants consider the commonality between the ideas they generated and assign titles that reflect the thread of meaning they perceive as running throughout the items in each category. Third, the structuring methodologies help participants to view their situation as a systemic whole, in which any single idea is viewed in light of the total set of ideas being discussed. Fourth, the methodologies promote an ordered sequence from which informed selections are made; the choices that participants make are, thus, informed by the choices they made already in previous discussions. Fifth, the methodologies support a creative process in identifying options for dealing with a situation. Although ideas may vary widely in their scope and feasibility, they all represent potential contributions to improving the situation. Because ideas are treated as possibilities rather than as final conclusions, participants are able to consider them without stifling creativity by overdue concern for feasibility or realism. Sixth, the methodologies support full participation in the planning process, as every participant's ideas can be included in the field for consideration by the group. Seventh, emphasis is given to tracking of the decision-making process, in that the choice-making methodologies display both the options selected by the group for implementation and the options that were not selected. By doing so, those involved directly in constructing a plan of action, as well as those not involved directly, can better understand the rationale for selecting a particular option because the other options that were considered simultaneously are also available for review. Eighth, any plan developed by a group using these methodologies represents an *alternative* plan for action that can be considered along with other alternative plans developed by different groups or by the same group at a different time. The availability of alternatives promotes consideration of a wide range of optional plans before choosing a final plan, and it allows for different plans to be developed for different scenarios. Finally, the plan of action that results for any scenario can be modified easily as conditions change and as the completion of some options results in new needs or possibly decreases the necessity of performing other actions that might have been selected initially. These characteristics, which allow creative idea generation, flexibility of organization, and involvement of a wide range of relevant stakeholders, are particularly helpful in protracted conflict situations, where participants need methodologies that help break destructive thinking patterns, open new avenues for thinking about the future, and involve a broad cross-section of society.

APPLICATIONS OF INTERACTIVE MANAGEMENT IN CYPRUS

The various applications of IM in Cyprus can be grouped into three primary stages.[5] The first stage consisted of the workshops conducted over a 9-month period with the core group of Greek-Cypriot and Turkish-Cypriot peace builders described earlier. Their work led to the second stage, when further workshops were conducted with targeted groups of young business leaders, young political leaders, and leaders of groups focused on women's issues. A third stage of IM work occurred after I left my residency as a Fulbright Scholar in Cyprus, when workshops were designed and conducted by local teams of Cypriots, through a "distance-learning" arrangement with me acting as their consultant.

During both the first and second stages, I served as primary facilitator for the workshops, and although I employed a team of facilitators from the core group during the work with targeted groups, it wasn't until I left Cyprus that IM work was conducted without my physical presence in the group. Teams conducting work in the third stage received their initial training through participation in the workshop sessions I had facilitated with the core group in the first stage, and they received "hands-on" experience in their role as part of the facilitation team for workshops with the targeted groups in the second stage. In addition, I returned to Cyprus at the end of 1997 to conduct a formal training workshop for new groups of facilitators, with a specific focus on learning the steps of the IM methodologies. Although I have continued to initiate and facilitate IM workshops focused on the Cyprus conflict, local facilitators have conducted most of the work that has taken place since I left Cyprus at the beginning of 1997. The following sections describe each of the three stages in more detail.

Stage 1: IM Workshops with the Core Peace-Building Group

The core peace-building group with which I worked during the first 9 months of my residency in Cyprus consisted of 15 Greek Cypriots and 17 Turkish Cypriots. There were 9 men and 6 women in the Greek-Cypriot group and 10 men and 7 women in the Turkish-Cypriot group. In both groups, ages ranged from the mid-twenties to the mid-fifties, with most of the participants in their thirties and early forties. They were professionals in various fields, including education (university professors and secondary school teachers), business, counseling, and civil service. Political affiliations

---

[5]This section, along with the one that follows, is an expanded version of a description of IM applications in Cyprus that appeared in Broome (2001).

ranged from the left/liberal to the right/conservative (including members of the ruling party in each community). For all of them, participation was voluntary and outside the scope of their normal job duties and family responsibilities. The group was self-selected, and everyone understood from the beginning that participation would require a significant commitment of time. Logistical assistance for making arrangements to meet together in the buffer zone was provided by the Cyprus Fulbright Commission (CFC); meeting space was arranged at various locations in each community, both with the help of the CFC and by members of the core peace-building group.

Workshops with the core group progressed through three design phases (for a description of the activities associated with each phase of work with this group, see Broome, 1997):

> Phase 1: Definition of the situation surrounding peace-building efforts in Cyprus
> Phase 2: Development of a collective vision
> Phase 3: Creation of an integrated set of activities

The three design phases resulted in several specific products representing group views. The most important products included: (a) a *problematique*—a graphical structure depicting each group's view of obstacles confronting peace builders in Cyprus, (b) a *vision statement*—a graphical structure representing the joint group's view of a desirable future for peace-building work in Cyprus, and (c) a *collaborative action agenda*—a plan of activities for accomplishing the aims of the group.

The joint collaborative action agenda consisted of 15 projects around which the group formed bicommunal teams. The projects consisted of bicommunal activities such as concerts and exhibitions, joint publications, special seminars, and workshops with targeted groups of young business leaders, young political leaders, educators, and women. To implement these projects, an "agora/bazaar" was scheduled, to which approximately 150 select individuals from both communities were invited. At this event, participants met initially as a large group and first heard a summary of each project. Participants then "shopped" at "booths" where they could learn more about each individual project. The purpose of this gathering was to "sell" the project ideas to individuals with an interest in working together with members of the other community. By organizing this agora/bazaar, the core group hoped to form an expanded circle of supporters and to increase the human resources available for carrying out the selected projects. Nearly all of those invited to the "marketplace" attended, and after combining a couple of projects and dropping one in which little interest was shown, 12 projects received sufficient support to form working teams, and plans were made for moving forward with implementation of the modified collaborative action agenda.

Although it is not possible in the space of this chapter to describe in detail the various obstacles the core group had to overcome to make forward progress (for initial observations, see Broome, 1997), it is important to note some of the difficulties experienced. Even in the monocommunal setting, there were significant differences between members within each group, including political disagreements, personality conflicts, and different ideas of what is meant by "peace" in Cyprus. Bicommunal meetings brought additional complications related to the history of separation between the communities, meaning that neither side possessed a very accurate view of the other's concerns; consequently, problems emerged because of both perceived similarities that did not actually exist between the groups and perceived differences that were not as great as everyone believed. In addition, because we could not obtain permission to work together, each community group had to spend a significantly amount of time working separately to complete the various phases of the facilitated process; this meant that each group's work often progressed in ways not well understood by the other group. There were several crisis points, when it was not clear if the work could continue, but, fortunately, a way was always found to overcome obstacles that threatened the breakup of the group. Partly as a result of these struggles, the group emerged as a strong unit that has remained to this day one of the driving forces behind bicommunal activities.

Stage 2: IM Workshops with Targeted Groups

As part of the implementation of the core peace-building group's collaborative action agenda, IM workshops were offered to several targeted groups. During the 2-year period following the agora/bazaar, design workshops were conducted with three groups: (a) young business leaders, (b) young political leaders, and (c) a women leaders' forum. These groups were targeted because of the critical role they will play in the future of Cyprus and because no previous rapprochement work had been conducted with these specific groups. In addition, we believed that the IM process would be the most appropriate tool to help them move forward.

Workshops with young business leaders. These workshops focused on "Issues Facing the Business Community in Working towards Economic Cooperation for a Future Federated Cyprus." The group consisted of 12 participants from each community, most in their early to mid-thirties. There were five women in the Greek-Cypriot group, whereas the Turkish-Cypriot group was all male. The majority of participants were young entrepreneurs in areas such as marketing and advertising, import-export management, computers and electronics sales, fashion design, and interior design; some were employees in large banks or manufacturing firms, whereas others owned small shops. For most, it was the first time they had the opportunity to meet individuals from the other community.

Funded by the CFC in late Spring 1995, the workshops started with separate weekend retreats at seaside hotels. The Greek Cypriots met for a 3-day period at a hotel near the port city of Larnaca on the south coast of the island; two weeks later, the Turkish Cypriots met at a beach resort north of the port city of Famagusta on the east coast of the island. Both groups met from Friday afternoon through Sunday afternoon. Participants shared all meals together and stayed overnight at the hotel, providing plenty of time for informal socializing between sessions. Following the initial 3-day monocommunal sessions, the two groups met together in the buffer zone to exchange workshop products. Over the next six months, the two groups met together in both bicommunal and monocommunal settings to continue their work. Most meetings were held on a weekday evening or Saturday afternoon in the buffer zone, but during one weekend, a special set of bicommunal meetings were held in which participants traveled together to each side of the island, something that normally is not possible for citizens of Cyprus. The group members also went together for a week-long trip to Brussels to learn more about the European Union.

During the workshop sessions, two primary questions guided the discussions:

> Question 1: "What are problems facing business leaders in working toward cooperation with the other community?"
> Question 2: "What opportunities do you see emerging for business leaders following an acceptable solution to the Cyprus problem?"

Group products resulting from the workshops included each community's problematique, or system of issues facing business leaders, and a support structure of opportunities for business leaders after an agreement is reached to end the current division of the island.

Workshops with young political leaders. These workshops focused on "Defining the Issues Facing the Youth of Cyprus in the Next Decade." The group consisted of 15 participants from each community, with ages ranging from the early twenties to mid-thirties. There were two women in the Greek-Cypriot group and four women in the Turkish-Cypriot group. Participants were members of the youth wings of the various political parties in each community, ranging from the far left to the far right; most were officers in their youth party structure, and some were affiliated with student political groups. Like the members of the business leaders group, very few of the young political leaders had been involved in bicommunal activities previously, and, consequently, for most, it was the first time they had the opportunity to meet individuals from the other community.

The workshops followed a pattern similar to that of the young business leaders. They started in late Spring 1996, with separate weekend retreats, again funded by the CFC. The Greek Cypriots met for a 3-day period at a hotel in the mountain village of Platres in the Troodos Mountains; two weeks later, the Turkish Cypriots met at a beach hotel near the village of Lapithos on the north coast of the island. Both groups met from Friday afternoon through Sunday afternoon. Participants shared all meals together and stayed overnight at the hotel, providing plenty of time for informal socializing between sessions. Following the initial 3-day session monocommunal sessions, the two groups met together in the buffer zone to exchange workshop products. Over the next six months, the two groups met together in both bicommunal and monocommunal settings to continue their work. Most meetings were held during a weekday evening or on a Saturday afternoon in the buffer zone, but during one weekend, a special set of bicommunal meetings were held in which participants traveled together to each side of the island. The group also went together for a week-long trip to Brussels to learn more about the European Union.

During the workshop sessions, two primary questions guided the discussions:

> Question 1: "What are issues (problems, challenges, threats, fears) facing the youth of Cyprus in the next decade?"
> Question 2: "What should be the goals toward which we (the youth leaders) direct our efforts to improve the future of youth in Cyprus?"

Group products resulting from the workshops included each community's problematique, or system of issues facing youth in Cyprus, and a support structure of goals for the youth of Cyprus.

Workshops with the women leaders' forum. These workshops were titled "Through the Eyes of Women: A Look at Pain and Suffering in Cyprus." The group, all women, consisted of 10 Greek Cypriots and 12 Turkish Cypriots; ages ranged from the late twenties to mid-fifties, with most participants in their mid-thirties and early forties. Participants were professionals involved in various nongovernmental organizations (NGOs) and community groups. Some had been involved in bicommunal activities in the past, but for many, it was the first time they would have the opportunity to meet individuals from the other community.

The workshops started in Spring 1996, with separate weekend retreats for each community group. The Greek Cypriots met for a 2-day period in the buffer zone, and immediately afterward, the Turkish Cypriots met at a restored Ottoman house in Nicosia. Participants shared meals together during the day, but unlike the young business leaders and the young political leaders, they did not stay overnight at a hotel, meaning they had no opportunity for informal socializing between sessions. Following the initial 2-day monocommunal sessions, the two groups met together in the buffer zone to exchange workshops products. Over the next six months, the two groups met together in both bicommunal and monocommunal settings to continue their work. Most meetings were held on a weekday evening or weekend afternoon in the buffer zone. Unlike the young business leaders and the young political leaders, we could not obtain permission for bicommunal meetings in which participants traveled together to each side of the island. It was also not possible to obtain funds for this group to go together to Brussels (although some members went the following year with a differently constituted women's group).

During the workshop sessions, two primary questions guided the discussions:

> Question 1: "What factors contribute to pain and suffering in Cyprus?"
> Question 2: "What are goals for our future that will help minimize pain and suffering in Cyprus?"

Group products resulting from the workshops included each community's problematique, or system of factors that bring suffering, and a vision statement for efforts to minimize pain and suffering on the island.

Each of the three groups briefly described in this section experienced many "ups and downs" as members worked together over the course of several months. The young business leaders, many of whom were entrepreneurs, were all very busy with their jobs, and it was not easy for them to take time away to attend workshops. Most of them were members of political parties that did not view positively bicommunal meetings and conflict resolution workshops, and ideas of rapprochement took time to cultivate. The young political leaders had to deal with differences in political orientation, both monocommunally and bicommunally, as well as differences in views that existed along community lines. In addition, because most of them had been well trained in the art of political posturing, asking them to engage in meaningful dialogue with the "enemy" was going far beyond their previous experience. The women leaders' group also dealt with an especially grueling topic—pain and suffering—and many were themselves victims of the very events they were discussing. The hurt and anger associated with these events were not easy to discuss, especially in a setting where their fellow group members consisted of individuals from the other community they believed had brought about the pain and suffering. In all groups, there was, at times, resistance to meaningful dialogue, with the willingness of one side to take steps toward reconciliation often countered by periods of greatest resistance by the other side. All these factors, however, simply reflected the story of Cyprus.

Unlike the core group of peace builders described earlier, whose work resulted in the design and implementation of many valuable projects, none of the three targeted groups progressed through the third phase of IM activity, which usually involves the specific design of an agenda for taking steps to address the situation being discussed. Thus, on the surface at least, one could conclude that the work of each group was incomplete. For the most part, this was the result of unavoidable and unpredictable external circumstances. The work of the young business leaders was interrupted by unfortunate timing, brought about by funding cycles, when, between the end of my initial Fulbright grant and the start of the second period, I had to return to the United States for a period of three months. That group was just starting with the third phase of its work and, at that point, my role as an outside third party was critical to the willingness of many individuals in the group to participate in the activities. My absence, thus, resulted in the work being put on hold. The members lost momentum at a crucial time, and we never fully recovered from that break. However, the work of the young political leaders and the women leaders' groups was subject to an even more difficult scenario: Both were in the "prime" of their work when tragic clashes occurred at the buffer zone and nearly brought about war. These events shut down the bicommunal activities for a period of time, and they created a very negative climate on the island, making it extremely difficult to continue the work of these groups, even in a monocommunal setting.

Despite these difficulties, the work of all three groups continued, and there have been clearly identifiable results from their activities. Many from the young business leaders group participated in a "Senior Business Leaders'" effort that was organized under an initiative by the U.S. diplomat Richard Holbrooke, who was appointed by President Clinton as a special envoy to Cyprus during 1998. Their earlier participation in our workshop activities helped them to make many positive contributions to the senior-level business group. Many from the young business leaders group also worked together in various European associations. From the young political leaders group, many have remained in contact, and several have cooperated in a regional consortium of youth organizations. Most of the participants in the women leaders' group became part of a larger women's initiative, sponsored by European Union funds, that has met outside Cyprus on several occasions. Participants from the various groups also undertook many individual initiatives; for example, one of the young political leaders obtained funds from the Council of Europe to send a bicommunal group of university students from Cyprus to Budapest for a week-long retreat. Overall, the work of the three targeted groups has manifested itself in a very different manner from the core peace-building group described in Stage 1, but it is easy to see the impact of the IM workshops on both individuals and follow-up activities of each group.

Stage 3: Extended Applications of IM by Local Facilitators

The workshops that had been conducted with the young business leaders, young political leaders, and the women leaders' forum not only helped to create forward movement and momentum within the specific groups but they also served as a training platform for the practice of IM in Cyprus. When I left my Fulbright position in Cyprus and returned to the United States in early 1997, there existed a small group of local citizens with experience both as participants in an extended series of IM sessions and as part of the facilitation team for various IM applications with other groups.

Even after I left Cyprus, I was soon able to work again with my Cypriot colleagues, facilitating a week-long workshop in Switzerland, held during July 1997, which we had organized together for a group of 24 individuals from Greece, Turkey, and the two communities of Cyprus. That positive experience convinced us that much more could be accomplished through the application of IM with various groups, and my colleagues started making plans for additional workshops. At that point, however, I had not offered any formal instruction in the process and we believed that this could be very helpful before my colleagues used IM to facilitate groups without my direct involvement. To complete the capacity-building process, I returned to Cyprus in December 1997 to offer a 2-week training program focused on teaching the specifics of the consensus-building methodologies we had been using, as well as on behavioral and process concerns in working with groups in a conflict setting.

This training served as the impetus for a number of projects that were launched by various local teams in both monocommunal and bicommunal settings. One project took place with a bicommunal group known as the "Citizens Group." This group had already existed for over a year when the IM sessions took place. Participants had been through a number of conflict resolution exercises, they knew each other quite well, and they had engaged in numerous discussions about the core issues of the Cyprus problem. The

IM sessions helped the members to better understand the similarities and differences in perceptions within their group, and they used the methodologies to develop a plan of activities. Another project took place with a university students group my colleagues and I had formed while I was still living in Cyprus. That group had a strong history of good relations among the participants (see Broome, 1999), but the IM workshops helped them to go beyond the friendly relations they had already created and provide a forum in which they were able to explore their differences and similarities in thoughtful and meaningful ways. Finally, IM workshops were held with other existing groups, such as one comprised of educators, mostly secondary school teachers, who had been working together for over a year.

In all the cases just described, my colleagues in Cyprus were offering IM sessions for groups that already existed and with which they had a good working relationship. A very different situation existed with another group to which an IM workshop was offered. Many have long believed that because of its unique location in the eastern Mediterranean, Cyprus could one day become a site for conflict resolution work that brings together groups from various Middle Eastern countries immersed in conflict, and several saw IM workshops as an appropriate way to work with some of these groups. A good start was made toward doing so during the late summer of 1999, when a group of Jewish and Arab Israelis, Lebanese, Egyptians, Greeks, and others from the eastern Mediterranean were brought to Cyprus for the purpose of helping to create a "Peace Village" on a plot of land that had been donated for building a new center where young people from throughout the Mediterranean could come for retreats and workshops. The project is in its beginning stages, and to build support for it in various countries, this group gathered in Cyprus, taking part in a week-long IM session to design the goals and objectives of the "Village." Although I provided some input into the design of the workshop, it was facilitated by my Cypriot colleagues. This work helped to build momentum toward the eventual realization of the idea, although, as of this writing, plans have not been fully implemented.

The work associated with the third stage of IM applications in Cyprus has not been without its challenges. Just after the December 1997 training sessions were completed, the political tide worsened on the island and a ban was put in place by the Turkish-Cypriot authorities on bicommunal gatherings. Without the possibility of meeting locally, it was almost impossible to continue with many of the workshops that were planned for various bicommunal groups. Some work could be accomplished in monocommunal settings, but without much hope for meeting with members of the other community, there was not a great deal of incentive to continue. This ban also meant that there were no opportunities for facilitators to work together across community lines, meaning that much of the potential learning from such work was no longer possible, and, thus, another primary motivating factor was lost. Although it was possible for bicommunal groups to hold workshops outside Cyprus, funds to meet abroad proved difficult to obtain. The resulting situation meant a loss of momentum and was a great setback to the process of creating local expertise in facilitating peace-building groups.

The third stage of IM work in Cyprus is still in its infancy. Given appropriate circumstances and some encouragement, it will continue to develop. Particularly when a political agreement is reached, and the buffer zone becomes more permeable, the need for IM workshops will increase. Ultimately, there may be a need to institutionalize its presence, building both educational and research components. When this happens, it might be necessary to describe a fourth stage of the work, which will have its own dynamics and promises for promoting peace in Cyprus.

Contributions of Group Facilitation to Building Peace in Cyprus

When the Cyprus IM applications started in 1994, a core group of individuals who were committed to promoting peace-building activities were already in place on both sides of the buffer zone. This group was small, consisting primarily of the 32 individuals who participated in the sessions described earlier, but over time, it grew in numbers. As the core group implemented its collaborative action agenda (which emerged from phase 3 of the IM sessions described in stage 1), participation expanded to include over 2,000 individuals who were meeting regularly in various groups.[6] Unfortunately, because of the political situation at the time, regular meetings in the buffer zone were stopped in early 1998.[7] However, contacts continued through a combination of meetings abroad, use of new technologies such as

[6]After I left Cyprus in 1997, several Fulbright scholars continued the emphasis on conflict resolution and peace-building activities. The work of Philip Snyder, John Ungerleighter, and Marco Turk was particularly important in the success of the subsequent bicommunal activities. In addition, the Cyprus Consortium organized several other workshops in the United States, and several bicommunal groups of teenagers, sponsored by the Cyprus Fulbright Commission, attended summer camps with Seeds of Peace and Experiment in International Living in the United States. All of these players made important contributions to the expansion of the bicommunal peace work.

[7]At its meeting in Luxemburg in December 1997, the European Union declined Turkey's request to be added to the list of candidates being considered for European

electronic mail and Web sites, and meetings held at two buffer-zone villages on the eastern side of the island where it is possible for meetings between Greek Cypriots and Turkish Cypriots to take place on a limited basis. Several projects developed by the core group went forward, and many related initiatives were developed and implemented by new groups. To this day, the activities continue in the face of numerous difficulties.

Although there is no way to know how the bicommunal efforts in Cyprus might have progressed without the IM sessions, and it is not possible to separate the effects of other factors, I believe that the IM sessions contributed in several ways to the growth of bicommunal peace initiatives in Cyprus. First, they helped the early participants, who would subsequently play the primary leadership role in the peace-building activities, to gain a deeper understanding of the situation they faced and the obstacles they must overcome. Without this careful examination of possible barriers to promoting peace, it would have been easy for this group to become discouraged when members encountered difficulties. Second, within each community and across community lines, the IM sessions promoted the development of teamwork, helping diverse groups of individuals to work together in spite of different motivations, languages, cultures, and ideas about peace. Several previous attempts to form cross-community alliances had not been successful, in part, because such teamwork had not developed sufficiently. Third, the sessions led to the creation of a collective vision statement by the core group that provided a crucial framework for its work, helping members to move forward with a single voice. Such a vision can help groups in their attempts to overcome past difficulties and to focus, instead, on where they can go together in the future. Fourth, the IM sessions produced a collaborative action agenda for the core group of peace builders in Cyprus that served as a structure for action, helping them to direct their energies in a more integrative manner, and probably helping them to avoid divergent and duplicative efforts.

Overall, I believe that the process in which the groups engaged, along with the products they produced, helped these courageous individuals to sustain their motivation over time, overcome numerous obstacles to their work, and act with a more unified voice during periods of crisis. However,

---

Union membership at that time, while simultaneously moving forward with accession talks with the Republic of Cyprus (the Greek Cypriots). The Turkish-Cypriot administration, unhappy with this decision, stopped granting permission for Turkish Cypriots to cross the checkpoint on their side of the buffer zone for meetings with Greek Cypriots. This effectively shut down the bicommunal meetings that had been taking place on a daily basis for dozens of groups. The checkpoint remained closed until May 2003.

even with the encouraging growth of bicommunal peace-building activities, the work that remains to be done is considerable, for only a small percentage of people in each community has taken part in bicommunal events, there is not widespread support for citizen-level initiatives in either community, and there is opposition in both communities to rapprochement efforts. However, if the bicommunal movement is someday judged as an important factor that helped to create peace in Cyprus, perhaps the group-facilitated sessions using IM described in this chapter will be viewed as having played a crucial role in that process.

FACILITATING GROUP COMMUNICATION IN PROTRACTED CONFLICTS: PROMISES, CONCERNS, AND LIMITATIONS

The IM applications in Cyprus provide an extended case study in the facilitation of group communication in a protracted conflict situation, from which many lessons can be learned. In this section, I briefly examine how the facilitated IM sessions helped to promote both improved communication among the participants and better information management within the facilitated sessions. I then discuss some concerns about the cultural appropriateness of the IM methodologies, as well as how these methodologies helped to manage the cultural differences among group members. Finally, I suggest a few cautions and limitations of facilitating group communication in situations of ethnic conflict.

Promoting Improved Communication and Information Management[8]

In protracted conflict situations, facilitators usually face numerous communication obstacles, including the presence of emotionally laden issues, hidden agendas, poor listening, premature evaluation, domination by high-status or vocal members, and unfocused group discussion. To be effective, facilitators need to manage the communication within and between groups in such a way that these obstacles are minimized.

Because of the complexity of most issues facing groups in conflict situations, group discussion may also be plagued by information-processing deficiencies, including information overload, over-attention to minor issues, and inadequate organization and display of information. Research shows that most unassisted groups faced with complex tasks have significant periods of disorganized activity (Poole, 1983, 1985; Poole & Doelger, 1986; Poole & Roth,

---

[8]This section is based on Broome (1995b).

1989). Similarly, as the task faced by groups becomes more complex, there is greater danger of cognitive overload (Miller, 1956; Simon, 1974). Groups also need assistance in dealing with their substantive, procedural, and relational problems (Hirokawa & Gouran, 1989), climate issues (Folger, Poole, & Stutman, 2001), and contextual influences (Friedman, 1989). Special methodologies are, thus, needed to help groups manage these issues, especially those groups involved in protracted conflict situations. In particular, methodologies are needed that are capable of helping group participants to generate, clarify, and structure ideas and to make informed choices among them.

Results from the IM sessions with citizen peace groups in Cyprus indicate that the facilitated process helped to structure their communication and manage information more effectively in a number of ways. First, the way in which the IM process structured dialogue to give every person an opportunity to contribute ideas and opinions prevented the more outgoing individuals from dominating discussion. Instead of constant interruptions typical in group discussion, individuals were allowed to finish their thoughts before others spoke. Theme-switching, typical of groups in general, was minimized, allowing discussions to stay on track and giving participants a chance to build on others' thoughts. Second, the process promoted learning through iteration in that ideas proposed during the early phases of the process were clarified, then related to one another, and used as building blocks for later phases. In this way, learning occurred at a gradual, deliberate pace, with constant opportunities for revision and reinforcement. Third, the process emphasized the integrated nature of outcomes in that ideas proposed by participants were discussed in light of the total set of ideas, and the process directly engaged participants in exploring the links between those ideas. Participants, thus, learned about the systemic nature of the problems they faced and, in that way, developed a holistic picture of potential ways to tackle those problems. Finally, the IM process promoted the development of "relational empathy" (Broome, 1993), in which parties involved in a conflict are able to create a shared communication space from which they can effectively interpret the situation confronting them and for which they produce alternatives for action that are possible and acceptable to all sides.

Considering the Potential Impact of Cultural Differences[9]

When facilitating group communication in protracted conflict situations, it is important to consider the fit between the culture of the participants and the facilitation practices one uses with the group. I have seen many facilita-

---

[9]This section is based partially on material from Broome and Murray (2002).

tors simply bring in approaches they have developed for use in their own cultural context and try to implement them without modification for working with local groups. Unfortunately, this can result in approaches that do not work effectively or, even worse, cause damage that may not be apparent until after the facilitator is safely back home. In my experience of facilitating group work in Cyprus, there were three primary areas where cultural differences had a strong impact on my work.

First, I had to make appropriate changes in my facilitation practices due to cultural differences between my Western value orientation and that of the eastern Mediterranean culture of the Cypriots. For example, I had to modify my expectations regarding the management of time, for we rarely started our meetings earlier than 45 minutes past the scheduled time for assembly, and yet we usually needed to stop by our scheduled ending time because people had other commitments. In addition, I always had difficulty bringing participants back from a break before at least 30 minutes had passed. Consequently, it took significantly more meetings to work through a particular methodology than I had expected. I soon realized that this was not a matter of lack of interest or commitment on the part of the participants; it was simply a way of working to which I needed to adjust. I also learned, however, that there were many benefits to this way of working; for instance, the social time at the beginning of sessions as everyone was slowly arriving, as well as during the long breaks, was an important means of building both group harmony and consensus on difficult issues (for a similar experience with groups in Poland, see Parrish-Sprowl, 2003).

Second, I had to consider the cultural appropriateness of both the sequence of activities and the techniques I applied for managing group communication. For example, when I decided to use a problem-definition, vision, and action sequence of activities that is common in applications with groups and organizations in the United States, I had to evaluate carefully its appropriateness for use in Cyprus. I was not sure it was possible to separate these phases of group work so clearly in a culture where multitasking is the norm. I considered whether it might be necessary to sequence the phases differently, work with different phases simultaneously, or follow an entirely different sequence of problem solving. I was also concerned about the specific methodologies associated with IM. The NGT, for example, uses an orderly turn-taking procedure, but there was no guarantee that it would work in a culture where people are used to a more free-flowing rhythm of conversation. ISM is also a computer-assisted process, and I was not sure how the groups would respond to the use of such technology.

Third, I was concerned about how cultural differences between participants from the two communities would affect communication. Greek Cypriots, in general, are more expressive than Turkish Cypriots, and when the two groups were together, this meant that Greek Cypriots tended to talk more and longer. One of my jobs as facilitator was to carefully monitor the dialogue, making sure that Turkish Cypriots had adequate opportunity to contribute. Greek Cypriots also tend to express their emotions more readily and visibly than do the Turkish Cypriots. Although the Turkish Cypriots with more bicommunal experience usually expected emotional responses from the Greek Cypriots, I often needed to remind Turkish Cypriots that the Greek Cypriots may not have meant what they said as strongly as it appeared to the Turkish Cypriots. Similarly, I often needed to explain to the Greek Cypriots that what they perceived to be an unenthusiastic response from the Turkish Cypriots might not mean the Turkish Cypriots were not interested in an idea. Turkish Cypriots tend to be much less impulsive and more cautious in considering proposals, thinking through consequences more carefully than Greek Cypriots before taking action. This cultural difference often meant that the Greek-Cypriot group was eager to move forward with an idea, whereas the Turkish-Cypriot group was inclined to wait longer. Finally, I found that Greek Cypriots were more proactive and future-directed in their thinking, whereas the Turkish Cypriots were more focused on the past. Greek Cypriots found this to be quite frustrating and grew tired of constantly listening to the Turkish Cypriots talk about the past; for the Turkish Cypriots, it was equally frustrating that the Greek Cypriots could not seem to acknowledge (to the satisfaction of Turkish Cypriots) the importance of past events.

In considering these cultural factors, I found it necessary to make a number of small modifications as I implemented the various IM methodologies. For example, the NGT term "triggering question," which is designed to stimulate the generation of ideas, did not carry the most positive connotations in a situation characterized by the extensive presence of military forces. A similar problem occurred in labeling the outcome of obstacle-structuring work in ISM. Because it graphically displays a group's consensus about how a set of ideas relate to one another, the ISM product is called a "structural map"; however, in Cyprus, referring to the outcome of our work as a "map" would raise suspicion among each community's authorities because territorial issues are one of the central concerns of the Cyprus conflict.

In spite of these and other modifications, most of the methodologies implemented in IM seemed acceptable to the participants and appeared to help mitigate some of the negative patterns of communication that existed between the two groups. For example, the NGT, with its emphasis on ordered turn-taking and clarification of ideas, made it possible to lessen the effects of some of the cultural differences in communication style between the more expressive and emotional Greek Cypriots and the more careful and reserved Turkish Cypriots. Overall, it is important to engage in mindful application of techniques and principles, doing one's best to implement them with the appropriate degree of cultural sensitivity, but it was my experience that many "imported" methodologies, if properly modified, can work in culturally different circumstances. For that to happen, however, it is very important to carefully monitor and evaluate the entire process at each step of the way to determine the cultural appropriateness of anticipated actions.

Cautions and Limitations

Although facilitated processes used with citizen groups can play an important role in protracted conflict situations, as this case study shows, it is necessary to acknowledge their limitations and shortcomings. First, successful implementation of facilitated group processes, such as IM, require a committed core of individuals who see the value of the process and are willing to devote a significant amount of personal time to take part. This dedication is required on the part of *both* the participants and the third-party facilitator. In most situations, because of their other commitments, neither participants nor third parties may be in a position where they can devote the time, energy, and other resources necessary for long-term success. Without such a commitment on the part of those involved, including those funding the work, it may be better to refrain from initiating a facilitated design project than to start something that could create false expectations or endanger the limited supply of goodwill that exists in such situations.

Second, we must recognize that no matter how successful a facilitation process might be with particular groups, it is not likely, by itself, to lead to the resolution of conflicts. Drawing up agreements between parties in conflict and making them work is a complex process, influenced by a host of factors and dependent on local, regional, and global political events. There is never a guarantee that the ideas generated in facilitated citizen groups will "filter up" the decision-making hierarchy in a way that significantly influences negotiations or strategizing at the top level. In addition, those ideas developed by groups for implementation at the citizen level can be either ignored or "shot down" by officials, the media, and others in power positions, making their accomplishment extremely difficult or impossible. Finally, even when citizen peace-building activities broaden to involve larger numbers of individuals and a broad cross-section of a society, they may not spread among enough of the population to significantly change societal perceptions about the other side.

In spite of the somewhat pessimistic tone of these cautions and limitations about facilitated group work in protracted conflict situations, there are plenty of reasons for optimism. I have seen many individual lives positively changed by such work.

CONCLUSION

Approximately 15 years ago, when I was first started teaching a graduate course in facilitating group communication, I had difficulty finding useful materials on the subject. In my discussions with colleagues, I learned that a number of communication scholars were engaged in facilitation activities but few were writing about their work. This led to a special issue of *Management Communication Quarterly* that I and David B. Keever edited in 1989 that focused on "Group Facilitation." This special issue was followed a few years later by Frey's (1995) edited text, *Innovations in Group Facilitation: Applications in Natural Settings,* which pulled together an impressive set of chapters describing facilitation of group communication with natural groups. As evidenced by the chapters in the current edited volumes, there is a growing sophistication of group communication facilitation methods and techniques, with applications in an increasing variety of situations.

Despite these advances, there are few examples in the literature of how group communication facilitation approaches have been applied in protracted conflict situations (for two exceptions, see the chapters in this volume by Albeck, Adwan, & Bar-On and by Moaz & Ellis). At the same time, there is probably no arena where such action is needed more urgently. I believe that communication scholars have much to contribute in the area of managing international ethnic conflict resolution, and I hope that this chapter provides a useful case study that shows how group communication facilitation can play a meaningful role in even the most difficult of conflicts. Although there is no single key to progress in such situations, culturally sensitive group facilitation practices can help parties in conflict to develop a richer understanding of the issues they face and to reach a consensus on how to move forward. There is never a guarantee that third-party interventions will be successful in protracted conflicts, and any attempt to work with groups caught up in age-old hostilities will be fraught with difficulties, but for those who are willing to take appropriate risks and make necessary sacrifices, there is probably no greater reward than being part of efforts to bridge the chasm of war and to help create a more humane future for people who seek to live in peace.

REFERENCES

Ackoff, R. L. (1981). *Creating the corporate future: Plan or be planned for.* New York: Wiley.

Alberts, H. (1992, March). *Acquisition: Past, present and future.* Paper presented at the meeting of the Institute of Management Sciences and Operations Research Society, Orlando, FL.

Argyris, C. (1982). *Reasoning, learning, and action: Individual and organizational.* San Francisco: Jossey-Bass.

Ashby, W. R. (1958). Requisite variety and its implications for the control of complex systems. *Cybernetica, 1*(2), 1-17.

Attalides, M. A. (1979). *Cyprus: Nationalism and international politics.* New York: St. Martin's Press.

Bahcheli, T. (1990). *Greek-Turkish relations since 1955.* Boulder, CO: Westview.

Bolukbashi, S. (1998). The Cyprus dispute and the United Nations: Peaceful non-settlement between 1954 and 1996. *International Journal of Middle Eastern Studies, 30,* 411-434.

Boulding, K. E. (1966). *The impact of the social sciences.* New Brunswick, NJ: Rutgers University Press.

Broome, B. J. (1993). Managing differences in conflict situations. In D. J. D. Sandole & H. van der Merwe (Eds.), *Conflict resolution theory and practice: Integration and application* (pp. 97-111). Manchester, United Kingdom: Manchester University Press.

Broome, B. J. (1995a). Collective design of the future: Structural analysis of tribal vision statements. *American Indian Quarterly, 19,* 205-228.

Broome, B. (1995b). The role of facilitated group process in community-based planning and design: Promoting greater participation in Comanche tribal governance. In L. R. Frey (Ed.), *Innovations in group facilitation: Applications in natural settings* (pp. 27-52). Cresskill, NJ: Hampton Press.

Broome, B. J. (1997). Designing a collective approach to peace: Interactive design and problem-solving workshops with Greek-Cypriot and Turkish-Cypriot communities in Cyprus. *International Negotiation, 2,* 381-407.

Broome, B. J. (1998). Overview of conflict resolution activities in Cyprus: Their contribution to the peace process. *Cyprus Review, 10,* 47-66.

Broome, B. J. (1999, September). Greek and Turkish Cypriot university students have more in common than expected. *Washington Report on Middle East Affairs,* pp. 82-84.

Broome, B. J. (2001). Participatory planning and design in a protracted conflict situation: Applications with citizen peace-building groups in Cyprus. *Systems Research and Behavioral Science, 18,* 1-9.

Broome, B. J., & Chen, M. (1992). Guidelines for computer-assisted group problem-solving: Meeting the challenges of complex issues. *Small Group Research, 23,* 216-236.

Broome, B. J., & Christakis, A. N. (1988). A culturally-sensitive approach to tribal governance issue management. *International Journal of Intercultural Relations, 12,* 107-123.

Broome, B. J., & Cromer, I. L. (1991). Strategic planning for tribal economic development: A culturally appropriate model for consensus building. *International Journal of Conflict Management, 2,* 217-234.

Broome, B. J., & Fulbright, L. (1995). A multi-stage influence model of barriers to group problem solving. *Small Group Research, 26,* 25-55.

Broome, B .J., & Keever, D. B.(Eds.) (1989). Group facilitation [Special issue]. *Management Communication Quarterly, 3*(1).

Broome, B. J., & Murray, J. S. (2002). Improving third-party decisions at choice points: A Cyprus case study. *Negotiation Journal, 18*, 75-98.

Burton, J. W. (1969). *Conflict and communication: The use of controlled communication in international relations.* London: MacMillan.

Calotychos, V. (Ed.). (1998). *Cyprus and its people: Nation, identity, and experience in an unimaginable community, 1955-1997.* Boulder, CO: Westview Press.

Christakis, A. N. (1987). Systems profile: The Club of Rome revisited. *Systems Research, 4*, 53-58.

Cleveland, H. (1973). The decision makers. *Center Magazine, 6*(5), 9-18.

Coke, J. G., & Moore, C. M. (1981). Coping with a budgetary crisis: Helping a city council decide where expenditure cuts should be made. In S. W. Burks & J. F. Wolf (Eds.), *Building city council leadership skills: A casebook of models and methods* (pp. 72-85). Washington, DC: National League of Cities.

Craig, R. T. (1989). Communication as a practical discipline. In B. Dervin, L. Grossberg, B. J. O'Keefe, & E. Wartella (Eds.), *Rethinking communication: Volume I: Paradigm issues* (pp. 97-122). Newbury Park, CA: Sage.

Craig, R. T., & Tracy, K. (1995). Grounded practical theory: The case of intellectual discussion. *Communication Theory, 5*, 248-272.

Cronen, V. E. (1995). Practical theory and the tasks ahead for social approaches to communication. In W. Leeds-Hurwitz (Ed.), *Social approaches to interpersonal communication* (pp. 217-242). New York: Guilford Press.

Deal, T. E., & Kennedy, A. A. (1982). *Corporate cultures: The rites and rituals of corporate life.* Reading, MA: Addison-Wesley.

Delbeq, A. L., Van De Ven, A. H., & Gustafson, D. H. (1975). *Group techniques for program planning: A guide to nominal group and Delphi processes.* Glenview, IL: Scott, Foresman.

Diamond, L., & Fisher, R. J. (1995). Integrating conflict resolution training and consultation: A Cyprus example. *Negotiation Journal, 11*, 287-301.

Doob, L. W. (1974). A Cyprus workshop: An exercise in intervention methodology. *Journal of Social Psychology, 94*, 161-178.

Feeg, R. (1988). Forum of the future of pediatric nursing: Looking toward the 21st century. *Pediatric Nursing, 14*, 393-396.

Fisher, R. J. (1992). *Peace building for Cyprus: Report on a conflict analysis workshop, June 1991.* Ottawa: Canadian Institute for International Peace and Security.

Fisher, R. J. (1997). *Interactive conflict resolution.* Syracuse, NY: Syracuse University Press.

Folger, J., Poole, M. S., & Stutman, R. K. (2001). *Working through conflict: Strategies for relationships, groups, and organizations* (4th ed.). New York: Addison Wesley Longman.

Frey, L. R. (Ed.). (1995). *Innovations in group facilitation: Applications in natural settings.* Cresskill, NJ: Hampton Press.

Friedman, P. G. (1989). Upstream facilitation: A proactive approach to managing problem-solving groups. *Management Communication Quarterly, 3*, 33-50.

Hadjipavlou-Trigeorgis, M. (1993). Unofficial inter-communal contacts and their contribution to peace-building in conflict societies: The case of Cyprus. *Cyprus Review, 5*(2), 68-87.

Hadjipavlou-Trigeorgis, M. (1998). Different relationships to the land: Personal narratives, political implications and future possibilities in Cyprus. In V. Calotychos (Ed.), *Cyprus and its people: Nation, identity, and experience in an unimaginable community, 1955-1997* (pp. 251-276). Boulder, CO: Westview Press.

Hirokawa, R. Y., & Gouran, D. S. (1989). Facilitation of group communication: A critique of prior research and an agenda for future research. *Management Communication Quarterly, 3*, 71-92.

Hitchens, C. (1997). *Hostage to history: Cyprus from the Ottomans to Kissinger.* New York: Noonday Press.

Joseph, J. S. (1997). *Cyprus: Ethnic conflict and international politics: From independence to the threshold of the European Union.* New York: St. Martin's Press.

Keever, D. B. (1989, April). *Cultural complexities in the participative design of a computer-based organization information system.* Paper presented at the International Conference on Support, Society and Culture: Mutual Uses of Cybernetics and Science, Amsterdam, The Netherlands.

Kemeny, J. (1980). Saving American democracy: The lesson of Three Mile Island. *Technology Review, 83*(7), 64-75.

Koumoulides, J. T. A. (Ed.). (1986). *Cyprus in transition: 1960-1985.* London: Trigraph.

Markides, K. C. (1977). *The rise and fall of the Cyprus Republic.* New Haven, CT: Yale University Press.

Miller, G. A. (1956). The magical number seven, plus or minus two: Some limits on our capacity for processing information. *Psychology Review, 63*, 81-97.

Mirbagheri, F. (1998). *Cyprus and international peacemaking.* New York: Routledge.

Mitchell, C. R. (1981). *Peacemaking and the consultant's role.* Farnborough, Hampshire, England: Gower.

O'Malley, B., & Craig, I. (1999). *The Cyprus conspiracy: America, espionage and the Turkish invasion.* New York: I. B. Tauris.

Parrish-Sprowl, J. (2003). Indexing the Polish transformation: The case of ECO-S from a bona fide group perspective. In L. R. Frey (Ed.), *Group communication in context: Studies of bona fide groups* (2nd ed., pp. 291-305). Mahwah, NJ: Lawrence Erlbaum.

Poole, M. S. (1983). Decision development in small groups II: A study of multiple sequences in decision making. *Communication Monographs, 50*, 206-232.

Poole, M. S. (1985). Tasks and interaction sequences: A theory of coherence in group decision-making interaction. In R. L. Street & J. N. Cappella (Eds.), *Sequence and pattern in communicative behavior* (pp. 206-224). London: Edward Arnold.

Poole, M. S., & Doelger, J. A. (1986). Developmental processes in group decision-making. In R. Y. Hirokawa & M. S. Poole (Eds.), *Communication and group decision-making* (pp. 35-62). Newbury Park, CA: Sage.

Poole, M. S., & Roth, J. (1989). Decision development in small groups IV: A typology of group decision paths. *Human Communication Research, 15,* 323-356.

Richmond, O. P. (1998). *Mediating in Cyprus: The Cypriot communities and the United Nations.* London: Frank Cass.

Rittel, H., & Webber, M. (1974). Dilemmas in a general theory of planning. *DMG-DRS Journal, 8,* 31-39.

Sato, T. (1979). Determination of hierarchical networks of instructional units using the ISM method. *Educational Technology Research, 3,* 67-75.

Savvides, P. K. (2002). *Cyprus at the gate of the European Union: Scenarios, challenges, and prospects.* Athens, Greece: Hellenic Foundation for European and Foreign Policy.

Simon, H. A. (1960). *The new science of management decisions.* New York: Harper & Row.

Simon, H. A. (1974). How big is a chunk? *Science, 183,* 482-488.

Stearns, M. (1992). *Entangled allies: U.S. policy toward Greece, Turkey, and Cyprus.* New York: Council on Foreign Relations Press.

Stoddard, P. H. (1986). An experiment in track two diplomacy. In D. B. Bendahmane & J. W. McDonald, Jr. (Eds.), *Perspectives on negotiations: Four case studies and interpretations* (pp. 139-143). Washington, DC: Center for the Study of Foreign Affairs, Foreign Service Institute, U.S. Department of State.

Talbot, P. (1977). The Cyprus seminar. In M. R. Berman & J. E. Johnson (Eds.), *Unofficial diplomats* (pp. 159-167). New York: Columbia University Press.

Theophanous, A. (1996). *The political economy of a federal Cyprus.* Nicosia, Cyprus: Intercollege Press.

Volkan, V. D. (1979). *Cyprus—war and adaptation: A psychoanalytic history of two ethnic groups in conflict.* Charlottesville: University Press of Virginia.

Warfield, J. N. (1976). *Societal systems: Planning, policy, and complexity.* New York: Wiley.

Warfield, J. N. (1994). *A science of generic design: Managing complexity through systems design* (2nd ed.). Salinas, CA: Intersystems.

Warfield, J. N., & Cardenas, A. R. (1994). *A handbook of interactive management* (2nd ed.). Ames: Iowa State University Press.

4

WORKING THROUGH INTERGENERATIONAL CONFLICTS BY SHARING PERSONAL STORIES IN DIALOGUE GROUPS*

Joseph H. Albeck
Harvard Medical School and McLean Hospital

Sami Adwan
Bethlehem University

Dan Bar-On
Ben Gurion University of the Negev

One of the most difficult tasks for 21st-century civilization is to find ways to diminish the pernicious long-term effects of past atrocities. After genocide, ethnic cleansing, oppression, and terror, can former enemies approach one another, not through the hatred and stereotypes taught to them by their societies but in open and honest dialogue? Perhaps most important for group communication facilitators, can we teach people how to do so?

   In this chapter, we describe our unique group encounter process and how we adapted from one context for use in others. A method of telling the story of one's personal experiences was initially developed in the "To Reflect and Trust" (TRT) encounters that brought together descendants of Holocaust

*This chapter is based on work reported in Albeck, J., Adwan, S., & Bar-On D. (2002). Dialogue groups: TRT's guidelines for working through intractable conflicts by personal storytelling. *Peace and Conflict: Journal of Peace Psychology, 8*, 301-322.

survivors and descendants of Nazi perpetrators between the years 1992-1998 (Bar-On, 1993, 1995a).[1] In 1998, the original TRT members invited individuals from Northern Ireland, Palestine/Israel, and South Africa who already were involved in peace-building efforts to join with them to test the possibility that the TRT storytelling method could be helpful in working through their current conflicts in a small group setting. In this chapter, we describe our TRT group process, first comparing it to other types of group methods tried in intractable conflicts. The guidelines for group work and facilitation that emerged from the TRT process are then explained, with a description of how they have been used in the current conflicts in Northern Ireland and in Palestine/Israel. In the process, we observed several important connections between unresolved issues in the German-Jewish and Israeli-Palestinian conflicts (Bar-On, 2000).

A Typology of Group Interventions for Working through Intractable Conflicts[2]

Group facilitation techniques that attempt to resolve ethnic conflicts can be classified into one of three approaches to such interventions: human relations groups, confrontational groups, and group encounters focused on the telling of individual and family stories. Each of these approaches is briefly explained below.

Human Relations Groups

This approach to resolving ethnic conflicts is based primarily on the *contact hypothesis* (Allport, 1954; Pettigrew, 1998), which assumes that under cer-

[1]The Nazi perpetrators' descendants began meeting as a self-help group in October 1988, as a by-product of research interviews the third author conducted with them in Germany (Bar-On, 1989). After following that group's work with admiration, as it was the only such self-help group confronting these issues at the time in Germany, Bar-On asked the group members if they would be ready to meet a group from "the other side." After they answered positively, he approached some students from his seminar on "The Psychosocial After-effects of the Holocaust on Second and Third Generations" taught at Ben-Gurion University in Beer Sheva, Israel. He also approached members of "One Generation After," an organization of descendants of Holocaust survivors in Boston, chaired then by Albeck. Volunteers from these three groups gathered for the first encounter in Wuppertal, Germany, in June 1992 (Bar-On, 1993).

[2]We thank Dr. Ifat Maoz of Hebrew University, Jerusalem, for her help in structuring this typology.

tain conditions, bringing people from different collectives into personal contact with one another will enable them to change their relations with one another for the better, and to learn how to apply their new relations to other situations. The assumption is that getting to know each other contributes to positive changes in stereotypic perceptions, attitudes, and relations.

There is a vast literature about this approach, but the results have not been consistently successful (for a review of results, see, e.g., Pettigrew, 1998). The problem with this approach is that by focusing on here-and-now interactions, such groups tend to disregard the historical background and the reality of generally asymmetric power relations between the larger communities in conflict. Although getting to know and understand individuals from the other side may have advantages in the short run, it usually has little long-term impact, as the external power relations and the hostile environment can overwhelm the positive effect created by the human relations group process (Maoz, 2000a, 2000b).

The Confrontational Model

The confrontational model of group approaches to resolving ethnic conflict was developed in Israel at Neve Shalom, a joint Palestinian-Jewish community, and at Givat Havivah, a learning center that runs Palestinian-Jewish encounters, as a critical response to the lack of success of the coexistence model of human relations groups based on the contact hypothesis (Maoz, 2001; Sonnenschein, Halabi, & Friedman, 1998). The confrontational approach focuses on strengthening a collective identity and the minimizing of asymmetric power relations between the parties in conflict; however, these foci occur at the expense of diminishing opportunities to create close personal relationships of trust and friendship between participants in the encounter group setting (Suleiman, 1997). Specifically, this strategy attempts to empower members of the minority group and to help members of the dominant group develop new insights into their own construction of identity and the effects of their respective positions of power (Maoz, 2000b; Sonnenschein et al., 1998; Suleiman, 1997). The facilitators of confrontation groups emphasize collective identities and try to undermine personal relationships and, thereby, support the minority group and help to empower its members.[3]

---

[3] Adwan's personal experience with such groups suggests that these goals are not always accomplished, as the process can sometimes reinforce the disempowerment of the minority group members when they realize the challenges they still face and the superiority of the majority group.

The rationale behind this confrontational model stemmed from work done by scholars such as Helms (1990), who viewed the problem of the asymmetry of power relations that arose in groups in conflict that met in encounters (e.g., between the white majority and black minority populations in the United States) as one of vagueness in the definition of the self among the majority members. This vagueness stands in sharp contrast to the gain in the strength of identity among members of an oppressed minority (e.g., the black minority, in the United States). Moscovici (1976) and Mugny and Pérez (1991) similarly maintained that in such encounters, members of the minority group develop more complex social self-representations than do members of the majority group. This happens because the minority has to differentiate (for its own survival) between its members' self-representation and that of the majority with whom the minority is often in disaccord; the hegemonic group, in contrast, usually has no clear representation of the minority group, as no such representation is needed for its survival. Therefore, during the first stages of the confrontational encounter, the minority group typically strives to use its relatively stronger construction of identity to its advantage, with the result being that the members of the majority group become aware of and begin to examine the vagueness and the internal contradictions in their own self-definition (Maoz, Bar-On, Steinberg, & Farkhadeen, 2002).

An outside observer of majority-minority confrontational group sessions sometimes feels that both groups come to the session as if they were walking along conflicting ethnocentric axes with no "meeting point" (Steinberg & Bar-On, 2002, p. 204). For example, when examining group sessions that employ the confrontational model between Israeli Jews and Palestinians who are also citizens of Israel, one observes the initial absence of a meeting point. Jewish participants generally are content with the political and social status quo and, therefore, approach their Palestinian co-citizens on an individual basis. In contrast, Palestinians need to improve on the status quo and, consequently, generally approach the Jews on a collective, or group, identity level (Sonnenschein et al., 1998). Thus, each side is motivated to try to frame the issue from its own perspective and to tip the scales toward its own axis. This has the effect of reinforcing group members' respective pre-encounter collective identities. Consequently, participants in confrontational groups tend not to examine the validity of, discover any internal contradictions and tensions within, or make any changes in their respective pre-encounter identities (Bar-On, 1999b).

A Third Option: Group Encounters Focusing on Sharing Family Stories

An alternative approach for working with groups in conflict—the TRT method—addresses some of the shortcomings of the two intervention models previously explained. In this method, members from two groups in conflict are asked to share their personal and family stories with the other participants in the group encounters (Zehavi-Verete, 2000). On the one hand, such stories vividly capture the emotional aspects of the personal and collective histories of the conflict from each side's perspective; on the other hand, the process of sharing these often dramatic stories promotes new connections between all those present, allowing more complex cross-group representations of the "self" and "other" to evolve and to be processed in the course of the group sessions. In the following section, we describe the development and application of the TRT group communication facilitation technique.

WORKING THROUGH THE HOLOCAUST IN THE TRT GROUP[4]

To understand the processes at work in TRT group encounters, the concept of "working through" is suggested as an alternative to the concepts of forgiveness and reconciliation. In groups confronting the Holocaust, we learned that participants can work through unresolved pain and anger related to past traumas through such group encounters (in addition to the working through that can occur in traditional one-on-one therapeutic situations, as well as in public or private symbolic acts of forgiveness or reconciliation; Bar-Tal, 2000). The concept of working through, which was initially developed by Freud (1953) to explain what happens in relation to individual psy-

---

[4]The idea of reconciliation between Jews and German was initially rejected by the Jewish postwar religious leadership (Bar-On, 2004; Dorff, 1992; Rittner & Ross, 2000). Dorff (1992) maintained that no primary conciliation of the members of the first generation (according to the Jewish tradition) was possible after the Holocaust, because the perpetrators and survivors of the Holocaust would never be able to honestly confront one another, especially since so few people exposed to the Nazi extermination process survived it, and because most of the Nazi perpetrators did not assume responsibility or express regret for their atrocious acts. According to Dorff, however, descendants of the victims and the victimizers, especially those who had worked through the silence that typically occurred and who acknowledged the traumatic or atrocious part of their family biography, could test the possibility of a secondary conciliation.

chotherapy between a patient and a therapist, has been used to describe the laborious psychological process that an individual must go through to come to terms with traumas that affect him or herself, his or her family, or others with whom the individual is close. Significantly more than a one-time insight is usually required, as the individual attempts to confront the meaning of the traumatic experiences, some of which may have been repressed. In the absence of a working-through process, unresolved psychological conflicts may continue to interfere with one's ability to adapt beliefs, attitudes, and behaviors to new life experiences and realities (Novey, 1962).

The concept of working through was later expanded to apply to social traumas and resultant Post Traumatic Stress Disorder (PTSD) symptoms (Danieli, 1988). After World War II, therapists borrowed the concept to describe how survivors coped with the traumas they suffered during the Holocaust. Later, it was used to frame the psychological processing of distress after the Holocaust as the essentially "normal" but delayed consequences of the very abnormal circumstances and terrible losses from which the survivors suffered during and after the Holocaust (Danieli, 1988). The original goal of the process of working through—letting go of the influence of repressed memories—was later supplanted by a more modest goal—the ability to "live with" the painful traumatic event in a better way than before (Lehman, Wortman, & Williams, 1987). The concept of working through also served those who wished to conceptualize the possibility of living with the feelings of loss and helplessness stemming from their experiences in an ever-changing post-Holocaust reality. Using working through in this way helped to explain why many survivors were able to normalize their lives, not showing any pathological signs for many years. However, survivors' repressed memories could suddenly surface and, thereby, threaten their

---

Dorff (1992) did address the question of whether, according to Jewish tradition and law, there is a possibility of reconciliation or forgiveness between the Catholic Church and the Jews and between Jews and Germans after the Holocaust. Unlike more conservative Jewish leaders, Dorff accepted neither their position that this is an act that the Gentiles have to accomplish all by themselves nor that the descendants of the victims have no right to be part of a process of reconciliation, on behalf of their parents. In this sense, Dorff, as a Jewish religious leader, broke a taboo after the Holocaust. According to his point of view, children of survivors have the right to act on their own, independent from the perspective of their parents. As he explained:

> If we see ourselves as part of an extended corporate entity known as the Jewish people, then we, as its present members, do have the right (indeed, the responsibility) to act on behalf of the group—past, present and future—in this issue as in all others. (p. 209)

adaptation, even if their functioning had been "normal" for many years (Davidson, 1980). Unfortunately, victims of social traumas are often haunted by their past suffering and trauma as they try to cope with their current reality (Adwan & Bar-On, 2001).

The concept of working through has also been used with the children of people who have suffered social traumas, including children of Holocaust survivors. Scholars have found that survivors' offspring are sensitive to their parents' avoidance strategies (such as telling details about what had happened to them without showing emotions or without telling the whole story; Albeck, 1994). This sensitivity often led to the creation of a "double wall" between the two generations (Bar-On, 1995a): Survivor parents did not talk about their wartime experiences, and their children usually did not ask. Even when one side wished to open up a "window" in its own wall, those individuals were usually confronted with the other's wall of avoidance. We have found very few spontaneous instances of both parties opening up windows in their avoidant walls simultaneously, allowing their feelings to be freely communicated to each other. Without such moments of open communication, parents and children were usually unable to help each other cope with their different but overlapping private struggles to come to terms with the meaning of the Holocaust in their lives. Talking with strangers from similar backgrounds usually proved more productive than efforts at direct intergenerational family discussion between survivor parents and their children. Furthermore, survivors were usually able to communicate more openly with their grandchildren than with their own children about their wartime experiences.

At present, there exists very limited psychological literature concerning the intergenerational effects of the Holocaust on the descendants of the Nazi perpetrators. Researchers have only recently begun to ask if one can speak of working through where descendants of perpetrators are concerned (see, e.g., Bar-On, 1990). Relevant questions include: To what extent have the atrocities that their fathers or grandfathers committed been transmitted to them through a "conspiracy of silence" enacted by their elders? How did such children start to confront and work through such silence (Hardtmann, 1991; Rosenthal, 1993)? We believe that the main reason it has taken so many years after World War II to pose these questions is because researchers and professional helpers have unconsciously avoided doing so, mainly because of their difficulty simultaneously conceptualizing that both groups of descendants—those of survivors and those of perpetrators—have been psychologically burdened by the Nazi era. If both groups of offspring were adversely affected, such a symmetric notion of the Holocaust's intergenerational effects would conflict with the presumed moral superiority of the victims over their victimizers (Bar-On & Charny, 1992). The resultant cognitive dissonance could account for the fact that so few attempts had been made to discuss these particular intergenerational victim-victimizer issues simultaneously, or to try and bring members of the two "sides" of this person-made catastrophe together into dialogue to examine its consequences. To help fill that gap, we now describe an example of how the working-through concept was applied to a multiyear series of group encounters that brought together descendants of Holocaust survivors and descendants of Nazi perpetrators.

SHARED STORYTELLING BETWEEN PARTIES IN CONFLICT: ACKNOWLEDGMENT AND WORKING THROUGH

TRT was formed to address and to attempt to work through the various levels of the conflicts and painful memories between Germans and Jews resulting from World War II. In 1992, descendants of Holocaust survivors from the United States and from Israel were initially brought together with descendants of convicted Nazi perpetrators from Germany (Bar-On, 1993). In 1995, after reviewing a British Broadcasting Corporation (BBC) documentary that had been made about TRT, in which the term "reconciliation" was used (Clay, 1993), TRT chose to describe its work through the alternative terms of "reflection and trust." The main reason for this shift in nomenclature was that some of the Jewish members of the group felt that they were not entitled to reconcile with, or forgive, the German descendants of the Nazi perpetrators, although they recognized that the offspring of the perpetrators had no part in their parents' crimes. This decision to move away from forgiveness and reconciliation terminology was also connected to clear differences between Jewish and Christian traditions concerning those concepts, especially after the Holocaust (these differences are discussed by Bar-On, 2004). We now turn to a more in-depth description and analysis of the TRT process.

Developing a Common Emotional and Conceptual Language across the Abyss

After some years of working with descendants of Holocaust survivors (Bar-On, 1995a) and interviewing descendants of Nazi perpetrators in Germany (Bar-On, 1989), a group setting was created in which members of these two groups could engage in a dialogue. The initiators of the group were interested in finding answers to a number of issues that they saw as important in this context. Specifically, the initiators wanted to learn if members of these groups would be able to communicate genuinely with each other; if the encounter would help each party to work through aspects that it could not work through in its separate home setting; and if, in the encounter, a common agenda would emerge, over and beyond the separate agendas of each side (Clay, 1993). Six encounters between a group of eight descendants of Holocaust perpetrators and a group of five U.S. Americans and four Israeli descendants of Holocaust survivors took place over six years, rotating between locations in Germany, Israel, and the United States. The meetings usually lasted 4-5 days, 8-10 hours each day. Except for the first encounter, which was planned by Bar-On and was devoted to getting acquainted, mainly by listening to each other's personal histories (Bar-On, 1993), the scheduling of the meetings was done by the group itself. The content of the six German-Jewish meetings focused on continued reflection about members' personal and family Holocaust stories.

During this joint working-through process, a common emotional and conceptual language evolved that was different from the affective terms and conceptual ideas that still characterized usage in the communities from which these group participants came. For example, the very concept of face-to-face meetings with descendants of Nazis was unacceptable to many family members of the Jewish participants, and the purpose of the meeting was initially concealed from some of them; reflecting together with descendants of Jewish victims had been similarly inconceivable to members of the perpetrator's families. Objections from friends and acquaintances to descriptions of TRT's activities, both before and after the initial encounter, were frequent and vocal.

The success of the converging approaches to dialogue from both victim and victimizer sides, however, created a dilemma for the two groups of descendants, for they had to struggle with the question: "Shall we become an isolated sect, as the communities we belong to cannot cope yet with our new mutual experience, or will we have to give up our joint, intergroup experience to remain active members of our original communities?" Although this issue was not initially discussed explicitly in the group sessions, it turned out that the TRT group chose to go in neither of these directions. Members were able to manage the tensions created from these options by using the TRT group for support during and between meetings to help them maintain their feeling of moral inclusion (belonging to an in-group, which has a moral privilege) (Optow, 2001). They hoped that their respective home communities would slowly move closer to each other and, thus, closer to the TRT group's newly created joint emotional "space" and worldview. As it turned out, the TRT process was relatively slow and painful, and was acknowledged and accepted by parts of the larger German and Jewish communities only after several years had passed.[5]

How did the process unfold? It was Bar-On's role (as an initiator of the TRT group, even though he clearly belonged to the Jewish group because of his family background and Jewish-Israeli identity) to present questions to the group members about where the group was heading in its process. He tried to formulate the questions so that members of both groups could identify with them and could associate the construction of their personal and collective experiences with these questions (examples of this procedure follow below). Clearly, everyone did not always agree with the original formulations and the questions consequently changed as a result of discussions in the group.

At first, members of both groups shared their stories about how, when, and in what ways they could trace the after-effects of the Holocaust within their own lives. For some, this was a daily struggle that was accompanied by sleeplessness, fears, and uncontrollable reactions. Often the stories were associated with the silence, repression, or other difficult reactions of their parents and members of their social network. In many cases, the acknowledgment of a personal relationship to the Holocaust was accompanied by a feeling of estrangement—internal (from oneself) as well as external (from one's social network). It took many years, both before and during the TRT encounters, for these members of the respective descendant generations to clarify and comprehend how these aspects of estrangement were associated with their personal relationship to the Holocaust.

A number of the Jewish members of the group suffered from physical uprootedness, as their parents had emigrated from Europe to the United States or to Israel after the Holocaust. This physical uprootedness was usually accompanied by psychological uprootedness, associated with the fact that their parents could not overcome the loss of so many family members and had difficulty integrating themselves into their new country. In contrast, most German members of the group did not experience physical uprootedness, as they usually continued to live in their original community or in other parts of Germany, but they shared the feeling of psychological uprootedness, albeit for different reasons than the Jewish members; as one of the German members said, "Due to the atrocities committed by my father, I feel that my roots had been poisoned." Thus, like the descendants of the survivors, they had to

---

[5]For example, recognition came when the German Federal Government gave Bar-On the "Cross of Merit" in 2001 for initiating this group and when Yad Vashem (The Israeli Memorial Institute of the Holocaust) invited Bar-On to be a fellow at its international seminar in 1999 and, thereby, acknowledged his work in Germany with descendants of Nazi perpetrators.

develop new psychological roots. The fact that some of the survivors' descendants felt that their own roots had been "tainted" by the intergenerational consequences of World War II suffering was yet another similarity between what the two groups endured in their respective home communities.

Struggling with feelings of estrangement and uprootedness was a major issue for members of both groups and brought up new questions that they addressed in the TRT group setting, such as whether they could allow themselves to live their own life, being neither dependent nor counterdependent on their parents' lives? The Jewish descendants' individuation from their parents was more emotionally difficult, as their parents often leaned on them; the descendants of Nazi perpetrators tended to counterreact and distance themselves from their parents and, thereby, suffered from an emotional void (Berger & Berger, 2001), a problem that became more severe over time, especially when their parents aged and caring for them became a necessity. Members of both groups reported struggling with dreams of death, being named after dead people (especially among the Jewish descendants of survivors), and having fantasies of sacrificing themselves for a noble human cause (especially among the descendants of Nazi perpetrators). As one member of the group commented, "We talk about our feelings, emotions, and ideas, but they all concern the dead people who are in the back of our minds." It should be pointed out that many members of the TRT group work in the helping professions; perhaps they chose these professions so that they could give special meaning to their lives, as if transmuting the shadows of death and evil in their family heritage into altruism.

Most members of the TRT group could readily establish a comfortable internal dialogue with the potential victim inside them. This was easy for both descendants of Jewish victims and descendants of Nazi victimizers, but it was much more difficult for members of both groups to identify and enter into a dialogue with the potential victimizer within, letting the victim and victimizer components of their identity "talk" with each other. Eventually, it became clear to most TRT members that both these potential roles were inside them. Only by openly acknowledging and entering into dialogue with one's own victimizer potential can its influence be controlled in future, unexpected situations, for a person cannot control his or her potential for engaging in victimizing behaviors if he or she denies the possibility of the existence of those behaviors. After most members came to this realization, another issue became salient: "What is left once we accepted the existence of both the roles of victim and victimizer within ourselves?" Trying to answer this question suggested the need for a different process of identity construction, one that was based not on negation of the "other" or on denying the existence of victimizer roles within oneself but on what had been worked through up to that point (Bar-On, 1999b).

Group members' attempts to deal with issues of identity construction invariably brought up the question of "Who suffered more?" Addressing this question made explicit the scaling of suffering indulged in by both sides. In the TRT group context, it became evident that members commonly assumed that there is a subjective scale of suffering. For example, Jewish members shared that there were families of survivors in which only the members who had been in Auschwitz (generally acknowledged as the worst of the death camps) were "allowed" to talk about their suffering in family gatherings, as if other family members' Holocaust experiences had no meaning in comparison to the horrors of Auschwitz. The scaling issue also came up in relation to the BBC filming of the TRT group—specifically, whether certain German members of the group were more important due to the fact that their fathers were prominent figures in the Nazi regime or whether their importance to the TRT group was associated with the fact that they had worked harder and longer on the meaning of their family's past, precisely because of their fathers' prominence (Bar-On, 1995b). Perhaps because extreme suffering induces helplessness, people may tend to feel more in control by scaling suffering. Members also learned that because some people cannot imagine the experiences their parents endured during the Holocaust, scaling suffering may help to make some sense of those experiences, if only in comparison with others' wartime experiences. It is much more difficult for people to relate to the suffering of others as just being different, neither more nor less, than their own torment. Thus, it became a challenge for the group how to maintain the legitimacy of grasping different stories without scaling them, as scaling, in itself, creates additional pain, alienation, and humiliation for those who might then feel "less than" the others.

TRT members eventually developed a feeling of mutual trust and respect that crossed ethnic lines, resulting in less scaling of suffering and more symmetry between the parties. However, this crossing of ethnic lines by no means erased the intergroup asymmetry that still existed in members' minds about their parents' roles during the Holocaust: one group being descendants of the victimizers and the other descendants of the victims. These types of scaled and unscaled, symmetric and asymmetric relationships were difficult to maintain simultaneously, but it was important for group members to find ways to navigate among them. The tensions between the difficult past and the complex, evolving present remain an ongoing challenge in this work.

Through the TRT group experience, it became clear that a positive outcome for participants was not to forget or to be done with the past, once and for all, but to find new ways to live with it. Successful working through, thus, meant living with it more consciously, but in less threatening and self-destructive ways than before. For descendants of survivors and of perpetrators, the Holocaust will always be in the background and they must forever deal with its after-effects; as one German member said, "The day we will feel that it is done with will mean that we went off our course."

Perhaps the most important result of the German-Jewish post-Holocaust encounters was the development of the TRT approach to working through the after-effects of violence during group encounters between descendants of former enemies. We thought that what we had accomplished, via group communication, had been very helpful for meeting this goal and began to wonder whether this approach might prove useful for opposing sides in some of the current generation of ethnic conflicts around the world (Kelman, 1999; Staub, 2000). We turned our attention, therefore, to facilitating other encounters.

Bringing in Practitioners from Current Conflicts

In 1998, after six years of work, the original TRT group decided to invite peace builders who had worked with victims and victimizers in the current conflicts in South Africa, Northern Ireland, and in Palestine and Israel to participate in a joint, week-long meeting (Bar-On, 2000). The purpose was to see whether the TRT group process of telling personal stories and reflecting on them in a trusting atmosphere could be relevant for these other conflict settings. It was clear to the organizers of the 1998 and subsequent TRT encounters that each conflict setting had its own "biography" that had to be carefully studied and taken into consideration. The TRT dialogue had, to that point, dealt exclusively with the Holocaust, an event that happened many years before and had a clear-cut division between victims and victimizers. Holocaust victim and victimizer descendants met with no current agenda, except for what was still burdening their minds and hearts. Still, on the basis of that experience, we thought that the TRT storytelling approach had relevance for practitioners struggling with the peace-building process in the particular conflicts noted above. We thought that such dialogue between members of the opposing sides might prove to be helpful in identifying psychologically deeper, underlying issues in ongoing group conflicts. The TRT experience suggested that combined political, legal, and financial (compensation for the victims) considerations may not be sufficient to comprehend and heal the critical intergenerational wounds developed from long-term intractable conflicts (Kelman, 1999). We, thus, believed that the TRT group approach for working through the legacy of the past might shed additional light on present-day dilemmas.

Testing the relevance of TRT concepts with peace builders from these current conflict areas, however, proved to be a challenge. First, the ongoing conflicts, especially the Palestinian-Israeli one, bringing together people who were personally related to the Holocaust (and who had made it their goal to work through it) and people who were related to the current conflict, might create a special problem for the Palestinian group. That group could easily feel that the Holocaust was being used by the Jewish and Israeli members of the group as a manipulation to undermine and minimize Palestinians' suffering inflicted on them by the Israelis (Rouhana, 2004). This could have seriously jeopardized the process of using storytelling procedures to address and work through the current conflict. In addition, the current violent Palestinian-Israeli conflict is being experienced by all generations simultaneously; consequently, group members' stories about the psychology and reality of intergenerational relations within their families are very different from the stories of descendants of Jewish Holocaust survivors from the United States. Our prior experience, therefore, provided little guidance in terms of how to facilitate working through these current violent group conflicts.

To plan the transformation from the initial, exclusively German-Jewish group to include an equal number of new practitioners working with conflict groups, we had to develop some new guidelines concerning the functioning of the TRT group. We provide a brief description of the guidelines that ultimately evolved.

TRT Group Guidelines and their Implementation in Current Conflicts[6]

The following guidelines were developed out of the experience of the initial TRT group process and are related to some more general aspects of storytelling (see, e.g., Sunwolf & Frey, 2001). Some of these guidelines were implemented in the 1998 multiconflict TRT seminar held in Hamburg, Germany, and in subsequent meetings held in Bethlehem, Palestine National Authority, and in New Jersey. Others were developed for "residentials" (a Northern Ireland term for short workshops in an isolated setting) organized in Northern Ireland by some of the TRT members there.[7] These guidelines were also later used by Bar-On and Fatma Kassem, a Palestinian-Israeli TRT member, when they cofacilitated a workshop designed for Jewish and

---

[6]An earlier version of these guidelines was presented by Albeck at three conferences: (a) the Psycho-traumatology Seminar at the Medical School in Tours, France, April 2001; (b) the Child Survivors meeting in Houston, Texas, in June 2001; and (c) the Conference on Refugees and Reconciliation at the United Nations in New York, in November 2001.

[7]In these residential meetings, held over a weekend, the TRT group brought together British ex-militaries and people from Northern Ireland (Catholic and Protestant) who had been involved in the "Troubles."

Palestinian Israeli students that took place at Ben Gurion University of the Negev in 2000-2001 (Bar-On & Kassem, 2004), and by Albeck in Arab-Jewish dialogue groups held in Boston, since 2000. Three categories of the guidelines are presented: principle guidelines, process considerations, and technical aspects. Although these categories partially overlap, differentiating them is useful for understanding the process.

A. Principle Guidelines

A.1. Specific and explicit goals. Concrete goals should be identified and acknowledged for each dialogue group utilizing the TRT approach. Examples of such goals include uncovering and working through past traumatic experiences, learning about the "other," learning about one's own collective identity in the conflict, empowering the weaker side in the conflict, and relating past events of the conflict to current psychosocial and political issues. It is also helpful to specify goals to be excluded from such a group process (e.g., intellectual or political discussions about the conflict and fund-raising for specific activities and projects related to the conflict).

A.2. Timing and time. Timing is an essential element in this type of dialogue group. As previously discussed, the initial TRT group started in 1992, after the German self-help group had worked on its issues for four years. In the United States, children of survivors groups had, by then, been in existence for 14 years. This extended time period coincided with the gradual emergence of a certain readiness in the Jewish community to encounter the "other side" in regard to the Holocaust. This illustrates that, to be successful, timing of "bottom-up" working-through efforts in conflict situations should be synchronized with "top-down" political change processes. Beginning a "bottom-up" encounter process too early may create frustration for participants, especially for those in active conflict settings, if they do not see any positive changes in the larger social scene; starting too late may mean that such an intensive, financially costly, and time-consuming undertaking is no longer necessary or relevant for the particular conflict context of concern.

A.3. Composition and screening. Ideally, when only two sides are involved, the dialogue group should be comprised of an equal number of participants from both sides of the conflict (Maoz, 2001). However, given that many intractable conflicts are often many-sided (Bar-On, 1999b), as many groups as possible should be represented and, whenever possible, a balanced number of participants from important subgroups within each "side" of the conflict should be included. For instance, when too few members of a particular gender, age, or minority ethnic/religious group are included, there is the risk of having their viewpoints submerged in the interest of "unity" or excessive "politeness." This consideration may sometimes result in choosing to leave out certain subgroups rather than having them underrepresented. For example, in the original TRT group, we decided to leave out Jewish-Germans (including in the meeting only Jewish descendants of survivors living in Israel and in the United States), as we believed that a Jewish-German group would introduce complexities that would make the TRT group agenda too burdened. In a different example, the current TRT group will be adding another Israeli citizen of Palestinian origin to the larger Palestinian-Israeli TRT dialogue group, because this subgroup's perspective is likely to prove critical to participants' understanding of the larger conflict. By previously having only a single representative of this subgroup, her thoughts, feelings, and behaviors were sometimes inappropriately submerged by both the Palestinian Authority members' and the Jewish-Israeli members' perspectives.

A.4. Facilitation and symmetry of power. In the original TRT group, there was no official facilitator; despite a search, no German facilitator was found for this unusual group, and Bar-On, who initiated and, to some extent, facilitated the encounter, was actually part of the Jewish group. This, however, should not usually be the case. Such groups should be organized and facilitated by two individuals, one from each side of the conflict (Maoz, 2001), because their joint work can serve as a model for the participants, their different reactions to issues discussed in the group are important for the group process, and because two facilitators give legitimacy to both sides, especially the weaker one (because, as is often the case, there are many more facilitators available from the dominant side). For example, in Northern Ireland, a Protestant and a Catholic were the organizers of the residential and the facilitators of the group meetings. At Ben Gurion University, two TRT participants, Bar-On, a Jewish-Israeli man, and Kassem, the Palestinian-Israeli woman previously mentioned, were the facilitators for the Jewish-Palestinian students' group. Furthermore, the facilitators should feel a *special responsibility* to provide support for the members of the "other" group, as this creates the feeling of trust and emotional security for the participants when they feel that the facilitator from the other group cares about them and what they feel, even when it is difficult for him or her to do so (Bar-On & Kassem, in press). Some asymmetries between the facilitators undoubtedly will exist (e.g., differences in perceived status), but such asymmetries should be considered "good enough" (Ross, 2000) and should be recognized and openly discussed in the group.

A.5. Choice of languages. During group meetings, the most well-known common language (e.g., English in Northern Ireland or in South Africa) or a neutral language should be used. Ideally, one of the criteria for choosing participants is their fluency in this common language. Even though this criterion is not always possible to meet, systematic or simultaneous translation should be avoided, as it takes a toll on the group process and disrupts the emotional working-through process; however, at times, short sequences of translation may be necessary, especially when some members are not completely fluent in the language used. The ideal of uniform language fluency cannot always be reached and, therefore, one may have to compromise on less-than-ideal solutions for the sake of involving those members who can represent a group or a subgroup in an authentic way, despite minor linguistic deficiencies. This may necessitate separate meetings (e.g., uninational in the Palestinian/Israeli case), using the respective native language, to process the intergroup sessions.

A.6. Confidentiality, ethics, and group norms. What members discuss in the meetings is confidential, unless specific permission has been granted to share information with others outside of the group. For some members, this is a difficult requirement to honor because they want to share the exciting things that happened to them with their family, friends, and colleagues. Therefore, group members should be told that they can discuss issues with outsiders only in general terms, without identifying personal details mentioned in the group. One guideline that emerged from this norm is that group members should avoid holding intergroup private sessions or sending e-mails between encounters that discuss controversial issues, although members should feel free to use intergroup private sessions or e-mails for debriefing, scheduling, and other noncontroversial matters. The reason for this guideline is that such private discussions often create more heat than light. Furthermore, attempting to "educate" the other side by sending unsolicited e-mails and internet materials can prove destructive. People who want to discuss "hot" issues between sessions should remember that the group itself is the optimal stage on which true dialogue can occur and that all other off-stage interactions should not replace what occurs during the face-to-face group encounters themselves.

Another ethical consideration is that if sound- or video-recording devices are to be used, every member present at the group meeting must agree to use them. A single person's objections must be respected, although the group can potentially make special arrangements to record the sessions (e.g., a person's face and body can be kept off camera). If such special arrangements cannot be agreed on, recording should not be permitted. If recordings are made, subsequent publication or other uses of them require the permission of all those involved. Any contact with the media by any member of the group also requires the consent of the group.

B. Process Considerations

It is usually easier to suggest that the group encounter process meet certain standards than to mandate that specific outcomes be reached (Maoz, 2001; Steinberg & Bar-On, 2002). The core of the process is building a safe space for dialogue and reflection together, based on mutual acknowledgement and respect of others, without giving up one's own beliefs and feelings.

B.1. Group decision making. The TRT group decided on its own agenda, starting from its 1993 (second) encounter. Before and during each encounter, members discuss, in a democratic fashion, the format for each session, additional membership criteria, and member entry and departure procedures. It is better if such decisions are made by consensus rather than by majority vote, even if it takes some additional time. Sometimes, if possible, a decision is made not to decide on a particular issue, so as not to force a minority of members to accept the majority vote.

B.2. Focusing on personal experiences and stories. In general, during group discussions, members, and especially the facilitators, should encourage participants to move away from intellectualized and politically polarized arguments about relevant issues, toward more personal perspectives on conflictual issues. Personal examples and memories shared in the group help to improve all members' understanding of the complex aspects of the conflict. This point can be a tricky one, because in some active conflict contexts, such as the Palestinian-Israeli one, getting members to focus on personal experiences and not to revert to well-known political arguments cannot easily be achieved (Bar-On & Kassem, in press). Outside events can influence the group encounters in an unpredictable fashion; examples might include bombings, military actions, or some other powerful event in the participants' home environment. The challenge is to keep these intrusions from taking over and destroying the trustful atmosphere that has been created and that is necessary for the sharing of personal stories. Although there is no simple way to ensure that it happens, over time, the group has found ways to make such shifts from political collective discourse back to personal sharing. If the ongoing political events are too emotionally powerful, the mission of the facilitators is then to gradually encourage a return to the sharing of personal stories as a priority, but not to exclude discussions of the outside events, as they, at times, become too important for some members to set aside.

If new members join an existing dialogue group, an "old-timer" should model the telling of a story for the benefit of these members, before the new members are asked to tell their stories. Old-timers rarely tell their own story exactly the same way twice, which makes retelling and rehearing them interesting, even for the old-timers themselves. This was the procedure used to conduct the TRT group encounter in the 1998 Hamburg seminar when new members from the current conflict groups were invited to join the process for the first time. However, one should be sensitive to the risk of old-timers overpowering new members with their family stories and not giving them a chance to share. Scheduling a brief period for questions and open discussion after each personal presentation allows for needed clarification and elaboration of each personal history.

Each person should have the opportunity to tell his or her life story, starting at least one generation back. Sometimes such sharing can feel easier for newcomers after engaging in some warm-up exercises (e.g., telling the story behind one's name, talking about a meaningful family object, drawing one's lifeline in the conflict, or telling a story based on pictures from one's family album; see Zehavi-Verete, 2000). Such exercises can help the facilitators to assess group members' willingness to be open and trustful. Family stories can subsequently be elicited. More elaborate preparation is sometimes needed, as was the case with the Jewish-Palestinian students' workshop. Participants were asked to interview members of their families (or representatives of their parents' and grandparents' generations), transcribe these interviews, and discuss them in the workshop. To accomplish these tasks, participants received special training on how to conduct such interviews (based on Rosenthal's, 1993, biographical method) and practiced the roles of interviewee, interviewer, and observer during the workshop before they conducted the actual interviews.

B.3. Improving participants' skills. Learning to listen to other people's life stories, especially when these individuals are members of a group that has traditionally been perceived as being "the enemy," is a difficult task. Such learning necessitates the acquisition of a number of skills. Participants must learn to listen to others' stories without interrupting them, except for brief requests for clarification of words or facts. Facilitators should seek to prevent situations in which one participant may be stimulated by the story of another to start sharing his or her own story, without leaving enough time for the group to react to the original story. Facilitators should also politely use the brief discussion periods between each person's presentation to clarify disagreements regarding historical accounts of the same events in the conflict, as seen from the differing perspectives represented in the room. When time and circumstances permit, those who have previously shared their story can add something to it briefly, if stimulated by something said by another member. In the TRT and in the Israeli-Palestinian workshop, the participants developed their own "rules" for responding to the stories shared. In the Northern Ireland group, the facilitators gave participants instructions about what could be an appropriate reaction to a personal story; for example, they asked participants not to shift too quickly to another topic but to try to listen to the feelings behind the presenter's spoken words.

The minimum time allotted to tell each personal story differs depending on the format used—20 minutes in the weekly sessions and 1 hour (on the average) in the full-day format. The groups, however, should meet long enough and often enough (in several-hour segments) so that each person gets the chance to tell his or her story by the end of the sessions. When sequencing story presentations in the group sessions, the different groups involved in the conflict should alternate telling stories. At university workshops, or in groups in which the format includes interviews with family members, it is important for the facilitators to follow what happens during the interviewing phase, meeting with participants at least once during the interview process to see how participants managed to conduct the interviews, transcribe them, and deal with the content that arose from the interviews (Bar-On & Kassem, 2004).

B.4. Uninational and binational sessions. When the conflict occurring outside the dialogue group is very violent, as it was, for instance, in October 2000, during the Israeli-Palestinian workshop, the facilitators should consider holding uninational meetings, in which each group meets alone with the facilitator from his or her group, in addition to the binational sessions. Such meetings may help to release any tensions that are built up during the binational meetings and to deal with the events outside the TRT group setting. As also previously mentioned, such meetings enable the minority group to use its own language, which may be especially important when the binational sessions are held in the language of the majority group or in a neutral language. Some participants may prefer to tell their story first in the uninational setting, as they may have more trust in participants from their own group, before exposing themselves to the other group.

B.5. External versus internal group priorities. There is built-in tension between those participants who urgently wish to act politically or socially outside the group context and those who prefer to first understand the other side and themselves via the group dialogue before engaging in further action outside of the TRT group context. This difference in viewpoint represents an ongoing dilemma for many TRT members. Several tactics can be used to help manage these tensions and dilemmas, including holding public "open house" presentations as part of, or between, dialogue meetings. Informal and formal meetings of ad hoc committees around specific public presentations or projects of interest to them as individuals can also be initiated. However, it is the responsibility of the facilitators to ensure that adequate time is preserved for dialogue-centered activities during the group sessions, without marginalizing those who feel a need for urgent action. In some cases, those members who are very interested in taking direct action can be encouraged to start a similar group process in another context, outside the dialogue group meeting times. This is what happened in the Northern Ireland residential programs organized for Protestants and Catholics (see footnote 7). It also happened in Israel and Palestine between Jews and Palestinians in the founding of the Peace Research Institute in the Middle East (PRIME) by Adwan and Bar-On, and in professional training programs organized by Albeck and Elia Awwad, a Palestinian member of the TRT. Similarly, it happened in Austria when Samson Munn, a son of Holocaust survivors and a member of the original TRT group, initiated a dialogue group for descendants of Austrian Nazis and Austrian Jewish Holocaust survivors.

B.6. External planned events. Once the group has become cohesive, outside speakers or presenters can be invited to the meetings. This tactic is useful when outside speakers can contribute important experience/knowledge to the group and help the members to put their own experiences into a wider context. Joint group visits to appropriate sites, when relevant and practical, can also be helpful, but need considerable time for preparation and discussion afterwards. The German-Jewish groups that worked on Holocaust-related issues jointly went to Yad Vashem (the Israeli historical museum and commemoration for the Holocaust, located in Jerusalem) during the group encounter in Israel and to Buchenwald and Bergen Belsen (the sites of concentration camps) during the second seminar in Germany (Bar-On, Ostrovsky, & Fromer, 1997); the entire TRT group also visited the Palestinian refugee camp at Dehaisha, the largest such camp in Bethlehem. These visits needed preparation before, as well as discussion sessions afterwards, but proved to be very powerful.

C. Technical and Practical Aspects of the Group Encounters

C.1. Adjusting the time arrangements to the format of the meetings. The TRT group process requires that enough time be reserved for the intensive group discussions to take place (the residential meetings had at least five days for each encounter). In addition, a significant amount of individual and group time is needed to digest the intensive events that occur within and between the encounter sessions. The facilitators also need adequate time to help prepare participants for subsequent sessions during the tightly packed 5-7-day residential schedule. Group facilitators should decide whether to schedule a format of a couple of hours per week or per month or to employ a format in which there are periodic meetings consisting of several long blocks of sessions held on consecutive days. The first format is more suitable for university seminars or high school settings; the second format is usually more convenient for adults who come from different locations and who have a busy agenda. Hence, the first format was used for the Israeli-Palestinian workshop and in the Arab-Jewish dialogue groups conducted in the United States and the second format was used for TRT meetings and in the Northern Ireland residential encounters.

C.2. Space and number of participants. For the storytelling, sitting in a circle in a relatively comfortable, quiet, and isolated room is required. Appropriate measures to protect the discussion time from outside interruptions are essential. Dialogue groups, such as the TRT, should not have more than about 18 participants, although plenary-style assemblies and "fishbowl" sessions, which allow for larger numbers of people to be present in the room, can sometimes be useful components of the overall program schedule.

C.3. Relaxation and recovery. Facilitators should make appropriate arrangements for food and beverages, breaks, sleep arrangements, and informal socialization during and between group sessions. There is a need to schedule ample time for rest, recovery, and informal socialization after each meeting, especially when using the format of long, consecutive, and intensive days. Many participants reported that the informal times between sessions and during meals and group outings proved very productive in forming new insights about the conflict and new relationships with members of the other side.

C.4. E-mail communication. Between meetings, group e-mail correspondence between members of the group can be extremely useful, but has the potential to become excessive. One guideline that has proved helpful is to agree to limit the use of a dialogue group's central e-mail list to items that are either written by or about the participants themselves. This protects members from much unwanted "education" and marginally relevant announcements. It also makes it more likely that important group e-mails will be read more carefully by the members.

CONCLUSION

In this chapter, we presented the TRT dialogue group process, initially developed for working through the Jewish-German conflict related to the Holocaust, which relies on storytelling and reflection. The TRT group encounters appear to be unique in their attempt to use group communication processes to "complete the historical circle" to promote working through the intergenerational and multigenerational aspects of large-scale historical conflicts. This intergenerational, psychological working-through process, facilitated by a storytelling and storylistening format conducted in a safe environment, capitalizes on the differing perspectives of the victims, the victimizers, and bystanders of the conflict in focus. Such sharing does more than simply juxtapose differing perspectives as they are told separately; it allows for gradual integration of those perspectives, especially when the members of the various groups and generations recount them in each other's presence.

Telling one's life story in such a TRT historical circle encounter can facilitate the evolution of a new, shared narrative among participants. Telling one's personal story to those from the "other side" also seems to help improve participants' subsequent ability to listen more deeply to the stories of those others. An Israeli TRT member aptly described the improvement in listening ability that regularly occurs after feeling that one's story has been heard as "getting the wax out of our ears." This surprisingly common phenomenon in TRT groups further strengthens the sense of a shared underlying humanity between parties whose perspectives had previously appeared to them to differ so greatly from one another. Even if such bonds between former enemies or parties in conflict are only temporary, it is necessary that they be forged and strengthened during the group encounter to prevent the complete collapse of efforts at dialogue when the inevitable explosive verbal conflicts do occur in the sessions. Successful resolution of such severe communication breakdowns is possible when specific misunderstandings can be identified by the group. Clarifying the basis of true misunderstandings powerfully facilitates further dialogue; however, failure to acknowledge and confront the genuine differences between individuals on different sides of a conflict is as detrimental to meaningful dialogue as is the more obvious failure to manage verbal clashes between group members.

The TRT group communication process is an ongoing endeavor. Currently planned encounters between former enemies will insure that it continues to evolve. However, there remains a long-term need for improvement in our understanding of the principles, processes, and techniques useful in promoting working-through processes of traumatic past and present conflicts, in both small group and in larger societal settings. The interface between bottom-up, small group activities, such as the TRT process, and top-down, governmental efforts will likely be our next area of focus for such encounters. We, thus, plan to invite to future meetings representatives from government and media sectors in current conflict areas.

The experience-based guidelines for the TRT group facilitation and storytelling approach described in this chapter helped to stimulate and structure additional workshops for groups in current intractable conflict situations. It took 10 years to formulate this group communication technique into guidelines that may be considered for use by facilitators in other, sometimes very different, settings. These guidelines for encounters between groups in conflict emerged only after a long process of experimentation and careful reflection on those facilitation experiences. This bottom-up, inductive approach is very different from the deductive, top-down process of formal theorizing that sometimes generates group facilitation practices (see Bar-On, 1999a). With respect to the domain of reconciliation and coexistence of parties in intractable conflicts, theory still lags far behind practice (Maoz, 2001). It is the duty of scholar-practitioners to try to reduce this gap by theorizing about their work and by testing the generalizability, applicability, and limitations of their theories and practices in other contexts. Although each conflict has its own biography, which potentially limits the applicability of guidelines from one context to another, such theory building and application may reveal certain principles that apply across conflict contexts. Some principles of symmetry, power sharing, and process-related interaction have been described in this chapter and in other studies (Maoz, 2001; Maoz & Ellis, this volume; Optow, in press; Ross, 2000) that may be relevant to more than just the TRT facilitation technique and storytelling approach. Further research is also needed to discover whether the guidelines described here have relevance for facilitating group communication in other intractable conflict situations.

The TRT group communication experience can be very useful for people who are trying to work through painful and long-lasting conflicts. We believe that through this group process, people can learn to live with the past and with a tense and painful present in a better way, and that it can help them to be more open to new ways to create a different future. Although we might wish otherwise, the TRT facilitation techniques likely will be needed for many years to come, as will other methods of group communication facilitation, because history has taught us that there will always be groups in conflict and that the victims and the descendants of the harsh consequences of these conflicts will have to find ways to work through them.

REFERENCES

Adwan, S., & Bar-On, D. (2001). (Eds.). *Victimhood and beyond*. Beit Jala, Palestine National Authority: Peace Research Institute in the Middle East.

Albeck, J. (1994). Intergenerational consequences of trauma: Reframing traps in treatment theory—a second generation perspective. In M. B. Williams & J. F. Sommer, Jr. (Eds.), *Handbook of post-traumatic therapy* (pp. 106-125). Westport, CT: Greenwood Press.

Allport, G. W. (1954). *The nature of prejudice*. Cambridge, MA: Addison-Wesley.

Bar-On, D. (1989). *Legacy of silence: Encounters with descendants of the Third Reich*. Cambridge, MA: Harvard University Press.

Bar-On, D. (1990). Children of perpetrators of the Holocaust: Working through one's moral self. *Psychiatry*, *53*, 229-245.

Bar-On, D. (1993). First encounter between children of survivors and children of perpetrators of the Holocaust. *Journal of Humanistic Psychology*, *33*(4), 6-14.

Bar-On, D. (1995a). Encounters between descendants of Nazi perpetrators and descendants of Holocaust survivors. *Psychiatry*, *58*, 225-245.

Bar-On, D. (1995b). *Fear and hope: Three generations of the Holocaust*. Cambridge, MA: Harvard University Press.

Bar-On, D. (1999a). *The indescribable and the undiscussible: Reconstructing human discourse after trauma*. Budapest, Hungary: Central European University Press.

Bar-On, D. (1999b). *Ha'acherim bitocheinu: Tmurut be'zehut hayisraelit mehaperspectiva hapshichologit* [The "other" within us: Changes in the Israeli identity from a psychosocial perspective]. Jerusalem, Israel: Ben Gurion University Press.

Bar-On, D. (Ed.). (2000). *Bridging the gap: Storytelling as a way to work through political and collective hostilities*. Hamburg, Germany: Koerber.

Bar-On, D. (2004). When are we expecting parties to concise or to refuse to do it? The triangle of Jews, Germans and Palestinians. In Y. Bar-Siman-Tov (Ed.), *From conflict resolution to reconciliation* (pp. 239-254). New York: Oxford University Press.

Bar-On, D., & Charny, I. W. (1992). The logic of moral argumentation of children of the Nazi era. *International Journal of Group Tensions*, *22*, 3-20.

Bar-On, D., & Kassem, F. (2004). Storytelling as a way to work-through intractable conflicts: The TRT German-Jewish experience and its relevance to the Palestinian-Israeli context. *Journal of Social Issues*, *60*, 289-306.

Bar-On, D., Ostrovsky, T., & Fromer, D. (1997). "Who am I in relation to the other?": German and Israeli students confront the Holocaust and each other. In Y. Danieli (Ed.), *International handbook of multigenerational legacies of trauma* (pp. 97-116). New York: Plenum Press.

Bar-Tal, D. (2000). From intractable conflict through conflict resolution to reconciliation: Psychological analysis. *Political Psychology*, *21*, 761-770.

Berger, A. L., & Berger, N. (Eds.). (2001). *Second generation voices: Reflections by children of Holocaust survivors and perpetrators.* Syracuse, NY: Syracuse University Press.

Clay, C. (Producer & Director). (1993). *Children of the Third Reich* [Television broadcast]. London: British Broadcasting Corporation.

Danieli, Y. (1988). Confronting the unimaginable: Psychotherapists' reactions to victims of the Holocaust. In J. P. Wilson, Z. Harel, & B. Kahana (Eds.), *Human adaptation to extreme stress: From the Holocaust to Vietnam* (pp. 219-238). New York: Plenum Press.

Davidson, S. (1980). The clinical effect of massive psychic trauma in families of Holocaust survivors. *Journal of Marital and Family Therapy, 1,* 11-21.

Dorff, E. N. (1992). Individual and communal forgiveness. In D. H. Frank (Ed.), *Autonomy and Judaism: The individual and the community in Jewish philosophical thought* (pp. 193-217). Albany: State University of New York Press.

Freud, S. (1953). *Standard edition of the complete psychological works of Sigmund Freud* (J. Strachey, Trans.). London: Hogarth Press.

Hardtmann, G. (1991). *Partial relevance of the Holocaust: Comparing interviews of German and Israeli students.* Report to the German-Israeli Fund, Jerusalem, Israel.

Helms, J. E. (Ed.). (1990). *Black and White racial identity: Theory, research, and practice.* Westport, CT: Greenwood Press.

Kelman H. C. (1999). Transforming the relationship between former enemies: A social-psychological analysis. In R. L. Rothstein (Ed.), *After the peace: Resistance and reconciliation* (pp. 193-205). Boulder, CO: Lynne Rienner.

Lehman, D. R., Wortman, C. B., & Williams, A. F. (1987). Long-term effects of losing a spouse or child in a motor vehicle crash. *Journal of Personality and Social Psychology, 52,* 218-231.

Maoz, I. (2000a). Multiple conflicts and competing agendas: A framework for conceptualizing structured encounters between groups in conflict—the case of a coexistence project of Jews and Palestinians in Israel. *Peace and Conflict: Journal Peace Psychology, 6,* 135-156.

Maoz, I. (2000b). Power relations in intergroup encounters: A case study of Jewish-Arab encounters in Israel. *International Journal of Intercultural Relations, 24,* 259-277.

Maoz, I. (2001). *Conceptual mapping and evaluation of Jewish-Arab coexistence activities in Israel: A summary evaluation report.* Jerusalem, Israel: Abraham Fund.

Maoz, I., Bar-On, D., Steinberg, S., & Farkhadeen, M. (2004). The dialogue between the "self" and the "other": A process analysis of Palestinian-Jewish encounters in Israel. *Human Relations, 55,* 931-962.

Moscovici, S. (1976). *Social influence and social change* (C. Sherrard & G. Heinz, Trans.). London: Academic Press.

Mugny, G., & Pérez, J. A. (1991(. *The social psychology of minority influence* (V. W. Lamongie, Trans). Cambridge, England: Cambridge University Press.

Novey, S. (1962). The principle of "working through" in psychoanalysis. *Journal of the American Psychoanalytic Association, 10*, 658-676.

Optow, S. (2001). Reconciliation in times of impunity: Challenges for social justice. *Journal of Social Justice, 14*, 149-170.

Pettigrew, T. F. (1998). Intergroup contact theory. *Annual Review of Psychology, 49*, 65-85.

Rittner, C., & Roth, J. K. (2000). Indifference to the plight of the Jews during the Holocaust. In C. Rittner, S. D. Smith, & I. Steinfeldt (Eds.), *The Holocaust and the Christian world: Reflections on the past, challenges for the future* (pp. 38-41). New York: Continuum.

Rosenthal, G. (1993). Reconstruction of life stories. Principles of selection in generating stories for narrative biographical interviews. *Narrative Study of Lives, 1*(1), 59-91.

Ross, M. H. (2000). "Good enough" is not so bad: Thinking about success and failure in ethnic conflict management. *Peace and Conflict: Journal of Peace Psychology, 6*, 27-47.

Rouhana, N. N. (2004). Reconciliation in protracted national conflict: Identity and power in the Israeli-Palestinian case. In A. H. Eagly, R. M. Baron. & V. L. Hamilton (Eds.), *The social psychology of group identity and social conflict: Theory, application, and practice* (pp. 173-192). Washington, DC. American Psychological Association.

Sonnenschein, N., Halabi, R., & Friedman, A. (1998). Legitimization of national identity and the change in power relationships in workshops dealing with the Israeli/Palestinian conflict. In E. Weiner (Ed.), *The handbook of interethnic coexistence* (pp. 600-614). New York: Continuum.

Staub, E. (2000). Genocide and mass killing: Origins, prevention, healing, and reconciliation. *Political Psychology, 21*, 367-382.

Steinberg, S., & Bar-On, D. (2002). An analysis of the group process in encounters between Jews and Palestinians using a typology for discourse classification. *International Journal of Intercultural Relations, 26*, 199-214.

Suleiman, R. (1997). Hamifgash hametuchnan bein yisraelim yehudim v'palestinay-im kemicrocosmis: perspectiva pyichologia chevratit [The planned encounter between Israeli Jews and Palestinians as a microcosm: A social-psychological perspective]. *Iyunim Bechinuch, 1*(2), 71-85.

Sunwolf, & Frey, L. R. (2001). Storytelling: The power of narrative communication and interpretation. In W. P. Robinson & H. Giles (Eds.), *The new handbook of language and social psychology* (pp. 119-135). New York: John Wiley.

Zehavi-Verete, T. (2000). Chasifa hadadit l'album hamishpachti: Kli ezer ledialog hyehudi-aravi [Mutual exposure to the family album: A helping device for Jewish-Arab dialogue]. *Dapim, 30*, 5-64.

5

FACILITATING GROUPS IN SEVERE CONFLICT

THE CASE OF TRANSFORMATIONAL DIALOGUE BETWEEN ISRAELI-JEWS AND PALESTINIANS*

Ifat Maoz
The Hebrew University of Jerusalem

Donald G. Ellis
The University of Hartford

The conflict between Israeli-Jews and Palestinians has been enduring and intractable. Abu-Nimer (1999) and others (e.g., Adwan & Bar-On, 2000; Kelman, 1995) have described the various efforts to facilitate meetings between Israeli-Arabs and Jews, or between Israeli-Jews and Palestinians. These encounters have ranged from single meetings to long-term contacts, and have involved participants from all levels of society, including teachers, students, journalists, and government officials (cf. I. Maoz, 2000a). These efforts have met with mixed results, but the commitment to resolution and reconciliation remains strong.

*The first author thanks the Solomon Asch Center for The Study of Ethnopolitical Conflict at the University of Pennsylvania for sabbatical support while writing the final version of this chapter. She also thanks the Israel/Palestine Center for Research and Information (IPCRI); Gershon Baskin, Israeli director of IPCRI; and Zakaria Al-Qaq, Palestinian director of IPCRI for assistance and support of the evaluation research described in the chapter.

In this chapter, we describe research on encounters between Israeli-Jews and Palestinians in grassroots dialogue groups that we observed and studied as part of a facilitation effort. We focus on the processes of group meetings that serve as a vehicle for change at the individual level. To set the stage for this discussion, we begin with a brief history of the Israeli-Palestinian conflict. One consequence of this history has been a deep-seated, zero-sum conflict concerning national identity and existence. Under such difficult circumstances, the parties began regular encounters to build trust and establish relationships, and the groups we describe emerged out of this process. In the chapter, we (a) place our work in the context of conflict resolution, (b) explain reconciliation-aimed dialogue groups, (c) describe the particular group communication facilitation procedures used, and (d) report evaluation results from these groups.

A BRIEF HISTORY OF THE ISRAELI-PALESTINIAN CONFLICT

The history of the Israeli-Palestinian conflict has known many dramatic turning points, with periods of severe violence followed by serious attempts at peace making and peace building. In the context of the current upsurge in violence between the sides, a peaceful solution does not seem any closer than it did 50 years ago. The origins of the conflict between Jews and Arabs can be traced to the end of the 19th century with the appearance of political Zionism that sought to establish a Jewish state in Palestine, a land Zionists considered the historical Israel, and the resulting waves of Jewish immigration to Palestine. However, the Arabs who lived on that same land had developed a Palestinian national identity. Consequently, a clash occurred between the Jewish and Palestinian communities over ownership of that land, the right to self-determination, and statehood. Violence between the two communities first erupted in the 1920s and has pervaded their relationship in various forms and with varying degrees of intensity since that time (see, e.g., Kelman, 1997; Rouhana & Bar-Tal, 1998).

The communal clash between Israeli-Jews and Palestinian-Arabs that characterized the first few decades of the 20th century escalated into a war that involved the neighboring Arab states when the area of Palestine was divided into two states—one Arab and one Jewish— in the United Nations (UN) Resolution 181 in November of 1948. The Palestinians rejected this UN partition plan and a war ensued between Israeli Jews and Arabs. Israel won the war, and the independent Jewish state of Israel was established in 1948. Almost half of the Palestinians who lived in Palestine fled or were expelled to neighboring Arab countries (M. Maoz, 1999a). The Six-Day War in 1967 brought the West Bank of the Jordan River and the Gaza Strip under Israeli control. Twenty years later, in 1987, there was an uprising (the Intifada) of Palestinians against Israeli occupation of this area that lasted until the signing of the Israeli-Palestinian Oslo peace accords in September 1993 (Rouhana & Bar-Tal, 1998).

Prospects for peace improved following the signing of the Oslo accords. There was hope that violence between the two sides would end and that reconciliation would begin (M. Maoz, 1999b), but these hopes were dashed a few years later when it became clear that Oslo was a fragile peace process (Rothstein, 2002). The assassination of Israeli Prime Minister Yitzchak Rabin and Palestinian terror attacks hindered the peace process. Neither side was able to assemble a peace coalition capable of governing its members (Shikaki, 2002); consequently, opposition to the Oslo accords hardened. Extremists on both sides demonized each other and stepped up acts of violence and revenge (M. Maoz, 2002).

The Camp David summit in July 2000 failed to produce a framework agreement on the status of the affected territories and other points of contention, leaving the Israeli-Jews and Palestinians at a difficult impasse (Shikaki, 2002). Since September 2000, and the eruption of the Al-Aqsa Intifada, relations between Israeli-Jews and Palestinians have further deteriorated and are characterized by the escalation of violent and armed clashes between them and by a halt of the peace process (Shikaki, 2002). Thus, the Oslo peace process has essentially collapsed, along with the degree of mutual trust and cooperation that had been achieved between the sides since the signing of the Oslo accords (M. Maoz, 2002).

Misperceptions, negative stereotyping, mutual delegitimization, and severe miscommunication are characteristic of such difficult and long-standing conflicts between groups (Bar-On, 1997; Bar-Tal, 1990). These problems contribute to the escalation of the conflict and hinder conflict resolution and reconciliation. Dialogue and encounter groups aimed at building positive relationships between the groups are one way to proactively seek resolution of such conflict (see Albeck, Adwan, & Bar-On, this volume). Examples of different forms of such planned group contacts, designed to help cope with living in conflict or its aftermath, can be found in Northern Ireland in large-scale projects conducted through schools and community agencies that focus on integration between Catholics and Protestants (Arthur, 1999; Cairns & Hewstone, 2002), in Cyprus with dialogues between Greek and Turkish educators and community members (Broome, this volume; Hadjipavlou, 2002; Saunders, 1999), and at the site of the groups described in this chapter (Ellis & Maoz, 2002; I. Maoz & Ellis, 2001).

TRANSFORMING GROUPS IN CONFLICT

Conflict resolution is under increasing criticism and has been shown to be inadequate for many situations—ethnic conflict, in particular. For instance, Avruch and Black (1990) and Abu-Nimer (1999) argued that deep-rooted conflicts (such as the Israeli-Palestinian conflict) have strong emotions at their core that are not easily restrained. Our work (Ellis & Maoz 2002; I. Maoz & Ellis, 2001) is consistent with this criticism in that we discovered that when given the opportunity, in planned intergroup conflict resolution events, Israeli-Jews and Palestinians exchange emotionally intense argument that seems to entrench their positions more than it tempers them. Conflict resolution has, thus, tended to privilege "rationality" by foregrounding communication that involves the orderly exchange of ideas and opinions and backgrounding emotions, power asymmetries, and the importance of culture and class.

It is clear that simply having bitter enemies sign peace treaties and then waiting for them to "work things out" is of limited value (I. Maoz & Ellis, 2001). Groups need help resolving conflicts and improving relationships. There is, of course, a long history of theory, research, and facilitation of interactive conflict resolution (cf. Kriesberg, 1997; Rothman, 1997). Interactive conflict resolution, however, is different from dialogue on a number of dimensions. Kriesberg (1991) reviewed the development of problem-solving techniques as they were introduced into international conflict settings and explained that in the same way that interactive conflict resolution was supposed to substitute for power-oriented and coercive techniques, dialogue seeks to redress weaknesses in power-oriented conflict resolution, as well as in interactive conflict resolution. For example, some interactive conflict resolution entails a third party assisting disputants to collaboratively solve problems. It demands abandoning power-oriented strategies and embracing analytical and noncoercive approaches to solving problems. There is no single agreed-on theory of conflict resolution practices, but the following principles are most characteristic of traditional interactive conflict resolution models: (a) conflict is natural but in need of management and control; (b) conflict is caused by numerous types of factors, including economic, political, and psychological; (c) communication is crucial for conflict management; (d) mutually agreed-on outcomes of conflict resolution tend to be better solutions than any imposed by one side; (e) the actual process of working on problems and managing conflict should be creative and seek to improve relationships between conflict parties; and (f) there are skills needed for conflict resolution (e.g., communication, group facilitation, analysis, and assessment) and these skills can be developed, taught, and learned.

Another common criticism of interactive conflict resolution practices is that relationships among individuals and between disputing groups often improve but that these rarely lead to political changes. Thus, interactive conflict resolution groups always have to face the problem of how long any changes will remain, and what the likelihood is that such changes will influence policy. Furthermore, some interactive conflict resolution (e.g., Kelman, 1995) has typically involved academics, journalists, and educators who have an advanced level of education and experience and are willing and prepared to negotiate; there are rarely groups comprised of average citizens. Finally, interactive conflict resolution is too influenced by facilitators and others who direct the experience (Bush & Folger, 1994), telling parties what is important and significantly shaping settlements and solutions. Hence, interactive conflict resolution tends to become overly directive, with the facilitator analyzing and diagnosing the problem, formulating a solution, and then trying to persuade the parties to accept it. As a result, the satisfaction of the parties involved is reduced because solutions do not emerge naturally from the conflicting parties themselves. The focus shifts from the concerns of the disputants to the interests of the facilitator. Moreover, the more a problem-solving specialist directs the resolution process, the more remote a solution becomes from the conflicting parties' true interests. Even when the facilitator's interests and influence are successfully masked, they still have an impact. Because of these criticisms and potential problems with interactive conflict resolution, and in an effort to find more innovative ways of transforming conflict and reconciling differences between parties, dialogue is posed as an important alternative.

RECONCILIATION-AIMED DIALOGUES

The concept of dialogue has received increased scholarly attention in recent years (cf. Abu-Nimer, 1999; Pearce & Littlejohn, 1997; Schoem & Hurtado, 2001), including attention from group communication scholars (Barge, 2002). Scholars in this field describe the dialogic process as designed to stimulate genuine personal change and growth for participating individuals (Gergen, 1999a, 1999b; Pearce & Littlejohn, 1997; Spano, this volume). Basically, the practice of transformative dialogue in conflict situations can be seen as a participatory process that tries to redress inequality, subjugation, and oppression by having conflicting parties engage in face-to-face interaction and trying to build new relationships. Arnett and Arneson (1999) claimed that dialogue is not meant to be an ethereal concept but a practice for parties to work through the gritty reality of achieving a common life together. Democracies, in particular, value diversity of persons, cultures, and religions, including the difficult task of constructing a community of common ground. This community can only be constructed through a type of communication that accentuates the co-creation of agreement. This is not conflict resolution or management per se but the working through of conflict, via dialogue, which creates new realities and relationships shared by the participants (see Albeck et al., this volume).

The notion of transformative dialogue, when used in the context of intergroup conflict, draws heavily from contact theory in social psychology (Allport, 1954; Amir, 1976). This theory states that contact that fulfills several conditions may be effective in reducing prejudice and improving intergroup attitudes. These conditions are specified as: (a) equal status of the two groups within the contact situation (as contact between groups of unequal status, especially where the traditional status imbalance is maintained, can perpetuate existing negative stereotypes); (b) personal and sustained communication between individuals from both groups; (c) cooperative interdependence, where members of both groups work together to achieve common goals that are best achieved collaboratively; and (d) consensus among the relevant authorities on social norms favoring equality. In a recent reformulation of the contact theory, Pettigrew (1998) added a fifth condition, stating that contact should bear the potential for the formation of friendship with members of the other group. Such groups have as their goal *reconciliation*, the process of individuals or groups accepting new relationships of cooperation and concession with formerly conflicting parties (Lederach, 1998; Saunders, 1999). Reconciliation includes the emotional and psychological components of forgiveness, reaching beyond past grievances, and taking responsibility for previous injustices.

Over the past decades, Allport's (1954) contact theory has inspired many studies examining planned contact as a means to reduce hostility and conflict between ethnic and national groups (cf. Abu-Nimer, 1999; Amir, 1976; Jackson, 1993; Pettigrew, 1998; for more detailed descriptions of these research trends, see I. Maoz, 2000b, 2000c). These studies have postulated that if members of two mutually hostile groups are brought together in a planned encounter, get to know each other, and interact under conditions of equal status, a mutual change toward more positive attitudes and perceptions of the other group will ensue. Consequently, most of these studies compare the attitudes of participants before and after intergroup contact to determine if contact that meets the required conditions is, indeed, effective in improving intergroup relations. These studies have yielded mixed results in that some support the predictions advanced by the contact theory, whereas others do not (Jackson, 1993). However, a recent meta-analysis of studies of contact effects by Pettigrew and Tropp (2000) found that contact and dialogue under the conditions stipulated by Allport do improve intergroup attitudes. Thus, contact between conflicting groups, such as Israeli-Jews and Palestinians, is necessary and desirable. However, the nature of the contact is equally important in that the successful management of conflict requires the harmonizing of interests between parties and the opportunity to acknowledge the perspective of the other. This, we believe, is accomplished by dialogic processes.

ISRAELI-PALESTINIAN DIALOGUE GROUPS: GOALS AND PRINCIPLES OF FACILITATION

We continue with a description of the major goals and principles involved in conducting and facilitating Israeli-Palestinian dialogue groups. This overview includes explanation of how these group encounters developed principles of this type of facilitation and evaluative results of these encounters.

History and Development of Israeli-Palestinian Planned Intergroup Contact

The first attempt to address the dispute between Israelis and Palestinians by means of structured communication meetings was in what Herbert Kelman of Harvard University called "interactive problem-solving workshops." These began in the early 1970s and have been conducted by Kelman and his colleagues since then (see Kelman, 1995). These workshops brought together politically active and influential Israelis and Palestinians to engage in face-to-face communication in small groups facilitated by unofficial third-party mediators.

Since the signing of the Oslo peace agreements in 1993, numerous programs of Israeli-Palestinian group meetings aimed at peace building have been conducted each year that are targeted at grassroots populations from both sides (see Adwan & Bar-On, 2000; I. Maoz, 2000a). These meetings have ranged from one-time events to long-term continuous series of meetings, and from youth encounters to dialogues among school teachers, university students, university professors, and other professionals (Adwan & Bar-On, 2000). The recent increase in violence between Israelis and Palestinians and the accompanying elevation of tensions between Jews and Arabs in Israel have created difficulties in facilitating encounter and dialogue activities between the sides. However, even in this severe situation, some Israelis and Palestinian dialogue projects continue to function, meeting in locations outside of Israel or Palestine, such as in Cyprus or in Turkey.

Goals of the Facilitation

Intergroup dialogues between Israeli-Jews and Palestinians represent grass-roots efforts in response to the challenges facing a fragile and acrimonious relationship between these two groups. In these dialogues, participants try to talk with one another directly, honestly, and sometimes harshly about the experiences they have had with members of the other group. It is easier to work with groups that have homogeneous experiences, including common goals, community activities, and problems, as such groups are able to maintain cohesion as they deal with differences because their members share so much in common. Israeli-Jews and Palestinians, however, as explained previously, are steeped in different sociohistorical legacies that have produced antagonisms, unequal social relations, negative stereotypes, and questions about the legitimacy and identity of the other; therefore, acknowledging differences between these groups is an important starting point for these dialogue sessions. The goal of the dialogue experience, as explained throughout this chapter, is to help participants begin to understand why there may be differences between the groups and to start to move beyond stereotypes of the other group. Moreover, participants are encouraged to see that their differences deserve respect and perhaps are not as divisive as originally thought. Eventually, this form of dialogue leads to the discovery of some common goals and values. Although it is important not to pose unrealistic goals for these groups, and group dialogue is not always successful, it does provide a good opportunity for accomplishing significant change, the type of change that transforms individuals such that they integrate their need for autonomy with a concern for others.

In brief, dialogue group sessions are conducted according to the following principles. First, dialogue is a process that takes time to allow participants to work through stages of change and to develop in-depth and nuanced understanding and meaning of the issues being discussed. Second, such groups employ a model of engagement, with exercises and techniques being used to encourage in-depth interaction. Third, group members agree to a long-term commitment, sometimes weeks or months, that ensures the conversation will continue. This commitment to engagement promotes trust among members and explicitly acknowledges that time is needed to process the complex information being shared. Fourth, because dialogue is fundamentally about relationship building among members, these groups are best conducted under a condition of confidentiality. The communication that occurs inside a dialogue group is not for gaining advantage with anyone outside the group; this is especially important when power relations are unequal, as in the case of the groups we describe. Fifth, such dialogue occurs on both an interpersonal and an intergroup level; consequently, the group dialogue experience must be sensitive to participants' background, values, customs, struggles, and histories. Dialogue promotes integration of individual and group identities and, thus, a mix of personal, intellectual, social, and political processes. Finally, facilitators are needed to coordinate and direct the groups according to the above principles (cf. Adams, Bell, & Griffin, 1997; Beale, Thompson, & Chesler, 2001).

These principles have guided the facilitation of Israeli-Palestinian dialogue groups that are focused on reconciliation and the reduction of prejudices (for related principles of storytelling dialogues with groups in conflict, see Albeck at al., this volume). On the basis of an extensive evaluation study of 47 programs of encounters between Jews and Palestinians in Israel, I. Maoz (2002) outlined the following additional principles for organizing and facilitating such dialogue groups:

Goals: Directors and facilitators of dialogue programs should clearly define the goals of these groups and specify the processes and practices used to achieve these goals.

Responsiveness: Intergroup dialogue projects must be responsive to the needs and abilities of the target populations. These needs and abilities may differ as a function of factors such as age, gender, religion, cultural background, and language.

Role Models: Those who lead such groups should have experience with facilitating dialogues and should know how to work through problems and emotional difficulties that may arise in such group processes.

Symmetry: There should be symmetry and equality between the participating groups with respect to members and facilitators; thus, there should be an equal number of facilitators and participants from each group present in the dialogue meeting, who hold a similar socioeconomical status.

Preparation: Preparation is necessary when participants in this type of process have never met the representatives from the other group. This might include prediscussion of attitudes about the conflict or the other group and expectations about what the group experience will bring.

Forms of Activity: There should be enough meetings between the groups to create a meaningful process of communication. A yearlong dialogue is desirable. Moreover, there should not be long periods of time between meetings. Finally, uninational discussions, where members talk only with members of their own national or ethnic group, can be beneficial and help to prepare participants for binational dialogue.

EVALUATION OF ISRAELI-PALESTINIAN DIALOGUE GROUPS

In this section, we describe research conducted to evaluate the effects of Israeli-Palestinian dialogue groups. The major goal of the dialogue groups was to improve mutual intergroup attitudes of Israelis and Palestinians. In that context, the research investigated whether participants actually did change their attitudes toward each other following participation in dialogue groups (for a more detailed description of this research, see I. Maoz, 2000a).

Research Site and Population

The workshops were conducted in the spring of 1998, during the post-Oslo peace agreement era, when the Likud Party, representing relatively hawkish positions in regard to working with the Palestinians, led the Israeli government. This time period was marked by difficulties stemming from both sides in implementing the Oslo agreements, and by stagnation in proceeding with the political process toward a lasting peace arrangement (M. Maoz, 1999b). A series of workshops were initiated with 15- and 16-year-old youths (10th graders) from pairs of Israeli and Palestinian schools. The workshops were held in various locations inside Israel, mainly of a mixed Jewish-Arab nature. One such location was Neveh Shalom, a joint Jewish-Arab village; another one was Tantur, a Christian compound situated on the outskirts of both Jerusalem and Bethlehem.

In the workshops, the youth from both sides met for two days to deal with social, cultural, and political issues through the sharing of personal narratives and discussions of the conflict. The sharing of personal narratives was expected by the workshop organizers to help the youth from both sides to transcend the national boundaries separating them by enabling them to listen, understand, and emphasize with the feelings, sufferings, fears, and hopes of each other. These workshops were organized and directed by the Israel-Palestine Center for Research and Information (IPCRI), a jointly managed Israeli-Palestinian nongovernmental organization (NGO) in the framework of a peace education project. Such NGOs often play a central role in peace education and peace-building activities directed at the grassroot level of populations in conflict. For various political and administrative reasons, governmental and official state offices on both sides of this particular conflict between Israelis and Palestinians, such as the Israeli and the Palestinian ministries of education, did not conduct extensive and systematic programs of peace education. Such work was, thus, left to NGOs and other similar groups and organizations.

In the period relevant to our work, over 100 Israeli-Palestinian peace-education and peace-building activities were conducted by dozens of NGOs, mostly financed by the United States and Europe (Adwan & Bar-On, 2000). A major part of these activities focused on developing dialogues between the sides. Moreover, even activities that focused on other joint efforts—such as study groups (in topics such as music, arts, drama, and religion), task groups (dealing with environmental tasks, arts and crafts projects, and writing curriculum, textbooks, and other educational materials), and productions of television programs and magazines—included in them Israeli-Palestinian dialogue as a major practice.

Structure, Content, and Language in the Dialogue Workshops

The workshops were similar in terms of structure and forms of activity to other Jewish-Arab coexistence-aimed group encounters conducted within Israel since the late 1980s (I. Maoz, 2000b, 2000c, 2002). The two days of encounters consisted of a series of dialogue sessions between the youth, with most of these sessions including mixed groups of Israeli and Palestinian youth. Two facilitators—an Israeli-Jew and a Palestinian—jointly led these group meetings. However, in some of the sessions, Israeli-Jews and Palestinians met separately in uninational groups, led by a facilitator of their nationality. Three workshops were studied. Each workshop included the following activities. After the opening plenary session, which included all the participants from each side, meetings were conducted in small mixed groups that included 5 to 7 Israeli-Jews and a similar number of Palestinians. At the end of the first day of the 2-day workshop, and again toward the end of the second day, Israeli-Jews and Palestinians from each subgroup met separately in a uninational group, led by a facilitator from the same nationality. The workshop ended with another plenary session. A typical schedule of the workshop is displayed in Figure 6.1.

Two practices within the workshops were particularly conducive to the creation of a transformative dialogue (Gergen, 1999a). First, the activities were planned such that a gradual transition occurred from activities centered on forming personal ties between Israeli and Palestinian youth to discussions of the conflict between the two national groups. Specifically, the first

Day 1

9:00-10:00a.m.	Opening in large mixed group (introductory remarks by facilitators)
10:00-11:30	Acquaintance in small mixed groups (ice-breaking exercises that include learning everyone's names and hobbies)
11:30-11:45	Break (frequent breaks are held to enable spontaneous interaction)
11:45-1:00	Acquaintance in small mixed groups continued
1:00-2:00	Lunch
2:00-2:45	Discussion in small mixed groups of the culture and traditions of each group, and differences and similarities between the groups.
2:45–3:00	Break
3:00-4:00	Discussion in small mixed groups of participants' experience of the conflict
4:15-5:00	Uninational meeting summarizing Day 1.

Day 2

9:30-11:00 a.m.	Participants tell about their lives in the conflict in small mixed groups
11:00-11:15	Break
11:15-12:30	Narrating lives in conflict in small mixed groups continued
12:30-1:30	Lunch
1:30-2:15	Processing and summary meeting in uninational groups
2:15-3:15	Summary of meeting in small mixed groups
3:15–4:00	Summary of meeting in the large group and concluding remarks of facilitators

Figure 5.1. A typical schedule of a Dialogue Workshop

day opened with getting-acquainted exercises, followed by a discussion of the culture and traditions of each side. Beginning at the end of the first day, a series of dialogues were conducted dealing with participants' experience of the conflict and the relations between the two sides. Project organizers and group facilitators chose this structure so that discussions of the conflict would begin only when the participants could manage them without jeopardizing the personal relations they had established with one another. Thus, participants discussed the conflict between them only after establishing a relationship and forming social and interpersonal ties (I. Maoz, 2000a; McNamee & Gergen, 1999). Second, the crux of the transformative communication process consisted of a series of dialogue sessions beginning at the end of the first day of the workshop, in which participants were encouraged to share with the other group members their experiences of living in the Israeli-Palestinian conflict (I. Maoz, 2000a). The practice of narrating personal stories was used in these dialogues to enable the youth to explore the individual and group realities of their own side and of the other side and, thereby, to make it easier for them to feel empathy, and to take into the self the experiences of the other (see Albeck et al., this volume; Sunwolf & Frey, 2001).

Most meetings were conducted in English. Given that a significant number of the Palestinian and Israeli participants had a fair knowledge of English, there was no notable advantage for one group over the other with respect to using this language. In some meetings, however, each side spoke its own language from the onset and the group facilitators translated their comments. Using English enabled a fairly smooth and coordinated conversation but occasionally contributed to discomfort, depending on participants' ease with the language. Translating the comments enabled wider participation but significantly slowed down the dialogue, disrupted its flow, and sometimes resulted in the wandering of the youth's attention when the language of the other side was spoken.

Research Methods

Data were collected and analyzed using both quantitative and qualitative methods. The first author, assisted by a research team of one Israeli-Jew and one Palestinian, collected the data and performed most of the analyses; the second author was an observer for one group and assisted later with textual data analysis. A questionnaire was administered to 52 Israeli and 48 Palestinian youngsters before and after their participation in the workshop. On their arrival at the encounter site, and before the beginning of workshop activities, participants were asked to complete the self-report questionnaires. This questionnaire examined the extent to which the youth had experienced contact with people from the other national group prior to their participation in the workshop, their stereotypic perceptions of the other national group, and various demographic questions. Immediately after the workshop ended, they again answered the same questions about their stereotypic perceptions and the demographic questions. The questions asked participants to indicate to what extent each of the following attributes characterized the other side: (a) considerate of others, (b) tolerant, (c) good-hearted, (d) honest, (e) intelligent, (f) broad-minded, (g) open to changes, and (h) willing to sacrifice for peace. Participants rated their agreement on a 5-point Likert-type scale (1 = *Not at all*, 5 = *To a very high extent*). Israeli participants received and answered the questionnaires in Hebrew; Palestinian participants received and answered the same questionnaires in Arabic after the questionnaires were translated from and back-translated to Hebrew to check for accuracy. Statistical analyses were performed by Maoz on the data derived from the questionnaires to assess the stereotypic perceptions of each group in regard to the other group and changes in these perceptions following participation in the workshop.

Interviews were also conducted at different points of the process with the Palestinian and Israeli participants, facilitators, and organizers of the workshops. These interviews were relatively open-ended and semistructured and were designed to elicit feelings and emotions from the participants. Interviewers took notes but did not audio- or videotape them to maintain anonymity. These data were not analyzed systematically but used qualitatively to discover major themes describing the facilitators' and participants' experiences in the workshop (Strauss & Corbin, 1990).

Maoz was the evaluator of the workshops and, together with her research group, fully observed and documented the facilitated group sessions; she also administered questionnaires and conducted interviews. The evaluation of the group dialogue workshop was a planned and integral part of the facilitation process but had to be essentially separate from the actual facilitation of the sessions to validly fulfill its functions for two reasons. First, technically, a facilitator could not fully document and evaluate the facilitation while being actively involved in the dialogue process; consequently, a separate evaluator was necessary. Second, part of the evaluation involved talking to and interviewing participants about their experience and perceptions of the facilitated process; being interviewed by a facilitator rather than a separate evaluator would have significantly increased opportunities for participants to give socially desirable responses, introducing bias on the part of the facilitator-interviewer, and might have led to degrading the effects of the group facilitation. Thus, keeping the evaluator separate was necessary for a more objective perspective.

Nevertheless, the two functions of facilitation and evaluation were closely related in the planned intervention. There was a process of mutual feedback between research and practice that included the following steps. The first was that the evaluation team interviewed the facilitators to understand the goals and guidelines of this facilitation. The second step was that the evaluation team observed, recorded, and documented the facilitation process and participants' experience. The third step had the evaluator provide feedback to the facilitators at various points of the workshop process that included description and interpretation of the facilitated process, assessment of the extent to which it met the predefined goals and guidelines, and descriptions of its strong and weak points. Finally, facilitators used the feedback to reassess and modify their facilitation practices. The role of the evaluator made it possible for the facilitators to monitor the process and make regular adjustments in their practices.

Changes in Attitudes and Perceptions Following Participation in the Workshops

To see whether participation in the dialogue activities that followed the group communication facilitation principles described previously actually transformed mutual perceptions, participants' accounts of their workshop experience and their stereotypic perceptions before and after their participation in the workshop were examined. The qualitative, as well as quantitative, results of the research showed that youth from both sides arrived at the workshops with very limited past acquaintance with members of the other side and held mutually negative stereotypes. Jewish-Israeli participants repeatedly described in their accounts an image of a violent and inhuman Palestinian terrorist; Palestinian participants prominently described the violent encounters between aggressive Israeli soldiers and Palestinian civilians. Thus, both Israeli and Palestinian youth arrived at the encounter threatened from the other side and traumatized as a result of the continuing violent encounters between the sides (I. Maoz, 2000a).

Qualitative analysis of major themes that were shared repeatedly during the workshop process showed that against the background of these negative emotions and experiences, the workshops' dialogical encounters enabled the youth to interact on a personal level. Processes of attitude change toward more favorable perceptions of the other side, based on the personalized interaction with the Palestinians, were prominently described by the Jewish-Israeli participants. Quotes from interviews conducted with Jewish-Israeli participants included (I. Maoz, 2000a):

> "The encounter showed me that the media are not always accurate, and that there are also human beings there, not like they describe them."

> "It is enough that I understood following the encounter that not all are mad and crazy like on the television. That there are people that are willing to speak logically."

> "In the beginning of the encounter, we generalized that all Palestinians are murderers, all are stone throwers, all are haters of Israel, but they showed the opposite side from what we thought."

> "I thought they were all against peace. This is what you see on television and at home. You grow up in a society where they say that

Palestinians are bad; that they all are the same. The media relayed to us only the negative things. Here I saw that they are really similar to us, identical. The same dreams, only that they live like in jail."

The Palestinians concentrated more on changing Israelis' perceptions of them, and of the conflict between the sides, so that the Jewish-Israeli would view Palestinians less as terrorists and more as individuals, and would understand and develop empathy toward the Palestinians' claims in the conflict (I. Maoz, 2000a).

Similar to the qualitative results, the quantitative results of the pre-post comparisons showed that after participation in the workshops, Israeli-Jews' perceptions of Palestinians became significantly more favorable; in addition, there was a significant favorable change in the attitudes of Palestinians toward Jews. There was a significant change for one of the two sides for each attribute reported here. Both Jews and Palestinians viewed each other as more "considerate of others," "tolerant," and "good-hearted" after participating in the workshop than before it. Specifically, Palestinians rated Israelis as significantly more considerate of others after the workshop than before it (before $M = 2.25$; after $M = 2.89$; $t(46) = 3.22$, $p < .002$), more tolerant (before $M = 2.22$; after $M = 2.89$; $t(45) = 3.61$, $p < .001$), and more good-hearted (before $M = 2.23$; after $M = 2.83$; $t(46) = 3.03$, $p < .004$). Similarly, Israelis rated Palestinians as significantly more considerate of others after the workshop than before it (before $M = 2.91$; after $M = 3.45$; $t(50) = 3.98$, $p < .001$), more tolerant (before $M = 2.69$; after $M = 3.65$; $t(51) = 5.61$, $p < .001$), and more good-hearted (before $M = 3.02$; after $M = 3.73$; $t(51) = 4.36$, $p < .001$). These attributes, on which favorable attitude change was found for both national groups, are directly relevant to processes of reconciliation and creating cooperative relations between the two sides, as more favorable perceptions of the other side's disposition toward others are essential for improving relations between groups in conflict.

In addition to the above attitude changes found for both Israeli-Jews and Palestinians, there were some favorable attitude changes demonstrated only for the Jewish participants. The results showed that following the workshop, Jewish participants also viewed Palestinians more favorably than before the workshop on attributes such as honest (before $M = 2.77$; after $M = 3.31$; $t(51) = 3.81$, $p < .001$), intelligent (before $M = 2.88$; after M = 3.65; $t(50) = 4.86$, $p < .001$), broad-minded (before $M = 2.90$; after $M = 3.46$; $t(49) = 3.13$, $p < .003$), open to change (before $M = 2.67$; after $M = 3.31$; $t(50) = 4.16$, $p < .001$), and willing to sacrifice for peace (before M = 2.65; after $M = 3.25$; $t(51) = 3.23$, $p < .002$) (I. Maoz, 2000a). Again, these attributes are highly relevant to building peace and cooperation between the sides.

Although the statistical findings showed positive attitude change on both sides following the encounter, there are differences in the degree of change demonstrated between Israeli-Jews and Palestinians. Jews showed significant favorable attitude change on eight dimensions in comparison to three dimensions for Palestinians. In addition, before-participation means showed that Palestinians arrived to the encounter holding more negative attitudes toward Jews than Jews held toward Palestinians (significant at $p < .01$) on the attributes of good-hearted, considerate, and willing to sacrifice for peace. Thus, in spite of the significant improvement of attitudes, Palestinian attitudes toward Jews following the encounter still remained quite negative in most of the dimensions assessed, and certainly more negative than the post-encounter attitudes of Jews toward Palestinians. This pattern of more favorable attitude change following the encounter in Jewish participants than in Palestinian participants suggests that the group dialogue experience was more effective in influencing the Israeli-Jewish majority, the group that holds more power and has more access to resources in the sociopolitical context of the Israeli-Palestinian conflict. Such a finding is consistent with, and would be predicted by, Moscovisi's (1985) dual process theory of social influence. Moscovisi's research on relationships between majorities and minorities showed that there is an expected influence of majorities in groups (in our case, the Israeli-Jews), but also, in some cases, an even more dramatic process of minority influence (in our case, the Palestinians) on majority group members. Moscovisi's studies and those conducted by others (e.g., Crano, 1994; Ellis & Maoz, 2002), found that minorities exert significant influence and affect attitude change in majority group members by confronting, challenging, and educating them. Consistent with the findings of our study, research on majority-minority influence processes has found that in certain cases, especially when conflict is discussed between the two groups, majority group members are more influenced by the interaction with the minority group than vice versa (I. Maoz 2000b, 2000c; Moscovisi, 1985).

CONCLUSION

The results of this work provide evidence that transformative dialogue group meetings are important in establishing the grounds for the members of the sides in acute conflict to understand each other and to cooperate (I. Maoz, 2000a). More specifically, our study demonstrates that such group facilitation is effective even under the conditions of extreme conflict that still exist between Israeli-Jews and Palestinians. These data also suggest that for dialogues to actually have a positive impact on intergroup relations, they should follow certain principles of effective facilitation and organization. Moreover, it is important that participants have equal status and standing within the confines of dialogue, a condition that leads them to confront the possibilities of relationships, communities, and nations. Such group facilitation encourages discussion that moves the theoretical ideas of equality and justice to a practical basis. When people begin on unequal footing but come together to confront their past, they end up examining the very issues of democracy. These facilitated dialogues, thus, create a space for members of diverse communities to live and work together in a manner that sustains everyone.

REFERENCES

Abu-Nimer, M. (1999). *Dialogue, conflict resolution, and change: Arab-Jewish encounters in Israel*. Albany: State University of New York Press.

Adams, M., Bell, L. A., & Griffin, P. (1997). *Teaching for diversity and social justice: A sourcebook*. New York: Routledge.

Adwan, S., & Bar-On, D. (2000). *The role of non-governmental organizations in peace building between Palestinians and Israelis*. Jerusalem, Israel: Peace Research Institute in the Middle East.

Allport, G. W. (1954). *The nature of prejudice*. Reading, MA: Addison-Wesley.

Amir, Y. (1976). The role of intergroup contact in change of prejudice and ethnic relations. In P. A. Katz (Ed.), *Towards the elimination of racism* (pp. 245-308). New York: Pergamon Press.

Arnett, R. C., & Arneson, P. (1999). *Dialogic civility in a cynical age: Community, hope, and interpersonal relationships*. Albany: State University of New York Press.

Arthur, P. (1999). The Anglo-Irish peace process: Obstacles to reconciliation. In R. L. Rothstein (Ed.), *After the peace: Resistance and reconciliation* (pp. 85-110). Boulder, CO: Lynne Rienner.

Avruch, K., & Black, P. (1990). Ideas of human nature in contemporary conflict resolution theory. *Negotiation Journal, 6*, 221-228.

Barge, J. K. (2002). Enlarging the meaning of group deliberation: From discussion to dialogue. In L. R. Frey (Ed.), *New directions in group communication* (pp. 159-177). Thousand Oaks, CA: Sage.

Bar-On, D. (1997). Israeli society between the culture of death and the culture of life. *Israel Studies, 2*, 88-112.

Bar-Tal, D. (1990). Causes and consequences of delegitimization: Models of conflict and ethnocentrism. *Journal of Social Issues, 46*, 65-81.

Beale, R. L., Thompson, M. C., & Chesler, M. (2001). Training peer facilitators for intergroup dialogue leadership. In D. Schoem & S. Hurtado (Eds.), *Intergroup dialogue: Deliberative democracy in school, college, community, and workplace* (pp. 227-246). Ann Arbor: University of Michigan Press.

Bush, R. A. B., & Folger, J. P. (1994). *The promise of mediation.* San Francisco: Jossey-Bass.

Cairns, E., & Hewstone, M. (2002). Northern Ireland: The impact of peace making in Northern Ireland on intergroup behavior. In G. Salomon & B. Nevo (Eds.), *Peace education: The concept, principles, and practices around the world* (pp. 217-228). Mahwah, NJ: Lawrence Erlbaum.

Crano, W. D. (1994). Context, comparison, and change: Methodological and theoretical contributions to a theory of minority (and majority) influence. In S. Moscovici, A. Mucchi-Faina, & A. Maass (Eds.), *Minority influence* (pp. 17-46). Chicago: Nelson-Hall.

Ellis, D. G., & Maoz, I. (2002). Cross-cultural argument interactions between Israeli-Jews and Palestinians. *Journal of Applied Communication Research, 30,* 181-194.

Gergen, K. J. (1999a). *An invitation to social construction.* Thousand Oaks, CA: Sage.

Gergen, K. J. (1999b, May). *Toward transformative dialogue.* Paper presented at the meeting of the International Communication Association, San Francisco, CA.

Hadjipavlou, M. (2002). Cyprus: A partnership between conflict resolution and peace education. In G. Salomon & B. Nevo (Eds.), *Peace education: The concept, principles, and practices around the world* (pp. 193-209). Mahwah, NJ: Lawrence Erlbaum.

Jackson, J. (1993). Contact theory of intergroup hostility: A review of the theoretical and empirical literature. *International Journal of Group Tensions, 23,* 43-65.

Kelman, H. (1995). Contributions of an unofficial conflict resolution effort to the Israeli-Palestinian breakthrough. *Negotiation Journal, 11,* 19-27.

Kelman, H. (1997). Group processes in the resolution of international conflicts: Experiences from the Israeli-Palestinian case. *American Psychologist, 52,* 212-220.

Kriesberg, L. (1991). Conflict resolution applications to peace studies. *Peace and Change, 16,* 400-417.

Kriesberg, L. (1997). The development of the conflict resolution field. In I. W. Zartman & J. L. Rasmussen (Eds.), *Peacemaking in international conflict: Methods and techniques* (pp 51-77). Washington, DC: U.S. Institute of Peace.

Lederach, J. (1998). Beyond violence: Building sustainable peace. In E. Weiner (Ed.), *The handbook of interethnic coexistence* (pp. 182-198). New York: Continuum.

Maoz, M. (1999a). From conflict to peace? Israel's relations with Syria and the Palestinians. *Middle East Journal, 53,* 393-416.

Maoz, M. (1999b). The Oslo agreements: Toward Arab-Jewish reconciliation. In R. L. Rothstein (Ed.), *After the peace: Resistance and reconciliation* (pp. 67-83). Boulder, CO: Lynne Rienner.

Maoz, I. (2000a). An experiment in peace: Reconciliation-aimed workshops of Jewish-Israeli and Palestinian youth. *Journal of Peace Research, 37,* 721-736.

Maoz, I. (2000b). Multiple conflicts and competing agendas: A framework for conceptualizing structured encounters between groups in conflict—the case of a coexistence project between Jews and Palestinians in Israel. *Peace and Conflict: Journal of Peace Psychology, 6*, 135-156.

Maoz, I. (2000c). Power relations in intergroup encounters: A case study of Jewish-Arab encounters in Israel. *International Journal of Intercultural Relations, 24*, 259-277.

Maoz, I. (2002). Conceptual mapping and evaluation of peace education programs: The case of education for coexistence through intergroup encounters between Jews and Arabs in Israel. In G. Salomon & B. Nevo (Eds.), *Peace education: The concept, principles, and practices around the world* (pp. 259-271). Mahwah, NJ: Lawrence Erlbaum.

Maoz, M. (2002). The Oslo peace process: From breakthrough to breakdown. In R. Rothstein, M. Maoz, & K. Shikaki (Eds.), *The Israeli-Palestinian peace process: Oslo and the lessons of failure—perspectives, predicaments, and prospects* (pp 133-148). Brighton, Great Britain: Sussex Academic Press.

Maoz, I., & Ellis, D. G. (2001). Going to ground: Argument between Israeli-Jews and Palestinians. *Research on Language and Social Interaction, 4*, 399-419.

McNamee, S., & Gergen, K. (1999). Relational responsibility. In S. McNamee & K. J. Gergen (Eds.), *Relational responsibility: Resources for sustainable dialogue* (pp. 3-48). Thousand Oaks, CA: Sage.

Moscovici, S. (1985). Social influence and conformity. In G. Lindzey & E. Aronson (Eds.), *The handbook of social psychology* (3rd ed., Vol. 2, pp. 347-412). New York: Academic Press.

Pearce, W. B., & Littlejohn, S. W. (1997). *Moral conflict: When social worlds collide*. Thousand Oaks, CA: Sage.

Pettigrew, T. (1998). Intergroup contact theory. *Annual Review of Psychology, 49*, 65-85.

Pettigrew, T., & Tropp, L. (2000). Does intergroup contact reduce prejudice? Recent meta-analytic findings. In S. Oskamp (Ed.), *Reducing prejudice and discrimination* (pp. 93-114). Mahwah, NJ: Lawrence Erlbaum.

Rothman, J. (1997). *Resolving identity-based conflict in nations, organizations, and communities*. San Francisco: Jossey-Bass.

Rothstein, R. (2002). A fragile peace: Could a "race to the bottom" have been avoided? In R. Rothstein, M. Maoz, & K. Shikaki (Eds.), *The Israeli-Palestinian peace process: Oslo and the lessons of failure—perspectives, predicaments, and prospects* (pp. 1-30). Brighton, Great Britain: Sussex Academic Press.

Rouhana, N., & Bar-Tal, D. (1998). Psychological dynamics of intractable ethnonational conflicts: The Israeli-Palestinian case. *American Psychologist, 53*, 761-770.

Saunders, H. H. (1999). *Public peace process: Sustained dialogue to transform racial and ethnic conflicts*. New York: St. Martin's Press.

Schoem, D., & Hurtado, S. (Eds.). (2001). *Intergroup dialogue: Deliberative democracy in school, college, community, and workplace.* Ann Arbor: University of Michigan Press.

Shikaki, K. (2002). Ending the conflict: Can the parties afford it? In R. Rothstein, M. Maoz, & K. Shikaki (Eds.), *The Israeli-Palestinian peace process: Oslo and the lessons of failure—perspectives, predicaments, and prospects* (pp. 37-46). Brighton, Great Britain: Sussex Academic Press.

Strauss, A., & Corbin, J. (1990). *Basics of qualitative research: Grounded theory procedures and techniques.* Newbury Park, CA: Sage.

Sunwolf, & Frey, L. R. (2001). Storytelling: The power of narrative communication and interpretation. In W. P. Robinson & H. Giles (Eds.), *The new handbook of language and social psychology* (pp. 119-135). London: John Wiley & Sons.

6

FACILITATING DIALOGUE AND DELIBERATION IN ENVIRONMENTAL CONFLICT

THE USE OF GROUPS IN COLLABORATIVE LEARNING

Gregg B. Walker
Oregon State University

Steven E. Daniels
Utah State University

Anthony S. Cheng
Colorado State University

Travel west from Denver, Colorado, and within two hours you will be surrounded by the White River National Forest (WRNF). As its Web site announces:

> The two and one-quarter million acre White River National Forest is located in the heart of the Colorado Rocky Mountains. The scenic beauty of the area, along with ample developed and undeveloped recreation opportunities on the Forest, accounts for the fact that the White River consistently ranks as one of the top five Forests nationwide for total recreation use. (U.S. Department of Agriculture-Forest Service, 2002)

Since 1997, the staff of the WRNF has engaged in a comprehensive planning process—the revision of the WRNF management plan. When the WRNF planning team released its draft plan in 1999 for public comment, "It was hailed as a precedent that would steer the agency [the Forest Service] toward emphasizing endangered species habitat and conservation over resource extraction and recreation" (Clarren, 2002, p. 3). After five years of planning; a cost of $5 million; dozens of presentations to groups, issue identification ("scoping") meetings, and open houses; and 14,000 comment letters, the final management plan has generated criticism from all sides. As Clarren reported, "In the several weeks since the [final] plan's release, wildlife and wilderness advocates, recreationists and water users have spouted enough rhetoric to dampen the 1,200 page document" (p. 3). The WRNF management staff observed that "the plan tries to give all sides a little bit . . . .'The fact that nobody thinks they got everything they wanted usually says we struck a good balance,' says Martha Ketelle, Supervisor of the White River National Forest" (Clarren, p. 3).

The WRNF land management planning situation reveals something seemingly inherent in major environmental and natural resource decision-making situations: conflict. As a conflict-laden, decision-making situation, the WRNF planning process and its outcome seem typical of environmental conflicts.

In this chapter, we address the arena of environmental conflict and the role that group communication facilitation can play in its management or resolution. We focus, in particular, on Collaborative Learning, a group-based approach developed to work through environmental and natural resource management conflict and decision-making situations.[1] We describe facilitated group activities we have used as part of Collaborative Learning applications and report data related to these activities. We conclude the chapter by noting the importance of group communication tasks in collaborative environmental decision-making and conflict resolution projects.

DEFINING ENVIRONMENTAL CONFLICT

In attempting to define "environmental conflict," Blackburn and Bruce (1995) asserted that "environmental conflict arises when one or more parties

---

[1]The term "collaborative learning" appears frequently in the education literature. We have not taken this term from the education arena nor have we drawn on the collaboration learning literature in education as a foundation for the theoretical or applied dimensions of our approach. We selected the term because it represents well the integration of systems thinking, working together, active learning, and managing conflict as part of an adaptive decision-making and management approach.

involved in a decision-making process disagree about an action that has potential to have an impact upon the environment" (pp. 1-2). Burgess and Burgess (1995) proposed that "environmental conflict refers to long-term divisions between groups with different beliefs about the proper relationship between human society and the natural environment" (p. 102).

These definitions reveal that environmental conflict involves some degree of incompatibility between groups of people arising from issues related to the environment rather than some other form of interpersonal or organizational conflict that merely happens to have arisen in the context of environmental decision making. The issues and incompatibilities in an environment conflict, as Crowfoot and Wondolleck (1990) noted, are "rooted in different values of natural resources and environmental quality, . . . incited by different stakes in the outcome of environmental and natural resource management decisions," and can be caused by "the uncertainly surrounding various environmental actions, and the different assessments of the risks associated with these actions" (pp. 6-7). Crowfoot and Wondolleck's insights, coupled with definitions of environmental conflict, imply two fundamental dimensions of environmental conflict: complexity and controversy.

Complexity

There may be no conflict setting more complex than environmental policy. Faure and Rubin (1993) identified a number of "distinctive attributes" of environmental negotiations: multiple parties and multiple roles, multiple issues, meaningless boundaries, scientific and technical uncertainty, power asymmetry, joint interest, negative perceptions of immediate outcomes, history, long time frame, changing actors, public opinion, institutionalization of solutions, and new regimes and rules. Consistent with these attributes, Daniels and Walker (2001) proposed seven sources of environmental conflict complexity: multiple parties, multiple issues, cultural differences, deeply held values and worldviews, scientific and traditional knowledge, legal requirements, and the presence of a conflict "industry" (people, organizations, or professions that may benefit from the persistence of conflict rather than its resolution; see also Walker, 2001).

The WRNF land management planning situation exhibits the sources of complexity Daniels and Walker (2001) identified, with a number of sources particularly salient. First, numerous parties—environmental organizations, motorized and nonmotorized recreation groups, local businesses, ski-area operators, timber and mining interests, and government officials—are concerned about WRNF management issues. Second, as the WRNF plan revision documents reveal, the planning process addresses a wide variety of issues related to human activity, biological diversity, ecosystem health, and economic vitality. Third, interests and positions regarding substantive issues reflect differences among cultural communities, such as urban and rural residents, younger and older generations, and those with modest versus high incomes. Fourth, the various groups and cultural communities involved in the WRNF situation hold strong values about place (e.g., a specific geophysical site) and the relationship of humans to the natural world. For example, local businesspersons may value the WRNF for its economic benefits, via tourism and commodity extraction, whereas a nonmotorized recreation group (such as birders or hikers) may associate natural beauty, quiet, and spirituality with the National Forest. Lastly, the many parties involved can pursue their often divergent goals and act on their different values in a variety of ways, such as by lobbying legislative leaders, appealing and litigating management decisions, protesting publicly, and participating in public involvement activities such as meetings and letter writing.

Both Faure and Rubin (1993) and Daniels and Walker (2001) concluded that given the complexity of environmental conflicts and negotiations, traditional alternative dispute resolution (ADR) practices, such as two-party mediation or conciliation, may not apply. Conventional ADR has focused on two-party situations and typically featured settlement-driven, problem-solving mediation. Just as this conventional ADR may display limitations in community and family mediation (Bush & Folger, 1994), its dominant approaches (e.g., arbitration and problem-solving mediation) do not account well for complex, fluid conflict situations that include many stakeholders. Instead, innovative approaches appropriate for multiparty situations need to be considered.

Controversy

In addition to their complexity, environmental conflict and decision-making situations are typically controversial for a variety of reasons. First, many different viewpoints exist concerning the array of issues in such situations. Second, tension or incompatibility between the parties in such situations may arise due to one or more of the following: contested facts, cultures, values, jurisdiction, history, personalities, relationships, and procedures (Daniels & Walker, 2001; Wehr, 1979). Third, parties often hold strong emotional ties to the issues and to the landscape (Brandenberg & Carroll, 1995; Cantrill & Senecah, 2001). Fourth, parties may display cognitive biases, such as overconfidence, fixed pie, and insufficient anchor adjustment, which contribute to competitive frames (Bazerman, 2002; Daniels & Walker, 2001). Fifth, in light of the previous four factors, the number of parties, varied sources of tension, and deeply held values, consensus may be very hard if not impossible to achieve.

The WRNF land management situation certainly demonstrates controversy. For example, citizens, interest groups, public officials, and government planners voice varied opinions about how the WRNF should best be managed and utilized. These divergent views may rely on different interpretations of WRNF "facts," such as recreation use statistics, economic benefit estimates, and habitat quality indicators. Not surprisingly, as Clarren's (2002) *High Country News* article on the WRNF management situation illustrated, consensus among the parties involved has remained elusive.

Policy decision-making processes need to be responsive to the complexity and controversy of environmental and natural resource management situations, such as the WRNF case. Although many decision-making methods exist (for reviews, see Daniels & Walker, 1999; Walker & Daniels, 1997), one approach that has been developed specifically to address complexity and controversy is Collaborative Learning.[2]

ADDRESSING COMPLEXITY AND CONTROVERSY: COLLABORATIVE LEARNING

Within the natural resource and environmental policy arenas, agencies and stakeholders are increasingly looking to collaboration and consensus-building processes for conflict resolution and decision making (Wondolleck & Yaffee, 2000). Collaborative Learning (CL) is one of many innovative approaches that may better meet natural resource and environmental policy public participation, conflict resolution, and decision-making needs than traditional public involvement activities.

As a facilitated approach that relies on small and large group interaction, CL seems particularly applicable to natural resource management, environmental policy, and other public policy arenas because it: (a) explicitly adopts a systems approach to a problematic situation and works to improve participants' understanding of it; (b) is more modest in its expectations for progress than the more frequently employed rational-comprehensive models

---

[2]Our development of Collaborative Learning began in 1991, with the first environmental conflict application occurring in Spring 1992 in southwestern Oregon. When we considered how to integrate systems thinking, conflict management, and experiential learning, we sought a name for our approach that emphasized collaboration. We considered labeling our approach "collaborative inquiry," but wanted the term "learning" in the name. We were optimistic that, even in challenging environmental conflict situations, people would not oppose learning.

that seek solutions; (c) expects and attempts to accommodate a wide range of worldviews about the relevant policy arena and the strategic behaviors that those worldviews are likely to generate in controversial situations; (d) utilizes a number of techniques to integrate technical (scientific) and traditional (indigenous, local) knowledge and, thereby, bring scientists and citizens together (Walker & Daniels, 2001); and (e) emphasizes constructive individual and group communication through dialogue, argument, and negotiation—the core of public deliberation and civic discovery (see Reich, 1988). The following sections explain the foundations of and the three levels associated with CL.

Collaborative Learning Foundations

CL draws on systems thinking and conflict management/ADR; systems thinking addresses complexity, whereas conflict management/ADR address controversy. More precisely, CL is a hybrid of soft systems methodology (SSM), experiential and adult learning theories, and the ADR areas of conflict resolution, mediation, and negotiation. Key notions of CL include:

- Redefining or reframing the task away from solving a problem to one of *improving a situation.*
- Viewing the situation as a set of *interrelated systems* as opposed to a linear cause-effect problem.
- Defining improvement as *desirable and feasible change* rather than simply a good idea. CL is action oriented but not solution driven; actions appear as implementable improvements rather than as solutions, improvements that emerge from the interaction among parties or stakeholders.
- Recognizing that *considerable mutual learning* about matters such as scientific information, substantive issues, and value differences will have to occur before implementable improvements are possible. Mutual learning emphasizes that all parties interact as teachers and learners rather than granting privilege to "experts" in an "inform and educate" setting. (Walker, 2001)

SSM provides the foundation for the emphasis on systems thinking and analysis in CL. Developed by Checkland (1981; see also Checkland & Scholes, 1990) and refined by Wilson and Morren (1990), SSM views environmental and natural resource management problems as "situations" comprised of "human activity systems." By focusing on environmental conflicts as human activity systems situations, CL encourages participants involved in such a conflict or decision-making situation to work through the situation's complexity by thinking systemically about the conflict at hand. From conflict management and ADR, CL incorporates communication methods designed to promote collaborative, mutual-gains negotiation. By respecting value differences, CL approaches provide opportunities for transforming positions into interests (Fisher & Ury, 1991). Systems thinking and conflict management/ADR principles and practices are brought together in an experiential learning environment (Kolb, 1984; Senge, 1990). By combining features of SSM and conflict management/ADR with an active, experiential learning emphasis, CL promotes *working through* issues and perspectives of a conflict situation (Daniels & Walker, 2001).

The Three Levels of Collaborative Learning

CL operates at three levels: philosophy, framework, and tactics or techniques. First, as a *philosophy*, CL emphasizes a particular orientation about what people's goal ought to be when engaging public policy or environmental conflict at a community level. Second, CL is a *framework* of five phases that comprise components of a comprehensive application. Third, CL features a *set of tactics* that have been used repeatedly by practitioners when trying to bring the philosophy and framework of CL to life in community-based facilitated projects. By looking at these three levels, we begin to understand both the intellectual roots of the approach and what it would look like in actual practice.

The Philosophy of Collaborative Learning

When we began to develop CL in 1991 within the environmental context, we sought to characterize environmental and natural resource conflicts in terms of a series of attributes. These attributes, in turn, gave rise to the following series of statements that began to define the following types of situations in which CL would have a high likelihood of making progress and having a positive impact:

1. *The task is to manage conflict, not resolve it.* Whereas much of the negotiation and mediation literature identifies the resolution of conflict as its primary goal and orientation, CL differs from that view by assuming that conflict is an ongoing inherent aspect of our civic lives and is endemic to public policy and environmental decision-making processes.

2. *People must make important decisions in the face of long-lived and deeply held values.* As a public policy arena, deep-seated values permeate natural resource and environmental management decisions (Daniels & Walker, 2001). Whether one's orientation is environmental protection or resource extraction/production, all parties involved in natural resource and environmental policy decision making seem to hold strong opinions that are derived from their core values. Consequently, CL presumes that the complex and controversial natural resource and environmental issues people face require confronting rather than avoiding the diversity of represented views.

3. *Consensus is not the only metric of satisfaction or success.* Attaining unanimous consent or agreement for environmental decisions may be problematic as a matter of principle. Many critiques of the community-based conservation efforts in recent years focus on the use of consensus as *the* metric of an acceptable outcome (e.g., Bingham, 1986; Wondolleck & Yaffee, 2000). Community-based collaborations that are consensus based generally grant a measure of veto power to each of the participants in the process; as a result, their "collaboration" may yield only lukewarm and tepid proposals that are acceptable to everyone in the room. It is, thus, unlikely that innovative or progressive strategies will emerge from such a consensus-based project (Wondolleck & Yaffee, 2000).

4. *Progress results from improvements rather than from solutions.* In environmental policy situations, there are significant constraints that are beyond the participants' ability to control. For instance, state and federal laws must be followed and may constrain decision alternatives. Natural factors are also inherent; for example, salmon restoration policies in the Pacific Northwest must account for conditions in the open ocean that have considerable effects on the viability of salmon populations. Because parties have limited control in many of these kinds of situations, invoking a "solution" frame may set them up for failure. However, giving parties the charge of "making progress" encourages them to identify and focus their efforts on those areas in which they do have some degree of control and self-determination. In our experience, asking people to solve the overall environmental problem of a community, watershed, or county tends to paralyze them in the face of overwhelming complexity, but if they are charged with making progress, they are able to generate a surprisingly large number of improvements, all of which collec-

tively constitute a tremendous amount of good work and forward-looking innovation.

5. *Improved decisions result from mutual and meaningful learning.* This fundamental feature distinguishes CL from many other approaches. Many formal public participation approaches are based in a legalistic orientation where improved decisions are presumed to be the result of adhering to a legally prescribed series of steps. In contrast, CL takes the philosophical orientation that mutual, shared learning provides the fundamental foundation for making high-quality decisions.

The Framework of Collaborative Learning

The goal of CL is to create opportunities for meaningful civic dialogue and deliberation, leading to good decisions. To do so, a comprehensive CL application to an environmental conflict situation features a two-dimensional framework, as illustrated in Figure 6.1. The outer circle presents the five

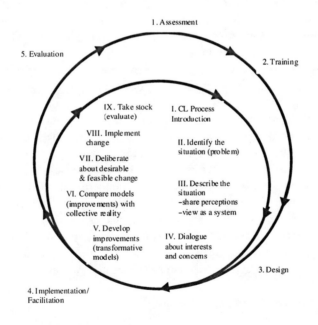

Figure 6.1. Collaborative Learning project phases and process stages.
Source: Daniels, S. E., & Walker, G. B. (2001). *Working through environmental conflict: The collaborative learning approach.* Westport, CT: Praeger, p. 18. Copyright ©2001 by Greenwood Publishing Group, Inc. Used by permission of Greenwood Publishing Group, Inc.

phases of a CL project: assessment, training, design, implementation and facilitation, and evaluation; the inner circle portrays the nine *stages* of a CL project, the first seven of which are addressed in a CL workshop.

Taken together, the five phases constitute a comprehensive CL *project* and the specific techniques featured in the design and implementation/facilitation phases define the CL workshop *process* core (Daniels & Walker, 2001). *Assessment* features a thoughtful evaluation of the potential for collaboration in a particular situation. *Training* emphasizes the development of an appreciation for collaboration among key organizational employees and stakeholders, as well as some grounding in the specific skills and techniques of CL. *Design* centers on the development of a situation-responsive strategy (e.g., CL community workshops) for involving participants in a meaningful collaborative process. *Implementation/facilitation* involves the direct conduct of meetings, field trips, workshops, and other activities designed to promote mutual learning; innovative, constructive debate; and decision making. Finally, *evaluation* includes gathering and reflecting on data to learn from participants what choices they made during the collaboration and what lessons can be learned for future collaborative projects.

As a public participation or planning team approach, CL encourages participants to acknowledge and work though conflict, think systemically, and learn from one another about a particular problem situation. The first few stages of a CL community-based, citizen workshop process (the inner circle of the figure) emphasize common understanding of the situation at hand; activities might include exchanging information, imagining best and worst possible futures, and constructing visual representations of the situation, perhaps through the use of "situation maps," an activity specifically designed to encourage workshop participants to view the situation as a system (Walker & Daniels, 2001). In the middle stages, CL participants focus on their concerns and interests regarding the specific situation, and how those concerns and interests relate to the concerns of other citizens; from those concerns, CL parties identify possible changes that could be made, termed "situation improvements." In latter stages, participants debate these improvements, addressing whether they represent desirable and feasible changes in the present situation. Following the workshop, agreed-on improvements are implemented and subsequently evaluated.

Tactics of Collaborative Learning

CL operates as both a philosophy and a framework, yet its real value is in its application. As of mid-2003, CL principles have been used to guide decision-making processes on some 9,000,000 acres of land administered by the U.S. Department of Agriculture's (USDA) Forest Service spread between

Pennsylvania and Alaska. Through our applications of CL, as well as our CL training programs for federal and state natural resource management agency personnel and organizational leaders, we have identified a variety of tactics or specific techniques that seem quite consistent with the philosophy and framework of CL (for a detailed discussion of these tactics or techniques, see Daniels & Walker, 2001). Key tactics include situation maps to promote systems thinking, guidelines or ground rules to foster constructive interaction, and worksheets as a basis for discussion.

The techniques employed as part of CL activities embody the following two tactical goals:

1. *Create a comfortable and safe environment for learning and interaction.* CL workshops bring people together to discuss issues about which they feel very strongly. Participants are often grounded in conventional public meeting experiences (e.g., public hearings and open houses) that typically foster heated, adversarial exchanges. To counter such behavior, CL emphasizes the construction of a safe environment for engaging in dialogue and learning by employing ground rules similar to mediation (see, e.g., Moore, 1996). CL workshops feature tactics such as selecting neutral sites for meetings, providing food, ensuring ample time for discussion, using round tables for participant interaction, and taking field trips that get participants out onto the land.

2. *Foster both dialogue and deliberation.* The goals of CL are shared understanding, discovering areas of both agreement and disagreement, developing policy improvements, and making good decisions. The generation of improvements—desirable and feasible actions or changes—hinges on constructive communication (Daniels & Walker, 2001; Walker & Daniels, 2001), which takes different forms at various stages in the CL cycle. In the early stages of a CL workshop process (see Figure 6.1)—when the goals are understanding the situation, viewing the situation systemically, and identifying concerns and interests—communication takes the form of dialogue. As dialogue, participant interaction is very open, with all ideas considered and respected; disagreement and comparative analysis is minimal and appears principally as inquiry. As participants in a CL process begin to generate improvements, their dialogue evolves into deliberation. Deliberative interaction is more decision oriented, with disagreement, constructive argument, comparisons, and discussion of priorities more likely to occur here than in the earlier dialogue period. As CL participants' interaction evolves from dialogue into

deliberation, they refine improvements, become advocates for actions, and decide what improvements can and should be implemented.

CL workshops use issue presentations, such as short talks given by agency specialists, to get information moving between experts and the general public, as well as among different interest groups. CL workshops employ active learning exercises based on physical and cognitive maps, the latter often as a situation map (Daniels & Walker, 2001), history wall (see Cheng, 2002), and/or computer simulation—whatever techniques help participants to acquire a deeper understanding of the issues at hand. Workshop participants often outline their ideas initially on a worksheet, which allows them to reflect quietly and thoughtfully on their ideas. By building a series of questions into the design of a specific worksheet, CL facilitators guide participants toward the more vexing aspects of the situation. The worksheet also provides a way for quiet and reserved participants to get their ideas into the mix, whereas at traditional hearing-style meetings, only the most vocal participants are recognized. Agency planning teams have also found that the worksheet technique provides more thorough and useful information than typically arrives through comment letters.

Dialogue and deliberation are fostered through "progressive discussion." Specifically, after CL workshop participants complete a worksheet about concerns, improvements, or similar matters, they form discussion pairs or groups in which each person shares his or her worksheet ideas with the other person(s). Discussion pairs evolve into larger groups of four to six or eight, where the ideas are shared and discussed further. Within these discussions, active listening, questioning, and voicing of different points of view are respected. People clarify and refine their improvements through dialogue. CL, thus, emphasizes "talking with" rather than "talking at." Through such progressive discussion, everyone's ideas are addressed and refined without rewarding the types of adversarial advocacy demonstrated at conventional public meetings (Walker, 2002).

In first-level or early-stage CL workshops (stages 1-4), participants' dialogic interaction does not require making decisions; instead, every person's concerns and improvements are acknowledged, respected, and discussed. A later-stage or second-level CL workshop emphasizes deliberative interaction, in which participants refine improvements by debating their desirability and feasibility and deliberating about what improvements should be implemented, how, and when; in doing so, workshop parties test ideas and make decisions.

THE USE OF GROUPS AND FACILITATION IN COLLABORATIVE LEARNING

As the discussion of tactics reveals, CL applications, particularly in the workshop process, rely on group activities. Small groups are a particularly important component of CL citizen workshops. Although CL workshops employ large group activities, as explained below, much of the meaningful learning occurs through small group interaction, where citizens communicate their concerns and talk about improvements or actions they propose.

Use of Large and Small Groups

CL workshops feature working in both large and small groups. Issue presentations, history time lines or walls, and situation maps are typically large group activities that involve all participants. For example, we have conducted situation mapping exercises at CL workshops with 15-120 participants. In such settings, we give each participant a "draft" situation map (one that is incomplete), place a transparency of the map on an overhead projector, and invite workshop participants, as a group of the whole, to improve the map. With transparency pens in hand, we listen to and record participants' additions to the map. This activity generally takes 45-60 minutes, with as many as 25 citizens suggesting changes to the map.

Worksheet activities provide a foundation for small group interaction. Rather than asking discussion groups to record ideas on flip charts, CL workshop participants first individually complete worksheets that identify their values and interests, critical concerns, policy improvement ideas, and action plans (Daniels & Walker, 2001). The worksheets typically include a sequence of questions that encourage participants to work their way through the systemic complexity of the situation being examined. For example, an "improvement" worksheet asks participants to describe their improvement idea, explain why it is desirable, consider how it is feasible, identify possible obstacles to its implementation, and list other parties and issues to which it relates. With their worksheet responses in hand, participants then share their ideas first in pairs and then in small groups.

The "policy improvement team" serves as another important small group element of the CL workshop process. Such teams are generally groups of 6-12 people who "debate" the improvements that CL participants generated at an earlier (first-level or tier) workshop. This activity occurs at a second-level CL workshop (stages 5-7), in which participants argue constructively about the desirability and feasibility of the proposed improvements (Daniels & Walker, 2001).

Large group and small group activities are, of course, interrelated. For example, after participants have worked with a situation map as a large group, they individually complete worksheets on their concerns about the environmental conflict situation they just "mapped." Following a small group discussion of their concerns, participants individually, via worksheets and then collectively again in small groups, develop ideas to improve the management of the situation. These improvements—actions, activities, projects, management plans, and so forth—are developed using questions that connect the improvements to the mapping and concerns activities. A 1-day CL citizen workshop typically culminates in participants writing about and sharing their ideas for improving the situation.

Regardless of the activity and group size, active learning through group interaction is an essential element of CL. Moreover, as explained below, all CL group activities, whether large or small, are facilitated, with facilitators directing the large group experiences and overseeing the small group interactions.

Facilitation of Collaborative Learning

Consistent with at least part of the discussion of facilitation that appears in Frey's introduction to this text, *facilitation* in a CL application refers to an impartial third party providing procedural guidance to group participants to promote competent interactional behavior, information exchange, learning, and collaborative negotiation. Facilitation can be provided by members of the convening party, local citizens (e.g., community mediation staff), and/or professional consultants who may reside outside the local community. In some cases, the facilitator might emerge from the workshop group itself, but if that occurs, the person should enact only the facilitator role (that is, "wear only one hat"). The choice of facilitators should be based on the interrelated factors of impartiality, fairness, and credibility; that is, regardless of who facilitates (e.g., internal, local, or external), CL participants need to view the facilitators as impartial on the issues and possible improvements, fair toward the parties and the process, and credible as skilled facilitators who understand the basic elements of the situation.

No matter what the environmental conflict situation, there are some general features of CL facilitation that include:

- *Do assessment work.* As an initial step in a CL application, both facilitators and project conveners need to develop a fundamental understanding of the environmental conflict situation, which likely includes general knowledge of the substantive issues of the situation and of the key parties involved.

- *Consider participants' needs, the room setting, and media resources.* Participants in a CL process benefit from a comfortable, appropriate work environment.
- *Plan for contingencies.* CL facilitators anticipate challenging (e.g., disruptive) behaviors and develop strategies and tactics for responding to them.
- *Work as part of a facilitation team.* Given the complexity of environmental conflict situations, a facilitation team can typically better direct a CL process than a single facilitator. Workshops may include many different parties and discussion groups may be large; if an individual participant becomes difficult, one facilitator can talk with that person individually as the other facilitator continues to direct the process.
- *Maintain flexibility in the process.* CL facilitators need to adjust things such as worksheet time and discussion group size based on the situation.
- *Employ, model, and monitor basic facilitation skills.* CL facilitators should possess and employ skills that are useful in conflict, team-building, and decision-making situations (for a detailed discussion, see Daniels & Walker, 2001). Key behavioral attributes include patience; active, supportive listening; keeping personal and substantive views in check; continual monitoring of self and others; modeling behaviors; and empowerment and recognition of participants' actions (Bush & Folger, 1994).

FACILITATING COLLABORATIVE LEARNING GROUPS: THREE CASE EXAMPLES

Although we have applied CL approaches in a variety of settings and projects, we focus here on three applications that have been particularly comprehensive and that include data collected from the groups. These cases span a decade and feature CL efforts in Oregon, Washington, and Colorado.

Case Example One: The Oregon Dunes National Recreation Area

The Oregon Dunes National Recreation Area (ODNRA) management situation represents one of the first comprehensive applications of CL in a natural resource management context (Daniels & Walker, 1996). This project included four of the five stages of a CL project: assessment, design, implementation, and evaluation.

Background

In April 1993, the first two authors received a call from the supervisor of the Siuslaw National Forest about holding CL workshops as a component of its new ODNRA draft management plan public participation activities. The ODNRA management process had been underway for more than two years, culminating in a Draft Environmental Impact Statement (DEIS) of alternative management strategies that was released to the public in April, 1993. Before the release of this statement, the Siuslaw National Forest held a public comment period during which it received letters and sponsored open houses on the DEIS alternatives. Many letters were critical of the DEIS's preferred alternative, and the open houses drew a lot of citizens who were upset with the Siuslaw National Forest's tentative plans. The ODNRA and Siuslaw National Forest leadership thought that a series of CL workshops might generate constructive citizen involvement and feedback in ways that other public participation activities had not. After a preliminary assessment of the situation, we decided to develop a CL project as part of the ODNRA public participation process.

The ODNRA consists of a strip of land approximately 40 miles long and, on average, 1.5 miles wide on the central Oregon coast between Florence in the north and North Bend-Coos Bay in the south; in all, there are 31,500 acres within the ODNRA boundary. The dunes system within the ODNRA has been part of the Siuslaw National Forest since 1908, when the Forest was established. By an act of the U.S. Congress, the dunes became a national recreation area in 1972; the legislation stated that the area "is to be administered by the USDA-Forest Service for the purposes of public outdoor recreation use and enjoyment . . . and the conservation of scenic, scientific, historic and other values contributing to the public enjoyment of such land and waters" (Siuslaw National Forest, 1993, p. I-1).

The ODNRA is a multiple-resource, multiple-use area. Major issue areas addressed in the planning process included off-road vehicle (ORV) management (e.g., access, noise, and safety); nonmotorized recreation activities (e.g., hiking, camping, and interpretation); vegetation (particularly non-native European beach grass); threatened/endangered species (e.g., the western snowy plover); wetlands; wild/scenic river designation; user population management; and local community impacts (particularly economic). Of these issues, the presence of ORVs in the ODNRA was the most contentious. Before the planning process, approximately 48 percent of the ODNRA was open to ORVs. The ORV community wanted more of the Dunes opened to motorized recreation; the dominant environmental organization in Oregon wanted ORVs excluded from the ODNRA.

CL workshops were conducted during the summer of 1993 as a supplement to the formal comment period. The workshops "were intended to provide a public forum, involving people with varied interests, in which [participants could] test ideas and develop collaborative suggestions for improvement of several planning issues at the [OD]NRA" (Siuslaw National Forest, 1994, p. 20).

Group Activities

Four CL workshops took place in four different communities. The first three (level one) addressed CL process stages 1-4 and the fourth meeting focused on CL workshop process stages 5-7. Facilitated group activities used included:

1. Large group activities: issue presentations, a panel discussion, a situation mapping exercise, and an improvements "go-round" (reporting out to the large group) at the end of the workshop.
2. Small group activities: concerns and interests worksheets and progressive discussion (1-2-8 persons), improvement worksheets and progressive discussion (1-2-8), and policy improvements analysis teams (groups of 10-12) at the fourth workshop (later-stage, second-tier meeting).

Participants' Evaluation of Facilitated Process and Group Activities

Participants were sent a questionnaire via mail after the first three workshops were completed. The questionnaire resulted in a response rate of 54 percent. Of the 54 survey respondents, 38 had participated in the entire day of a full-day workshop; the remainder attended either the morning or afternoon session only.

The questionnaire included a number of Likert and Likert-type scale items pertaining to the CL workshop process and facilitated group activities; these items were part of a more comprehensive survey of ODNRA CL workshop participants (Daniels & Walker, 1996). Tables 6.1 and 6.2 present the Likert scale results for the relevant items: Table 6.1 features items about the CL workshop process; Table 6.2 focuses on items that address small and large group workshop activities (these results were originally reported in Daniels & Walker, 1996).

As these tables show, ODNRA CL workshop participants clearly wanted an open and accessible public process to be part of ODNRA management planning. Participants reported that the CL workshops fostered open discussion and provided attendees with an opportunity to deliberate about issues and concerns. Participants thought that the group activities were important and valued the presence of outside facilitators.

Table 6.1. Participants' Evaluation of the ODNRA Collaborative Learning Workshop Process.

Item	Mean	SD	N
The ODNRA management process should include activities that involve the public as openly and completely as possible. (1 = SD, 5 = SA)	4.72	.54	50
ODNRA workshops encouraged open discussion and evaluation of ideas. (1 = SD, 5 = SA)	3.96	1.03	48
ODNRA workshops involved the public in ways different from other public meetings. (1 = SD, 5 = SA)	3.96	1.15	46
ODNRA workshops included opportunities for participants to argue constructively about issues, concerns, and recommendations. (1 = SD, 5 = SA)	3.74	1.15	47
Importance of the Collaborative Learning process during the afternoon of the ODNRA workshops. (1 = NI, 5 = HI)	4.31	.84	45
Importance of the use of outside facilitators. (1 = NI, 5 = HI)	4.17	1.29	48
Willingness of Forest Service and other agency employees to participate in the ODNRA workshops (1 = NI, 5 = HI)	4.82	.43	51
Preference for collaborative discussions as a process for achieving ODNRA goals. (1 = SO, 5 = SP)	4.38	.77	47

Note. SD = *Strongly disagree*, SA = *Strongly agree*, NI = *Not important*, HI = *Highly important*, SO = *Strongly opposed*, SP = *Strongly preferred*

Table 6.2. Participants' Evaluation of the ODNRA Collaborative Learning Workshop Group Activities.

Activity	Mean	SD	N
Issue presentations (large group)	4.04	1.04	47
Panel discussion (large group)	2.98	1.20	45
Creating a situation map (large group)	3.26	1.22	38
Identifying concerns and interests about ODNRA issues (small group)	3.92	1.06	39
Developing ODNRA situation improvements	4.09	.98	35

Note. On all items, 1 = *Did not help*, 5 = *Helped greatly*

Most noteworthy was the importance participants placed on active involvement in the workshop of agency (in this case, Forest Service) employees. In the questionnaires, as well as in assessment and evaluation interviews we subsequently conducted with a number of key stakeholders, citizens noted that they wanted agency employees in the discussion groups with them rather than standing at the back of the room observing. In this and in other projects that we have designed and facilitated, citizens and agency personnel alike have consistently reported the value of citizen-agency employee interaction through small and large group workshop activities.

ODNRA workshop survey respondents evaluated the large group and small group activities quite differently. Of the three large group activities, they valued the issue presentations—formal talks given by content experts—more highly than the panel discussion and situation map exercise. Perhaps this preference reflected their prior experience with more formal public meetings, where content is typically conveyed through formal talks given by scientists, agency administrators, and specialists; perhaps they valued the situation map exercise less than the issue presentations because they were experiencing the exercise for the first time.

Respondents evaluated the small group activities very positively. The improvements exercise was the highest-rated activity, perhaps because it was action oriented. Citizens told us during the assessment and evaluation interviews we conducted that they want to accomplish something meaningful when they attend public meetings. The improvements exercise enabled people to generate action ideas that they knew would be considered by the ODNRA planning team.

Case Example Two: Wenatchee National Forest Fire Recovery Planning, 1994-1995

CL workshops took place relatively late in the ODNRA planning process, after a DEIS had been released to the public. In contrast, the first two authors got involved in the Wenatchee National Forest Fire Recovery Planning project at its inception.

Background

For Wenatchee National Forest Service personnel, the summer of 1994 in central Washington started out as a typical season. With its proximity to both the Puget Sound area and to Spokane, recreation activity in the Forest was high. Wenatchee National Forest employees looked forward to the summer, their "project season," when they could do much of their work out on the ground; by the end of that summer, however, "out on the ground" had taken on a much different meaning.

For many years, the risk of fire throughout the forests of central Washington had been building. Fire suppression had been a forest management priority throughout much of the 20th century, and many stands of trees that might have been thinned naturally through fire had become thick with younger trees. Fuel loadings in the Wenatchee National Forest were high, and with another summer of hot weather and drought conditions predicted, forest managers were concerned. Not only was the fire risk genuine but throughout the 1980s and early 1990s, an increasing number of people had built primary or secondary residences in or on the edge of the forest. A fire, Forest Service officials feared, would potentially destroy property and could put people's lives in danger.

Their fears were realized in the summer of 1994. On Sunday evening of July 24, a lightning storm moved east across the Cascade Mountain range of Central Washington. The storm followed in the wake of record-breaking summer temperatures in forests suffering from years of drought-like conditions. It ignited numerous fires; 41 in the Wenatchee National Forest alone. By late July, four significant fires were burning simultaneously in the Chelan County portion of the Wenatchee National Forest: the Tyee Creek Fire, the Rat Creek Fire (which was human caused), the Hatchery Creek Fire, and the Round Mountain Fire. Collectively, the fires burned over 181,000 acres, temporarily closed major highways, destroyed 37 homes, involved over 8,000 firefighting personnel from 25 states, and cost almost $70 million to suppress (Wenatchee National Forest, 1994). Although the fires were generally contained by mid-August, some high-country areas continued to burn through September.

In late August, Wenatchee National Forest managers launched short-term rehabilitation efforts to thwart erosion, reduce the risk of floods, and maintain public safety. As these efforts proceeded, forest-level and ranger district management began to plan for the long-term health of the forests. They realized that rehabilitating the forests required a comprehensive fire recovery planning effort. This effort needed to be grounded in ecosystem-based management, combining the best available scientific knowledge with thorough public involvement. To draw on the best available science, the forest leadership supported the development of a science team organized by the Wenatchee Lab of the USDA-Forest Service Pacific Northwest Research Station. The science team's charge was to incorporate data from these and previous fires to determine management scenarios that would maintain forest ecosystem health.

The forest supervisor, the forest rehabilitation director, and district rangers decided that the fire recovery public involvement situation offered an opportunity for innovation. They recognized that forest restoration activities could be controversial and that different views about fire recovery and forest health created the potential for conflict. Consequently, they decided to employ a CL approach, and solicited our participation to do so.

Group Activities

Six CL workshops took place in three different communities. The first four (level one) featured CL process stages 1-4; the fifth and sixth meetings (level two) focused on CL workshop process stages 5-7, using a worksheet tied to possible planning alternatives. The workshops employed the same facilitated large and small group activities used in the ODNRA process, with three modifications. First, issue presentations took place in a separate meeting on an evening just prior to the day-long CL workshops. The issue presentations were summarized as part of a planning process talk at the CL workshops. Second, no panel discussion took place. Third, the level-two workshops were site specific, focusing on specific areas of the forest, and featured small group interaction throughout.

Participants' Evaluation of Facilitated Process and Group Activities

Participants were surveyed at the end of the 4-day-long CL workshops (see Blatner, Carroll, Daniels, & Walker, 2001). Seventy-two people completed the questionnaire, generating a response rate of approximately 50 percent. The questionnaire included a number of Likert and Likert-type scale items pertaining to the CL workshop process and facilitated group activities; many of these items were patterned after items employed in the ODNRA project (Daniels & Walker, 1996). Tables 6.3 and 6.4 present the results for the relevant items (for more detailed results, see Blatner et al.).

Wentatchee CL workshop process evaluations were similar to the ODNRA results. Participants rated all of the process factors rather highly, particularly the CL activities, the use of external facilitators, and the willingness of Forest Service personnel to participate actively. As was the case with the ODNRA survey results, this last item received the strongest favorable response from workshop participants.

When asked about specific Wenatchee CL workshop group activities, survey respondents rated all of them favorably. Large group issue presentations received the highest rating, but both the concerns/interests small group discussions and the situation improvements small group discussions were seen as being helpful. The situation map large group activity, although viewed positively, received the lowest rating of the group activities. As was the case with the ODNRA project, this evaluation might be attributable to the newness or novelty of this particular exercise.

Table 6.3. Participants' Evaluation of the Wenatchee National Forest Fire Recovery Planning (WNF-FRP) Collaborative Learning Workshop Process.

Item	Mean	SD	N
Constructive communication occurred. (1 = SD, 5 = SA)	4.10	.70	67
WNF-FRP workshops allowed every party's interests to be considered. (1 = SD, 5 = SA)	4.30	.70	70
WNF-FRP workshops involved the public in ways different from other public meetings. (1= SD, 5 = SA)	4.40	.90	66
WNF-FRP workshops included opportunities for participants to argue constructively about issues, concerns, and recommendations. (1 = SD, 5 = SA)	3.90	1.20	68
Importance of the Collaborative Learning process during the WNF-FRP workshops. (1 = NI, 5 = HI)	4.50	.70	70
Importance of the use of outside facilitators. (1 = NI, 5 = HI)	4.50	.80	70
Willingness of Forest Service and other agency employees to participate in the WNF-FRP workshops (1 = NI, 5 = HI)	4.70	.60	71

Note. SD = *Strongly disagree*, SA = *Strongly agree*, NI = *Not important*, HI = *Highly important*, SO = *Strongly opposed*, SP = *Strongly preferred*

Table 6.4. Participants' Evaluation of the WNF-FRP Collaborative Learning Workshop Group Activities.

Activity	Mean	SD	N
Issue presentations (large group)	4.00	.90	56
Creating a situation map (large group)	3.60	1.0	66
Identifying concerns and interests about community specific issues (small group)	3.90	.90	67
Developing community specific situation improvements	3.90	.90	65

Note. On all items, 1 = *Did not help*, 5 = *Helped greatly*

Although the Oregon Dunes and Wenatchee National Forest CL workshops occurred at different points in the overall planning process, participants' evaluations of group-related activities and the process as a whole generally were similar. This may have been due to the similarity in the design of these workshops, as the Wenatchee National Forest project CL workshops were patterned after those employed with the Oregon Dunes planning effort. As with the Wenatchee National Forest project, the final case we present features CL workshops at the outset of a planning effort. Guided, in part, by the efforts of the third author, this project features a different group activity at each one of a series of meetings, as well as progressive group discussion across meetings.

Case Example Three: Landscape Assessments on the Grand Mesa, Uncompahgre, and Gunnison National Forests, 2001-Present

This case describes an ongoing collaborative process occurring on the 3.1-million-acre Grand Mesa, Uncompahgre, and Gunnison (GMUG) Consolidated National Forest in western Colorado. The process, in which the third author is involved, uses a combination of individual, small group, and large group CL activities to simultaneously build competencies for effective public involvement and to produce outcomes that are regarded as scientifically credible and socially legitimate.

The CL process is a central part of the GMUG Core Planning Team's (CPT) landscape assessment, part of a prelude to revision of the forest plan. A *landscape assessment* is a document that describes historic and current conditions, identifies issues and opportunities, defines a range of desired future landscape conditions, sets measurable indicators and outcomes for achieving those future conditions, and proposes management opportunities and actions. In essence, a landscape assessment frames a situation and lays out the basic framework for decision alternatives about projects on a specific landscape; by doing so, it sets the parameters for potential decisions.

The GMUG landscape assessment work is subdivided into five geographic areas, each with its own Landscape Working Group (LWG). The LWGs serve as a forum for bringing together resource specialists and public stakeholders. This is a marked departure from traditional landscape assessments, which are developed primarily by a team of resource specialists and almost exclusively emphasize the biophysical features of the landscape, with little or no collaborative public involvement. The LWGs' work will occur on a 6-month schedule staggered over 18 months. This discussion focuses on the first LWG, the Uncompahgre Plateau Working Group (UPWG).

Landscape Working Group Framework

Because of the size of the Uncompahgre Plateau (1.2 million acres) and related travel distances within that area, two UPWGs have been convened in

the significant communities adjacent to the Plateau: the Norwood/
Naturita/Nucla and Grand Junction/Delta/Montrose communities. The average attendance for each community group has ranged from 40 in
Norwood/Naturita/Nucla to 90 in Grand Junction/Delta/Montrose. To contribute meaningfully to landscape assessment, the UPWG organizing team
has identified five competencies that the group activities used during the
meetings are designed to emphasize and foster:

1. Group management: small group self-facilitation, interpersonal
   communication, ensuring equal participation, and conflict management
2. Inquiry: asking questions and exchanging ideas with and among
   scientists, specialists, local knowledge experts, and other participants
3. Conceptual: systems thinking, especially with respect to understanding and appreciating multiple perspectives on a situation
4. Spatial: identifying geographic locations and potential interrelationships of landscape attributes and values
5. Deliberation: identifying interrelationships of parties, issues, and
   policies; potential overlaps and conflicts; and effectively presenting and justifying viewpoints

The two UPWGs meet every 3-4 weeks and are coordinated by an organizing team. One of the central design features of the working group process
is that every meeting includes small group activities intended to foster dialogue and contribute substantive information to the geographic area assessment. Thus, it is necessary for each discussion table to appoint a participant-
facilitator and to record its contributions. This central design feature has
taken participants a while to get used to, as most are used to participating in
large groups managed by a professional facilitator. On the one hand, using a
professional facilitator frees stakeholders to speak openly; however, in
doing so, stakeholders are under little or no obligation to actively listen and
learn from others in the small group setting. In contrast, via participant facilitation and the trading off of facilitation duties, stakeholders share the
responsibility of creating a group environment where listening and learning
can occur. The development of such self-facilitation skills has proven to be
vital in sustaining meaningful involvement throughout the UPWG process.

Landscape Working Group: Small Group Activities

Each meeting focuses on simultaneously building a set of competencies
among members and contributing substantively to one or more components

of the geographic landscape area assessment. As of June 2002, four UWG meetings have taken place in both locations (eight meetings in total), each involving a unique small group activity. Each activity is described below, followed by data collected from participants (see Table 6.5).

LWG activity one: Shared history timeline. The shared history timeline is employed primarily as an ice-breaker among members, but also to develop a "community history" of the Uncompahgre Plateau. The timeline is designed to foster participants' understanding and appreciation of the many perspectives about the Uncompahgre Plateau and to illustrate that there is no one correct way of defining the Plateau's historic, current, and possible future conditions.

At the first meeting of the UPWG, several large butcher block sheets were posted around the meeting room. Each sheet featured a general timeline; a horizontal line at the very top of the sheet starting from the last Ice Age and ending at the present year. Significant events were provided on the timeline as reference points, such as the establishment of the Forest Service, the Great Depression, the end of World War II, and placing a person on the moon. UPWG meeting participants sat at tables of no more than eight participants. On post-it notes, participants wrote down key events, conditions, and transitions that would contribute to someone's understanding of the Plateau's natural and human history. After sharing their post-it note ideas with other group members, participants attached their notes to one of the posted timelines. Once all post-it notes were attached to the timelines, participants were given an opportunity to walk around and read what others had put up. Following this activity, participants took part in a large group discussion of the timeline material, facilitated by one of the UWG organizing team members.

LWG activity two: Issue identification and prioritization. The LWG CL-based process extends beyond simply providing an opportunity for stakeholders to articulate their issues and concerns, as is typically the case in hearings, open houses, or letter writing. Quite often, public involvement stops at this "feedback" point and the CPT is left to sort through the piles of unorganized issue statements. The LWG process, in contrast, provides public stakeholders with the unique opportunity to work with one another and offers CPT members a chance to identify and prioritize issues using their own words. This narrower set of high-priority issues will then be documented in the final landscape assessment.

Participants at the second UPWG meeting focused on issue identification and prioritization. Eight issue headings derived from a series of focus group interviews that took place prior to the LWG process were used: communi-

Table 6.5. Participants' Evaluation of the Uncompaghre Plateau Working Group (UPWG) Workshop Small Group Activities.

Evaluation Question	History Timeline (N = 143)	Exercise Issue Ident. & Priority (N = 87)	Geographic Mapping (N = 81)	Desired Future Conds. (N = 58)
Your participation in this working group process will contribute to shaping GMUG management priorities.	2.54	3.67	4.05	4.33
You learned something new about the Uncompahgre Plateau landscape tonight.	3.66	3.36	4.01	3.91
Tonight's activity gives you a better understanding of the challenges for managing GMUG.	3.47	3.87	4.16	4.64
Tonight's activity helps clarify different perspectives among stakeholders.	3.59	3.99	4.33	4.43
Tonight's activity helps clarify common perspectives among stakeholders.	3.95	3.33	3.52	4.38
The objective of tonight's activity was clearly explained.	2.64	4.0	4.28	2.47
The pace of tonight's meeting was adequate.	2.91	4.21	4.07	3.93
The objectives of tonight's meeting were effectively achieved.	3.03	4.08	4.06	3.88
Tonight's meeting was a good use of your time.	3.12	4.03	3.89	4.09
Everyone was able to participate equally tonight.	3.85	4.36	4.16	3.76
Tonight's meeting left me feeling energized.	3.06	3.72	3.89	3.79
Tonight's meeting was well-run overall.	3.84	4.26	4.22	4.19

Note. On all items, 1 = *Strongly disagree*, 5 = *Strongly agree*

ty/economy, recreation, special designations, travel/roads, vegetation/ ecosystem health, water, wildlife, and others. Participants chose their eight-person table groups based on their primary issue preference. They identified one or two relevant issues/concerns about the Uncompahgre Plateau, wrote them on post-it notes, and presented the ideas to their table group for discussion. After discussion, participants reviewed all of the issues/concerns and looked for similar themes. The group then selected and prioritized the top 6-10 issues/concerns, recorded them on flip-chart paper, and reported them to the large group.

The final part of the exercise involved all participants. Participants were given seven colored dots and asked to place a dot on the appropriate flip-chart paper for each issue/concern that was the most important to them. They could use all seven dots on one issue or distribute them across various issues. This small group activity was designed to foster group management, inquiry, and conceptual skills. By then asking participants to explain *why* they highlighted a particular issue or concern, they could clarify their own perspectives and gain an understanding of others' perspectives. At the end of the meeting, the stakeholders had identified an extensive list of issues and concerns and had participated in two prioritizing phases, a new experience for many UPWG participants.

LWG activity three: Geographic mapping. Because the LWG process is centered on a series of *geographic* area assessments, the process includes understanding and interpreting broad issues and concerns so that they can be placed on geographic locations. This was achieved at a third UPWG meeting using large, laminated maps of the landscape, colored grease pencils, and post-it notes. Similar to the issue identification and prioritization activity, tables were divided into eight preselected issue topics and participants chose the issue table where they wanted to work. Each group worked with the top six issues and concerns generated from the previous exercise. Group members located sites on the map where each issue or concern occurred; for example, wildlife issues and concerns were written on the wildlife map and recreation issues on the recreation map. Participants could then go from issue table to issue table to work on geographically locating high-priority issues and concerns. This enabled participants to see for the first time the interconnectedness of the landscape.

Products from both the issue identification and prioritization and the geographic mapping small group activities have subsequently been incorporated into three spreadsheet matrices developed by the CPT: aquatics, human dimensions, and terrestrial. Each matrix spreadsheet features stakeholders' issue statements, geographic location, the CPT's interpretation of stakeholder issues, further questions, responsible management authority, and draft desired future condition (DFC) statements corresponding to the issue statement. The spreadsheet matrix displays how stakeholders' input about issues has been interpreted and translated into DFC statements by the CPT; these DFC statements form the critical component of the landscape assessment and will provide the basis for defining plan alternatives.

LWG activity four: Diagramming relationships between desired future conditions and improvements/actions. Developing a range of desired future landscape conditions is the central component of the landscape assessment. Ideally, the DFC statements capture issues and concerns and are based on credible information about historic and current resource conditions. However, translating issues and concerns into DFCs is somewhat of a conceptual leap. Issues and concerns typically refer to a current situation, with implications for the future; defining possible future landscape conditions is typically not a task public stakeholders are asked to do.

The foundation for translating issues and concerns into a range of DFCs is the spreadsheet matrix developed by the CPT; the matrix was presented as a "first cut" of this translation. The exercise was divided into two steps. First, small groups worked through a prepared worksheet that was formatted as a matrix, with column headings of issue statement, why this is an issue, desired condition, and possible improvement/action. Table group participants received a set of worksheets and the spreadsheet matrices developed by the CPT and were asked to focus on at least two issues that they identified in the issue identification and prioritization exercise and to determine if the CPT translation captured the essence of these issues; if it did not, they could reword the DFC statement. The purpose of the activity was not to judge the validity of the issue statements but to evaluate the relative accuracy of the translation to DFC statements. Participants then shared their worksheets with others in their small group.

The second step of the exercise involved the entire UPWG. With members of the organizing team serving as facilitators, each table group was asked to define a DFC and possible improvements or actions that would contribute to achieving it. DFCs were written on butcher block paper. With each successive DFC and improvement/action statement, the facilitators asked the group to define any relationships with other DFCs and with their improvement/action statements. The work generated a diagram with arrows and labels indicating potential positive, adverse, and neutral relationships for achieving DFCs. Through this activity, stakeholders and resource specialists identified and explored relationships and interconnections between DFCs and potential improvements/actions. In this way, public stakeholders could begin to understand and appreciate the challenge of making trade-offs among DFCs and arriving at a feasible set of alternatives. The exercise encouraged participants to employ inquiry, conceptual, and deliberation skills and went several steps further into a collaborative public involvement process than the participants had typically experienced. The CPT plans to employ the diagramming exercise through the rest of the landscape assessment work and into the decision-analysis phases of the planning process.

Participants' Evaluation of Facilitated Process and Group Activities

The small group activities taking place as part of the GMUG's collaborative landscape assessment process have been largely experimental. The average number of participants at each UPWG meeting has stabilized after a slight drop-off from the initial meeting, indicating that public stakeholders view the process as meaningful. However, are the activities having their desired effect and do participants truly perceive their input as being meaningful and contributing to a substantive outcome?

To gauge the relative effectiveness of each set of activities, a 12-item questionnaire has been distributed at the end of every meeting. Table 6.5 displays the summed mean values of participants' responses to items germane to and across the four specific meetings, defined by their primary activity. Although the items differ from those used in the Oregon Dunes and Wenatchee cases, they, too, provide insights about the value of facilitated group process in natural resource management and environmental policy situations.

Several observations emerge from these responses. First, participants are clearly moving from "disagree" to "strongly agree" in response to the item, "Your participation in this working group process will contribute to shaping GMUG management priorities." This shift suggests that participants are likely seeing the overall direction of the LWG process and are responding to it positively. Second, participants are gaining a better understanding of the Uncompahgre Plateau landscape, and an appreciation of the challenges involved in managing GMUG. This understanding and appreciation of the complexity of the management situation are central to collaborative learning among diverse stakeholders because it will lead stakeholders to be less likely to advocate for a single solution or policy position and to recognize that managing a complex situation can entail many possible improvements and actions to reach many possible outcomes.

Third, the initial activities that focus on issues and concerns tend to highlight differences among stakeholders rather than commonalities. Not until the desired future condition activity do participants begin to see common perspectives. If the small group activities stopped at issue identification and prioritization, and geographic mapping, participants would be left with an understanding of one another's differences but would not discover their common ground. Moving toward activities that focus on future conditions, thus, appears to be a critical step in the CL-based LWP process.

Finally, the evaluation questionnaires provide feedback on the quality of activity instructions and facilitation. When participants clearly understand the objectives and instructions of the small group activities, they tend to agree that the meeting and the entire working group process are useful. The questionnaire responses also indicate, however, that there will always be individuals involved who are not completely satisfied with the collaborative process, although, overall, UPWG participants appear to be satisfied with the process thus far. These initial results from the UPWG experience will inform the subsequent LWGs and offer a model for applying CL and engaging stakeholders in small group activities.

DISCUSSION OF RESULTS FROM THE THREE CASES

The small and large group activities that form the basis of a CL application seem to accomplish their intended effects. Specifically, the activities provide participants with opportunities to learn about the situation and understand it more fully, share their voice, build skills, and contribute meaningfully to the substance of natural resource management decision situations.

From the Oregon Dunes and Wenatchee National Forest projects, and the ongoing UPWG process thus far, we draw five tentative "lessons" about group facilitation processes, in general, and the CL approach, in particular. First, group activities, both large and small, seem to achieve their desired effects when participants understand where those activities fit into the specific meeting and the planning process generally. In the Oregon Dunes and Wenatchee projects, such knowledge was provided both in the issue presentations and in the group activities themselves.

Second, group activities must produce tangible products that are clearly incorporated into the policy-decision process. In the ODNRA and Wenatchee cases, citizens saw their ideas addressed in planning documents and in correspondence they received from the Forest Service following the meetings. In the UPWG case, every meeting has generated a paper product that gets posted on the GMUG Web site and is available for distribution. The products are also part of the official administrative record and will be published in all decision documents. The cumulative effect of these products is to demonstrate what, where, how, and why public stakeholder input is being used.

Third, clear description, facilitation, and debriefing of small and large group activities seem essential. The organizing team of a process, such as the LWG, needs to sufficiently prepare and clearly explain instructions to reach a general audience. Facilitators must work to create an environment of open exchange and help participants to draw out clear themes and points without being too heavy-handed. In the UPWG project, for example, the overall objective of the facilitation is to promote discovery, learning, and critical deliberation of issues and future conditions.

Fourth, small group activities should be designed to foster learning about a wide array of topics, skills, and competencies. In the ODNRA and Wenatchee projects, situation mapping and worksheet activities encouraged participants to engage in systems thinking and understanding of the complex and controversial nature of the situations at hand. The basic assumption underlying the UPWG process design is that through group-based learning activities, adults build a knowledge and experiential base germane to the analysis and planning process. In all three applications, meetings emphasized small group work, but varied to the extent that they asked for individual work and large group interaction. In addition, each meeting sought the full involvement of all participants, including having them manage the group. The meeting agendas and activities also moved from one topic to the next without significant redundancies. Together, the meeting design, generally, and group activities, specifically, may foster improved relationships between stakeholders. In the case of the GMUG application, the LWGs are explicitly working partnerships, with a significant amount of effort asked of all involved in the collaborative process.

The fifth and final lesson from these projects is that although some in the community and in agencies may see the small group activities as a tedious and time-consuming public meeting option, those activities are a vital feature of innovative, collaborative public involvement in public lands management decision making. CL and its group activities differ dramatically from traditional public involvement processes, which primarily ask stakeholders only to identify issues, concerns, and ideas; rarely are stakeholders asked to contribute to the prioritization, interpretation, and translation of issues/concerns/ideas into resource management goals, objectives, and actions. Generating such meaningful contributions from public stakeholders takes time and requires a certain amount of skill building for both the stakeholders and the resource specialists. Once stakeholders understand that their contributions are being used to shape substantive outcomes, there is a higher likelihood that they will continue to be engaged in the CL-based process. After decades of conventional public involvement, public lands management stakeholders have been conditioned to participate in a certain manner—oftentimes confrontational and adversarial (Walker, 2002). Working in small groups is one small, but important, step in altering participation behavior towards something more collaborative.

CONCLUSION

Collaborative Learning brings together existing conflict management theories and techniques in new ways. It builds on a foundation of work in environmental mediation and negotiation and complements this foundation with principles and practices from learning and systems theories. The integration of these perspectives provides facilitators, stakeholders, and decision makers with a more robust approach for addressing the complexity and controversy of natural resource and environmental decision making than each perspective would alone. In doing so, Collaborative Learning intentionally attempts to reorient how facilitators, stakeholders, and decision makers address natural resource and environmental policy conflicts.

Group communication is an essential part of a Collaborative Learning strategy. Through both designed and facilitated large and small group activities, parties experience a method for managing conflict rather than seeking to eliminate it. Through group interaction, participants articulate their deep-seated value and opinion differences and recognize the validity of those differences. Once differences are acknowledged and respected, stakeholders can discuss those differences in ways that enhance learning about the situation and that generate meaningful improvements. Collaborative Learning process participants discover that actions can be taken—improvements implemented—without achieving consensus per se. If at the end of a CL process stakeholders have improved their collective understanding of the situation and have developed desirable and feasible changes, progress has been made. In turn, stakeholders with an improved shared understanding of the situation may eventually formulate decisions that would have been previously unimaginable. Although we certainly do not view Collaborative Learning as a quick-fix, "silver bullet" method, we do believe that by using a CL approach, environmental policy and natural resource agencies and their stakeholders can make significant progress toward improving problematic situations.

REFERENCES

Bazerman, M. H. (2002). *Judgment in managerial decision making* (5th ed.). New York: John Wiley.

Bingham, G. (1986). *Resolving environmental disputes: A decade of experience.* Washington DC: Conservation Foundation.

Blackburn, J. W., & Bruce, W. M. (Eds.). (1995). *Mediating environmental conflicts: Theory and practice.* Westport, CT: Quorum Books.

Blatner, K. A., Carroll, M. S., Daniels, S. E., & Walker, G. B. (2001). Evaluating the application of collaborative learning to the Wenatchee fire recovery planning effort. *Environmental Impact Assessment Review, 21*, 241-270.

Brandenberg, A. M., & Carroll, M. S. (1995). Your place or mine? The effect of place creation on environmental values and landscape meanings. *Society and Natural Resources, 8*, 381-398.

Burgess, G., & Burgess, H. (1995). Beyond the limits: Dispute resolution of intractable environmental conflicts. In J. W. Blackburn & W. M. Bruce (Eds.), *Mediating environmental conflicts: Theory and practice* (pp. 101-119). Westport, CT: Quorum Books.

Bush, R. A. B., & Folger, J. P. (1994). *The promise of mediation: Responding to conflict through empowerment and recognition.* San Francisco: Jossey-Bass.

Cantrill, J. G., & Senecah, S. L. (2001). Using the "sense of self in place" construct in the context of environmental policy making and landscape planning. *Environmental Science and Policy, 4*, 185-204.

Checkland, P. (1981). *Systems thinking, systems practice.* New York: John Wiley.

Checkland, P., & Scholes, J. (1990). *Soft systems methodology in action.* New York: John Wiley.

Cheng, A. S. (2002). *Use of small group exercises in collaborative landscape assessments on the Grand Mesa, Uncompahgre, and Gunnison National Forests, Colorado.* Unpublished manuscript, Colorado State University, College of Natural Resources, Fort Collins.

Clarren, R. (2002, July 8). White River forest plan friend to all—and to none. *High Country News*, p. 3.

Crowfoot, J., & Wondelleck, J. (1990). *Environmental disputes: Community involvement in conflict resolution.* Washington, DC: Island Press.

Daniels, S. E., & Walker, G. B. (1996). Collaborative learning: Improving public deliberation in ecosystem-based management. *Environmental Impact Assessment Review, 16*, 71-102.

Daniels, S. E., & Walker, G. B. (1999). Rethinking public participation in natural resource management: Concepts from pluralism and five emerging approaches. In *Pluralism and sustainable forestry and rural development: Proceedings of an international workshop* (pp. 29-48). Rome: Food and Agriculture Organization of the United Nations.

Daniels, S. E., & Walker, G. B. (2001). *Working through environmental conflict: The collaborative learning approach.* Westport, CT: Praeger.

Faure, G-O., & Rubin, J. (1993). Organizing concepts and questions. In G. Sjostedt (Ed.), *International environmental negotiation* (pp. 17-26). Newbury Park, CA: Sage.

Fisher, R., & Ury, W. (with Patton, B.). (1991). *Getting to yes: Negotiating agreement without giving in* (2nd ed.). New York: Penguin Books.

Kolb, D. A. (1984). *Experiential learning: Experience as the source of learning and development.* Englewood Cliffs, NJ: Prentice-Hall.

Moore, C. W. (1996). *The mediation process: Practical strategies for resolving conflict* (2nd ed.) San Francisco: Jossey-Bass.

Senge, P. M. (1990). *The fifth discipline: The art and practice of the learning organization.* New York: Doubleday/Currency.

Siuslaw National Forest. (1993). *Draft environmental impact statement for the Oregon Dunes National Recreation Area management plan.* Corvallis, OR: U.S. Department of Agriculture-Forest Service, Pacific Northwest Region.

Siuslaw National Forest. (1994). *Record of decision: Dunes management plan.* Corvallis, OR: U.S. Department of Agriculture-Forest Service, Pacific Northwest Region.

U.S. Department of Agriculture-Forest Service. (2002). *White River National Forest.* Retrieved December 5, 2002, from http://www.fs.fed.us/r2/whiteriver/

Walker, G. B. (2001). Working through environmental conflict: Citizens' views of collaboration. In C. B. Short & D. Hardy-Short (Eds.), *Proceedings of the Fifth Biennial Conference on Communication and Environment* (pp. 105-123). Flagstaff: Northern Arizona University School of Communication.

Walker, G. B. (2002). The Roadless Areas Initiative as national policy: Is public participation an oxymoron? In M-F. Aepli, J. W. Delicath, & S. P. Depoe (Eds.), *Proceedings of the Sixth Biennial Conference on Communication and Environment* (pp. 31-43). Cincinnati, OH: University of Cincinnati, Center for Environmental Communication Studies.

Walker, G. B., & Daniels, S. E. (1997). Collaborative public participation in environmental conflict management: An introduction to five approaches. In S. Senecah (Ed.), *Proceedings of the Fourth Biennial Conference on Communication and Environment* (pp. 271-289). Syracuse: State University of New York College of Environmental Science and Forestry.

Walker, G. B., & Daniels, S. E. (2001). Natural resource policy and the paradox of public involvement: Bringing scientists and citizens together. *Journal of Sustainable Forestry, 13,* 253-269.

Wehr, P. (1979). *Conflict regulation.* Boulder, CO: Westview Press.

Wenatchee National Forest. (1994, September 12). *Forest information sheet.* Wenatchee, WA: National Forest, Pacific Northwest Region.

Wilson, K., & Morren, G. E. B. (1990). *Systems approaches for improvement in agriculture and resource management.* New York: MacMillan.

Wondolleck, J. M., & Yaffee, S. L. (2000). *Making collaboration work: Lessons from innovation in natural resource management.* Washington DC: Island Press.

7

WHO OWNS THE JAZZ FESTIVAL?
A CASE OF FACILITATED INTERGROUP
CONFLICT MANAGEMENT

Richard W. Sline
Weber State University

> Have a dialogue between the two opposing parts and you will find . . .
> that they always start out fighting each other. . . . As the process of
> encounter goes on, there is a mutual learning until we come to an
> understanding, and an appreciation of difference, until we come to a
> oneness and integration of the two opposing forces. Then the civil
> war is finished, and your energies are ready for your struggle with the
> world.
>
> —Perls (1969, p. 69)

In June 2000, the Park City International Jazz Foundation contracted me as
a consultant to clarify its vision and mission, as well as to analyze and suggest a structure for the Foundation, its Board of Directors, and its operations. Since 1998, the Foundation, a 501(c)(3) nonprofit organization established for the purpose of promoting jazz music through performance and
education opportunities, had produced jazz festivals each August in the ski
resort town of Park City, Utah. Each annual festival, spanning three days of
concerts and workshops, attracted thousands of jazz enthusiasts and had
grown in scope to become an event costing $300,000 in 2000.

I partnered on this project with Anna C. Boulton, Coordinator of
Community-State Partnerships for the Utah Arts Council, who has many

years of experience working with nonprofit arts and cultural organizations. In the discovery process of our consultation, we quickly learned that the underlying core problem facing the Foundation was a basic conflict over ownership and control of its highly successful annual jazz festival. In its relatively brief, 3-year existence, the Fidelity Investment's Park City International Jazz Festival had grown beyond anyone's expectations to become an extremely successful money-making event, attracting nearly 10,000 attendees each year. At the time of our consultation, the ownership of the event (and its significant budget residue) was in dispute between the Foundation, which had originally conceived the Festival, and the Park City Chamber-Bureau, a combined chamber of commerce and convention/visitor/tourism bureau that had been providing the organizational infrastructure necessary to run the event since its inception. The title sponsor of the event, Fidelity Investments Corporation, had provided the Foundation with a special grant to hire a consultant in hopes of resolving this growing conflict by finding some common ground between the parties that could successfully address the interests of the community, the Foundation, and the local businesses that benefited from the Jazz Festival.

Embedded within this substantive intergroup conflict was significant affective conflict (Nicotera, 1997; Walton, 1987) between the Foundation cofounders and the Chamber-Bureau staff person who codirected the Jazz Festival, a conflict that was beginning to interfere with the functioning of the staff and volunteers who produced the festival. What follows is a description of the group communication facilitation we used to help the Foundation and Chamber-Bureau begin to fix their intergroup conflict problems by creating a supportive climate that allowed them to collaborate successfully in the production of their popular annual event.

I begin the chapter with a description of my background and orientation toward organizational communication consulting, which helps to explain our approach to this group communication facilitation project. I then describe the case in detail, beginning with the discovery process used to gather information, followed by our findings, including the two Festival ownership perspectives that emerged, an analysis of the advantages and disadvantages of each perspective, and the recommendations that we made to the Foundation Board. The next section describes the group communication facilitation process we used to report the results and recommendations from our research in a "confrontation meeting" (Beckhard, 1967) involving key Festival stakeholders. I then provide an overall analysis of the facilitation, drawing on relevant literature from intergroup conflict meeting facilitation. I conclude the chapter with a description of the outcomes from this consulting intervention, including an update on the status of the organization two years later.

GROUP PROCESS CONSULTATION

I began my work as a part-time organizational communication consultant in the early 1980s while working as an administrator at the University of Michigan (UM). I was fortunate to become involved with Ron Lippitt Associates, a group of individuals from a variety of disciplines and careers that Lippitt had formed to work with him on community action interventions after his retirement from UM's Institute of Social Research. Lippitt, one of the founders of organizational development (OD), along with one of his associates and my mentor, Kathleen Dannemiller, introduced me to the traditional OD approach to consulting. Organizational development, often referred to as "organizational renewal," involves "the process of initiating, creating, and confronting needed changes so as to make it possible for organizations to become or to remain viable, to adapt to new conditions, to solve problems, and to learn from experiences" (G. L. Lippitt, 1982, p. xiv).

G. L. Lippitt and Lippitt (1986) defined consulting as "a two-way interaction process of seeking, giving, and receiving help aimed at aiding a person, group, organization, or larger system mobilizing internal and external resources to deal with problem confrontations and change efforts" (p. 1). The consulting work we did in the early 1980s was mostly pro bono and was designed to facilitate organizational and community change. Since that time, I have continued both as a paid and a volunteer consultant on a limited basis with for-profit corporations and nonprofit organizations.

My present work as an organizational communication consultant primarily takes the form of process (Schein, 1969) or collaborative (Block, 1981) consulting. Schein (1969) first coined the term "process consulting" to differentiate it from other types of organizational consulting, such as *expert resource consulting*, where a consultant uses his or her expertise to solve a problem for a client, or *pair-of-hands consulting* (Block, 1981), where a consultant is used simply as a tool to implement decisions previously made by a client organization. In contrast, *process consulting* involves helping organizations to solve their own problems by teaching members about their organizational processes, the consequences of those processes, and how to change them if needed (Schein, 1969; see also Milburn, Kenefick, & Lambert, this volume). Schein argued, in particular, that process consultation is most appropriate for interventions designed to confront conflict experienced in groups and organizations, as well as those focused on structural suggestions pertaining to group membership, communication, and the allocation of authority and responsibility.

Consistent with a traditional OD approach, we implemented with the Jazz Foundation four of the six steps of an action research intervention model

(French & Bell, 1984). First, through conducting a precontract interview and subsequent informal conversations held with those who contracted our services, we made a preliminary diagnosis of the problem. Second, we systematically gathered data from the client group to assess and document the nature of the problem. Third, in the facilitation that is described later in the chapter, we provided the Foundation with data feedback, and fourth, analytically led a group composed of key stakeholders through a process of data exploration in a day-long confrontation meeting (Beckhard, 1967). After the confrontation meeting, the group implemented the remaining two steps of the action research model: action planning followed by action execution.

The action research model was first initiated by Kurt Lewin as a means of generating standards for measuring human progress and for enacting social change. Lewin (1946) argued that "realistic fact-finding and evaluation is a prerequisite for any learning" and that "social research should be one of the top priorities for the practical job of improving inter-group relations" (p. 35). Given the intergroup conflict that existed in this nonprofit organization, and the corresponding need for organizational change, the action research model was deemed most appropriate (Coates, 1997). In the case described in this chapter, we used a third-party mediation approach to facilitate a resolution to the intergroup conflict between supporters of the Jazz Foundation and those of the Chamber-Bureau. Third-party mediation focuses on finding a mutually agreeable compromise with respect to the content of the conflict, with improved relationships between the disputing parties hopefully being a by-product of the satisfactory resolution of the conflict (Keashly, Fisher, & Grant, 1993; Putnam & Poole, 1987; Wall, 1981).

THE DISCOVERY PHASE

Data-Collection Methods

We employed four strategies in the discovery phase of the project: (a) document analysis; (b) survey questionnaires completed by Foundation members, Chamber-Bureau staff, and key Festival volunteers; (c) attendance at the Festival; and (d) one-on-one follow-up interviews with Festival stakeholders. First, we analyzed over 20 documents to ascertain information about the Foundation and the Chamber-Bureau. We examined formal documents, including the Articles of Incorporation for both the Foundation and the Chamber-Bureau, Foundation by-laws, Foundation Board of Trustees meeting minutes, Festival sponsorship agreements, Festival profit/loss statements, and Festival employment contracts. In addition, we reviewed informal documents, such as internal and external Foundation and Chamber-Bureau correspondence.

Second, prior to the 2000 Festival, we constructed and sent a questionnaire to 22 Festival stakeholders, including Foundation Board members, staff, and members of the Park City Chamber-Bureau and Festival volunteers, asking respondents open-ended questions about their perceptions of the values, vision, and mission of the Foundation and the Festival. Third, although we both had attended Festival concerts in 1999, we were provided with an "up-close" opportunity to experience many of the events associated with the 2000 Festival, including a benefactor and sponsor prefestival reception, concert performances, educational workshops, and free jazz performances on Park City's historic Main Street. Finally, after the 2000 Festival, I conducted in-depth, semistructured, one-on-one interviews with 19 Festival stakeholders to gain a deeper understanding of the issues identified from the responses to the survey questionnaire.

General Findings

The Park City International Jazz Foundation is an example of a "social enterprise," or "social purpose organization," one of four classes of nonprofit organizations identified by Young (2001). *Social enterprises* are organizations that undertake entrepreneurial projects and commercial activities to advance a social cause or contribute to the public good. Social enterprises are "driven by a mission other than profit making; however, commercial revenue and business activity are seen as strategic means to generate income to support the mission, or to carry out mission-related functions expeditiously" (Young, p. 152). Given its mission "to promote jazz music through performance and educational programs" (Park City International Jazz Foundation, 1997), the Jazz Foundation clearly falls into this category of nonprofit organizations, also referred to as "commercial" nonprofits (Hansmann, 1980, pp. 840-841).

Our attendance at both the 1999 and 2000 Festivals left us extremely impressed with the professionalism of the productions. Indeed, the Festival organizers had presented what appeared to be a very successful event from the perspective of an audience member. On the surface, the Park City Jazz Foundation appeared to be a very successful social enterprise nonprofit organization. However, as one member of the Board said in an interview, "The success of the Festival this year [2000] was beyond our expectations and sometimes in spite of us," referring to the general dysfunction of the Foundation as an organization.

Contrary to research that has found considerable variability in stakeholders' judgments of organizational board effectiveness (e.g., Herman, Renz, & Heimovics, 1997), near unanimous agreement was noted among Jazz Festival stakeholders interviewed about the ineffectiveness of the Jazz Foundation Board. On the basis of what we learned from the discovery phase of the project, we too were appalled at how dysfunctional the Foundation was as a nonprofit organization. For example, several Board members expressed concern about not being kept informed, the lack of meetings, sketchy minutes of the few meetings held, not being consulted on important issues, and not having a chance to review budgets and financial reports. Some of the non-Board members we surveyed didn't even know the Foundation existed until they received our questionnaire. To be blunt, the Foundation was an organization in name only. It was described by many of those interviewed as the "Luke and Andrea show," referring to Luke and Andrea Feldstein, the husband and wife cofounders of the Festival and Foundation, who, along with a small group of supporters, had attempted to maintain close control over the operations of the Festival. It seemed that the rapid success and growth of the Jazz Festival created a set of organizational problems that have plagued other nonprofits with similar fast-growth experiences, including "ill-defined authority, confusion of roles, lack of organization and planning, ineffective hiring, inadequate supervision, and poor communication" (Lakey, Lakey, Napier, & Robinson, 1995, p. 59). This discovery allowed us to understand the disparate responses to the survey questions about the Foundation's mission and vision and motivated us to try to understand more about the many organizational paradoxes described below.

The primary purposes of the survey questionnaire we administered to Foundation members and other Festival stakeholders were to ascertain their (a) personal values that motivated their involvement in the organization, (b) perceptions of the organization's purpose or mission, (c) vision for the organization, and (d) perceptions of key issues that needed resolution for the mission and vision to be realized. Two of the survey questions asked about the reasons why people were involved with the Jazz Foundation and/or Festival and the aspects of their involvement that gave them the greatest satisfaction. The reason we asked about these things was because we have come to believe from our experience with nonprofits that personal values are the primary reason why people get involved with nonprofit organizations and that being convinced that members have shared values is the primary reason why they stay involved. Many times, the real conflict in an organization is that members are involved to fulfill personal values that are incongruent with those of other members, and this appeared to be the case with this organization.

Although the vast majority of questionnaire respondents stated that they were involved with the Foundation because of their belief in its mission, an interesting pattern of exceptions emerged. Some members stated that they were involved primarily to protect the interests of the organizations they represented, whereas others stated that their involvement stemmed from a desire to share their professional expertise and to give back to their community. Follow-up interviews with questionnaire respondents further revealed that the discrepancy in values that existed among participants could be categorized as a love for jazz versus a desire to promote the business interests of the Park City community.

Although we must admit to being naïve in our ignorance that a problem of ownership and control of the Festival was even an issue until we actually got into the interview phase of the discovery process, it quickly became apparent that ownership and control of the Festival was a significant contested question of fact and conjecture (see Gouran, 1982, 1997) that had to be addressed immediately. In an effort to facilitate this process, our report included the two perspectives we identified in the discovery process, along with a third alternative we recommended for the organization's consideration. These three alternatives are explained below.

Origin of the Festival and Foundation—Which Came First?

After we had learned that the ownership of the Jazz Festival was in dispute between the Jazz Foundation and the Festival's primary custodian, the Park City Chamber-Bureau, we assumed that understanding the chronology of the Festival and Foundation origins would help to clarify the dispute. Most people we spoke with were confused about which came first—the Foundation or the Festival. Although our research produced an accurate chronology of the evolution of both the Festival and the Foundation, unfortunately, it did not clarify the legal ownership of the event, as we had anticipated it would.

The idea to produce a jazz festival in Park City was first championed by Luke and Andrea Feldstein in 1996. The Feldsteins were semiretired, "straight-ahead" jazz enthusiasts from the eastern United States who had relocated to Park City for its clean mountain air and world-class skiing. Their dream was to share their love of jazz with the citizens of Park City through a festival, and although many people were attracted to the idea of creating an annual, internationally recognized jazz festival in the mountains, it took some time to muster the financial support to make Luke and Andrea's dream a reality. Hence, consistent with what frequently occurs with similar nonprofit organizations, the Jazz Foundation began as a result of the vision of its cofounders, who formally established the organization with little doubt that they would run it under the authority of a small board of trusted friends (Andringa & Engstrom, 1998).

At some point in 1997, Nicole London, then Special Events Director of the Park City Chamber-Bureau, identified Fidelity Investments Corporation as a potential title sponsor for such a jazz festival. Early in the planning stages of the first Festival, London resigned her position with the Chamber-Bureau and was replaced by Brenda Callahan, who had previously worked as an independent contractor for the Chamber-Bureau. Callahan assumed the role of "event director" for the first Festival and worked with the Feldsteins, Fidelity representatives, and a group of volunteers to produce the Festival. Although the first Festival was planned and organized within the Chamber-Bureau's office, it was understood by all parties involved that the Chamber-Bureau's philosophy and unwritten policy had been to start events and support them for up to three years, after which they needed to become self-sufficient. The Chamber-Bureau budgeted $10,000 to support the first Festival, similar to the amount of start-up support it had provided to other stand-alone community events, such as the Sundance Film Festival, World Cup Ski Races, and a Senior PGA Tour Golf Tournament.

Consistent with the Chamber-Bureau's policy, it was recognized early on by Festival organizers that a foundation with 501(c)(3) tax-exempt status would be needed to eventually manage the Festival; consequently, the Park City International Jazz Foundation was officially incorporated in the State of Utah on November 20, 1997, nine months *before* the first Festival. However, the Foundation did not receive tax-exempt status under section 501(c)(3) of the Internal Revenue Code until December 9, 1998, four months *after* the first Festival, adding further confusion as to which came first, the Festival or the Foundation. Consequently, the question of which came first remained a disputed point between supporters of the respective perspectives of the Foundation and the Chamber-Bureau.

Festival "Ownership" — Perspective #1: The Chamber-Bureau Should Own the Festival

The staff and members of the Chamber-Bureau felt strongly that the Park City International Jazz Festival should be an ongoing tourism event sponsored by the Park City Chamber-Bureau. They believed that if the Jazz Foundation existed at all, its role should primarily be ancillary, focusing on educational programming and related fund-raising. The probable mission of the Festival under this scenario would be for it to exist as an auxiliary of the Chamber-Bureau for the purpose of producing an annual destination music festival to maximize tourism revenue for Park City, with the Festival Event Director remaining a staff person of the Chamber-Bureau.

The members and staff of the Chamber-Bureau were extremely motivated to have the Festival become a destination event and believed that to grow the Festival, the music genres presented at the Festival needed to expand and become more popular and contemporary rather than remain focused on traditional, straight-ahead jazz. Such a debate about jazz is an ongoing dialectical tension at many jazz festivals throughout the country (see Jenkins, 2002).

Proponents of this perspective cited several points to support their viewpoint. First, they argued that the Chamber-Bureau had covered the deficit that was created from the first Festival in 1998. Although it had generally been agreed that, from the perspectives of delivering a fabulous selection of performers, a world-class stage, and a wonderful educational component, the 1998 inaugural Festival was a great success, the event was not a financial success, ending with a $25,000 deficit. This deficit notwithstanding, the Chamber-Bureau Executive Committee had recommended that the event was worth saving because of its encouraging potential as a signature destination marketing event for Park City. Although cofounder Luke Feldstein indicated that he was willing to take out a personal loan to cover the shortfall, he was told that wouldn't be necessary because the Chamber-Bureau believed it could cover the loss by way of a $7,500 cash contribution and a $17,500 loan against the following year's Festival profits.

This was, indeed, what occurred, as the Festival was able to pay off the $17,500 loan from its subsequent year's (1999) Festival budget and still accumulate a positive balance of approximately $31,000, which was rolled into the 2000 event. Therefore, although the Chamber-Bureau did, as one representative put it, "bail out" the Festival, it did so with full purpose as a partner in developing the Festival, certainly not because it had to, as had been implied by some Chamber-Bureau representatives who were interviewed.

A second piece of evidence supporting the argument that the Chamber-Bureau owned the Festival was that the staff members who organized and ran the Festival were employees of the Chamber-Bureau, not the Jazz Foundation. Connie Walton was hired as the first full-time Festival Event Director in the Spring of 1999, well after the planning for the 1999 Festival was underway. Although Walton proposed her fee structure as the Event Director for the 2000 Festival in a September 15, 1999 letter to "Luke Feldstein, Park City International Jazz *Foundation*" [italics added], a copy of the independent contractor agreement between the Jazz Festival and Connie Walton as "contractor to act as the Event Director in conjunction with the Executive Committee of the Jazz Festival," was signed by Walton, as the contractor, and by Brenda Callahan, in her capacity as Special Events Director for the Chamber-Bureau. Consequently, it appeared as if Walton was legally a contracted employee of the Park City Chamber-Bureau, not the Jazz Foundation.

Probably the strongest evidence supporting the Chamber-Bureau's claim for Festival ownership was the fact that all financial management responsibility for the Festival had been assumed by the Chamber-Bureau. Until May 2000, all deposits made in the name of the Park City International Jazz *Foundation,* as well as those made payable to the Park City International Jazz *Festival,* were transacted through Park City Chamber-Bureau auxiliary accounts; correspondingly, all payments on behalf of the Festival were made from these same accounts. The first bank account in the name of the Park City International Jazz Foundation was not opened until May 2000, well after the first two Festivals. Only one deposit had been made to that account and only one check had been written from it—a check made payable to the Chamber-Bureau. Consequently, it appeared that the Chamber-Bureau did, in fact, have custodial control of the Festival; as Biff Martin, Executive Director of the Chamber-Bureau, put it, "We take the financial risks, we write the checks. . . . If we're not going to direct it [the Festival], why should we take the risks?"

There were several perceived advantages to Chamber-Bureau ownership of the Jazz Festival that were claimed by its proponents. First, they believed that it would provide for maximum efficiency and control, as Chamber-Bureau staff, rather than a committee, would control all Festival policy and programming decisions, and a volunteer organizing committee would primarily be associated with Festival program implementation rather than with policy decisions. Second, with the Chamber-Bureau controlling the event, the potential to grow the Festival would be unfettered by the straight-ahead jazz mission desired by the cofounders of the Foundation. A third perceived advantage of this alternative was the potential to use Festival proceeds to support other Chamber-Bureau events that were not as able to pay for themselves. Some also believed that if the Chamber-Bureau controlled the Jazz Festival, it would increase the ability to attract more business sponsorships, because the Festival's mission would be to promote the business interests of Park City. Finally, on a related matter, the Chamber-Bureau staff believed that its ownership of the Festival would help to fulfill the Chamber-Bureau's mission; as Executive Director Biff Martin put it, "We're judged by how many butts we put in beds," referring to the Chamber-Bureau's charge to fill hotel rooms and rental condominiums, particularly during the summer off-season. This was an especially salient argument, because concern had been expressed about the future revenue base of the Chamber-Bureau both during and immediately after the 2002 Winter Olympics. Some had speculated that the Olympics might actually have a negative effect on the number of "skier days" during and after the 3-week event. If destination skiers stayed away from Park City because of the Olympics, it would have a negative effect on the occupancy rates during the Olympics, which, in turn, would mean less transient room tax revenue—the mainstay of the Chamber-Bureau's budget.

Festival "Ownership"—Perspective #2: The Foundation Should Own the Festival

Understandably, most of the Park City International Jazz Foundation Board members who participated in this project believed that the Jazz Festival should be the primary performance program of the Foundation. Under this arrangement, all policy decisions regarding the Festival would be made by a volunteer Board of Trustees, with day-to-day management decisions continuing to be controlled by a volunteer Board Executive Committee, and with program implementation support from the Foundation's Festival Director, the Chamber-Bureau's Special Events Director, and an Event Organizing Committee.

There were several points made by Foundation members in support of this perspective. First, they argued that the Chamber-Bureau's mission had never before included the ongoing control and management of community events. As stated previously, its unwritten policy had historically been to seed such events for a maximum of three years, and several Foundation members testified in the interviews conducted that they had heard Chamber-Bureau Executive Director Biff Martin reiterate this policy at a public meeting soon after he had been hired.

Second, they argued that as a tax-exempt nonprofit organization, the Foundation had the ability to attract diverse sustainable funding sources (e.g., foundations, government agencies, and individuals desiring a tax write-off) for the Festival and for other Foundation programs in a way that was not possible for the Chamber-Bureau, for although it was a nonprofit organization, the Chamber-Bureau was not eligible for tax-exempt status. This point assumed, of course, that all Festival funds would be managed by the Foundation rather than by the Chamber-Bureau.

A third point supporting Foundation ownership of the Festival was also related to Festival finances. If the Chamber-Bureau retained control of the Festival, it was very probable that the Festival would lose significant in-kind services that currently were being donated to support the mission of a tax-deductible nonprofit organization. For example, the graphic design and printing firms that handled all Festival publication and advertising design and printing work on a pro bono basis did so because of their respective owners' commitment to the Foundation's mission of promoting jazz music through performance and education. Such services, with an estimated value of $75,000 in the year 2000 alone, would probably not be donated to a Chamber-Bureau-controlled Festival, particularly if the Festival's mission and music format changed, as had been threatened. A related problem with Chamber-Bureau ownership of the Festival was anticipated sponsor concern about the potential of Festival proceeds being diverted to other Chamber-Bureau programs, as had been suggested by Chamber-Bureau staff members.

A fourth line of reasoning in support of Foundation ownership of the Festival was related to the general community's perception and support of the Festival. Many members of the Park City community supported the Jazz Festival, in part, because the Foundation had the mission of promoting the general public interests of all citizens of Park City; in contrast, the Chamber-Bureau's mission was focused more narrowly on meeting the business interests of the city. If the Chamber-Bureau wrestled away control of the Festival from the Foundation, it had a real potential of becoming a public relations problem for the Chamber-Bureau by being perceived as having commandeered the idea of community-minded citizens. As one influential citizen stated, "If the Festival is owned by the Chamber-Bureau as a commercial enterprise, I would feel betrayed, or co-opted. This shouldn't happen to people like Luke and Andrea Feldstein." Such a perception could stifle the community-minded spirit of citizens and discourage them from coming forward and partnering with the Chamber-Bureau on new ideas that might promote its mission. Chamber-Bureau ownership of the Festival also potentially increased the possible loss of long-term volunteers who might not be willing to be involved in the planning and implementation of a Chamber-Bureau-controlled Festival. Estimates suggested that two-thirds of the roughly 150 volunteers who worked the Festival did so, at least in part, because of their commitment to Luke and Andrea Feldstein's vision for the community.

In summary, a substantive intergroup conflict over ownership and control of a prestigious, money-making jazz festival existed between the Jazz Foundation and the Park City Chamber-Bureau. Ironically, the concept of "ownership" is completely foreign in 501(c)(3) nonprofit organizational law, in that there can be no "owners" of a nonprofit organization because such an entity is intended to serve a broad public purpose, and the law is clear in specifying that ownership (with concomitant private gain) is incompatible with such public purpose (Wolf, 1999). Although we found no evidence that individuals associated with the Festival had realized private gain, nonprofit organizational law relates to the issue of Festival ownership in other ways. If, indeed, the idea for a festival was conceived as a way to further the cultural milieu of Park City, as had been claimed by its cofounders, there appeared to be an obligation to seriously consider this "public trust" when making any decisions regarding the future of this highly successful event.

Our analysis of the ownership issue led us to the conclusion that neither perspective was viable on its own; instead, a blending of both perspectives was necessary for the short- and long-term benefit of the Festival and the Park City community. We believed that although the Chamber-Bureau had more material, or legal, evidence to support its claim of ownership, the Foundation should ethically maintain ownership and control of the event it had founded. However, the Foundation was not yet in a position as an organization to independently manage the Festival as a stand-alone event; it needed the continued support of the Chamber-Bureau. The problem was that each party in this intergroup conflict viewed ownership and control of the Festival as an "all-or-nothing" issue. As the Chamber-Bureau Executive Director stated, "Either it comes inside the Chamber-Bureau completely or it should be on its own separate from the Chamber-Bureau." Our challenge, thus, was to facilitate a compromise between these two disparate perspectives.

Our Recommendations

Given that there was sound evidence in support of and against both the Foundation's and the Chamber-Bureau's positions on Festival ownership, we presented a third alternative for these groups' consideration: that the Park City International Jazz Festival be the primary performance program of a *transformed* Park City International Jazz Foundation. The Board of Trustees of such a new Foundation would need to be expanded to include a broader representation of both the Chamber-Bureau and the community at large. Because one of the key responsibilities of board members of a nonprofit, charitable organization is to provide a communication link with the local community, it is important that a diversity of backgrounds and interests be represented on such a board. When a wide diversity of partners and segments of the community are represented on a board, each group sees the organization as its own and this increases the support in both tangible and intangible ways.

Although ideally, all members of this new Foundation Board would have a passion for jazz and its related music forms, this might not always be possible. If not, it was recommended that the Board be composed of some individuals who had this passion, some individuals with particular professional expertise needed (e.g., financial and law), and some individuals who simply had the time and desire to contribute to the betterment of their community. Our purpose for recommending that the Board have members with specific areas of expertise was not to encourage those particular members to become involved in the day-to-day activities that are staff responsibilities but, rather, to provide a monitoring capability for the Board. Members with such expertise can provide important background information needed to establish policy, understand staff recommendations, and make informed decisions. We also suggested that various Board members should be familiar with the programs and activities that the Foundation sponsors and should support the organization's mission.

To encompass the values and interests of both its original founders—Luke and Andrea Feldstein—as well as those of its steward—the Chamber-

Bureau—we also suggested that the newly transformed Foundation have a broader superordinate mission that addressed the values and needs of *both* perspectives we had discovered in our research: bringing live jazz performances to the community *and* promoting the business interests of Park City by attracting out-of-town tourists. We argued that such an expanded mission would symbolically insure that the event retained the integrity of its original vision and encompassed the Chamber-Bureau's need for the Festival to grow to become a successful destination event, not only for the economic well-being of the community but for everyone's need for the future sustainability of the Festival. Under this scenario of a transformed Foundation, we also recommended that policy be established by the Foundation Board regarding the "aesthetic core" of the Festival, specifying the breadth of the genre being programmed and how event-performing artist budgets should be allocated (e.g., 25% on traditional jazz, 25% on international jazz, 35% on contemporary jazz, and 15% on "new age" jazz). We also recommended that memoranda of understanding, or partnership agreements, be prepared and signed by all the partners (e.g., the primary sponsors, the Chamber-Bureau, and the Foundation) clarifying representation, roles, and expectations on this new Board.

Another recommendation we suggested was that the newly transformed Foundation should hire an executive director to run the day-to-day functions of the organization, including the Festival, rather than having this person only be responsible for the Festival. We believed that if the Foundation hired a person to be responsible for the daily decisions related to all Foundation programs, including the Festival, many of the communication problems between Board members, Chamber-Bureau staff, and Festival volunteers would be eliminated. However, for this truly to work, we suggested that the roles of Board members and an executive director required clarification, because the relationship between the Board and the staff (volunteer or paid) is critical to the successful operation of a nonprofit organization (Wolf, 1999).

Another issue identified by many who we interviewed was the question of future leadership of the Foundation and the Festival. Most people interviewed were strong supporters of the Foundation founder and president, Luke Feldstein, as a visionary, public relations schmoozer, fund-raiser, people person, and advocate for the mission of the Festival and for the Foundation. However, nearly everyone also acknowledged that administrative leadership of the Foundation had been lacking since its creation. For example, there was no record that the Board had met more than twice since it was created, which potentially threatened the Foundation's 501(c)(3) nonprofit designation. Such leadership problems are actually quite common for young nonprofit organizations (Robinson, 2001). As Wolf (1999) explained:

> Nonprofit organizations often encounter special personnel challenges
> with regard to founders who ultimately become chief executives. It is
> often the case that the individual with the vision, imagination, and
> entrepreneurial energy to be a founder is not the best person to be an
> organization's chief executive after a number of years. (p. 133)

Our research and analysis of the organizational health of the Jazz Foundation led us to the clear conclusion that founders Luke and Andrea Feldstein needed to step aside as the primary leaders and managers of the organization if the Foundation was to have any chance of survival. Consequently, we recommended that a new Board president be elected as soon as possible and that Luke and Andrea Feldstein each retain the title of "CoFounder," remain on the Board for as long as they chose to be contributing members, and serve in roles commensurate with their particular skills.

We believed that there were several advantages to this third alternative of a transformed Foundation. First, the Foundation would retain the ability to operate as a 501(c)(3) nonprofit organization and, thereby, reduce the fiduciary risk of Board members. As such, the Foundation would retain the ability to diversify sustainable funding sources that require a 501(c)(3) recipient. Such an organization would be able to attract future partners and donors focused on promoting Park City tourism, as well as donors interested in promoting jazz and related art forms, and, thereby, bring together in a true collaboration the interests of those in the arts with those in commerce. The new Foundation would also have greater potential for receiving continued donations of in-kind services in support of its nonprofit mission, along with the ability to preserve and increase the loyalty of the community and continued volunteer support.

The means for presenting our recommendations had been stipulated in the consulting contract issued to us by Luke Feldstein when he specified that "the 'client' in this consulting relationship is the Foundation Board in its entirety, and that a written report, including all recommendations, will be directed with full disclosure to the entire Board simultaneously." In fulfillment of this expectation, we designed a day-long adaptation of Beckhard's (1967) *confrontation meeting*, in which an entire group "generates information about its major problems, analyzes the underlying causes, develops action plans to correct the problems, and sets a schedule for completed remedial work" (French & Bell, 1984, p. 176). DeWine (2001) argued that "a process consultant is needed to run a confrontation meeting . . . where two conflicting groups come together and work through their tensions and frictions that have built up over an extended period of time" (pp. 161-162). What follows is a description of the design and facilitation of this confrontation meeting.

THE CONFRONTATION MEETING FACILITATION

Design of the Meeting

We designed the confrontation meeting to fulfill each of Seibold and Krikorian's (1997) four meeting functions: (a) The meeting was intended to *inform or instruct* participants about the findings and recommendations from our research, (b) we wished to *solicit opinions* from participants about our recommendations, (c) we wanted the meeting to become a forum for conflicting groups to *solve problems and make decisions*, and (d) we truly hoped that the meeting would be a beginning step in helping to *create unity* between the two groups in conflict. Our approach to designing the meeting also considered several of the factors for participative learning outlined by R. O. Lippitt and Schlindler-Rainman (1975); specifically, the meeting included process work on group problems, conflict resolution, and the development of collaboration between the two groups. We wanted to model a more effective means for group communication than members of the Foundation had reported experiencing in the past as we implemented a process for the group to address its conflict in a collaborative way that maximized the best interests of the Park City community.

The design of our intervention essentially followed most of Keltner's seven stages of a mediation process:

1. *setting the stage* (establishing rapport and credibility);
2. *opening and development* (identifying ground rules and building trust);
3. *exploration of the issues*: isolation of basics (when the relative importance of issues is decided and clients state opening positions);
4. *identification of alternatives* (identification of other options);
5. *evaluation, negotiation, and bargaining* (matching needs with criteria previously established);
6. *decision making and testing* (when parties begin to make commitments);
7. *terminating the process* (mediator reviews the decisions made) (as cited in DeWine, 2001, p. 164).

Meeting Participants

We paid close attention to insuring that the right mix of participants would be present at the facilitated confrontation meeting. In addition to the entire

Foundation Board of Trustees, we strategically invited select staff and members of the Park City Chamber-Bureau to attend. It was important to get all the key players together in one meeting to discuss our report and to maximize acceptance of any decisions they made regarding the future ownership of the Jazz Festival and the corresponding existence, purpose, role, and structure of the Jazz Foundation, for we knew that "when individuals help determine the solution, they have already made a commitment to make sure it works" (DeWine, 2001, pp. 210-211).

We thought about several factors when comprising the confrontation meeting group and the activities we planned for it (Napier & Gershenfeld, 1989; Seibold, 1979). We considered how the participants would:

> differ with regard to power; status; experience with the issue under discussion; concern about the problem; interpersonal relationships with other group members; hidden agendas (i.e., personal goals for the session); [and] communication skills . . . [because] the homogeneity/heterogeneity of the group along each of these dimensions can affect the interpersonal and task dynamics which ensue during the meeting (e.g., conflict, participation, time it takes to solve a problem and number of alternatives considered, quality of the decision, mode of decision making, and members' satisfaction with the group). (Seibold, 1979, p. 6)

No Pre-Meeting Agenda

Standard procedures for meeting preparation suggest that an agenda and any materials to be reviewed should be distributed to participants sufficiently in advance of the meeting date to allow them to come to the meeting prepared for discussion and decision making (DeWine, 2001; Seibold, 1979, 1995). Seibold (1979) argued that "if members can anticipate the purposes, goals, and issues which form the basis for their meeting, as well as their own responsibilities for its conduct, they may come better prepared and more motivated" (p. 6).

Although Seibold's claim is logically warranted, in this particular situation, we intentionally wanted members to come *without* being fully prepared to discuss the issues we were going to raise about the Jazz Foundation and the Chamber-Bureau. Given the nature of the intergroup conflict and corresponding strong feelings participants had regarding their respective positions, we deliberately did not distribute our report in advance of the meeting. Strong negative feelings of anger, distrust, resentment, fear, and rejection had built up over a 2-year period between the Foundation cofounders and the Chamber-Bureau staff who coordinated the Festival, which, as our questionnaires and interviews showed, was having a ripple effect on everyone associated with the Festival production. Therefore, we wanted all of the participants to confront both the information contained in our report, as well as one another, without a further build-up of premeeting resistance and defensiveness, because, as Seibold (1979) explained:

> The dynamics which accompany controversy about an issue (listening in order to refute rather than to understand; polarization and further entrenchment in one's position; selective search for facts which support one's own view and refute others') mitigate against objective, collective problem-solving. (p. 9)

Meeting Location

We thought carefully about an appropriate location for the confrontation meeting (Seibold & Krikorian, 1997). Rather than using the Chamber-Bureau's meeting room, which was the normal location of meetings associated with the Jazz Festival, we selected a location that we considered to be neutral—a dining room at the Park City Mountain Ski Resort that was available because the meeting occurred just before the resort opened for skiing. The dining room was large enough to allow for a primary meeting setup along with four table groupings distributed throughout the room for subgroup discussions. To maximize group dialogue, participants sat at tables arranged in an open "U" shape facing us, the facilitators, who stood at the front of the room next to two flipchart easels we used for taking notes. Separate tables were used for food and beverages and for a display of the artifacts we had examined in the discovery phase of the project (e.g., Articles of Incorporation, employment contracts, and correspondence between the Foundation and the Chamber-Bureau). We wanted participants to examine these documents during breaks to confirm for themselves the claims we had made in our report, and several participants took advantage of this opportunity.

The Meeting

We began the confrontation meeting with introductions of ourselves as the facilitators, followed by all 20 participants introducing themselves. In addition to Foundation Board members not knowing some Chamber-Bureau representatives, there were actually some Foundation Board members who had never met one another. We then articulated and displayed the purpose of the meeting on flipchart paper as follows:

> To share findings and recommendations regarding the relationship between the Foundation, its ancillary partners (Chamber-Bureau/Jazz Festival), educational efforts, and the annual presentation of the Jazz Festival, including a definition of the appropriate makeup and roles of all Board members. (Sline & Boulton, 2000, p. 1)

We also stated our hope that participants would be able to reach a consensus agreement about the future structural relationship between the Foundation, the Chamber-Bureau, and the Festival.

Using a group call-out procedure, in which participants are asked to state their ideas in a free-form fashion, we had participants identify their expectations and suggest explicit norms for the day's meeting, which we recorded on flipchart paper and displayed prominently on the wall for reference throughout the day. Although this procedure seemed quite foreign to most of the participants, I have found great value in having groups go through the process of agreeing on meeting ground rules before proceeding with their task, particularly when conflict is anticipated, as it was in this case. As Bradford (1975) argued, "Norms of behavior for individuals and the group are like scaffolding of a building" (p. 117).

Once participants were clear about their expectations and norms for the meeting, we strategically divided the group of 20 into four buzz groups—a means of dividing a large group into smaller subgroups to maximize participation in discussions and decision making (Seibold & Krikorian, 1997)—and explained the process we were going to use for everyone to come to a shared understanding of the data and recommendations in our 43-page report. We attempted to insure that each 5-person buzz group had the maximum mix of Foundation and Chamber-Bureau supporters to minimize conversational control by either faction in the buzz group discussions (Dannemiller, 1988; Dannemiller et al., 1990). In addition, we strategically placed key individuals whom we knew had problems with one another in different buzz groups.

The Facilitation Innovation

Our written report was divided into four sections. The first section described the consulting contract and the discovery process we used to gather information. The second section described our findings, including a summary of the responses given on the survey questionnaire and in the follow-up interviews, and our corresponding observations about those responses. The third section contained a description of the two perspectives that emerged regarding the "ownership" relationship between the Foundation, the Chamber-Bureau, and the Festival, along with our initial analysis of the advantages and disadvantages of each perspective. The final section of the report presented our recommendations for the participants' consideration.

The process we used to work the group through the sections of our report was referred to by one participant as like "peeling back the layers of an onion" (C. Landis, personal communication, April 26, 2001). Rather than give participants a full copy of the report to review, we distributed the report section by section to them. The reason we did this is because my experience has been that when given a lengthy report, client groups typically go immediately to the executive summary and then pour through the recommendations without understanding and seriously considering the credibility of the data on which the recommendations are based. We wanted to circumvent this tendency.

Participants were given approximately 10-15 minutes to read the first section and then another 15-20 minutes to discuss their reactions in their buzz groups. When the buzz group discussions seemed complete, we reconvened all participants as one group to summarize and discuss their buzz group conversations and to ask us questions of clarification regarding that section. After brief breaks between each phase, the process was repeated with the second, third, and fourth sections of the report.

After participants had worked through the last section of our report, we facilitated a general discussion about appropriate next steps that could be taken. Founder Luke Feldstein offered no resistance to our recommendation that he step down as Board Chair; in fact, he seemed relieved to pass on this designated leader responsibility. The group appointed an interim Board Chair and a restructuring committee, and established a time line for considering each of our 10 recommendations, most of which were subsequently implemented.

ANALYSIS OF THE FACILITATION INNOVATION

The conflict in the Jazz Foundation case included both substantive content conflict over the ownership and control of the organization—its structure, goals, and policies—as well as affective conflict in the form of emotional and personal conflict among the individuals involved (DeWine, 2001; Nicotera, 1997; Walton, 1987). These types of conflict are quite common in nonprofit organizations, "which as fragile coalitions of diverse interests, must constantly struggle for the consensus which enables them to do their work" (Hall, 1990, p. 156).

The intergroup nature of the conflict in this case provided an opportunity to examine the dynamics of group boundary spanning by key members of both groups, as well as the relationships between two or more bona fide groups (Putnam & Stohl, 1990, 1996), a somewhat rare opportunity for group communication scholars (Poole, 1999; for some examples, see the case studies in Frey, 2003). Factions existed among Jazz Festival stakeholders; some were Foundation loyalists, whereas others represented the interests of the Park City Chamber-Bureau.

The affective conflict was primarily between Foundation cofounders Luke and Andrea Feldstein and Chamber-Bureau staff member Brenda Callahan, with strong negative feelings having built up over a 2-year period between these organizational representatives. Although we did a good job of designing and facilitating a problem-solving process that allowed meeting participants to resolve the substantive conflict issues, it was impossible in such a limited time period to help those experiencing interpersonal conflict to effectively restructure their perceptions and work through their negative feelings. The process did, however, at least make the affective conflict problem and its impact more "public" and, thereby, set the stage for improved management of this conflict in the future.

Given that the purpose of this confrontation meeting was both "problem oriented" and "solution oriented" (Seibold, 1979, p. 8), we believed that the design for the session needed to be carefully crafted. This meeting's primary purposes were both to inform participants about the problems of organizational and interpersonal conflicts between the Jazz Foundation and the Chamber-Bureau and to facilitate their management, as the goal of the session was for participants to receive and take action on our report. To accomplish this dual purpose, we used different adaptations of problem-solving meeting procedures outlined by Seibold (1979) to "help circumvent [the] inefficiency, delay, confusion, redundancy, and occasional frustration [of unstructured meetings] by coordinating members, focusing their attention on common issues, and guiding them through jointly understood aspects of problem diagnosis, solution selection, or implementation" (p. 9). First, our written report was structured much like the two-column method, in that it included a summary of each party's argument, outlining the pros and cons of each, along with a "third column," which was the third alternative we submitted for the group's consideration. Second, we used a variation of rational reflection when we guided participants through a "series of predetermined 'reflective' phases intended to address specific aspects of a problem in 'rational' fashion" (Seibold, p. 9). Third, much of this work was accomplished by placing participants in maximum-mix buzz groups, which facilitated full participation.

These meeting procedures also allowed sufficient time for a learning curve to develop for participants, and for the client groups to begin to take ownership of their problems and make plans to follow through with their collective commitments (Coates, 1997). We believe that the process of having participants systematically "peel away" our findings and recommendations allowed some of the emotionally controversial dimensions of the issue to be approached in a more objective manner through open discussion, helped to minimize member divisiveness around each position, and enabled both sides of the issue to be appraised more realistically and cooperatively (Maier, 1963; Seibold, 1979). One participant agreed that this was the case when she wrote to us in an e-mail message following the facilitation:

> You and Anna were just marvelous. I become dubious and jaded when I hear the word "facilitator" because often it's just a regurgitation of information. You were in a very delicate position and handled the day with such finesse, objectivity, and optimism. I also like the way you presented your findings in increments rather than the whole packet of information, which would have been overwhelming. (J. Chournous, personal communication, November 13, 2000)

Similar to what was reported by Coates (1997) in his recommendations for facilitating change in nonprofit organizations, when participants were able to systematically read and discuss the consultants' feedback report, including specific quotes from one-on-one interviews conducted with participants, first in buzz groups and then as a collective group, a climate was created where members felt comfortable to open up and share their thoughts and feelings quite freely. As Coates explained, and as we experienced in this case, "The intensive discussions provided an emotional catharsis and appeared to lay the groundwork for more open communication among [participants]" (p. 163). As another participant wrote to us in a follow-up e-mail message:

> You guys were terrific! I enjoyed the content of what you did, but was also keenly aware of your methodology. The task of objectively presenting the results of your findings, then moving us to honest discussion was tricky. But your methods worked in checking potential destructive conflict and instead brought to light the issues that needed to be dealt with in a rational, calm fashion. I am very optimistic that we can create a structure that will obtain buy-in of all parties. THANKS!! (L. Bonnell, personal communication, November 10, 2000)

Indeed, we were fortunate that the intergroup conflict remained constructive rather than destructive. As such, each of Papa and Canary's (1995) three stages of conflict—differentiation, mutual problem description, and integration—was evident in the substantive intergroup conflict over Festival ownership that occurred throughout this project. The Foundation was in the stage of differentiation when we were hired, in that the Foundation Board committee that hired us clearly recognized that there was a problem. We then created a forum for mutual problem description through the confrontation meeting we designed and facilitated. In the meeting, participants were able to understand the factors that contributed to their respective perspectives regarding ownership of the Jazz Festival and began to collectively construct a mutually beneficial solution, which finally came together and was achieved in the integration stage of the conflict.

The substantive conflict between the Foundation and the Chamber-Bureau stemmed primarily from differences in values. Foundation supporters placed a priority value on presenting and promoting traditional, straight-ahead jazz music, whereas supporters of the Chamber-Bureau placed a greater value on presenting a music festival with more wide-appealing music genres that would attract overnight tourists to Park City. As Gouran (1997) argued, value-based conflicts are not easily resolved because of the passionate feelings associated with people's beliefs and attitudes. To manage such conflicts, some higher order, shared value must be identified that minimizes the divisive influence of the values in conflict.

The third alternative we recommended for Festival ownership—the creation of a transformed Foundation—attempted to capitalize on higher order shared values, or superordinate goals, "those that have compelling appeal for each group but that neither group can achieve without participation of the other" (Sherif, 1966, p. 89). Sherif argued that superordinate goals "must arise from the relationships between groups in a fashion so compelling that they can be recognized within each group" (p. 147). However, Sherif qualified the effectiveness of achieving superordinate goals for resolving intergroup conflicts when he concluded from his research that:

> superordinate goals are possible only when two or more groups find a purpose toward which each can strive without sacrificing the most cherished aspirations of its members. When this is not possible, group conflict continues despite efforts to forestall its ultimate consequences and despite practices that appear legitimate to each group. (p. 107)

In the case of the conflict between the Jazz Foundation and the Chamber-Bureau, the creation of a new Foundation with an expanded Board of Trustees and a revisioned mission served as a superordinate goal that did not require either group to significantly sacrifice its aspirations.

Some conflict management scholars have argued that the unique background and characteristics of each organizational conflict suggest that resolution processes must be customized to meet the needs of each situation. Ertel (1991) argued that those who attempt to facilitate the resolution of conflict need first to understand the core issues that have inhibited its resolution so as to make informed decisions about designing a facilitation process for conflict management. Such a process must help those in conflict to understand each party's underlying interests, because "while positions may be in conflict, underlying interests need not be" (Ertel, p. 31). I believe that the facilitation described in this chapter enabled both parties to see that their underlying interests were not in as much conflict as they had previously perceived based on their extremely different positions regarding ownership and control of the Festival.

The facilitation method used to manage this intergroup conflict met many of Ertel's (1991) criteria for an effective conflict management process. First, through thorough research by us as the consulting team, the process was able to *clarify the interests* of each party. Second, the process paid considerable attention to *building a good working relationship* between the members of the Foundation and those of the Chamber-Bureau. Third, the process *generated good options* for each party to consider. Fourth, the process was *perceived as being legitimate* by participants in that the public's interests were kept paramount and because the process instilled in both parties a sense that the solutions they produced together would be fair and equitable. The process also *improved communication* between Foundation members and Chamber-Bureau staff by encouraging the questioning and testing of each party's underlying assumptions, facilitating the understanding and discussion of mutual perceptions, and establishing effective two-way communication between those involved in and able to resolve the conflict. Finally, the process led to *wise commitments* between the Foundation and the Chamber-Bureau that have enabled the new transformed Foundation and its Jazz Festival to flourish in the three years since the process was implemented.

The confrontation meeting we designed and facilitated proved to be extremely successful. The outcomes met each of the criteria for evaluating the success of any conflict management method: "(1) good substantive outcome, (2) improved relationship so that future differences are handled more collaboratively, and (3) general efficiency of the method" (Keashly et al., 1993, p. 390). The reasons for this success may be the same as the underlying dynamics that contribute to the effectiveness of other intervention techniques, such as those discussed in this section of the text, for resolving inter-group conflicts (French & Bell, 1984). First, the process we designed for the meeting provided a structure—a lockstep procedure for working through our report, section by section—that allowed us as the facilitators to maintain a type of control that kept the parties from merely arguing and defending their respective positions. Second, the intervention was based on thorough data that was made public during the meeting. French and Bell argued that:

> for joint problem-solving to take place, all the actors who are part of the problem or part of the solution must share the same data, [and that] knowing the scope of the issues and having a comprehensive understanding of them is probably a necessary ingredient in making a group (or an individual) move from a defensive posture to a prob-lem-solving stance. (p. 161)

Our meeting process required all of the participants to discuss and come to a shared understanding of not only our recommendations but also the data on which they were based.

A third reason why French and Bell (1984) suspected that such interven-tions are effective in managing intergroup conflict is that the controlled nature of the structured group process enables participants to experience successful communication with the other group rather than engage in volatile verbal displays of conflict. Our use of maximum-mix buzz groups allowed participants to listen to and be heard by others as they discussed each section of the report prior to bringing the whole group back together to process the information in a collective discussion. This method of systemat-ically processing emotionally charged, complex information allowed "feel-ings of anxiety, apprehension, and hostility [to] start to give way to feelings of competence and success as the early stages of the interventions produce better communication and understanding than the participants had expected" (French & Bell, p. 161).

Finally, the constructive, problem-solving tone that we set at the outset of the meeting is a fourth possible reason why this intervention was successful. We created a clear problem-solving climate by having participants agree on explicit norms at the outset of the meeting.

CONCLUSION

The group communication facilitation described in this chapter is an exam-ple of an intergroup conflict consulting intervention that proved successful.

If truly candid, however, most group facilitation consultants will acknowledge that the results of many interventions are often much less effective. Although the potential effectiveness of group interventions is partly due to chance, a consulting facilitator can increase his or her chances of success by carefully planning and structuring the process used to share the results of the research phase of the consultation intervention with the client group. Of course, the client group must agree to engage this process; when this is not the case, the results may be very different. For example, in another intervention with a different nonprofit organization, the client group was not willing to spend the time needed to participate in a meeting to carefully review my report. I was essentially given less than an hour to present the results of the report to the group without the advantage of having members carefully consider the data on which the recommendations were based. Consequently, the results of that intervention were far less effective, as the group focused almost exclusively on the recommendations that were controversial and different from what they wanted and expected. This proved to be a no-win situation; the group felt that its investment in an external consultant was a waste of time and money, and as the consultant, I felt disconfirmed and ineffective. I did, however, learn an important lesson from that experience.

Much of the success of the intergroup conflict intervention with the Park City Jazz Foundation can be attributed to careful adherence to the six-step action research process for consulting. The facilitation innovation of this intervention was our decision to deviate from standard meeting planning guidelines. We did not provide the report to the group in advance, which helped to reduce defensive coalition building before the meeting. Our decision to distribute the report to participants in buzz groups, section by section in a controlled manner, enabled participants to see the logic supporting our recommendations and helped to de-emotionalize flammable issues. Our innovation was particularly useful in getting the decision makers to reflect on and discuss the data we generated in the discovery process and in achieving collective sense making of our recommendations.

Many of our recommendations were accepted and implemented. The Chamber-Bureau relinquished full ownership and control of the Jazz Festival to a newly constituted Jazz Foundation with an expanded Board of Trustees with superordinate goals shared by both groups. Three Board members who were appointed by the Chamber-Bureau's Board were added, along with three additional members from the community. The new Foundation repaid the Chamber-Bureau an equitable amount of money for its past support of the Festival and ultimately opened its own office in Park City from which it has produced successful Festivals in each of the four subsequent years since this intervention. The Park City Jazz Foundation is now a fully stand-alone 501(c)(3) nonprofit organization committed to fulfilling its mission to promote jazz music through performance and educational programs that continue to attract more and more people to Park City, Utah, each summer. In Perls's (1969) words, the two groups truly found oneness and integration through dialogue. Their civil war is finished and their combined energies are now focused on making their Festival among the best in the world.

REFERENCES

Andringa, R. C., & Engstrom, T. W. (1998). *The nonprofit board answer book: Practical guidelines for board members and chief executives.* Washington, DC: National Center for Nonprofit Boards.

Beckhard, R. (1967). The confrontation meeting. *Harvard Business Review, 45,* 149-155.

Block, P. (1981). *Flawless consulting: A guide to getting your expertise used.* San Diego, CA: University Associates.

Bradford, L. P. (1975). Creating a learning environment. In K. D. Benne, L. P. Bradford, J. R. Gibb, & R. O. Lippitt (Eds.), *The laboratory method of changing and learning: Theory and application* (pp. 111-138). Palo Alto, CA: Science and Behavior Books.

Coates, N. (1997). A model for consulting to help effect change in organizations. *Nonprofit Management & Leadership, 8,* 157-169.

Dannemiller, K. (1988). Team building at a macro level, or "Ben Gay" for arthritic organizations. In W. B. Reddy & K. Jamison (Eds.), *Team building: Blueprints for productivity and satisfaction* (pp. 107-115). Alexandria, VA: National Training Laboratory Institute for Applied Behavioral Science.

Dannemiller, K. D., Albert, R., Jacobs, B., Lerner, A., Loup, R., Dannemiller, K. C., Gabrion, J., Jones, K., & Thompson, B. (1990). *Interactive strategic planning: A consultant's guide.* Ann Arbor, MI: Dannemiller-Tyson.

DeWine, S. (2001). *The consultant's craft: Improving organizational communication* (2nd ed.). Boston: Bedford/St. Martin's Press.

Ertel, D. (1991, Summer). How to design a conflict management procedure that fits your dispute. *Sloan Management Review,* 29-42.

French, W. L., & Bell, C. H., Jr. (1984). *Organizational development: Behavioral science interventions for organization improvement* (3rd ed.). Englewood Cliffs, NJ: Prentice-Hall.

Frey, L. R. (Ed.). (2003). *Group communication in context: Studies of bona fide groups* (2nd ed.). Mahwah, NJ: Lawrence Erlbaum.

Gouran, D. S. (1982). *Making decisions in groups: Choices and consequences.* Glenview, IL: Scott, Foresman.

Gouran, D. S. (1997). Effective versus ineffective group decision making. In L. R. Frey & J. K. Barge (Eds.), *Managing group life: Communicating in decision-making groups* (pp. 133-155). Boston: Houghton Mifflin.

Hall, P. D. (1990). Conflicting managerial cultures in nonprofit organizations. *Nonprofit Management & Leadership, 1*, 151-175.

Hansmann, H. (1980). The role of nonprofit enterprise. *Yale Law Journal, 89*, 835-901.

Herman, R. D., Renz, D. O., & Heimovics, R. D. (1997). Board practices and board effectiveness in local nonprofit organizations. *Nonprofit Management & Leadership, 7*, 373-385.

Jenkins, W. (2002). Seeking the jazz truth. In G. Stamler (Ed.), *Inside arts* (pp. 26-30). Washington, DC: Association of Performing Arts Presenters.

Keashly, L., Fisher, R. J., & Grant, P. R. (1993). The comparative utility of third-party consultation and mediation within a complex simulation of intergroup conflict. *Human Relations, 46*, 371-393.

Lakey, B. M., Lakey, G., Napier, R., & Robinson, J. (1995). *Grassroots and non-profit leadership: A guide for organizations in changing times*. New Haven, CT: New Society.

Lewin, K. (1946). Action research and minority problems. *Journal of Social Issues, 2*, 34-46.

Lippitt, G. L. (1982). *Organizational renewal: A holistic approach to organizational development* (2nd ed.). Englewood Cliffs, NJ: Prentice-Hall.

Lippitt, G. L., & Lippitt, R. O. (1986). *The consulting process in action* (2nd ed.). San Diego, CA: University Associates.

Lippitt, R. O., & Schindler-Rainman, E. (1975). Designing for participative learning and changing. In K. D. Benne, L. P. Bradford, J. R. Gibb, & R. O. Lippitt (Eds.), *The laboratory method of changing and learning: Theory and application* (pp. 189-212). Palo Alto, CA: Science and Behavior Books.

Maier, N. R. F. (1963). *Problem-solving discussions and conferences: Leadership methods and skills*. New York: McGraw-Hill.

Napier, R. W., & Gershenfeld, N. K. (1989). *Groups: Theory and experience* (4th ed.). Boston: Houghton-Mifflin.

Nicotera, A. M. (1997). Managing conflict communication in groups. In L. R. Frey & J. K Barge (Eds.), *Managing group life: Communicating in decision-making groups* (pp. 104-130). Boston: Houghton Mifflin.

Papa, M. J., & Canary, D. J. (1995). Conflict in organizations: A competence-based approach. In A. M. Nicotera (Ed.), *Conflict and organizations: Communicative processes* (pp. 153-179). Albany: State University of New York Press.

Park City International Jazz Foundation. (1997, November 20). *Articles of incorporation*. Park City, UT: Author.

Perls, F. S. (1969). *Gestalt therapy verbatim*. Lafayette, CA: Real People Press.

Poole, M. S. (1999). Group communication theory. In L. R. Frey (Ed.), D. S. Gouran, & M. S. Poole (Assoc. Eds.), *The handbook of group communication theory and research* (pp. 37-70). Thousand Oaks, CA: Sage.

Putnam, L. L., & Poole, M. S. (1987). Conflict and negotiation. In F. M. Jablin, L. L. Putnam, K. H. Roberts, & L. W. Porter (Eds.), *Handbook of organizational communication: An interdisciplinary perspective* (pp. 549-599). Newbury Park, CA: Sage.

Putnam, L. L., & Stohl, C. (1990). Bona fide groups: A reconceptualization of groups in context. *Communication Studies, 41*, 248-265.

Putnam, L. L., & Stohl, C. (1996). Bona fide groups: An alternative perspective for communication and small group decision making. In R. Y. Hirokawa & M. S. Poole (Eds.), *Communication and group decision making* (2nd ed., pp. 147-178). Thousand Oaks, CA: Sage.

Robinson, M. K. (2001). *Nonprofit boards that work: The end of one-size-fits-all governance.* New York: John Wiley.

Schein, E. H. (1969). *Process consultation.* Reading, MA: Addison-Wesley.

Seibold, D. R. (1979). Making meetings more successful: Plans, formats, and procedures for group problem-solving. *Journal of Business Communication, 16*(4), 3-20.

Seibold, D. R. (1995). Developing the "team" in a team-managed organization: Group facilitation in a new-design plan. In L. R. Frey (Ed.), *Innovations in group facilitation: Applications in natural settings* (pp. 282-298). Cresskill, NJ: Hampton Press.

Seibold, D. R., & Krikorian, D. H. (1997). Planning and facilitating group meetings. In L. R. Frey & J. K. Barge (Eds.), *Managing group life: Communicating in decision-making groups* (pp. 270-305). Boston: Houghton Mifflin.

Sherif, M. (1966). *In common predicament: Social psychology of intergroup conflict and cooperation.* Boston: Houghton Mifflin.

Sline, R. W., & Boulton, A. C. (2000, November 8). *In search of common ground: A structural analysis of the Park City International Jazz Foundation.* Unpublished report to the Park City International Jazz Foundation Board of Trustees.

Wall, J. A. (1981). Mediation: An analysis, review, and proposed research. *Journal of Conflict Resolution, 25*, 157-180.

Walton, R. E. (1987). *Managing conflict: Interpersonal dialogue and third-party roles* (2nd ed.). Reading, MA: Addison-Wesley.

Wolf, T. (1999). *Managing a nonprofit organization in the twenty-first century* (Rev. ed.). New York: Simon & Schuster.

Young, D. R. (2001). Organizational identity in nonprofit organizations: Strategic and structural implications. *Nonprofit Management & Leadership, 12*, 139-157.

III

FACILITATING GROUP CONVERSATION AND DISCUSSION

8

THEORY AND PRACTICE IN PUBLIC DIALOGUE
A CASE STUDY IN FACILITATING COMMUNITY
TRANSFORMATION

Shawn Spano
San José State University
Public Dialogue Consortium

On a sunny afternoon in the Fall of 2001, over 120 people gathered together for a large public forum at the Quinlan Community Center in Cupertino, California. For over seven hours, city residents, public officials, and city staff talked together and listened to one another about their concerns and visions for their city and community. The format consisted of a series of small and large group activities, each of which was designed to enable participants to openly discuss the most pressing issues and topics facing the city. Trained facilitators guided participants through the activities by enacting a set of communication techniques they had learned in a facilitation workshop held two weeks prior to the forum.

At first glance, this event might seem commonplace, in line with any number of town hall meetings or community forums regularly held in cities and towns across the United States. A closer look, however, shows that the event was carefully crafted to produce conversational structures based in a distinctive yet underutilized form of public communication. This event was unique, in part, because it was explicitly designed as a "public dialogue."

This was not the first public dialogue to be held in Cupertino. Indeed, the event just described, and explained in more detail later in this chapter, is part of an ongoing community project that was initiated in 1996 through the efforts of the Public Dialogue Consortium (PDC), a nonprofit organization comprised of communication practitioners, consultants, theorists, and researchers (Spano, 2001; for information on the PDC, see www.publicdialogue.org). From its inception, the Cupertino project was designed to create new opportunities for residents of the city to participate with local government officials in public decision-making processes. In addition to several large, city-wide public dialogue forums, the project has evolved through a series of focus group meetings, intergenerational interviews, team-building sessions, and training workshops conducted in collaboration with the local city government, public schools, and other community service organizations. Although clearly oriented toward achieving practical outcomes, the Cupertino project is also guided by well-defined and coherent communication theory and methodology. As Cissna and Anderson (2002) noted, "The Cupertino project is an excellent example of how a practical application of dialogue, in this case of sustained community self-awareness and community building, can be at the same time theoretically informed" (p. 229).

In this chapter, I describe the methodology, theory, and research orientation underlying the PDC's approach to the facilitation of public dialogue. Using the Fall 2001 Cupertino public dialogue forum as a case study, I then demonstrate how the methodology works in practice. A cornerstone of the Cupertino project, and public dialogue more generally, is that it seeks to bridge the academic concerns of communication theorists with the practical demands of government institutions and public organizations. Although these efforts present unique challenges, at both theoretical and practical levels, they also have enormous potential to create applied approaches that simultaneously advance communication theory and help to improve the quality of group communication facilitation and public decision making. In the final section of the chapter, I highlight some implications of the PDC's approach to facilitating public dialogue in light of the theoretical and practical challenges we encountered as a result of our work in Cupertino.

A METHODOLOGY FOR FACILITATING PUBLIC DIALOGUE

The PDC methodology is rooted in a constellation of theoretical perspectives that call forth the social, communicative, pragmatic, and systemic qualities of group facilitation. Social constructionism (see, e.g., Gergen, 1999; Shotter, 1993; Shotter & Gergen, 1994) provides the broad philosophical grounding for conceptualizing communication as the primary social process through which humans collectively create, maintain, and recreate social reality. Within the social constructionist perspective, the individual is replaced as the primary unit of observation privileged in other social-psychological approaches with a conversational metaphor, thus drawing attention away from individual behaviors to the joint actions people perform together (Shotter, 1993). Recent developments in the coordinated management of meaning (CMM) theory (Cronen, 1995a; W. B. Pearce, 1989; W. B. Pearce & Pearce, 2000a) have extended the interpretive framework of social constructionism into the realm of practical action and applied intervention techniques. Consequently, CMM functions in the PDC methodology as the theoretical infrastructure that informs the communicative actions of facilitators as they engage with group participants to create new social practices.

The goal of the PDC methodology is to produce a coherent set of communicative practices and an accompanying theoretical discourse that enables community members to engage in positive social change. The theory, which consists of vocabulary terms, linguistic distinctions, principles, models, and metaphors, does not come before the practice nor is it treated as a separate process; rather, the theory arises out of situated practices, enacted within localized settings, that reflexively assists in contributing to the ongoing development of the practices. Although generalizability is not a primary goal, the methodology can potentially contribute to other facilitation practices that are enacted in different local settings and group contexts.

The approach described above is an example of "practical theory" in the emerging tradition of systemic-pragmatic inquiry (see Barge, 2001b; Cronen, 1995b, 2001). As defined by Cronen (2001):

> A practical theory informs a grammar of practice that facilitates joining with the grammars of others to explore their unique patterns of situated action. The proximal reason for joining is the cocreation of new affordances and constraints for creative participation in the instrumental and consummatory dimensions of experience. Practical theory itself is importantly informed by data created in the process of engagement with others. (p. 26)

This approach to inquiry is clearly interventionist in that practical theorists purposefully engage with community members to help change, alter, and modify problematic social practices. Although this goal of transformative practice (Barge, 2001b; Spano, 2001) through facilitating group interaction may be possible without the benefit of a theoretical perspective, it is not desirable, in this case, because it would not be sufficiently practical. The value of theory in this approach is that it provides a comprehensive framework for integrating particular aspects of the situation together (Cronen,

2001). Theory assists the facilitator in making sense of the situation at hand and in offering alternative scenarios that invite community members to move forward in light of the consequences of the actions that they and others have taken and will take.

Guided by practical theory, the PDC seeks to facilitate social change through the use of dialogic communication (Littlejohn & Domenici, 2001; W. B. Pearce & Pearce, 2000b; Spano, 2001). As we conceptualize it, *dialogue* is a form of communication (W. B. Pearce, 1989) that relationally situates interactants in such a way that they are able to stay in the tension between holding their own ground and being profoundly open to others (Buber, 1958; W. B. Pearce & Pearce, 2000a). This conceptualization calls forth an additional set of dialogic qualities: (a) an emphasis on listening as much as speaking; (b) the free and honest expression of views and opinions; (c) the ability to seriously consider other peoples' views and opinions, no matter how different they might be from one's own; and (d) a focus on mutual understanding and coordination, not winning and losing (Spano, 2001).

Important questions arise as we consider the methods used to facilitate dialogic communication: Dialogue for whom? To what end? Under what circumstances? Answers to these questions point to the "strong" democratic principles (Barber, 1984) embedded in the methodology, and to a consideration of what it means to theorize and practice *public* dialogue. Whereas private dialogue is focused solely on the micro (interpersonal) level, public dialogue is distinct in that it operates at both macro (community) and micro levels. At the macro level, communities are viewed systemically, as being comprised of complex webs of interconnected conversations. At the micro level, public dialogue seeks to foster collaboration, relational development, and mutual understanding among community members in concrete, situated, face-to-face encounters. As such, public dialogue entails the intermingling of bottom-up and top-down patterns of communication in that opportunities are created at the grassroots level for community members to directly engage decisions in a bottom-up fashion, and simultaneously, city officials, community leaders, and others at the top are encouraged to support initiatives from the bottom and to respond and act in ways that create opportunities for ongoing participation by community members. Ultimately, the goal is to create coordinated speaking and listening opportunities between and among community leaders and community members so that everyone has the chance to express his or her views and to hear the views of others.

Public dialogue projects are enacted based on the interests, needs, concerns, and perspectives of particular community members. In line with community-based action research, the purpose "is to assist people in extending their understanding of their situation and thus resolve problems that confront them" (Stringer, 1996, p. 9). The facilitator's role is not one of content expert, called in to diagnose the situation and solve the problem; rather, the facilitator is a resource person who assists in the design and implementation of processes that will enable community members "to investigate systematically their problems and issues, formulate powerful and sophisticated accounts of their situations, and devise plans to deal with the problems at hand" (Stringer, p. 15). As such, action research and public dialogue embody the principles of participatory democracy—strong democracy—in that they encourage the active participation of community members in decision-making activities that directly affect them (Greenwood & Levin, 1998; Spano, 2001).

Principles of participatory democracy are also embedded in the PDC methodology through the development of training programs that guide community members in learning to design and facilitate public dialogue events. One of the many insights coming out of the early stages of the Cupertino project was the need to share our skills and knowledge as communication specialists with local participants. This focus on educating and training community members for the purpose of building their capacity to serve as facilitators themselves increases opportunities for people to engage in dialogic communication, reduces the need for outside experts, and enhances the likelihood that public dialogue projects will become self-sustaining—that is, directed by the community members themselves.

PUBLIC DIALOGUE FACILITATION MODEL

The public dialogue process model developed by W. B. Pearce and Pearce (2000b) grew out of the work engaged in as part of the Cupertino project. One of the key implications of the model is that it extends conceptualizations of facilitation beyond the micro skills used to manage group processes. As the model indicates, specific facilitation skills and techniques are situated within the context of larger event and strategic process designs. This expanded view of public dialogue requires that we enlarge the domain of facilitation beyond isolated events and single group interactions. I now turn to an examination of each of the three levels of the model.

Level 1: Strategic Process Design

Strategic process design, the broadest of the three levels, locates individual events and activities that are part of a public dialogue project within an ongoing sequence of events that build off one another. When facilitators work with community members to map out the broad contours of a project—how it will evolve over a series of stages or phases—they are working at this level.

Public dialogue strategic designs have a number of distinctive features when compared to other forms of public communication. For example, in the traditional top-down model of public decision making, leaders formulate the issues in advance and on their own and then set out to persuade the public to accept their conclusions, recommendations, and preferred courses of action (Yankelovich, 1991). By contrast, public dialogue strategic designs involve community members early in the process, as issues are formulated and options are developed. This means that the public is invested in the process from the very beginning. Moreover, public dialogue projects are organic in that each phase grows out of the preceding phase, while simultaneously setting the context for the phases to follow. This means that the process evolves, usually over an extended period of time, in such a way that particular outcomes cannot be determined in advance.

Although there is a good deal of variation in how public dialogue projects are designed, most typically include the following six stages: (a) issue identification, (b) eliciting different views, (c) framing the issue, (d) generating options for action, (e) deliberating and deciding, and (f) implementing public agreements. The pace, duration, and scale of these stages differ depending on the nature of the community, the issues and topics under consideration, and the resources and skills of the participants.

As shown in Figure 8.1, a typical public dialogue strategic process design evolves through stages that expand and contract based on whether the discussion is oriented toward divergence (opening up possibilities) or convergence (narrowing choices). Eliciting Different Views (stage b) and Generating Options for Action (stage d), for example, are accomplished by designing events and facilitating discussions that call forth competing perspectives, multiple alternatives, and diverse opinions. As such, these stages promote divergence among participants. Framing the Issue (stage c) and Deliberating and Deciding (stage e), in contrast, are accomplished by focusing events and discussions on areas of convergence, commonality, and consensus among participants. In Implementing Public Agreements (stage f), the goal is to maintain continuity in the decisions that were made in the previous stage, and simultaneously to create a space for issues and implementation strategies to develop and change.

The uneven lines that frame each of the stages signify that the process evolves in nonlinear, unpredictable, and imprecise ways. Because there is no exact formula that can guarantee results, there will inevitably be points in the process where the facilitators and participants experience confusion, frustration, and paradox. Moreover, the stages differ in terms of their challenges and possibilities. A stage that is designed around openness and divergence, for example, will operate differently from one that seeks commonality and convergence. In this regard, each stage in the process creates its own

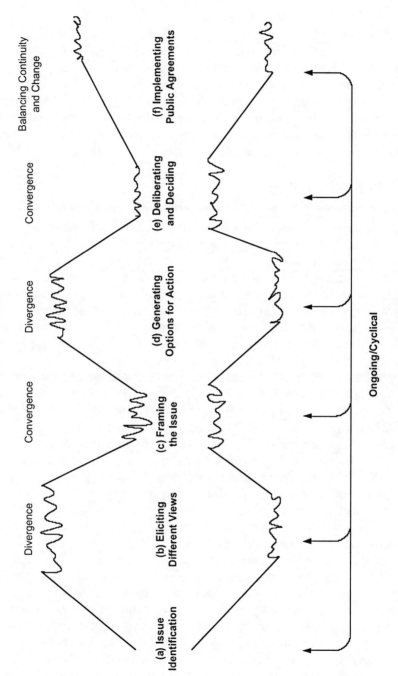

Figure 8.1. Sample strategic design process

unique set of affordances and constraints. Finally, public dialogue processes do not end simply because a public agreement has been decided or implemented; issues, topics, and concerns evolve and change over time as a result of having gone through a public decision-making process. We conclude from this that public dialogue stands the best chance of being successful in managing issues and making decisions when facilitators and community members attend to them in an ongoing and cyclical fashion.

Level 2: Event Design

The design of a given dialogue event is shaped by its placement within the overall strategic process. For example, if the stage of the strategic process is to deliberate and decide on a particular course of action or policy recommendation (stage e), facilitators might work with community members to develop one or more events that are explicitly designed to accomplish this goal. Typically, public dialogue events are centered on small groups, including focus groups, deliberation groups, study circles, and other similar groups. Even in the case of large public forums, with 100 or more attendees, the PDC designs events to include opportunities for small group interaction, in addition to large group plenary discussions. Depending on the particular phase of the strategic process, a public dialogue project might also include one-on-one interviews between the facilitator and community members. Such interviews and other similar activities are especially helpful in the early stages of a project as a way to elicit perspectives and concerns that can then be discussed in subsequent small group and large group contexts.

In addition to their placement in the overall strategic process, public dialogue events must be carefully designed to balance structure and openness. Events that are overly structured limit creativity, spontaneity, and the generation of new ideas, options, and alternatives; by the same token, events that are not adequately structured often fail to harness a group's collective contributions toward the accomplishment of common goals and other outcomes and decisions. This tension between structure and openness is not, of course, an either/or proposition; rather, public dialogue events should be designed to include episodes that oscillate between *both* opening up possibilities *and* narrowing choices (Spano, 2001). Of course, the level of structure and openness also depends on where a given event fits within the overall strategic process. Typically, in the early stages of a project or event, the activities will be geared toward openness; in later stages, there is a move to create more structure as participants begin deliberating options, making decisions, and implementing action plans.

Level 3: Event Facilitation Skills

Event facilitation skills refer to the actions facilitators perform "in the moment" as they work with group participants. Consistent with the other two levels of the PDC facilitation model, the selection and enactment of these skills depend on the particular event in which they will be used. For this reason, facilitators must use good judgment in choosing skills that fit the parameters of the event, and they must have the ability to perform these skills, moment to moment, in response to changing group dynamics. As W. B. Pearce and Pearce (2000b) stated:

> The success of the event as public dialogue hinges on such subtle things as the difference between asking a question or making a comment at a particular moment, or the way a question is phrased, or the timing with which it is asked. (p. 416)

To facilitate public dialogue, thus, requires a heightened awareness and ability to act into and out of multiple contexts. Hence, facilitators respond to what is being said and done at a particular point in time, and they must also simultaneously adjust their actions to fit within the unfolding logic of the larger event design.

In addition to the standard facilitation skills that apply in most situations, such as time keeping and recording, there are several other skills that are keyed more directly to public dialogue. In what follows, I briefly describe six of the main techniques used by PDC facilitators in the Cupertino project and elsewhere to promote dialogic communication: neutrality, curiosity and wonder, dialogic listening, appreciative questioning, systemic questioning, and reflecting and reframing.

Neutrality refers to the position facilitators take relative to the topic and content at hand. It is crucial that facilitators not impose their views and opinions on the group but, rather, let participants themselves determine the content. One technique for achieving neutrality is taking the "not-knowing position," in which facilitators are mindful of their own assumptions and careful not to let their preconceptions unnecessarily influence their interpretations and actions.

Leading with curiosity and wonder refers to facilitators' active engagement of neutrality and taking the not-knowing position. Facilitators demonstrate through their verbal and nonverbal communicative acts that they are open to and capable of eliciting the multiple perspectives that are present in the group. Ideally, facilitators' actions should establish an inclusive group context where everyone's input is welcomed and where all participants are recognized as having something valuable to add to the dialogue.

Dialogic listening entails moving from one's own conception of a situation to another person's side of the conversation to understand it from that person's perspective. As Stewart and Logan (1998) noted, it is listening designed to cultivate a shared understanding of meaning. Sometimes referred to as "empathic" or "active listening," facilitators engage in this form of listening by nonverbally attending to those who are speaking, asking questions that help to enrich the other person's perspectives and stories, and summarizing and paraphrasing what participants say to ensure mutual understanding.

Appreciative questioning is a technique that facilitators use to help participants uncover the positive resources that exist in a group, community, or organization (Cooperrider, Barrett, & Srivastva, 1995; Littlejohn & Domenici, 2001). By asking questions that call forth the qualities and values that enrich life in a given community, facilitators can construct other questions that help participants develop ways to extend those qualities into the future. Barge (2001a), for example, articulated a stage model of affirmative community conflict that begins by asking participants to consider the core values that represent the "best of what is in the community." Subsequent stages move progressively through a series of appreciative questions that ask participants to envision an idealized future followed by the actions they need to engage in to create it.

Systemic questioning is a technique that facilitators use to draw out connections and relationships in the perspectives and stories that participants tell. Because they target perceptions of difference (W. B. Pearce, 1995; Selvini, Boscolo, Cecchin, & Prata, 1980), systemic questions invite people to compare their views with the views of others. For example, a facilitator might ask a group participant how another participant's position on a given issue is different from his or her own. The facilitator might follow this up by asking what would need to happen for one or both of them to change their position in the future. One of the advantages of systemic questioning is that such questions treat difference, disagreement, and conflict as socially constructed sites for exploration and growth.

Finally, *reflecting and reframing* are techniques that facilitators use to foster new understandings among group participants. After carefully listening to the various perspectives and stories shared in the group, for example, a facilitator might reflect back to participants his or her interpretations of what he or she heard. The purpose of such reflections are to offer the group a co-constructed account of what the members have produced together. This is normally accomplished by the facilitator drawing together common themes, highlighting points of contention, and surfacing implicit assumptions. Reframing goes one step beyond reflecting by placing the facilitator's interpretive accounts into a significantly different context than that put forth by group members (Andersen, 1982). For example, if a group has talked about an issue as a past problem, the facilitator might reframe the discussion by suggesting ways in which it might lead to future possibilities. In both reflecting and reframing, facilitators' accounts are not offered as factually correct statements—the "Truth"—but, rather, as stimulants to create additional discussion based on new and different understandings by group members.

CASE STUDY: EXAMINING THE PDC METHODOLOGY IN PRACTICE

To provide an illustration of the PDC methodology, I describe below a dialogic communication training program and public dialogue event held in Cupertino in October, 2001. The purpose of the training program was to teach participants how to facilitate dialogic communication within the context of the particular community event, a large public forum in Cupertino that was designed and facilitated via the methodology and public dialogue model described earlier.

Dialogue Facilitation Training

The training program was conducted over a 2-day period. The 26 participants consisted of city residents and members of the Citizens of Cupertino Cross Cultural Consortium (5Cs), graduate students from the Department of Communication Studies at San José State University, and volunteers from the Peninsula Conflict Resolution Center, a sister organization of the PDC located in the San Francisco bay area. A PDC training manual on facilitating dialogic communication (K. A. Pearce, 2001) was mailed to participants in advance. Four PDC members served as trainers (Suzette Merchant, Darshana Nardkarni, Barnett Pearce, and me).

The first day was a 4-hour, afternoon session consisting of informational presentations by the trainers, group exercises, and group discussions. Participants first completed a self-assessment questionnaire and activity that encouraged them to critically reflect on their experiences with group facilitation and facilitation-related activities (K. A. Pearce, 2001). This activity was framed as an opportunity for each participant to "create his or her own facilitator story" and to envision ways in which he or she might use the training to chart a path for ongoing personal growth and professional development. In keeping with our theoretical orientation, participants co-constructed their stories in groups. As each person shared his or her reflections about the items on the self-assessment questionnaire, the other group members listened and asked questions to help extend and enrich the story being told.

Participants were then introduced to the conceptual foundations of group facilitation as it is practiced by the PDC and were led through an activity designed to demonstrate the theoretical principles. The conceptual foundations included an overview of the social constructionist perspective, an introduction to the qualities and characteristics of dialogic communication, and a preview of the three-level public dialogue facilitation model, including specific event facilitation skills. The demonstration consisted of a critical analysis of a videotape of a non-PDC public meeting held several months prior in Cupertino. The meeting consisted of a rather lengthy series of presentations by city officials and outside experts on the city's General Plan, followed by audience questions and comments. The design and facilitation of that public meeting prefigured an adversarial relationship between the presenters and participants, who, during the audience question segment, repeatedly accused the officials and experts of "not listening" to residents or taking their concerns into account. This was clearly not a public *dialogue* event; it constituted what we would call a "negative" example.

In a large group discussion, training participants engaged in a critical analysis of the Cupertino General Plan meeting. Trainers used the following descriptive and evaluative questions to guide the analysis: (a) What is the strategic process being used? When are members of the public involved? How are they involved? (b) What is the event design? How is the meeting structured? What is the sequence of the episode—what comes first, second, etc.? How does it end? (c) What is "being made" at this event? (d) What event facilitation skills are being utilized? On the part of the leaders? On the part of the audience? What skills are not being practiced—what are the leaders and the public not doing? (e) What is your evaluation of this event? Does it foster mutual understanding? Does it contribute to community building and civic engagement? Does it lead to effective decision making? (f) How could the event be made better? What specific suggestions do you have?

The second day of the training was a 7-hour session consisting of a series of experiential activities—role plays—designed to give participants practice at facilitating and recording the types of conversations they were likely to encounter at the public dialogue forum. This approach highlights the PDC's focus on event-specific training. In our experience, we have found that facilitation skills and competencies are best learned in situations that are directly relevant to participants (Spano, 2001). One way to achieve such relevance is to key the acquisition of facilitation skills directly to their application in a particular event. For example, the role-play activities conducted at the training session mirrored in every way possible the different small group discussions planned for the public dialogue forum; this included developing written scenarios and detailed descriptions for each of the role-play activities.

Another feature of the PDC facilitation training model evidenced here is the emphasis on moving participants into different "person positions" (W. B. Pearce, 1994; Spano, 2001). As participants learned "about" facilitation, they assumed a third-person position; that is, they were positioned "outside" the skills and processes being taught. When participants practiced being "in" the role of facilitator, they experienced directly what it is like to actually enact the skills and processes and, thereby, assumed a first-person learning position. In addition, the role-play activities included opportunities for critical reflection, in which the PDC trainers led the groups in a discussion about the role plays—for example, by asking what the successes and challenges were and what the facilitators might do differently to improve. This type of critical reflection involved a combination of both first- and third-person positions in that participants reflected "about" a process that they actually engaged "in."

Public Dialogue Community Forum

The day-long public dialogue forum was held one week after the dialogue facilitation training workshop. Participants from the training served as table facilitators and recorders. This particular forum was the fifth in an annual series of large public meetings that the PDC helped to design and facilitate. In keeping with the previous four events, the overarching goal was to create a context that would enable residents and city officials to explore community issues utilizing a dialogic form of communication. The stated outcome for the forum, as indicated on the agenda and invitation letter, was to give residents, the city council, and city staff the opportunity to meaningfully discuss current issues relevant to the city and community.

Following the official welcome by the mayor, a member of the PDC team provided context-setting remarks and a preview of the event design. This has become a standard feature in the way the PDC organizes and conducts events. By articulating the strategic process and event design at the very beginning of a public dialogue forum, we seek to establish with participants a common set of expectations and agreements. As noted earlier with the case of the nondialogic Cupertino General Plan meeting, the conventional structure of many public participation meetings consists of informational presentations and panel discussions, with time thrown in at the end for audience comments and questions. Other types of public participation events, such as city council meetings, are legally prescribed and overly structured in terms of rules and procedures; typically, members of the public are given an allotted period of time at the microphone to state their opinion, with the result being a series of often disconnected monologues. At public dialogue events such as the Cupertino forum, it is, therefore, crucial that participants understand the event design and how it differs from the conventional format of most public participation meetings.

In setting the context for the event, the current public dialogue forum was described in terms of how it fit within the larger strategic process design of the Cupertino project. This was accomplished by providing an historical account of the previous four large public meetings and how they evolved to create the present situation. The PDC team member went on to explain:

> The questions guiding us today are: Where do we go from here? Are last year's topics still relevant? Are there new issues? What are they? And given the issues, what are you—residents, city council members, and city staff—going to do about them? How are you all going to work together—to collaborate—to identify and resolve the issues that you face? Nobody's exactly sure what anybody is going to say here; there are no preplanned topics. The only issues that we will talk about are the ones that you and the other participants identified at last year's public forum. So today's meeting builds off prior meetings; it continues the tradition of moving the community forward.

The rest of the context-setting remarks were focused on describing the micro-level communicative practices and outcomes of the forum:

> We will establish some ground rules for your table discussions so that everybody will be operating out of a common set of agreements. We will emphasize listening as much as speaking. Most people are pretty good at stating their views and opinions, and everybody here today will indeed have the chance to say what is important to them. The missing piece—the piece that gets emphasized at these public forums—is listening. The real challenge, and this is not easy, is to listen, and I mean really listen, to someone who is saying something that you disagree with. We will also emphasize understanding more than winning and losing, which means that the focus is on collaboration more than competition. We will work to uncover what our differences are, but we will seek to do this is a climate of trust and respect. Finally, we will work to develop a set of recommendations and action plans. The goal is to leave the meeting today with some specific steps that you and the city can take to address the issues and concerns you identify as important.

The event design for the public dialogue forum consisted of small group, table discussions strategically intermixed with a series of fishbowl discussions conducted in the large group setting. After a brief introduction activity, table facilitators guided participants through an open discussion designed to elicit what they perceived to be the most relevant topics and issues in the city. Facilitators framed the discussion as an opportunity to hear everyone's views about the current state of the city; at the same time, facilitators had been instructed during the training to gently guide discussion away from solutions and actions. The views expressed at each table were summarized and recorded on large sheets of paper and posted around the room in preparation for participants to take a "gallery walk." It is critical to note here that the content for the entire public dialogue event, in the form of community topics and issues, was developed during this first small group discussion activity. All of the subsequent discussions and activities were designed, in one way or another, to extend, elaborate, refine, and narrow these topics and issues.

The next segment of the forum consisted of a series of interconnected discussions that moved back and forth among different sized groups. Employing a conversational metaphor, the design called for the groups to build off each other's conversations as the movement shifted between fishbowl discussions in the large group setting and the small group, table discussions. The first fishbowl was comprised of participants selected from the various small groups. Sitting on a special stage erected on one side of the room, these participants were guided by a PDC facilitator as they reflected on the topics and issues shared in their small groups and compared these with the topics they read during the gallery walk. Cupertino city council members then moved into the fishbowl and, with the help of the same facilitator, they were asked to respond to the topics that had been identified and to weave their own views, issues, and topics into those expressed in the previous fishbowl. From here, the focus shifted back to the small group, table discussions. All participants were first given an opportunity to respond to what they had heard in the two fishbowls and were then asked to begin narrowing the list of topics and issues by choosing the two or three that they felt were most important. Facilitators asked participants to discuss the advantages, disadvantages, and tradeoffs in making their selections and encouraged each group to make decisions on the basis of consensus instead of majority rule.

The remainder of the forum was spent developing action plans for each of the issues that had been selected. This was accomplished through a modified version of open space technology (Owen, 1992), which is an event design that allows participants to choose their own topics and construct their own groups. Participants at the forum self-selected into different groups corresponding to the five issues that had been generated: housing, traffic and transportation, city government communications, systemic decision making, and youth issues. Facilitators and recorders were assigned to each of these issue-specific groups; a city staff member was also assigned to the groups to serve as an information resource. Groups spent approximately 90 minutes developing their action plans, which were recorded on specially designed template forms to ensure consistency. The questions posed by facilitators in this segment were: (a) How does the issue impact the Cupertino community? (b) What are the challenges and opportunities the issue presents to the city? (c) Who should do what, with what resources? (d) What should be done first? After each issue group reported the results of its discussions in the large group setting, the city council members moved back into the fishbowl format and responded to the action plans. The mayor gave the closing remarks.

METHODOLOGICAL IMPLICATIONS AND CHALLENGES IN FACILITATING PUBLIC DIALOGUE

At the core of the PDC methodology is a grammar of practice (Cronen, 1995b, 2001) that enables us as facilitators to develop our abilities and ways of working by joining with the grammatical abilities of others. The "others" with whom we join obviously include community members, such as city residents, city staff, government officials, and community leaders. At the same time, our grammar of practice is also informed by our engagement with social theorists, action researchers, communication consultants, and others who are not directly tied to the local community in which the facilitation takes place. PDC members purposefully join with these different types of conversational partners to develop both our theoretical understandings of and practical skills in facilitating public dialogue in real-world situations.

As I explained, we seek to employ dialogue as the primary process through which we join our grammar of practice with the grammars of others. As Bernstein (1992) noted, to be in dialogue requires participants to be open to each other and to the differences that are inevitably experienced as a result of their encounter. In learning from their differences, participants can construct new understandings and new grammatical abilities that allow them to create and participate in new communicative practices. In this regard, members of the PDC view the development of our methodology as a co-constructed activity that is formed by bringing together different grammars—different ways of communicatively organizing and constructing social reality.

In what follows, I identify four theoretical implications of the PDC methodology and point out some of the challenges these pose for facilitating public dialogue. In the spirit of practical theory and dialogic communication, each implication joins the PDC methodology—our grammar of practice—in relationship with the other grammars we have encountered both inside and outside of local, applied settings.

Praxis and Methodological Openness

The methodological and practical approach to public dialogue facilitation outlined throughout this chapter advances an open-ended, organic form of inquiry that is responsive to social and structural change. This approach is made possible because of the PDC members' awareness of and attention to the reflexive relationship between theory and practice, an approach that Stewart (2001) aptly described as falling within the domain of *praxis*. For the PDC, the methodology is validated to the extent that the theory successfully informs communicative practices, and the practices, in turn, lead to the continual and ongoing development of the theory. Staying "close to the ground" in this manner enables us—indeed, requires us—to adapt to changes both in and out of the research setting.

One of the challenges in working with an open-ended approach to inquiry is maintaining continuity, coherency, and focus. The danger here is that the methodology might be perceived by community members, social theorists, and communication practitioners as lacking a center or core purpose because it can be so easily modified in response to changes in the practical setting. A common but misguided response to this challenge is to try to formalize the methodology. However, as Stohl and Cheney (2001) pointed out, attempts to formalize an inherently informal process produces a paradox that can ultimately undermine the ability of a methodology to adapt to changing situations. Instead of imposing an a priori structure or procedure, the PDC's response is to conceptualize public dialogue strategic processes as developing in an ongoing, cyclical manner, not a step-by-step, linear one. For the PDC, an open-ended methodology is one that weaves together the actions, meanings, and outcomes of various events. Each event in the process, therefore, overlaps and builds off other events. This is a critical dimension in the way we work because it enables public dialogue projects to evolve organically rather than having to follow a pre-established protocol.

The claim that public dialogue evolves organically does not preclude facilitators from establishing empirical markers of success. Indeed, the PDC methodology suggests a range of fairly well-defined outcomes, including mutual understanding, relationship building, and the coordination of meaning and action, which facilitators can use to make judgments about the success of a given strategic process, event design, or facilitation technique. It is important to recognize, however, that these judgments are always context bound, polysemic, and, thus, open to multiple interpretations and reconstructions as contextual circumstances change. As Stewart (2001) noted, the ends of *praxis* are constantly revised as facilitators and community members engage in the serious work of "making-it-up-as-they-go-along" (p. 239).

Having to respond to change is inevitable in community-based research and practice. Working in Cupertino, for example, the PDC has had to adapt to a new city manager, turnover of city council members, and other personnel changes in city hall staff. The community residents who participated in the public forums constantly changed, as various people dropped in and out of the project. Larger developments, such as the recent economic downturn in Silicon Valley, also affected the public dialogue process, at least indirectly. The relevant community issues have changed as well. In the early stages of the project, the main concern centered on cultural diversity, an issue that emerged because of dramatic changes in the ethnic composition of the city's Asian and Chinese population in the 1980s and early 1990s. By the end of 1999, there was a good deal of evidence indicating that the communication processes and structures developed and implemented by the PDC were successful in helping residents and city officials to manage this particular issue constructively (Spano, 2001). As the cultural diversity issue subsided, other issues, including housing, education, and traffic and transportation, came to the forefront.

These changes point to an interesting and important dimension of *praxis* and methodological openness: The means of intervention and inquiry used to facilitate and study public dialogue must be responsive to an environment that is continually changing, in part, due to the methodology itself. In this regard, public dialogue processes and skills must ensure a framework for reconstructing themselves. This re-creation never produces an exact replica, of course, given that the communicative practices that result from an intervention are in response to situations that are continually evolving and changing. The early success of the Cupertino project in dealing with the cultural diversity issue, for example, created opportunities for the PDC to facilitate public dialogue on other community issues and, thereby, expanded our repertoire of grammatical practices. Recently, we have had occasion to revisit our methodology in light of the cultural diversity issue, which has surfaced again through a series of heated public exchanges involving city council members, city officials, and community residents. As we respond to this latest development, we are finding that the issue itself has changed, the community has changed, and so has the relationship between the city and the PDC.

Connecting Facilitation to Academic Research

The second implication addresses the ways in which the PDC methodology contributes to scholarship. Although clearly oriented to the pragmatic demands of the public sector, the methodology is also designed to respond to the traditional scholarly requirements of academic research. One of the ways we achieve this is by extending the position of the facilitators as practitioners into the role of theorists. First, consider that facilitators, as practitioners within an applied setting, are the people uniquely positioned to help participants coordinate and understand the dissimilar grammars that are in play within their group, organization, or community. Simultaneously, facilitators must also weave their own grammar into the mix by virtue of the fact that they are active participants in the discussion. Building off that, we can now describe how facilitators move out of the applied group context to connect their grammatical practices to theoretical formulations articulated by professional academics. In making this shift, it is critical that we avoid falling into a dualistic trap that establishes sharp boundaries between the facilitator-practitioner and facilitator-theorist (Cronen, 2001). The key is to connect, in a dialogic manner, the different worlds and grammars that public dialogue facilitators inhabit.

The shift from practitioner to theorist is accomplished by locating facilitators as moving in an ongoing fashion between inside and outside research positions. The inside research position foregrounds facilitators within the applied context, where the focus is on the generation of practical knowledge, or what Shotter (1990) called "knowing from" (p. 12). For example, the successful enactment of the event facilitation skills described earlier depends on facilitators' practical knowledge to make "in-the-moment" judgments about how to act and respond to others. In the outside research position, facilitators step away from the applied context and direct communication with the group participants to reflect on the communicative actions and practices that were performed by making sense of them in light of social constructionism, CMM, and other relevant theoretical concepts and perspectives. The critical feature is not either one of the positions alone but, rather, the movement between the two (Penman, 2000). Each research position both shapes and is shaped by the other.

One way of conceptualizing the movement between these two positions is to envision facilitators as participating in different discourse communities, each with its own relatively distinct vocabulary, grammar, and rules. Accordingly, the facilitator-practitioner engages one set of discourse communities in the applied context, whereas the facilitator-theorist engages a different set of discourse communities in the academic setting. These are not separate activities but different aspects of the same methodological approach. Indeed, PDC members are committed to joining our theoretical formulations, conversational practices, and grammatical abilities with all of the different discourse communities we encounter in our professional work. Practitioners who do not theorize their practice are ill equipped to engage and learn from academic discourse communities; by the same token, theorists who operate solely within the realm of abstract conceptual systems are ill equipped to enact practical actions that improve conditions in the applied setting. Theory building in the PDC methodology, thus, results from reflexive engagement with both local participants and social theorists.

This approach to inquiry raises interesting questions concerning the form of academic research. If the content of traditional, theoretical-based scholarship is expanded to include practical action and social intervention, then what is the purpose of a research report and what structure should it take? One answer is to frame a research report not as the end point but as one conversational turn in a series of turns. In this way, a research report serves as a form of social action that facilitators enact in response to prior actions and as a condition or invitation to future actions. This means that the report should provide a retrospective account of the facilitation practices, in the form of description, explanation, and critique, from an outside research position; at the same time, the report should also include particular actions and practices that might be enacted prospectively from the inside research position.

Another factor influencing a public dialogue research report is the intended audience. Given that the PDC methodology is co-constructed in collaboration with different discourse communities, it follows that our research reports should benefit multiple audiences, including both local participants and social theorists. In some cases, a report might be framed for the benefit of scholarly audiences, as in the case of W. B. Pearce and Pearce's (2000b) essay, in which the Cupertino project was used as a basis for extending the CMM theory. Another option is to appeal to different audiences within a single report by demonstrating connections between different grammars and discourse communities; my account of the Cupertino project (Spano, 2001), for example, is designed for public professionals, communication practitioners, and communication scholars. Regardless of the particular audience(s), the research report should be framed as a vehicle through which facilitators "translate" theory into practice and practice into theory (Petronio, 1999).

Engaging Nondialogic Forms of Communication

Paradoxically, even as the PDC methodology emphasizes dialogue, it requires an engagement with and responsiveness to nondialogic patterns of communication. Our experiences in Cupertino have led us to conclude that public dialogue cannot be sustained equally throughout the various stages of a project, or even within the context of a single event. There is an ebb and flow in public communication that requires the creative positioning of dialogue alongside more traditional top-down and argumentative/debate forms of interaction. This is necessary, in part, because most public institutions and community organizations operate within a framework of technical rationality that privileges efficiency, effectiveness, and productivity. As former Cupertino City Manager Don Brown (2001) noted, public professionals "view themselves as problem solvers and experts. They are trained to find 'correct' answers that are based on a technical evaluation of information" (p. x). In addition to formal problem-solving methods, the prevalence of technical rationality is also evidenced in argumentative/debate forms of communication where disputants marshal evidence and weigh opposing views to determine which side is correct or true.

The institutionalization of technical rationality in modern organizations (see Stohl & Cheney, 2001) is a powerful force that pushes dialogue away from the center of public life. It does so by promoting a view of communication based on the transmission of information, not the co-construction of meaning (W. B. Pearce & Pearce, 2000a; Spano, 2001). Whereas dialogue seeks the development and transformation of relationships and meaning within contexts that are open to emergent unintended consequences (Cissna & Anderson, 1994), the transmission model upholds the autonomy of individuals to accurately convey information and achieve immediate and certain results. Time and again, PDC members have found ourselves in situations where our conception of dialogic communication as a co-constructed activity has come into conflict with the transmission view. When faced with public officials and community members who hold the transmission view, how should public dialogue facilitators respond? How are we to engage with others who act out of a conception of communication that, on the surface at least, appears to be incompatible with dialogue?

The PDC has formulated two ways of responding to nondialogic forms of communication. The first, which was developed early in the project, is to be proactive and explicit in teaching and modeling dialogue to others. This approach forms the basis of our facilitation training programs, which, not coincidentally, typically include a discussion of the transmission view and how it differs from social constructionist and dialogic approaches. In addition, the PDC seeks to teach dialogue through modeling and demonstration. This combination of teaching and modeling is a powerful tool in providing a framework for meta-communicatively talking about dialogue and simultaneously enacting behaviors that are indicative of dialogue. For example, on a number of occasions, community members have criticized dialogue for being "too soft," "too touchy-feely," and "not focused enough on immediate results." Our response in these situations is to demonstrate curiosity and openness by acknowledging the concerns as legitimate and by inquiring into them. The key is to respond so as not to polarize or antagonize others by pointing out that their view is wrong but, rather, to invite them into a process that enables the exploration and understanding of our different conceptions of communication.

No matter how successful we are in designing and facilitating dialogic processes and events with community members, it is unrealistic to expect ourselves or others to maintain communication in a dialogic frame indefinitely. This was a learning that came to us as the Cupertino project unfolded and we noticed that there were always instances of nondialogic communication at play in the events we facilitated, including events that we felt were highly successful in promoting public dialogue. Stepping back, we came to the realization that dialogue cannot be facilitated in all places at all times, which, in turn, led to us to develop a second approach to dealing with nondialogic forms of communication.

The second approach calls for the careful development of strategic processes and event designs that create an overarching context that establishes the preconditions for dialogue. In the moment-to-moment interactions within a group, there will invariably be instances where participants do not engage in actions that constitute dialogic communication. A participant might become dogmatic, for example, or another might make a personal attack. In Buber's (1958) poetic language, these participants have fallen off the narrow ridge of dialogue that enables them to stay in the relational tension between self (holding one's own ground) and other (being profoundly open to other views). In these situations, facilitators are tasked with helping the group situate nondialogic actions within the dialogic episode—that is, within the larger context or event in which the participants are acting (W. B. Pearce & Pearce, 2000a). This approach only works, of course, if the larger context is sufficiently structured to call forth dialogue, participants are aware of and have accepted the context as legitimate, the facilitators are skillful enough to reframe the nondialogic actions in light of the larger dialogic episode, and if participants are able to reconstruct the episode along with the facilitators.

Dialogue and Ideologically Neutral Facilitation

A final implication of the PDC approach arises from the focus on ideologically neutral facilitation. This approach to facilitation is embedded throughout the PDC methodology, especially at the level of event facilitation skills. When facilitators suspend their preconceptions and assumptions and take the not-knowing position, this enables them to be open to the differently positioned voices in a group, organization, community, or larger social context. Importantly, we are not suggesting that facilitators can actually discard their ideological presuppositions altogether or act in ways that are completely free of ideological meaning and intent. What we do promote is the willing suspension of a particular point of view that would predispose facilitators to take sides on the topics under discussion.

Neutrality, as described here, does not imply passivity; it points, instead, to the responsibility of facilitators to actively promote *all* the points of view that are relevant to a given issue. In this regard, facilitators are not against anybody or any view but are for everybody and all views. Social constructionism provides the theoretical grounding for this particular stance on neutrality. As Gergen (1999) stated:

> Constructionism furnishes a mandate for feminists, ethnic minorities, Marxists, gays and lesbians, the elderly, the poor, and indeed all of us to challenge the "truth" and "the facts" of the dominant order. There is respect for all traditions of value—religious and spiritual, political, social. However, constructionism does not select a victor among the competing voices. . . . All positions may possess legitimacy in their own terms. (p. 231)

One of the most important tasks of public dialogic facilitation, then, is to strive to create the conditions that promote the full and rich expression of all the various voices that exist within a community. Support is demonstrated when facilitators engage with the grammars of different perspectives in an attempt to make them intelligible and understandable, particularly to those who not share them. Although this engagement entails exploring the underlying values that inform a particular point of view, it does not obligate facilitators to make value judgments about a given perspective. To the contrary, public dialogue facilitators are obligated to create an inclusive, safe, and respectful environment so that all voices can be expressed and heard, including those that are both in and out of the mainstream, as well as those that some might find strange, objectionable, radical, or too conservative or too liberal.

The issue of facilitator neutrality also raises important questions concerning power, authority, and leadership. Given the dominant framework of technical rationality, described earlier, public organizations operate much like their private counterparts in that they structurally position people into hierarchical relationships. The question, then, is whether it is possible to have dialogue in situations of unequal power. Is it politically naïve to think that those at the top will relinquish some of their authority by entering into horizontal relationships and shared decision-making activities? Although it is impossible to avoid power differences when working in community settings, it is possible to explicitly acknowledge these differences within the dialogue itself. How power is defined and how it will or won't be exercised within a public dialogue project are topics that can and should be addressed by the participants, including those who hold different positions of authority. If those at the top are unwilling or unable to engage in this type of conversation, or if there are institutional constraints prohibiting it, then a public dialogue project cannot go forward. When faced with these situations, the PDC will either agree to do the necessary prework that will enable participants to engage in a dialogue about power or we will decline to offer our facilitation services.

Facilitators must, of course, choose to initiate public dialogue in groups, organizations, and community settings as they are currently constituted, not as they wish them to be. Moreover, there can be no presumption at the outset that public dialogue will result in a radical restructuring of institutional authority and power. I recognize that not all theorists will agree with this claim. Bachrach and Bostwinick (1992), for example, argued that participatory democracy in the workplace "cannot be accommodated in the present political system. . . . The system itself must be changed in the course of the class struggle to achieve workplace democracy" (p. 15). Rather than accept structural change as a precondition for public dialogue, PDC facilitators are committed, instead, to designing processes that enable participants to openly question the basis on which institutional power and authority rests. There must be, as Gergen (1999) noted, a genuine opportunity to "to challenge the 'truth' and 'the facts' of the dominant order" (p. 231). Under these conditions, dialogue might produce new insights that lead participants, including those who assume traditional positions of power, to consider how current institutional arrangements subvert democratic participation and silence marginalized voices. Dialogue might lead participants to develop new strategies, including structural realignment or alternative forms of resistance, or it might lead to other types of solutions or actions that none of the participants have yet envisioned. There is also the possibility, of course, that dialogue might produce only modest changes, or perhaps no changes at all. The point to be made here is that the outcomes, whatever they might be, cannot be determined at the outset without compromising the open-ended, organic quality of the public dialogue process.

The success of public dialogue projects, however, strongly depend on the extent to which those at top of the hierarchy exercise collaborative forms of leadership. This means, in the case of community projects, that city officials and other leaders must have the knowledge, skill, and motivation to assist others in designing processes and events that create genuine opportunities for public participation. Typically, this requires someone in a leadership role to step forward and champion the project, and to do so in a way that fosters public participation rather than controlling it him or herself (Stohl & Cheney, 2001). This is a delicate, difficult, and often risky balancing act. Too much control from the top will prohibit public dialogue, yet without the right leadership and guidance from those who have authority, there is little hope that public dialogue will ever get off the ground, much less succeed. In our experiences working in Cupertino, we found that city officials and community members were more likely to assume collaborative forms of leadership to the extent that they understood the ideologically neutral stance of public dialogue facilitation and were comfortable enough in their professional positions to share decision-making responsibilities. In other words, collaboration by those at the top is made possible when leaders are not bound to a predetermined outcome and when there is a willingness to openly consider alternative sources of power and authority.

CONCLUSION

Cronen (2001) concluded one of his articles on practical theory by asking readers to consider the essay itself as an "instrument" that encourages "new practical inquiries" (p. 32). I would like to do something similar by suggesting that this chapter be treated as a compass for navigating the theoretical, methodological, and practical complexities of facilitating public dialogue with community groups. In this regard, I intend the chapter to serve as a directional device for conceptualizing, designing, and facilitating public dialogue projects. I did not provide an exact formula, map, or blueprint that can simply be superimposed on a particular community, problem, topic, or issue. Because every social situation is defined by a unique set of contingencies, there is no guarantee that a strategic process, event design, or facilitation technique that worked in one situation will be successful in another.

What I hope this chapter offers is a sense of direction for scholars and facilitators that helps them to move forward in the development of public dialogue theory, method, and practice. Specifically, the methodological compass provided here points facilitators in the direction of open-ended out-comes, not predetermined results; charts a path for connecting the pragmatic needs of community groups and public institutions with academic research; directs facilitators to engage with nondialogic forms of communication, not to silence them or argue against them; and sends public dialogue theory and practice along a trajectory of ideological neutrality, collaborative leadership, and the inclusion of all the representative voices within a community. By using this compass, dialogue facilitators can help to develop communication structures and processes that enhance public participation and improve the quality of group decision making.

REFERENCES

Andersen, T. (1992). Reflecting on reflecting with families. In S. McNamee & K. J. Gergen (Eds.), *Therapy as social construction* (pp. 54-68). Newbury Park, CA: Sage.

Bachrach, P., & Bostwinick, A. (1992). *Power and empowerment: A radical theory of participatory democracy*. Philadelphia: Temple University Press.

Barber, B. R. (1984). *Strong democracy: Participatory politics for a new age*. Berkeley: University of California Press.

Barge, J. K. (2001a). Creating healthy communities through affirmative conflict communication. *Conflict Resolution Quarterly, 19*, 89-101.

Barge, J. K. (2001b). Practical theory as mapping, engaged reflection, and transformative practice. *Communication Theory, 11*, 5-12.

Bernstein, R. J. (1992). *The new constellation: The ethical-political horizons of modernity/postmodernity*. Cambridge, MA: MIT Press.

Brown, D. (2001). Foreword. In S. Spano, *Public dialogue and participatory democracy: The Cupertino community project* (pp. ix-xii). Cresskill, NJ: Hampton Press.

Buber, M. (1958). *I and thou* (R. G. Smith, Trans.; 2nd ed.). New York: Scribner.

Cissna, K. N., & Anderson, R. (1994). Communication and the ground of dialogue. In R. Anderson, K. N. Cissna, & R. C. Arnett (Eds.), *The reach of dialogue: Confirmation, voice, and community* (pp. 9-30). Cresskill, NJ: Hampton Press.

Cissna, K. N., & Anderson, R. (2002). *Moments of meeting: Buber, Rogers, and the potential for public dialogue*. Albany: State University of New York Press.

Cooperrider, D., Barrett, F., & Srivastva, S. (1995). Social construction and appreciative inquiry: A journey in organizational theory. In D-M. Hosking, H. P. Dachler, & K. J. Gergen (Eds.), *Management and organization: Relational alternatives to individualism* (pp. 157-200). Aldershot, England: Avebury.

Cronen, V. E. (1995a). Coordinated management of meaning: The consequentiality of communication and the recapturing of experience. In S. J. Sigman (Ed.), *The consequentiality of communication* (pp. 16-75). Mahwah, NJ: Lawrence Erlbaum.

Cronen, V. E. (1995b). Practical theory and the tasks ahead for social approaches to communication. In W. Leeds-Hurwitz (Ed.), *Social approaches to communication* (pp. 217-242). New York: Guilford Press.

Cronen, V. E. (2001). Practical theory, practical art, and the pragmatic-systemic account of inquiry. *Communication Theory, 11*, 14-35.

Gergen, K. J. (1999). *An invitation to social constructionism*. Thousand Oaks, CA: Sage.

Greenwood, D. J., & Levin, M. (1998). *Introduction to action research: Social research for social change*. Thousand Oaks, CA: Sage.

Littlejohn, S. W., & Domenici, K. (2001). *Engaging communication in conflict: Systemic practice*. Thousand Oaks, CA: Sage.

Owen, H. (1992). *Open space technology: A user's guide*. Potomac, MD: Abbot.

Pearce, K. A. (2001). *Facilitating dialogic communication: Basic facilitation training manual*. Unpublished manuscript.

Pearce, W. B. (1989). *Communication and the human condition*. Carbondale: Southern Illinois Press.

Pearce, W. B. (1994). *Interpersonal communication: Making social worlds*. New York: HarperCollins.

Pearce, W. B. (1995). Bringing news of difference: Participation in systemic social constructionist communication. In L. R. Frey (Ed.), *Innovations in group facilitation: Applications in natural settings* (pp. 94-116). Cresskill, NJ: Hampton Press.

Pearce, W. B., & Pearce, K. A. (2000a). Combining passions and abilities: Toward dialogic virtuosity. *Southern Communication Journal, 65*, 161-175.

Pearce, W. B., & Pearce, K. A. (2000b). Extending the theory of coordinated management of meaning (CMM) through a community dialogue process. *Communication Theory, 10*, 405-423.

Penman, R. (2000). *Reconstructing communication: Looking to a future*. Mahwah, NJ: Lawrence Erlbaum.

Petronio, S. (1999). "Translating scholarship into practice": An alternative metaphor. *Journal of Applied Communication Research, 27*, 87-91.

Selvini, M. P., Boscolo, L., Cecchin, G., & Prata, G. (1980). Hypothesizing, circularity, neutrality: Three guidelines for the conductor of the session. *Family Process, 19*, 3-12.

Shotter, J. (1990). *Knowing of the third kind: Selected writings on psychology, rhetoric, and the culture of everyday social life*. Utrecht, Netherlands: ISOR.

Shotter, J. (1993). *Conversational realities: Constructing life through language*. Thousand Oaks, CA: Sage.

Shotter, J., & Gergen, K. J. (1994). Social construction: Knowledge, self, others, and continuing the conversation. In S. A. Deetz (Ed.), *Communication yearbook* (Vol. 17, pp. 3-33). Thousand Oaks, CA: Sage.

Spano, S. (2001). *Public dialogue and participatory democracy: The Cupertino community project*. Cresskill, NJ: Hampton Press.

Stewart, J. (2001). Dialogue in the Cupertino community project. In S. Spano, *Public dialogue and participatory democracy: The Cupertino community project* (pp. 237-243). Cresskill, NJ: Hampton Press.

Stewart, J., & Logan, C. (1998). *Together: Communicating interpersonally* (5th ed.). New York: McGraw-Hill.

Stohl, C., & Cheney, G. (2001). Participatory processes/paradoxical practices. *Management Communication Quarterly, 14,* 349-407.

Stringer, E. T. (1996). *Action research: A handbook for practitioners.* Thousand Oaks, CA: Sage.

Yankelovich, D. (1991). *Coming to public judgment: Making democracy work in a complex world.* Syracuse, NY: Syracuse University Press.

9

FACILITATING CULTURAL CHANGE
A CITIZENS GROUP CONFRONTS
DEHUMANIZATION IN THE SCHOOLS—
THE LAST OF THE REDSKINS

Sharon Howell
Oakland University

Bernard Brock
Wayne State University

Kenneth Brown
University of Michigan

The gunshots in the halls of the high school in Columbine, Colorado ripped through suburban communities across the United States, shattering the belief that wealthy, suburban districts were immune to violence. In the wake of those killings, parents, students, teachers, and school administrators across the country confronted the question, "Could it happen here?" Many school districts acknowledged that it, indeed, could. As community leaders began to look more closely at life within the walls of their schools, a picture of bullying, harassment, violence, and social tensions emerged.

This study analyzes our facilitation of a group created within a school district charged with the responsibility of assisting a local school board in developing a safe and respectful environment in a high school. The group's decision-making process about how to improve relationships within the school lasted for over a year and culminated in a series of recommendations made to the school board about how to alter its policies and practices. The first issue the group chose to bring to the board for action was a resolution to abandon the name of the high school mascot—Redskins. In this study, we describe the facilitation process we used with the group, as well as efforts by the group to create a community consensus to support its recommendations to create more inclusive relationships in the high school (Johnson, 2002a).

The study examines our facilitation of this group through three interrelated theoretical perspectives. First, we draw on concepts from the bona fide group perspective (Putnam & Stohl, 1990, 1996: see also Frey, 2003), especially to explore the relationship between social context and the development and functioning of the group. Second, we use structuration theory as a general approach to understand group functioning, emphasizing the emergence of rules within the group studied that encouraged open, democratic processes and the use of resources to expand the range of options available to achieve this group's goals (Poole, Seibold, & McPhee, 1985). Third, efforts of the group to develop consensus in the community for the recommendations made are interpreted through a dramatistic perspective, exploring contrasting rhetorical visions of the community posed by the group in public deliberations (Bormann, 1972).

These theoretical perspectives provide the framework for exploring the facilitation techniques we employed to explicitly bring the social context into the group's communication and decision-making processes and to help group members move from a focus on individual identity to one of group identification (Cheney, 1983). These facilitation techniques were informed by our work in social action, feminist, and antiracist organizations. In this study, we emphasize facilitation strategies in three areas: (a) expanding the group members' shared social context and problem identification through the use of focus groups, (b) developing group identification through a balance of the engagement of conflict and the use of stories to create connection, and (c) enhancing the group's commitment to democratic, transparent processes in the public campaign to create community consensus.

This work began when Ken Brown and Shea Howell were invited by the school district to assist in forming a community group to work on the diversity component of a newly created strategic plan for the district. Brown and Howell were recommended to the district by the superintendent of a neighboring school district because of their work in defusing tensions that had emerged within that district. Shortly after the formation of this group, we, as the facilitators, and the group members discussed together our feeling that something significant was developing. Brown, an historian, framed the group's intended efforts as "a practice of democracy at its best." Members commented that the group was significant to them and to their community because they believed they were beginning to address issues that had long divided the community. Members decided to document their efforts and, as a result, we became participant observers, serving as facilitators for the group. We attended all meetings, prepared the agenda, facilitated and participated in discussions, interviewed group members before and after the group sessions, and kept detailed notes of both the internal group processes and the interaction between the group and the larger community. Local newspapers covered the campaign to get the school board to change the name of the high school mascot, providing a record of the strategies and statements of the group.

We begin this study with a discussion of the strategic goals for group interaction in each of the three areas of creating a shared social context, balancing conflict and connection, and creating community consensus. We examine the facilitation techniques we designed and implemented to achieve those goals, and conclude with lessons learned from reflecting on this group communication facilitation effort.

CREATING A SHARED SOCIAL CONTEXT

The bona fide group perspective emphasizes the relationship between the contexts in which a group is embedded and the evolution of that group. Relevant contexts include, among others, the historical, economic, cultural, and demographic conditions that influence the development of a group and its ability to achieve its goals (Putnam & Stohl, 1990, 1996; Stohl & Putnam, 1994). Social context, however, is an illusive concept. It does not refer to an objective, agreed-on reality but to the perceptions, observations, and values of those who experience it. Moreover, it differs not only by individual but also by social and cultural experience (Barge & Frey, 1997; Pearce, 1994).

One goal of this facilitation effort was to find ways to create a shared understanding among members of the larger social context. This task was especially difficult as the group consisted of individuals from very different cultural backgrounds whose perspectives on the history, role of education, and the changing nature of the community were often contradictory. Diversity in membership, although valuable for complex group decision making (Hoffman, Harburg, & Maier, 1962; Ling, 1990; Triandis, Hall, & Ewen, 1965), does not necessarily lead to a broadened perception of the context by group members, even in heterogeneous groups. Individuals identifying with the dominant culture often set the boundaries for group discussion, defining the relevant aspects of the broader historical and social contexts from their own perspective, whereas those who do not identify themselves as being part of the dominant culture remain silent (Adair & Howell, 1986). Facilitation strategies were therefore, developed to encourage the group members to have an evolving, enriched, and shared sense of their social context.

A second strategic goal of the facilitation was to overcome the contextual pressure to deny problems created by increasing diversity in a school or community. One of the primary difficulties in helping a community to explore important issues confronting it is to find ways for people who identify with the dominant culture to acknowledge problems in their community. Those in the dominant culture don't experience these problems in the same ways as those outside of that culture and they typically have little direct information about these problems (Martin, Nakayama, & Flores, 1998). When those in the dominant culture do recognize and acknowledge such problems, there is often a shared sense of dis-ease among those individuals. The challenge we confronted as facilitators was to bring into view the full social context of those both within and outside the dominant culture so that this group could become aware of the depth of the tensions in the community. This expanded awareness would enable the group to determine what problems needed attention and, ultimately, lead to better group decisions (Cox, 1993).

Changing the name of the high school mascot was a highly charged issue in the community. Two years earlier, a high school student had gone to the school board with a request that the name Redskins be dropped because, as a person of American Indian heritage, she found the term offensive.[1] The subsequent controversy over the request consumed the school district. Public meetings attracted hundreds of people. Proponents of the name change were harassed and received death threats. The town finally exhausted itself and the school board refused to take action on the mascot issue (Elvin, 2002a).

Over the course of the next two years, a new superintendent, school board, principal, and administrative staff began to take a more critical look at the overall educational plan of the district and at the relationships among its students. The district was experiencing tremendous growth. Once a highly rural area, noted for its forests and lakes, Huron Valley had become one of the fastest-growing communities in the metropolitan Detroit area. Upper middle-class professionals, looking for small town or rural settings in which to raise

---

[1]The elders with whom we worked on this project asked that we use the term "Indian" to describe the indigenous people of the United States rather than the more commonly used term "Native American." Although the word *Indian* is often associated with a Eurocentric perspective, the people with whom we worked use it to emphasize the sovereign status of Indian nations.

families, fueled much of this growth. Farmland was giving way to subdivisions and public services were experiencing the strains of growth. Schools, at all levels, were overcrowded and their facilities needed to be upgraded.

Along with the tensions associated with rapid growth, the school board and administration were keenly aware of the similarities between their community and those around the country that were experiencing violence in the schools. Because of these conditions, the school board expressed a new willingness to reevaluate its schools (Johnson, 2002a).

In 1999, the school leadership created a citizens group to develop a strategic plan to assess the school system and to set goals for improvement. A major aspect of the plan was to address issues of diversity and tensions among students arising from diversity within the district. Two specific tasks from the community planning process were to formulate a diversity action committee (DAC) to advise the school board on issues of diversity and to encourage the board to revisit the mascot issue.

The school board and the superintendent of schools contacted the National Conference on Community and Justice (NCCJ) to facilitate the process of developing a community consensus about actions that should be taken to address diversity issues within the school. NCCJ facilitators worked with a volunteer group of 23 citizens, school personnel, and students to identify and address tensions within the school. Group members became convinced that the history of the community as unwelcoming to people of color and the recent controversy over the high school mascot compelled them to reintroduce the question of the mascot as the first priority and to assist the school board in creating a community consensus to abandon the name Redskins.

Brown and Howell worked with this citizens group for more than a year, guiding the group in an investigation into the life of the school, helping to shape a coherent group perspective on diversity, and developing strategies to bring issues before the public (Lee, 2001). We used census data, interviews, and focus groups to create a shared consciousness in the DAC about issues surrounding diversity, inclusion, and safety.

The focus groups conducted did not employ random selection of participants, as is typical in survey research (Cragan & Shields, 1995), but were created, instead, with the aim of providing a picture of the life of the community from multiple perspectives. We, thus, engaged in a more ethnographic approach, using the focus groups to find deeper patterns of meaning, memory, and collective stories in the community (Bass & Young, 2003).

To create the focus groups, we reviewed the demographic make-up of the geographic area and investigated its history. The town has an historical society, a local newspaper, and is covered by metropolitan and county newspapers. The recent census documented the intensified growth patterns in that part of the county. This information informed the one-on-one interviews we first conducted with a number of key leaders in the school and in the community. These interviews were conducted in a very open-ended fashion, asking the leaders to talk about how they came to the community, what they knew of its history, and what they saw as the main issues facing the community and its schools.

A number of themes emerged from these interviews. The first theme was the commitment of people to preserving the wilderness aspects of the area. Almost everyone chose to live in the Huron Valley area because of its natural beauty and undeveloped land. Unlike other areas in the rapidly growing corner of Southeastern Michigan, almost one-third of the land in Huron Valley is reserved as public parks and recreation. Thus, development is limited and the rural character of the area is protected. This sense of a place of natural beauty and a healthy atmosphere for families was universally valued. Population growth was seen as inevitable, but unlike the case in surrounding communities, it was limited by public lands restricting the availability for development.

The second theme was the acknowledgment that the area did not historically welcome people of color or people who were in any way different from the dominant culture. A common reference was that many people had "moved here from Detroit to get away." Although rarely explicitly stated, it was understood by all that this meant white people getting away from people of color. The view of the community as a place of escape from diversity was underscored by the image that prior to the 1960s, the area was well known as a stronghold of the Klu Klux Klan.

In the last decade, however, new residents had arrived, not to get away from cities but simply in search of a more rural lifestyle. Although sharing with current residents an appreciation for the natural beauty of the district, these newer arrivals were concerned that the area lacked cultural diversity. Increasingly, these new residents were themselves members of diverse groups. African American, Latino, and Asian American professional, middle-class families moved to the area and gay men and lesbians became more visible, opening businesses in town. These newer groups expressed concerns about the image of the area as white and unwelcoming of diversity.

The final theme to emerge from these interviews with key community leaders was the history of the earlier struggle around the name of the high school mascot. All leaders interviewed agreed on the basic story, recounting the open hostility that met the efforts of the high school student to change the name. People both in favor of and opposed to the name change blamed outsiders, especially national Indian organizations, for the division. No one, not even the strongest advocates for the name change, wanted to repeat that experience (Johnson, 2002b).

These themes provided a foundation for identifying key individuals and segments of the community to serve as participants in the focus groups. Alumni of the high school, newer residents, parents, and downtown business owners were identified as especially important to the process. These themes also provided the background for forming the questions posed to the focus group members, who were officially invited to participate by the school administration for the express purpose of exploring perceptions of the school and community.

Using the techniques outlined by Cragan and Shields (1995), focus groups were structured to allow for flexibility. We established the purpose of the meeting as providing a picture of the community to help organize efforts to make the high school a safe and inclusive place for all students. We asked a series of open-ended questions designed to draw out focus group members' experiences and perceptions of the school system and of the community. We asked participants about the history of the school district and how the area had changed over the last decade and to identify any tensions they saw in the community. Notes were taken of the comments made, with participants informed that they would not be identified with particular comments, although the conclusions from the focus groups conducted would be made public.

Coupled with the earlier themes from the one-on-one interviews, the picture of the community emerging from the focus groups became more vivid. Although participants continued to echo their love of the natural beauty and wildness of the area, they identified a clear division between the newer residents and the "redneck, good old boys" who were in control of the life of the community, enforcing their beliefs through intimidation and violence. Community people offered several examples of such intimidation. In one focus group, held shortly after the attack on the World Trade Center in September 2001, one woman reported that her Chaldean neighbor was afraid to allow her daughter to attend school because she feared her daughter would be attacked as an Arab. Another person reported problems her daughter experienced in kindergarten because the daughter had friends who were of a different color than she.

The tension points the focus group participants identified in the community emphasized a number of areas. First, participants talked about the racial tensions that were becoming obvious as some whites reacted negatively to people of color moving into the area. Many participants reported negative comments made by the good-old-boys group in the community about the changing population. Participants also knew of instances in the schools where they or others had been harassed because of their race. One African American man talked about his son finding a noose inside his car, hanging from the mirror. Others talked of frequently hearing the term "nigger" spoken in schools and other public places.

Along with racial tension, people talked about problems of sexual harassment and tensions around gender. One father said that he felt like he was sending his daughter "off to the wolves" when she went to school because of the pressure for girls to be sexually active. Moreover, adults and youth alike agreed that it simply was not safe for an individual to come out and identify him- or herself as gay or lesbian; all were aware that the current phrase for being an outcast or loser in high school and in middle school was "Oh, that's so gay."

The issue of the school mascot, however, proved to be the one that most animated all of the focus groups. Everyone was aware of the previous controversy and the issue seemed to embody the differing views of how the community saw itself. Keeping the name Redskins was associated with retaining the traditions and values of the past; dropping the name was viewed as embracing change and diversity.

The focus group process provided language, images, and stories that enabled us, as the facilitators, to bring an expanded social context into the DAC. In particular, the experiences and perceptions of people in the community who were normally kept on the outside of and by the dominant culture were incorporated into the fabric of the DAC's group interaction. By incorporating these voices, group members came to have a shared sense of life in their community and of the meaning of the effort to change the mascot's name. These shared perceptions formed a foundation that united the members of the DAC. Shared meaning, essential to effective group functioning and a sense of identity among members (Eisenberg & Goodall, 1993), was, thus, created through the introduction of the perceptions, stories, and ideas that were originally articulated by the participants in the focus groups.

FACILITATING THE DIVERSITY ACTION COUNCIL

The interviews and focus groups helped to identify the categories of people needed for the DAC. Parents, teachers, students, members of the business community, and the police were considered the most important; there were no religious leaders or public institutions that had a significant impact on the cultural life of the area. The school administration, in consultation with us as the facilitators, invited 23 people to a meeting to ask them to commit to being members of the DAC for a year. Sam Osborn, a school administrator, welcomed everyone and explained the process by which they were selected. He talked about the strategic plan created by over 300 citizens and about the commitment of the school administration and the school board to create safe, inclusive schools. He also introduced us as the facilitators for the process.

Most people welcomed the opportunity to provide leadership in their community on issues of diversity. Some, however, voiced concerns over the intentions of the school administration; specifically, they asked if there would be any real change resulting from their efforts. Some people felt that they had previously been asked for their time and ideas and that those ideas had been disregarded. In response to these expressed doubts, Osborn kept referring to the strategic plan and its accompanying mission. He also gave people a view of the longer process of reinventing the schools, of which this step to create a more inclusive environment was just a part. His knowledge of the history of the district and his reputation as a fair and effective high school principal were critical elements in gaining initial trust in the process by members of the DAC.

At this first meeting, we shared the findings from the interviews and focus groups we had conducted. This information became a key element in how the DAC defined its mission and the problems the members believed needed to be addressed. In this presentation, comments that had been made about intolerance, racial and gender tensions, and incidents of verbal and physical violence were grouped together. This thematic, graphic organization of phrases and examples helped group members to recognize that there were serious and pervasive problems in their schools and community. The focus group information enabled the members to hear in a coherent and organized form phrases and images that circulated in fragmented ways through conversations in their community. As a result, the group was able to move quickly to discussions of problems of inclusion and safety in the community. There was widespread recognition that the community was in transition, moving away from its image as a redneck area to a more welcoming and diverse community. The high school mascot issue provoked the most intensity of any discussion, with many people feeling that the reintroduction of this issue was central to any effort to improve the climate in the schools. Group members reflected later that the information from the focus groups helped to "strip away" objections and defenses of some of the individual members of the DAC and enabled them as a group to commit to seeking solutions to the issues confronting their schools and community.

Our facilitation strategies for the group meetings were rooted in processes designed to encourage democratic dialogue and decision making, engaging citizens with one another to explore issues, differences, and similarities. In addition, we had to find ways to move the members of the group from a focus on their individual identities to a collective identification with the group. This was especially challenging, as many members had been invited to participate precisely because of their identification with a particular social, cultural, or historical perspective. Finally, we needed to find ways to develop trust and confidence among members as prerequisites for the group making public proposals that were bound to create controversy in the community.

In approaching these challenges, we developed facilitation strategies that attempted to balance the need for engaging in conflict and controversy between group members with the opportunity for promoting connections among members through the sharing of personal stories and experiences. We provided conceptual and historical frameworks for the interpretation and evaluation of these stories and experiences. This facilitation work was also informed by feminist theory that emphasizes the sharing of personal stories and confronting power relationships as explicit processes (Kirk & Okazawa-Rey, 1998). The work by Brislin (1981, 1986) and Murphy (1995) on inter-group dialogue was also especially helpful in pointing out to the DAC members the importance of establishing relationships of equality. Finally, our strategic choices attempted to overcome the biases of the dominant culture, which was organized to repress tensions, conflicts, and differences (Adair & Howell, 1988).

All of the DAC members attended a day-long diversity training where these strategies guided our facilitation of the group's interaction. The goals of the meeting were to create a common language about diversity, develop the basis for working together as a group, and decide on actions to be taken. We began the day with an overview of the process, stressing our facilitator role as one of helping the group to think about its mission and the actions it could take toward creating safe, inclusive schools. Group members were asked to articulate ground rules for what they needed to have a safe, supportive atmosphere in which to do their best thinking about the issues under consideration. Along with predictable responses about openness, honesty, listening, and humor, the group agreed to acknowledge that there would be different points of view and that members did not have to agree with one another, as long as they were willing to engage each other and respect differing opinions. This explicit acknowledgment that the group was going to deal with controversial issues reflected the influence of the community's prior experience with the mascot issue. Members knew that honest conversation had the potential to alienate fellow members; as a way to avoid divisiveness, they acknowledged that differing views were valuable to the group.

This discussion proved to be important for the group, as it helped to forge cohesion among members without demanding agreement and, thereby, fostered a climate of collaborative decision making. As facilitators, we stressed the importance of conflict as a source of growth, clarity, and strength (see Nicotera, 1993, 1994). However, to balance the potential of conflict to become destructive and divide the group, we explicitly discussed the elements necessary for creating a supportive group climate (see Gibb, 1961) and reinforced instances of them as they occurred in the interactions. Specifically, group members were encouraged to be descriptive rather than evaluative, focus on the problem and the process rather than on individuals, and participate in a spirit of openness and honesty. We also acknowledged differing points of view and invited differing ideas.

The explanation of these ground rules was followed by a series of exercises enacted in smaller groupings of 6-7 DAC members. The exercises were based on questions designed to draw out experiences and personal stories as the basis for looking at larger conceptual issues about difference. The power of personal narratives to create connection across difference has been discussed widely in reference to groups and organizations (see, e.g., Pepper, 1995; Sunwolf & Frey, 2002). People were first asked to describe their cultural heritage and to name one thing about their culture that was important to them and one thing that was problematic. They were also asked to discuss what the people who raised them did for a living and how they and their family were influenced by the experience. After the questions were first addressed in small groups mixed by age, ethnicity, and gender, they were discussed in the larger group comprised of all the DAC members.

Discussion of these issues served a number of functions for the group. First, it enabled people to see that diversity is much more complex than issues of race divided along lines of black and white, something that is especially critical to acknowledge in the metropolitan Detroit area, as it is one of the most racially segregated areas in the nation. Discussion of these issues also provided a basis for exploring the concept of race. As facilitators, we pointed out that race is a social and political construct, not a biological category. Drawing on the work of Roediger (2002) looking at the social and political construction of whiteness, we invited people to think about themselves and others in more complex cultural terms. In particular, by asking people to look at ways of making a living, we introduced issues of economic difference into the discussion without creating defensiveness. Finally, this exercise, through the stories it evoked, enabled people to connect with one another in an open-hearted way and, thereby, helped to produce an atmosphere of trust in the group as members came to know something more about one another.

One of the stories shared during this exercise was critical in helping the group as a whole to understand that different social and ethnic groups have very different realities. One woman, a Puerto Rican mother who recently moved to the area, related a story of a conversation she had with her youngest son. He had come home from school upset, and asked his mother to explain why he looked the way he did; that is, why he was the color he was. The mother explained to the group that she had taken a deep breath, closed her eyes, and hoped that this would be the last time she would have this conversation with one of her children.

The group was moved by her experience and her efforts to help her son value his heritage. As facilitators, we considered it to be important to help the group respond not only to the emotional impact of the particular situation being described but to recognize that this is a core experience for every person of color in the United States, one that is never shared by members of the dominant culture. We talked about how people who identify as white never have to explain their color or their difference, as being white is considered to be "normal" and, therefore, never requires explanation. Such differences in experience create at the core of our being different perceptions about our sense of self and the role of race and culture in individual identity. One of the main tasks of our facilitation was, thus, to balance acknowledgment and respect for individuals' experience with helping people to move from that experience to seeing larger social dynamics (Pratt, 2002).

A second exercise we employed in smaller groups that drew on people's experience was asking members to reflect on their earliest memory of when they saw someone treated unfairly because of difference. People recalled situations from childhood that carried with them the emotional impact of the experiences themselves. As people shared these memories with one another, we again facilitated the conversations to acknowledge the individual stories and, at the same time, to draw attention to patterns, shared assumptions, and larger social dynamics. Brown, as a professor of history specializing in immigration, was especially able to acknowledge individual situations and to provide people with a larger historical context in which to understand the experiences shared; for example, when a man talked about being excluded from the social life in his town because his family was Irish and Catholic, Brown presented information about the treatment of both groups during the late 1800s and early 1900s in the United States.

The second phase of the diversity training was designed to develop a specific set of concepts for the group regarding diversity. Basic terms essential for talking about issues of difference and multicultural issues were discussed. Distinctions were made between *prejudice* (referring to attitudes), *discrimination* (referring to actions), and *"isms"* (referring to prejudice plus the social, cultural, political, and economic power to enforce it). We also looked at concepts of privilege, oppression, target groups, and allies. Each of these terms, as well as the stories shared during the earlier exercises, helped members to talk about the climate in their school and in their community in ways that directed attention away from the intentions of the school, students, and staff and toward the consequences of the culture and climate.

The third phase of the diversity training examined attitudes of inclusion moving along an eight-point continuum beginning with repulsion as the most negative attitude and moving to celebration as the most positive attitude. We combined this attitude analysis with an exercise created by Judy Bryant of the NCCJ designed to help group members identify their own biases and places where they felt they still had work to do in relation to a particular "ism." We also used this discussion to draw distinctions between personal beliefs and the public responsibility of institutions.

Finally, the diversity training concluded with decisions about what actions to take as a group and the type of structures needed to carry out those actions. We encouraged thinking first about tasks or responsibilities and then what was needed to accomplish them, rather than beginning with set committees and defining the work in relation to such structures.

The group developed a series of recommendations to the board of education that included providing training to the school board and staff on diversity issues, reviewing curriculum, re-examining policies and procedures, promoting diversity in the schools, and changing the name of the Milford High School mascot. The group unanimously decided that its first step should be the recommendation that the school board abandon the name Redskins. The group discussed the previous attempt to change the name of the mascot, wanting to be sure that this time the effort was seen as coming from local citizens, not from a group of outsiders, and believing that the issue had to be addressed because of both its symbolic implications and its real harm within the school in terms of fostering negative stereotypes, arrogance, and insensitivity toward differences. Until the community was willing to confront this issue, the DAC believed that any other effort to address diversity would be seen as self-serving. The group, consequently, began to plan strategies for taking the mascot issue to the school board.

As a result of the session, DAC members gained a deeper understanding of one another and themselves. They listened to each other's stories, examined important issues and concepts, and assessed their community schools based on this shared information and enlarged perspective. The group members, consequently, believed that they had a responsibility to raise the mascot issue to the board. However, this decision began to erode the trust that had been created in the group. As the group discussed strategies, school administrators shifted perspective from their membership in the group to their roles within the school system. Sam Osborn indicated this shift in perspective when he said that he wanted to see all materials before they were forwarded to the board. Several members heard this remark as a call for censorship or manipulation of the group, especially the people of color in the group, who had little trust in the administration and its intentions. Although Osborn insisted that he only wanted to see the materials to help determine how to present them, the group member who identified himself as a member of a local Indian nation refused to continue with the group under such a condition. His decision to leave the group saddened the remaining members but also strengthened members' resolve to carry the mascot issue forward to the school board.

The group met in November and made final plans for presenting the recommendation to the school board to drop the name of the mascot. The DAC established a publicity committee to develop a strategy for the board meeting, create a Web site, write fact sheets, and circulate ideas via e-mail. The group also set up a process to develop and rehearse presentations. Group members engaged in these extensive activities to make clear their overall mission of creating safe, inclusive schools, and because they wanted to generate community-wide support to change the name of the high school mascot.

The group decided to organize its presentation by having two people speak, one high school student and one adult member of the DAC. Tara, the high school student, would begin the presentations by talking about the climate in the schools from her perspective. Dave, a respected business leader in the community, would then give an overview of the process the DAC had gone through, talk about the long-term goals of the DAC, and introduce the mascot issue as part of a larger process of creating a safe, inclusive high school and community. We, as the facilitators, emphasized the importance of strategies for organizing other people to come to the meeting, so that the school board could see that many people in the community were interested in creating a more inclusive climate in the schools.

As the time for the presentation to the board grew near, tensions started to become apparent between the DAC and the school board. School administrators who were members of the DAC thought that the board was becoming concerned about the possible political fallout of changing the name of the mascot. The DAC was committed to advocating change and was mistrustful of the board's political will. As these tensions mounted, Osborn gave the group a sense of standard board procedure and focused members' attention on what they could realistically expect from the board in response to the presentation. The most likely response was a simple "thank you" for the work the DAC had done, as the board never took immediate action in response to recommendations, no matter what they were. Osborn's comments were key in helping the group to see the board as supportive of the DAC's goals and mission and in forestalling disappointment because of a lack of immediate action on the part of the board. Debbie Squires, president of the school board, also attended DAC meetings to pledge her support for both the short-term goal of the mascot name change and for the longer range concerns about promoting a healthy climate in the school. She asserted that the board agreed with her on these issues and said that the usual slow processes of the board should not disappoint the group.

On the night of the board meeting in December, virtually all of the members of the DAC attended. The school board meeting was held in a large auditorium of the local high school with over 100 people attending; the size of the meeting was so large because it was the time for the annual holiday presentations from selected schools. When the DAC item was reached on the agenda, Osborn introduced it by referring to the strategic plan and to the earlier citizens group. He then introduced Tara, who said:

> From the outside, high schools appear to be pretty good for students . . . but they're not. I'm Tara, a junior . . . and I am privileged enough to see what really goes on. Students are still harassed; there is racism, sexism, and a million things that go on behind closed doors and sometimes right out in the open. Students are not any meaner; there is just a lot of ignorance and fear. This committee is here to change this, to teach students, staff, and the community acceptance and, at the very least, tolerance for our differences.

Dave Armstrong followed Tara and began by referring to the strategic plan and its goal to "develop a plan for helping each student to feel more valued and worthy while implementing a program targeting diversity." He explained that action steps accompanying this goal mandated a review of all "team names, logos, and mascots to ensure that they reflect cultural awareness with sensitivity." He then said:

> It is the unanimous opinion of the Diversity Action Council that the high school name Redskins and its accompanying graphics do not pass the test of cultural awareness and sensitivity and we hereby recommend to the board . . . that the name be changed. . . . In an era when we teach our children that it is wrong to judge or categorize people by the color of their skin, one of our high schools uses a name based on just that. . . . The term itself is derogatory and inflammatory to countless people.

As predicted, the school board simply received the recommendations without comment and without acting on them (Johnson, 2002d). After the meeting, the DAC members met for the first time informally at a local restaurant. Tara talked about a conflict she had with Osborn, who had objected to a part of her speech about sexual harassment and left it out of the written text he had forwarded to the board. This conflict, reminiscent of the earlier group fears of manipulation and censorship, eroded some of the group members' feelings of accomplishment. At the same time, however, both Tara and Osborn were willing to talk about the issue. Osborn explained his motivation fully, stating that he simply did not want to put forward in writing comments about sexual harassment that might be construed out of context. He said he had no objection to what Tara said, only to putting that particular phrase in a written document. The DAC members were critical of Osborn's action, but a level of trust had developed such that the members regarded this conflict as growing out of the dual roles he played in the group, not out of a motive to censor or control the group. Osborn's open communication with Tara and the group helped everyone to work through the conflict and to continue to work together.

The conflict also served as a reminder to the group that the school board, as an elected body, had concerns that went beyond the issues raised by the DAC. As the group assessed its presentation to the board meeting, members began to identify the importance of strengthening the political consensus in the community for change (Johnson, 2002a). They, thus, started a process designed to create a community consensus for the mascot name change.

CREATING COMMUNITY CONSENSUS FOR CHANGE

As the DAC approached the task of creating a consensus in the community, members decided to rely on the principles and practices that had emerged within the group as guidelines for how to approach the larger community. They emphasized the importance of their vision of the community (Bormann, 1985); concern for processes of fairness, openness, and honesty; the willingness to engage in conflict; and the importance of speaking about their own experiences and sharing important personal stories about diversity.

At its next meeting in January, the DAC reflected on what had happened since the school board meeting. Members reported on conversations they had within the community, letters to the editor published in the local newspapers, and other media coverage. The students in the group reported on the current climate in the schools following the proposal and what they heard their classmates saying about the name change. From these evaluations, the members concluded that community opposition to the name change at the moment seemed minimal, but that the school board was less than 100 percent behind their efforts and, furthermore, many of the students, especially those in the high school, were opposed to the name change (Johnson, 2002b).

To address these potential problems in changing the mascot's name, the group decided to employ a number of strategies. First, members discussed the framing of the issue to the community. Group members emphasized that dropping the school mascot name was a symbol for the kind of community they wanted to become. They, thus, decided to pose the issue in terms of two competing visions of the community: remaining a place that was isolated and unwelcoming of change versus a progressive, welcoming community that was willing to confront and overcome its past. This second vision had sustained the DAC in its deliberations, and members thought it would be compelling to others in the community (Bormann, 1985). They decided to present this position at a public meeting where citizens could voice their opinions. The group agreed to monitor the follow-up public response, watching for letters written to the local newspaper editor and news stories published about the proposal, and to attend school board meetings so that arguments in support of the name change could be advanced. Members took specific responsibilities and developed a process to check in with one another as time passed to the next meeting. In this way, the group thought it could effectively stop efforts by the opposition to define the attempt to change the mascot's name as one initiated by outsiders.

Public Meeting

The public meeting was scheduled in February and we (Brown and Howell) were to facilitate the meeting. After much discussion, it was agreed that the DAC members would sit together in front of the room and would explain their thinking and respond to direct questions, but they would not try to debate opponents. Instead, this was designed to be an open meeting where all views were welcome and encouraged. To promote that goal, it was agreed that we, as the facilitators, would begin the meeting with an overview of the process; Tara and Dave would then essentially repeat to this new audience their presentations to the school board; and citizens would then be encouraged to speak. We would facilitate the meeting by having alternate speakers, asking for a person in favor of the change and one against it to speak. Roseanne would conclude the meeting by talking about her experiences as a mother of students who had firsthand experience with the lack of tolerance in the schools. Members left the organizing meeting clear about their roles and the need to encourage other community members to attend the public meeting. The publicity committee developed and distributed flyers, prepared fact sheets on the rationale for the name change, and provided other supporting materials that included an explanation of the history of the DAC (Johnson, 2002c).

The meeting was held in the cafeteria of the high school. About 300 people attended, with local newspapers and television stations sending reporters and Indian organizations from the area sending representatives. Former high school students attended wearing their Redskins jackets; current students opposing the change did the same in protest.

We began the meeting by welcoming everyone on behalf of the DAC. Brown gave the welcome and Howell went over the purpose and process for the meeting, stressing that everyone who wanted to speak would be given an opportunity. Each person would be given a maximum of three minutes, except for the opening remarks by the DAC members, repeating their presentations to the school board, followed by alternating speakers with one person speaking for the proposed name change followed by one person opposed to it.

As the meeting began, it seemed that most people in the room were either in favor of the name change or were open to listening to the reasons why such a change was being considered. There was virtually no organized opposition. Students who spoke against the change did so with a sense of inevitability, as though the decision had been made and there was little they could do about it. Several prefaced their remarks with statements such as, "I know this has already been decided, but . . . ." Although members of the DAC reiterated that the school board had made no decision, most students in opposition regarded this as a temporary bureaucratic response.

Those in opposition argued that the name was a term of honor and that no offense was intended and, therefore, none should be taken. They also said that the name was a tradition and that many students looked forward to graduating as Redskins. Finally, they argued that cost was a concern, saying it would be expensive to change uniforms, signs, and symbols.

The most vocal opposition came from a local family whose members identified themselves as members of a local Indian tribe. The father said that he, his wife, and his children were proud to have attended a high school that had an Indian symbol. The wife and mother of that family talked about how important it was to her to drive up to the school and see the large symbol of an Indian chief in the building. Other members of the family, however, voiced support for the name change and questioned the authenticity of their relatives. Additional support of the change came from other Indians associated with the local tribe or from Detroit, and many spoke of their ties to the high school.

Those in favor of the change argued that the name was an embarrassment to the school district and represented values with which they did not want to be associated. One woman spoke about her experience of taking her daughter to visit a nearby university that had recently been the scene of a bitter fight over a similar issue. She described how her daughter, getting out of the car for a campus tour, pulled off her Redskins jacket and threw it into the back seat, saying that she didn't want people on the campus to think that she was racist.

After about an hour of back-and-forth discussion, one of the most respected town elders stood up. He said he remembered 1955 when the first name change was enacted. Prior to that time, the school name had been the Trojans. He made a joke about why they had changed to Redskins, wanting to distinguish the school from a popular method of birth control, and talked about how, for many years, he had been proud of the school and its accomplishments. He then said that the whole controversy had forced him to ask himself a simple question: "If we were to pick a new name now, is this the one we would pick?" He said it seemed to him that the obvious answer would be "no." That being the case, he said he did not see how or why they should continue using the name, given this opportunity to change it.

On a few occasions, members of the DAC spoke. They affirmed that they were all members of the community, had come to the decision to recommend the name change after much careful thought and deliberation, and were concerned that such a decision be made using an open and public process. One member, who represented the teachers' union, said that the union had voted unanimously in favor of the change.

Only a few more people wanted to talk as the meeting drew to a close and no new opposition speakers were identified. The meeting concluded with Roseanne speaking as a mother and as a member of the DAC, thanking people for participating and sharing her personal hope that the name change would happen so that all students felt welcome and safe. She, thus, gave voice to the vision that had brought the DAC to its position. Her comments appeared in the local newspaper:

> Why focus on the mascot issue? I realize that for many, myself included, this issue at first appears less significant than others related to education, the economy and even global issues. The time of when to deal with certain issues is often not ours to choose. . . . We know the term "redskin" is derogatory to many, whether we know them personally or not. . . . Our kids are watching and waiting to see how we handle this. . . . Do we use this teachable moment to act on our deep commitment to have an inclusive and accepting environment in our community and schools for all people? Or, do we say it's just a word whose meaning has never affected "us"? That tradition is more important than doing what is morally right. That is because we always thought we were honoring the North American Indian; we are justified in ignoring the information we now have. . . . Change is tough, but change is do-able. . . . This is a teachable moment for our kids. They get to see a process of request for change, a process of community dialogue and exchange of different ideas and beliefs, and a process of educated decision making by the elected representatives of our community. Most importantly, they have seen their community make a commitment to raise our differences and our sameness—our diversity—to a level of inclusiveness for all. (Garcia, 2002, p. 21A)

Telling Stories in High School

In the week following the public meeting, some of the members of the DAC met to evaluate the public forum. The group asked Robert O'Brien, superintendent of the school district, to attend and also invited Adrienne Bryant, an Indian elder who had participated in the forum. Group members agreed that the weakest part of their strategy had been their lack of attention to having discussions with the high school students. Adrienne said she thought that in a few days time she could organize six or seven other Indians to join her in an effort to talk to every class in the high school. O'Brien said he thought that it was important to make all classes available for discussion of the reasons for the proposed name change. He stressed that agreement from all students was not necessary but that the group needed to be able to say that it had taken every step possible to insure that the name change process was open and fair. After a brief discussion of logistics, two days were set aside for class meetings with Indians, organized by Adrienne, with a DAC representative accompanying each team of presenters.

These meetings with classes received mixed reviews from students and faculty. Some presenters were more skilled than others and some classes were more attentive or interested than others. In the end, however, DAC members and school personnel thought the meetings went well and that students were appreciative of the effort to engage them in serious discussion (Higgins, 2002).

School Board Vote

Before the board meeting to formally consider the recommendation to drop the name Redskins, the DAC was concerned that the board might be pressured from other citizens and turn down the recommendation or vote to defer it. DAC members organized through e-mail exchanges and held a session to discuss inviting supportive people to the school board meeting to give public comments if needed and to continue forwarding responses to the media.

On March 21, 2002, the night of the school board meeting, the room was packed with citizens and local media. After the usual preliminary processes, the board moved to consider the recommendation to change the name of the mascot. One member asked for a role call vote and each member of the school board gave his or her vote, accompanied by prepared remarks that explained the reasons for his or her vote. Debbie Squires, board president, talked about her journey from opposing the name change to deciding it was the right thing to do. She said, "I've come to recognize that terms not intended to harm can be hurtful." In the end, the board unanimously supported the change (Elvin, 2002a; Johnson, 2002d).

Superintendent O'Brien summed up the importance of the vote for the community, again echoing the symbolic significance of the decision. As O'Brien's (2002) article in the local newspaper explained:

> This issue is a defining moment for Milford High School and our community. Defining moments have no second acts. We get one chance to determine our response, "united or divided," "cast blame or propose solution," "self interest or a common good"; each requires a specific action or effort. It is ours to choose, but "no second act." . . . Our world has changed since the current symbol of Milford High School was selected in 1947. Change that we embrace and change that we reject. . . . Our current mascot . . . must change because we all want our future to be defined by what we know is right. (p. 13A)

Aftermath

In May 2002, the student body of Milford High School voted to become the Mavericks, officially leaving behind the name Redskins forever (Elvin, 2002b). The DAC met formally twice after the board meeting where the final name-change decision was made. One of those meetings was devoted to developing strategies for offering summer activities, organizing committees to begin to look at other areas of concern, and discussing acknowledging the actions of the school board. The group decided to ask the state legislature for a resolution honoring the board for its actions. On June 20, such a resolution was presented by the state representative to the school board, acknowledging its courage and leadership and recognizing the significance of the decision to the community.

CONCLUSION

This study reflects the potential of small groups to provide a safe public space where diverse individuals can work together to address difficult problems and to create meaningful change. In particular, we demonstrated that in groups comprised of individuals representing differing ethnic, social, and cultural experiences, facilitators can use such differences as a source of strength.

First, the use of focus groups to expand the social context of the diversity action council was especially important in expanding the shared perceptions of the dimensions and depth of the problems the group faced. The information gained from those focus groups helped to enrich the social context and provided a basis for building relationships among DAC members based on trust and commitment to the group.

Second, a climate of openness and honesty was established in the group through an explicit emphasis on processes and norms that encouraged the expression of disagreement and differing points of view. Conflicting ideas, placed in appropriate social, historical, and cultural contexts, were sources of group unity rather than division, enabling the members to expand the basis on which they understood and evaluated issues and one another. Facilitation strategies that encouraged members to share personal stories provided a foundation for approaching conflict in ways that strengthened the group and contributed to an atmosphere where members were willing to confront each other and to share their concerns with the group. As facilitators, we played a key role in validating the importance of conflict as a valuable process and in framing the tensions in meaningful social and cultural terms.

This facilitation experience suggests that processes that are valuable and productive within a small group setting can be the basis of principles of interaction in larger civic relationships. Clarity of process, commitment to fairness, willingness to listen to one another, encouraging conflict, and the sharing of personal experiences are healthy and productive practices that have the potential of helping diverse and often opposing factions to make decisions about important issues that matter to them.

Finally, this experience reinforced the interaction between facilitating or guiding a group and leadership provided by members of the group itself. By the time of the school board vote on the name change, several DAC members had emerged as public spokespersons, engaging in leadership within the group and within the larger community. This facilitated group communication experience, thus, provided a good foundation for the ongoing work that the DAC now faces in sustaining activities designed to continue improving relationships in its schools and community.

REFERENCES

Adair, M., & Howell, S. (1988). *The subjective side of politics.* San Francisco: Tools for Change.

Armstrong, D. (2001, December 13). Speech presented at the Huron Valley School Board, Milford, MI.

Barge, J. K., & Frey, L. R. (1997). Epilogue. In L. R. Frey & J. K. Barge (Eds.), *Managing group life: Communicating in decision-making groups* (pp. 340-342). Boston: Houghton Mifflin.

Bass, R., & Young, J. (2003). Borders of identity: Stories of the self. In R. Bass & J. Young (Eds.), *Beyond borders: A cultural reader* (2nd ed., pp. 13-16). Boston: Houghton Mifflin.

Bormann, E. G. (1972). Fantasy and rhetorical vision: The rhetorical criticism of social reality. *Quarterly Journal of Speech, 58,* 369-407.

Bormann, E. G. (1985). Symbolic convergence theory: A communication formulation. *Journal of Communication, 35*(4), 128-138.

Brislin, R. (1981). *Cross-cultural encounters: Face-to-face interaction.* Elmsford, NY: Pergamon Press.

Brislin, R. (1986). Prejudice and intergroup communication. In W. B. Gudykunst (Ed.), *Intergroup communication* (pp. 74-85). London: Edward Arnold.

Cheney, G. (1983). The rhetoric of identification and the study of organizational communication. *Quarterly Journal of Speech, 69,* 143-148.

Cox, T., Jr. (1993). *Cultural diversity in organizations: Theory, research, and practice.* San Francisco: Berrett-Koehler.

Cragan, J. F., & Shields, D. C. (1995). Using SCT-based focus group interviews to do applied communication research. In L. R. Frey (Ed.), *Innovations in group facilitation: Applications in natural settings* (pp. 233-256). Cresskill, NJ: Hampton Press.

Elvin, A. (2002a, March 22). Milford High ditches Redskins nickname. *Oakland Press.* Retrieved August 9, 2002, from http://www.theoaklandpress.com

Elvin, A. (2002b, May 11). It's the Milford Mavericks, *Oakland Press.* Retrieved August 9, 2002, from http://www.theoaklandpress.com

Eisenberg, E. M., & Goodall, H. L., Jr. (1993). *Organizational communication: Balancing creativity and constraint.* New York: St. Martin's Press.

Frey, L. R. (2003). Group communication in context: Studying bona fide groups. In L. R. Frey (Ed.), *Group communication in context: Studies of bona fide groups* (2nd ed., pp. 1-20). Mahwah, NJ: Lawrence Erlbaum.

Garcia, R. (2002, March 14). Council gives their closing remarks. *Milford Times,* p. 21A.

Gibb, J. R. (1961). Defensive communication. *Journal of Communication, 11,* 141-148.

Gravlyn, T. (2001, December 13). Speech presented to the Huron Valley School Board, Milford, MI.

Higgins, L. (2002, March 14). Indian culture and high school tradition: Milford examines nickname. *Detroit Free Press.* Retrieved August 9, 2002, from http://www.freepress.com

Hoffman, L. R., Harburg, E., & Maier, N. R. F. (1962). Differences and disagreement as factors in creative group problem solving. *Journal of Abnormal and Social Psychology, 64,* 206-214.

Johnson, E. (2002a, January 10). Berels, Borich face prospect of Redskin name change for second time. *Milford Times,* p. 2A.

Johnson, E. (2002b, January 31). Redskins nickname decision will come by end of school year. *Milford Times,* p. 2A.

Johnson, E. (2002c, February 7). Redskins may be history. *Milford Times,* pp. 1A, 2A.

Johnson, E. (2002d, March 28). Board gives boot to Redskins. *Milford Times*, pp. 1A, 4A.

Lee, A. (2001, December 27). Milford urged to change mascot name. *Detroit News*, p. 17A.

Ling, S. C. (1990). *The effects of group cultural composition and cultural attitudes on performance.* Unpublished doctoral dissertation, University of Western Ontario, London, Canada.

Kirk, G., & Okazawa-Rey, M. (1998). *Women's lives: Multicultural perspectives* (pp. 450-456). Mountain View, CA: Mayfield.

Martin, J. N., Nakayama, T. K., & Flores, L. A. (1998). History and intercultural communication. In J. N. Martin, T. K. Nakayama, & L. A. Flores (Eds.), *Readings in cultural contexts* (pp. 93-96). Mountain View, CA: Mayfield.

Murphy, B. O. (1995). Promoting dialogue in culturally diverse workplace environments. In L. R. Frey (Ed.), *Innovations in group facilitation: Applications in natural settings* (pp. 77-93). Cresskill, NJ: Hampton Press.

Nicotera, A. M. (1993). Beyond two dimensions: A grounded theory model of conflict-handling behavior. *Management Communication Quarterly, 6*, 282-306.

Nicotera, A. M. (1994). The use of multiple approaches to conflict: A study of sequences. *Human Communication Research, 20*, 592-621.

O'Brien, R. (2002, April 4). HVS superintendent comments on mascot issue. *Milford Times*, p. 13A.

Pearce, W. B. (1994). *Interpersonal communication: Making social worlds.* New York: HarperCollins.

Pepper, G. L. (1995). *Communicating in organizations: A cultural approach.* New York: McGraw-Hill.

Poole, M. S., Seibold, D. R., & McPhee, R. D. (1985). Group decision-making as a structurational process. *Quarterly Journal of Speech, 71*, 74-102.

Pratt, M. L. (2002). Arts of the contact zone. In R. Bass & J. Young (Eds.), *Beyond borders: A cultural reader* (2nd ed., pp. 249-261). Boston: Houghton Mifflin.

Putnam, L. L., & Stohl, C. (1990). Bona fide groups: A reconceptualization of groups in context. *Communication Studies, 41*, 248-265.

Putnam, L. L., & Stohl, C. (1996). Bona fide groups: An alternative perspective for communication and group decision making. In R. Y. Hirokawa & M. S. Poole (Eds.), *Communication and group decision making* (2nd ed., pp. 147-178). Thousand Oaks, CA: Sage.

Roediger, D. R. (2002). *Colored white: Transcending the racial past.* Berkeley: University of California Press.

Stohl, C., & Putnam, L. L. (1994). Group communication in context: Implications for the study of bona fide groups. In L. R. Frey (Ed.), *Group communication in context: Studies of natural groups* (pp. 285-292). Hillsdale, NJ: Lawrence Erlbaum.

Sunwolf, & Frey, L. R. (2001). Storytelling: The power of narrative communication and interpretation. In P. Robinson & H. Giles (Eds.), *The new handbook of language and social psychology* (2nd ed., pp. 119-135). New York: John Wiley & Sons.

Triandis, H. C., Hall, E. R., & Ewen, R. B. (1965). Member heterogeneity and dyadic creativity. *Human Relations, 18*, 33-35.

10

EMPIRICALLY DERIVED TRAINING TECHNIQUES FOR FACILITATORS OF GROUP DISCUSSIONS

Beatrice Schultz
University of Rhode Island

Patricia Kushlis
University of New Mexico

Interest in group facilitation has grown significantly over the past several decades as organizations have seen the need to use groups to solve problems, make decisions, and improve employee morale. There also appear to be a growing number of formal and informal groups created to respond to a continuing demand, perhaps even a hunger, for discussion, whether in book clubs formed among friends and neighbors or small groups that meet to discuss controversial issues. Many of the people who join these groups seek human interaction, sometimes under the guidance of an assigned facilitator. More significantly, people probably use such groups as a way to relate to others after years of experiencing the ennui of the suburbs, the breakdown of the family, and the dominance of television and other forms of one-way-only passive communication. These isolating factors in U.S. society doubtless have diminished the opportunities for dialogue, a void that discussion groups help to fill.

In this chapter, we examine a training program we conducted for moderators/facilitators of discussion groups whose task it is to discuss controversial, international issues in monthly luncheon meetings. These group discussion sessions are sponsored by the Council on International Relations (CIR), a Santa Fe, New Mexico, affiliate of the World Affairs Councils of America

(WACA), whose major purpose is to promote a better understanding of international issues and the implications of these issues for U.S. foreign policy among self-selected participants from Santa Fe, Albuquerque, and Los Alamos.

The luncheon discussions are held monthly from September to June with an average attendance of 80 members at each discussion. The format for these luncheons is that of a speaker who first presents an analysis of a current international issue to attendees, and then participants sit at a round table of eight over a working lunch for approximately an hour and discuss that issue with the help of a moderator who facilitates the discussion. The discussion session concludes with a 15-minute question/answer period with the speaker or comments offered from representatives of the various group table discussions. Some of the topics of recent luncheon presentations have been globalization, the Middle East crisis, terrorism, U.S. policy in Colombia, and the Indian/Pakistan conflict over Kashmir, each of which has implications for future U.S. foreign policy.

Prior to each luncheon, CIR moderators participate in a preparatory session where the speaker addresses the content of the upcoming discussion that moderators are being asked to facilitate. This preparatory session also includes a short review of some processes and problems involved in moderating the group discussions. The speaker presents an analysis of the topic followed by discussion with the moderators about the potential issues for group discussion. The moderators and the speaker also formulate possible questions to help stimulate table discussions.

As the people responsible to CIR for the luncheon discussion programs, we designed a special training program for moderators that involved a review of some practical group facilitation techniques and their theoretical foundations. We implemented the training program with nine specially selected moderators, who, over the past three years, had moderated five to eight luncheons. Almost all of the moderators selected had previously attended one or two training sessions we had offered that explored the functions moderators of discussion groups should provide. The specific focus of this chapter is on our facilitation training of the group discussion moderators we selected and the subsequent facilitation techniques they used in directing the participation of members of these discussion groups.

Each moderator was given a handout to study prior to the special training session (see Appendix A). This handout was a more elaborate and detailed analysis of the functions of group facilitation than had been the focus of prior training sessions and included topics such as the value of participant introductions; the necessity of establishing the "rules of the game"; an in-depth discussion of processes and procedural interventions that encourage participation; the usefulness of mediation techniques such as reframing, reminding, and summarizing; and the problems or obstacles moderators may encounter and possible measures for overcoming them. The training session lasted three hours and included an elaboration of each moderator function with examples and role plays of problems encountered in group discussions.

One week after this special training session, the nine participants served as moderators for the next monthly luncheon discussion. After the discussions were completed, they were asked to record in written form the facilitation functions they performed and to evaluate whether or how well these techniques worked for them. One week later, the moderators met with us for a 3-hour debriefing session in which they described orally what they had learned about group facilitation and also submitted written evaluations of their experience as a moderator. The next section of the chapter explains the specific techniques of group discussion facilitation that were presented in the handout and examined in the special training session, and moderators' impressions and reactions to the facilitation techniques they employed, including the extent to which they were useful for facilitating group discussions, followed by comments offered by us as the facilitators of the special training program. We conclude the chapter by examining some of the lessons learned from this process for facilitating group discussions.

ANALYZING THE DEBRIEFING SESSIONS

Participant Introductions and Forecasting Rules

When moderators met the group of seven other members at their discussion table, they had been asked to perform two important tasks. The first task was to ask each participant to tell something about him or herself, such as the person's reason for coming to that particular luncheon, his or her knowledge or interest in U.S. foreign policy and international relations, or something about his or her background that would be relevant to the group discussion.

The training handout stressed the need for this function to help participants understand the discussion process. In the training session, we asked moderators to open the group discussion period with a statement similar to the following:

> We would like to give everyone an opportunity to participate, to express his or her views and perspectives. Our talk activities (whether problem analysis or interactions among members) mean that each of us is talking to the group as a whole and that members

should refrain from engaging in "side-bar" (talking to one person only) conversations. We welcome your ideas, thoughts, uncertainties, criticisms, and feelings, as these are all part of an ongoing discussion, with one proviso: No attacks on anyone's personal views, not even comments such as "You've got to be kidding" or "I guess everyone is entitled to his or her opinion."

The use of this type of "icebreaker" at the beginning of the group discussion was intended to build a warm and open atmosphere in the group, and we explained to moderators that the literature showed that such introductions helped to create a positive climate for learning and interacting (Culbert, 1972).

The second task, after the relatively brief introductions, was for moderators to explain the rules of the group discussion session. As Shimanoff (1992) observed, "In a healthy group, rules should facilitate group processes . . . making members feel more at ease and increasing listener responses" (p. 257). If participants know the rules in advance, the moderator can help to move the discussion along and to make it more likely for participants to express their views (Chilberg, 1989). Moderators also asked participants to be considerate of all group members at the table—specifically, to speak sufficiently loudly for all to hear and to show respect for differing opinions and perspectives. In addition to emphasizing the need for participant interaction, moderators were asked to explain their role by saying that they would try to keep group discussion at an appropriate level of interaction, add vitality to the discussion (by reflecting on what a participant said or asking for other opinions), and act as a referee in cases where one participant was either too aggressive or too domineering (Keltner, 1989). We especially stressed in the training session with moderators that group participation would be the key to making the group discussions a meaningful learning experience for members.

Moderators' comments (Participants' actual names are used by permission).

Harry: I find this [the introduction] very important as an icebreaker. I also use it to assess how my group is going to behave, especially in identifying the "high talker" and the "low talker," and anybody with particularly relevant personal experience. In stating my role as moderator, I simply point out that it is my job to facilitate and to ensure that everyone have a chance to participate and to keep us more or less on the subject.

Helen: The first person to introduce himself or herself sets the pattern for others—the length, depth, detail, subject area, etc. I try to choose someone I know to begin the introductions or I start. I try to build group cohesion. I point out to the group subthemes or commonalities, or, for example, "This group seems to include four of you with children married to Chinese citizens." Forecasting rules works well and I stick to them. If a side conversation starts, I bring the entire group to a halt.

Linda: Before the introductions, I set the stage for the discussion by acknowledging what a special group we have assembled. I introduce myself (name and connection with the organization or topic) and I ask participants to do the same. When all have spoken, I outline the procedure for the discussion. I strive to be friendly and pleasant without losing the attention or control of the group.

Paul: Introductions are important. They need to be relaxed, welcoming, and as informative as possible, but brief. It is also very helpful to lay out the purpose and goal of the table session.

George: I think I did a better job on 5/22 [the May luncheon discussion] following the moderators' training session of setting the stage for discussion than I had previously done by emphasizing the need to speak to the person across the table, avoiding side-bar conversations, and urging all to participate. This was perhaps the most important improvement I made as a result of our training session.

Facilitators' analysis.

The moderators' reflections indicate that they were concerned both with setting the ground rules and with how the discussion group members would respond to an intervention when it became necessary to enforce the rules. Their concern was with how to deal with participants when there was a side conversation or a domineering individual interfering with the discussion process, and to do this without seeming to criticize a particular participant. Moderators were also concerned with the extent of group members' participation, especially the give and take of their interaction, asking to what extent they should fill in when group members were not too responsive. Despite these initial concerns, moderators' comments indicated that they had accepted a process that seemed to be helpful for initiating a group discussion session and that they had absorbed some useful techniques, such as introducing themselves and having group members do likewise, that made them feel more comfortable with this introductory process.

Procedural and Content Interventions

A key instruction to moderators in the training session was to help them think about when to intervene in the ongoing group discussions and with what frequency. We asked them to consider the promise of better interaction among the participants because of the type of procedural or content inter-ventions they used, but also pointed out some disadvantages of intervening. For instance, although facilitators can enhance group deliberations through their interventions, interventions also mean potentially interrupting the flow of conversation, which may not be acceptable or helpful in some groups. We discussed specific procedural intervention strategies for encouraging better participation by members, such as asking the group the questions, "Why do you think that proposal will work?" "What about this perspective?" "Haven't we overlooked?" or "Shouldn't we give some thought to . . .?" Such questions can also serve as content interventions because they can motivate more communication. We stressed that to be an effective facilitator is to have access to many such strategies (Culbert, 1972).

We also used several concepts from the relevant literature to underpin the value of this instruction. For instance, we cited Janis's (1982) prescription that those who can be truly devilish by raising new issues in a conventional, low-key style can help a group to offset majority dominance. We also stressed that when the discussion is off-focus, any intervention, as Keltner (1989) noted, should be made with great care; although it is important to help a group, it is also necessary to anticipate how a group will respond to any such intervention.

We advised moderators about the complexity of the facilitation process, including the need to examine their own expectations as a moderator. We emphasized some necessary procedural functions of facilitation, such as providing acknowledgement of everyone's contributions to the discussion and assisting the group to perform more effectively by making sure that all members have an opportunity to contribute to the discussion. In addition, we advised that one of the more critical tasks for moderators is selecting the issues on which to focus (Gersick, 1988).

We also talked about what moderators should not do. Although they are key to moving a group discussion forward, moderators were instructed not to assume the dominant position, for they are neither the content expert nor the appointed leader of the group; rather, they should think about the goals they would like their discussion groups to achieve and develop appropriate strategies for achieving those goals. We discussed at length how much con-trol they should exert, and when and how often to intervene. We suggested that if group members were actively involved in the discussion, there was little need for intervention. On the other hand, we discussed how a modera-tor could make a procedural or content intervention without seeming to be too directive, such as stating in a straightforward way, "I think we are drift-ing away from the topic" or asking the question, "Are we ready to consider another issue related to the topic?"

We explained that discussion groups need not be asked to follow the type of formal decision-making procedure, often recommended by group communication scholars for decision-making groups, such as using a sequential pattern of identifying the problem, examining potential alternatives, and then choosing a solution from among those alternatives (Chilberg, 1989). Indeed, in CIR discussion groups, issues pertaining to the topic are the focus of the table discussions; consequently, these discussion groups were not expected to come to a decision, although they often speculate about possible solutions and, thereby, express a need for closure about the issues. These groups are, thus, more likely to follow a process described by Scheidel and Crowell (1964), in which one member may advance an idea, the group discusses it at length, and after the group expresses approval, the members move onto the next idea or cycle back to a previously discussed issue for further discussion and elaboration.

Moderators' comments.

Harry: I use content interventions mostly to elicit thoughts from low talkers. I watch their faces to judge whether or not they are going to have any thoughts at all on a particular point. If it's negative, I wait for another opportunity. Content or procedural intervention is necessary also when we get off on a tangent. Then I make a statement such as, "This is very interesting and I wish we had time to pursue it, but for now, let's get back to the subject at hand." Then I recall the last relevant point someone made.

Bob: Usually, the purpose of decision-making group discussions is to solve a problem or, at least, to agree on a recommendation for a solution. In the case of CIR discussions, the purpose is twofold: to allow participants an opportunity to learn more about the topic and to express their personal views on the topic. Consequently, moderators need to encourage a productive exchange of views while keeping the experience pleasant. Although all the guidelines for being an effective moderator are useful and valid, I have a difficult time thinking of them in a formal manner. I go to the table and do what needs to be done.

Linda: In the beginning, I don't have enough knowledge or the expertise, interests, or points of view of the participants. To some extent, I must rely on intuition. I notice that there is usually someone whom the others respect, or whose opinion they respect. I tend to let the strongest (read: the most informed, most eager to speak) begin the discussion. In the introductions, I like to call on people out of order—in other words, I like to avoid going clockwise or counterclockwise. I sometimes rephrase the statements of a speaker before going to the next person. I pay attention to the group to see who seems eager to speak. Sometimes I coax (in a pleasant and gentle way) a response from a reticent speaker. I thank speakers for their opinions or comments, I acknowledge differences of opinion and points of agreement, and I solicit amplification of statements if I think the group has not quite grasped a speaker's message.

Nan: Listening to everyone alertly, encouraging everyone to talk during introductions, feeding back if they cannot be heard distinctly, helping to make the connections between what's being said and what others have already said, and showing interest—all of these work to connect the group for me.

Facilitators' analysis.

Moderators reflected that they were engaged continuously in monitoring the interaction of group members. Poole and Baldwin's (1996) appraisal of what takes place in a group discussion has relevance for the processes these moderators observed, in that how groups function depends on many contingencies. As Poole and Baldwin explained, group interaction is like "a series of intertwining threads of activity that evolve . . . in different patterns over time" (p. 222). These threads of activity include problem analysis and the substantive issues being dealt with by the group, but also social activities, such as sharing personal stories and showing respect for one another's views. In these groups, there is not typically pressure to conform as there is in decision-making groups; instead, members seem intent on building a cooperative atmosphere in which they can discuss the issue on the table.

Moderators reported that their procedural and content interventions in the group's discussion focused on how to encourage participation and interaction, especially in assisting low or reticent talkers to participate, asking participants for their reactions, paraphrasing a participant's point, and creating an atmosphere for a productive exchange of views. Moderators believed that participants actually wanted to engage in problem analysis and are more likely to do so when they think they may examine an issue in an in-depth manner. Moderators considered that they had helped their discussion groups in ways similar to a perspective expressed by Schwartzman (1989) as necessary for effective group discussion: by helping participants to find out the facts, build group solidarity, and meet individual members' needs for status and social relations.

Reframing, Reminding, and Summarizing

The literature from mediation training programs offers advice about particular communication techniques for helping parties in conflict to manage the situation. We made clear to moderators during the training session that mediation training programs emphasize listening skills, such as paraphrasing, asking questions, providing feedback, and other forms of active and reflective listening, which are depicted as ways to comprehend both the issues and the personalities in a dispute. We suggested that these skills would be useful for moderating the discussion groups (Schultz, 1989).

Mediators are also trained to use the specific techniques of "reframing," "reminding," and "summarizing" to improve the communication exchanged during a mediation process. Because of the controversial issues examined in the CIR discussion groups, we recommended to moderators that these techniques could be helpful for facilitating the discussion process. We illustrated the technique of *reframing*, defined as restating a proposal to make the idea more understandable or using relatively neutral language to alter a stymied group discussion. As an example, if a proposal for a solution is made that is immediately criticized, reframing would help participants to see the proposal in a different way, leading to a more inquiring response. Restating a proposal in this way helps to reduce the effect of inflammatory statements that members may express intentionally or unintentionally. Literally, reframing means restating issues without overgeneralized accusations and free from excessive criticism in an effort to find some positive value in what a participant said. By altering a message—either by changing the syntax or wording of a message or by clarifying the meaning of a viewpoint—one can help group members to re-examine their differences and perhaps acknowledge more commonality in their views than they previously believed there to be.

We discussed with moderators the reminder function as another approach for changing the dynamics within the group. The *reminder* in a group discussion could be any group member, although more likely it would be the moderator/facilitator, who processes what is going on in the group and makes a suggestion or a comment that deals with group process. For instance, if group members are stalled in their discussion of a controversial issue, the reminder could make a statement such as, "Why don't we hold the discussion on that issue? Because of time constraints, we should move onto another issue that also needs discussion." As another example, if a member makes an assertion but does not provide backing for it, the reminder can ask the group to consider what data support the assertion.

The reminder function is conceptualized as a continuous process that involves questioning a group's interaction, indicating constraints on time, offering the suggestion that members conclude the session with a summary of what was learned, or other similar behaviors (see Schultz & Ketrow, 1996). This function may improve the quality of group members' contributions by pointing out some of the processes that help a group to engage in a more satisfying discussion. When a moderator suggests, "Think about this . . .," "Let's go back to an earlier issue that may have relevance now," or "Can we compare these two concepts?," group members are reminded about some ways to conduct and improve the group's discussion. In addition, we advised moderators that interventions are better expressed in a questioning tone than in a declarative sentence, such as, "Is there another point of view on that issue?" or "Does anyone want to add to that?," but also to be mindful that having a sense of humor and having fun are important for building group cohesion and solidarity, especially in discussion groups. As Chilberg (1989) pointed out, a facilitator should have a comprehensive knowledge of various types of interventions to confront various group dynamics problems because that person is supposed to be both a model and an instructor of effective group interaction.

Finally, we advised moderators that after the discussion has reached a midpoint, it is probably wise for them to suggest that the group summarize what has been accomplished thus far. This intervention is based on the recognition that there are "breakpoints" in a group's discussion, where there is a need to change direction, consider additional issues, or move to some endpoint (see Fisher & Stutman, 1987). Asking the group to summarize from time to time, rather than waiting until the end of the discussion period to do so, is also a reminder of how much has been done and what remains to be done. This type of intervention in a group's discussion may encourage a reconsideration of some of the issues discussed and perhaps lead to formulations of some conclusions about what was learned from the discussion process (Fisher & Stutman, 1987).

Moderators' comments.

George: At the last table, my group included an opinioned and aggressive participant. This gave me several opportunities to reframe with such statements as, "I think Joe is saying . . ." and "Does anyone have a different view he or she would like to express?" I kept referring back to that person's point so that he knew he had been heard. It seemed to work very well. Also, I emphasized turn-taking as a way to deal with that aggressive member. By calling on people who said little or nothing, and saying we are interested in your views, I was able at least temporarily to derail the aggressive one, as he would have been embarrassed not to cooperate in that context.

I did not become frustrated by my "problem" participant but used him as a challenge to see if I could keep everyone else interested and involved. On other occasions, I have used summarizing as a method of changing directions when things stagnate; for example, "I think we have achieved a consensus on that point" or "Should we now consider . . .?" In summary, I felt like I had reasonable success, mostly through using reframing statements and encouraging turn-taking.

Harry: I tend to use summarization. Even framing the summary on the outrageous side tends to provoke members into talking. I find that summarizing stimulates some further discussion or makes it clear that it's futile to pursue the issue any further. In the case of CIR discussions, there are always plenty more sub-issues to take off on. I often will initiate one by a question directed at a high talker just to get things moving again.

Paul: As we all understand, the purpose of our table discussions is not to provide information; rather, it is on the basis of the information we share that we have an opportunity to express our personal opinions about policies to be developed and our reactions to be taken with respect to certain developments. Think of the process as a unit beginning with the title and the topic. The moderator should frame or reframe the issues in such a way that people see themselves as members of a single team working together to understand the topic.

Linda: One of the most challenging aspects of moderating is getting the group to zero in on a manageable part of the topic. At CIR events, the issues are frequently so enormous that it (sometimes) makes discussions get off to a slow start. When it comes to international affairs, there are so many pressing issues that people don't always know where to begin. I think it is okay to remind group members at the start of a session that we will only be able to touch the surface of a small part of the issue. What shall we do? Look for solutions? Express our opinions? Our frustrations? As a reminder, the facilitator can ask what the group sees as the desired results of discussions such as those undertaken at CIR luncheon events: Community? Camaraderie? World peace?

Bill: The tables like direction. There is a need to ask every person at the table something, but how to do so without being overly directive? It would be good to remind the group members that we want to hear their views. Sometimes the facilitator can ask, "What do you think about that?," or call on people randomly throughout the session.

Nan: I do reframe, restate—in different words—people's points of view quite often. I find this helps to both focus and channel the group.

Helen: Reframing works particularly well for monopolizers. These folks have a problem; they need to express their viewpoint and they need attention and power. It helps to reframe their diatribe into recognizable foreign policy problems and then refer to this several times during the discussion. If that doesn't satisfy them, another participant may tell them to be quiet, which is more powerful than if I do it. Then there is always the ploy of "Hold that while we get other viewpoints," but you have to remember to get back to them. (Alas.)

Paul: It is important for the group to stay on subject and not be allowed to wander afield. Of course, we must not stay mired in difficult questions but having heard enough on a question, the group must be helped to go on to the next question. Reframing and summarizing are very important in this regard; the ability to do this is a test of the skill of a moderator. Finally, we should remind ourselves and the table participants that we are here for a very short period of time, to enjoy one another's company and to learn something new—from the presenter and from one another. We want to go away thinking, "This was worthwhile."

Facilitators' analysis.

What impresses us are the strong feelings that moderators expressed about using reframing and summarizing, seeing their value not only in offsetting aggressive and dominant participants and as measures for keeping group members from going off on tangents but also for building group cohesion and for wanting every member to leave with feelings of having learned something of value and an appreciation of the discussion process. The technique of reminding, however, although used by some of the moderators, seemed to be a more difficult intervention for them to apply. Perhaps this function is more appropriate for decision-making groups, where, for instance, facilitators seek to challenge groups when they reach for a solution too quickly and when a delay may improve the quality of the group process and the decision (Maier & Hoffman, 1960). In addition, given the relatively short time period for discussion (1 hour), moderators said that they did not feel comfortable challenging group members about the backing for an assertion or suggesting other approaches for discussing the topic.

Nevertheless, these comments affirm that facilitation benefits from having a fundamental understanding of specific techniques that are useful for guiding meaningful interaction among participants. Moderators' comments also emphasized that a meaningful discussion adds to participants' education not only about the topic but also about how to interact with other members. What also seems apparent in moderators' comments about the facilitation process is that they used intervention techniques that group members could also learn. This potential for learning the techniques that moderators demonstrated could lead group members to consider playing an important role in group facilitation. This evolving process of learning about facilitation is not unlike what scholars have prescribed for effective leaders, in that they are considered to be people who help groups to reach a point at which members themselves are the primary source of help to the group (Anderson, 1985).

Dealing with Obstacles

We explained to the moderators at the training session that every group encounters some type of group dynamics problems, such as a lack of participation, competitive or aggressive behavior, lack of tolerance for other views, fear of opposing a dominant member, or an overly cohesive group. Obviously, individual differences and abilities that members bring with them to a group can play an important role in how the group experiences such problems. We suggested, therefore, that the introductions and forecasting of rules might include an explanation that groups may encounter some cognitive and relational constraints that can affect the discussion process.

The lack of sufficient information about different backgrounds and perspectives, or knowledge of the issues, can interfere with group members' understanding of the implications of their discussion of a topic. Similarly, when relationships among members become a dominant concern, or when members are overly concerned with gaining approval from the group, these factors may influence a premature unity in the group. Thus, by understanding that there are relational and cognitive constraints, moderators learned that they would need to be attentive to these influences and to take steps that could prevent or counteract such constraints by employing techniques such as questioning ideas, playing devil's advocate, asking for expressions of disagreement, or assessing the group's understanding of the issues (see Gouran & Hirokawa, 1996).

Moderators' comments.

Bob: I believe that every table has a personality and my objective is to help develop this personality. I am not as interested in the individual comment, per se, but in nurturing what the group as a group is doing. I believe that personalities are as important as the topic for discussion. I do not tend to focus on rules for individuals as much as I try to build the total group. Therefore, I engage in catalytic activity to stimulate or provoke conversation. My understanding of being a moderator is similar to the concept of "Gaia"—that the whole earth can be looked at as an integrated organism and that every individual is included in that organism. I try to create a situation in which everyone participates and, in this way, all the selves are taken care of. Sometimes, however, I do get a "table from Hell." I once had a woman at the table who would contradict the speaker and everyone else in the group. In that case, I had to say to her that if she didn't calm down, I would have to send her on a retreat for 30 minutes.

Harry: Side-bar conversations are a problem and, in such situations, I use questions to call attention to the need to address the whole group. In most groups I have facilitated, there has been a dominant person. Sometimes it is necessary to simply interrupt and pose a question to someone else on whatever point was being made. Additionally, the subject itself causes problems. Where to start? Again, by asking questions, seeing where a response seems to be, such as, "I see you nodding. What do you think of what "N" said?" But if no one responds initially, the moderator may begin.

Linda: Sometimes the table is composed of knowledgeable professionals, sometimes shy, uninformed people with varying amounts of curiosity; other times, groups of people who know one another quite well, and, at other times, strangers. I feel that there are problems with the seating; for example, a group of "experts" sitting together when it would be better for them to share their expertise with other tables. In CIR, members can spot cliques. Another issue is that couples sit together; one seems to be afraid to speak up when the other is present. They would learn more and add to the tables if they separated. Can't we ask spouses and friends to sit at different tables or with people they do not know?

Nan: The issue of side-bar conversations is crucial and I've begun to stress it at the beginning. My conflict is that people often come to these luncheons expecting a somewhat free-floating, nonfocused discussion, and we as moderators are gradually structuring and formalizing the process. I have felt a bit uneasy about this. Sometimes this keeps me from being as good a "rules forecaster" as I think I should be.

Helen: Most people don't have an "inner grid" (really a conceptual framework) on which to hang the material, a way of learning a construct to help understand what is going on. If speakers provide a clear example, moderators can mirror it at the table. I would add, however, that the more I moderate, the less I find I need to say. I wonder what's going on? More nonverbal communication? Increased comfort level?

Facilitators' analysis.

A frequent response from moderators to the question, "What problems have you experienced and how did you handle the problems?" has been "I play it by ear." In attempting to elicit the tacit knowledge behind that statement, moderators generally agreed that playing it by ear simply means that they try to appraise how the discussion is going, and only if they see a need to intervene, such as when the discussion has been taken over by side-bar conversations or when one person seems to dominate, do they step in with a suggestion or a reminder that "We all would like to hear what you are saying" or "There are other people who would like to comment." We also advised moderators that when they perceive obstacles to continuing a group discussion, it is necessary for them to consider whether to address that issue or to change direction by suggesting another point that needs clarification.

The important lesson is that moderators will have to learn to differentiate when an intervention is necessary from when it is not. As one of the moderators pointed out, the role of facilitation is sometimes a matter of intuition:

> Sometimes a discussion starts on a good path and stays there with everyone contributing. The moderator can then keep a low profile, intervening only to do a little steering toward new directions for the discussion. On other occasions, the moderator must deal with dominant speakers, reticent people, side conversationalists, etc., in which event, the moderator needs to play a more active role and apply some of the techniques discussed at the training session and the debriefing session.

LESSONS LEARNED FOR FACILITATING GROUP DISCUSSIONS

The training session helped the moderators to feel more confident facilitating group discussions, and they looked forward to trying some of the techniques examined in the training session. One often-repeated comment from the debriefing session, and later confirmed in moderators' written evaluations, was the concern that moderators had for finding ways to ensure that all group discussion participants had an opportunity to contribute, and they stated explicitly that the training session had given them more confidence in using facilitation techniques to accomplish this goal of increasing participant participation.

A concurrent concern was how to manage group interaction so that a group spirit would develop that motivated the members to keep processing information so as to gain insight about the topic, and moderators found that certain techniques were especially useful for motivating participants to stay engaged in the discussion. The emphasis on turn-taking, for instance, was a way to gain maximum participation, but also became a means for confronting dominant or aggressive participants. Similarly, reframing was helpful for disarming a possible hostile reaction to a particular point of view. Another technique, using frequent summaries during the discussion, also helped the groups to move in a new direction or to see that a prolonged discussion over a troubling issue would not be resolved at that time.

Both the mediation techniques of reframing and summarizing proved to be effective facilitation techniques for altering the tactics of competitive participants, as well as effective measures for changing the dynamics of the group, in that they encouraged more active participation among members who initially tended to hold back their comments and increased participants' willingness to disagree with a particular view. The reminder function, although found to be useful for improving decision quality in decision-making groups, was not used by moderators as frequently in the luncheon group discussions as were the other mediation techniques. In the debriefing session, moderators suggested that because there was only a short time for discussion, and because groups were not expected to come to a decision, they did not feel it was necessary to interrupt too often. They also believed that they might be seen as too directive by engaging in such behavior, and they hesitated to intervene in this manner because they were not sure how effectively they could use the reminder function.

An important consideration that moderators expressed in the training session was the education of group participants about the facilitation process. In addition to building a cohesive group of participants, they hoped to achieve the goal of participants gaining insight about the topic and the issues being discussed. They expressed the desire that participants would leave the discussion feeling that it had been a learning experience, as well as a socially worthwhile and enjoyable experience. In addition, moderators indicated a serious concern for the interpersonal relations of group members. Good interpersonal relationships in dyads make people feel better about each other, themselves, and their work; by extension, the nature of the interaction between a moderator and each group member doubtless has important effects on group processes and members' morale (Basadur, Graen, & Green, 1982). The ability to motivate participants' interaction in groups should have important implications for how long group members will sustain their deliberations and continue to search for explanations and rationales for particular viewpoints.

The self-reports given by the moderators in this study redirect attention to the importance of examining the relationship between the moderator, participants, and the discussion setting. An understanding of this relationship offers a viable approach for applying facilitation techniques in all types of discussion groups. In this particular case, the format of the luncheon discussion programs is designed to acquaint members with the fundamental issues generated by the topic under review in the hope that an understanding of these issues will lead participants to seek further information about the topic.

The luncheon discussion format, however, also has an equally important social purpose that provides people interested in international issues with a chance to interact in a structured, but nonacademic or judgmental forum. Thus, here again, these discussion groups have a different set of activities than do decision-making groups. For example, at the moderators' preparatory session, the moderators and the speaker develop and refine a set of questions devoted to the specific luncheon topic; the moderators then use these questions selectively to stimulate and focus discussion among the members of the group and, thereby, help participants to better analyze the complex issues pertaining to the session's topic. In contrast, members of decision-making groups typically generate the format.

Although the group discussion focused on a task—the discussion of an international issue—it is clear that members also engaged in these discussions because of the social component, and it is this component that moderators tried to address by setting a welcoming tone, encouraging members to participate, and assuring them that their views and perspectives are important. Hence, in contrast to decision-making groups, where the emphasis is on accomplishing the task at hand, with relationships among members considered to be of secondary concern, moderators of discussion groups, such as CIR discussions, see a broader mission of paying attention to the relationships among members because of the setting. Thus, this study shows that the integration of task and interpersonal concerns is vital for conducting successful group discussions of this type and may also offer insights into the utility of encouraging high-quality relationships among members of task-oriented, decision-making groups.

In summary, there were a number of themes about group communication facilitation that appeared with some frequency in the training session and in the self-reports given by moderators:

- The importance of personal introductions as a critical element in guiding the group discussion that followed. Introductions were seen as a way of taking early stock of the personalities to be engaged, their backgrounds, and the group's likely character.
- Setting minimum guidelines or ground rules for the conduct of the discussion was considered crucial for success; in particular, participants needed to know that they would be heard and that others needed a chance to express themselves.
- The implicit recognition of the need for moderators to be keen observers of the behavior of group members throughout the discussion period and to adjust the facilitation techniques they used as needed as the discussion progressed.
- The need to use various intervention techniques to move the group discussion along, especially reframing and summarizing, and the need to introduce new themes when conversation

appeared to be lagging by refocusing and calling on individuals who might themselves redirect the conversation in interesting ways.

- The importance of establishing fellowship—such as by listening to others, sharing perspectives, acknowledging contributions, and building group cohesion—is an important relational consideration that influences the process and outcome of the group discussion.

- The need to examine one's own goals as a moderator/facilitator and to understand that the purpose of that role is to assist the group discussion process so that members gain insight into the topic and the perspectives of others.

- The recognition that the aid of a knowledgeable facilitator, a good group climate, and a productive group can lead to a group discussion that becomes a fulfilling experience. As one moderator put it, "What is fun for me is gaining insight into the opinions of others. There is a kind of fellowship that happens every time, at every table, that fills me with a wonderful feeling about the kindness, graciousness, fears, and apprehensions that we all seem to share."

CONCLUSION

The increase in formal and informal discussion groups in U.S. society is perhaps most reflective of people's longing to escape the isolation that has resulted from the breakdown of the nuclear family, the flight to the suburbs, and the imposition of one-way-only communication through an homogenized mass media. Many people appear to be increasingly concerned by what they see happening around them but feel powerless to affect change. They, at the very least, want to express their ideas and feelings to others in a non-threatening group environment.

Well-moderated group discussion sessions while breaking bread with others allow people to do just that. The techniques that the CIR moderators tried and discussed in some detail that we reported and analyzed in this chapter provide some basic methods for successfully facilitating such group discussions. It is our hope that these techniques can assist others engaged in facilitating similar kinds of group discussions.

APPENDIX A: AGENDA FOR MODERATORS' TRAINING

1. *Introducing Ourselves: An Important Step in the Process of Moderating*: The introductions are an important part of the procedures that allow a group to understand the functions of a discussion group and the functions of a facilitator/moderator. Here is the place for moderators to *forecast* how the discussion will be run, that is, the rules of the game, such as, "We would like to give everyone an opportunity to participate, to express their views and perspectives. Our talk activities (problem analysis, solution evaluation, working relationships among members) mean that each of us is talking to the group as a whole, and that group members will refrain from engaging in a side-bar conversation (translation: no two people pairing off for their own conversation). We welcome your ideas, your thoughts, your uncertainties, your criticisms, your feelings—these are all part of an ongoing discussion, with one proviso: no attacks on anyone's personal views, not even such comments as, 'You've got to be kidding' or 'I guess everyone is entitled to his or her opinion'."

2. *Advising Moderators About Process*: Consider the following: What are your expectations as a moderator? How would you like a moderator to carry out his or her tasks? What would you not like moderators to do? Some important functions of a facilitator/moderator are to (a) provide a perspective on the contributions of members to the discussion, (b) keep group tension at an optimum level, (c) provide vitality to the group's discussion, and (d) act as a referee. Essentially, the functions of facilitation help a group with sense making; with meeting the individual needs of members for recognition, status, and power; and for solidification of the group.

3. *A Basic Assumption of Facilitation*: The art of facilitation is assisting the group in performing more effectively. How? By making sure that all members have an opportunity to contribute to the discussion. Consider also what moderators should not do. While moderators are key to moving a discussion along, they are not to assume the dominant position. Rather, they will need to develop strategies for intervention, such as: When should I intervene? How often? If the discussion is off-focus, what is to be my focus? How much control should I exert? How should I relate to my group? What are my assumptions about being a moderator?

4. *The Key Process Questions and Statements that Influence a Group's Discussion*: The essential characteristic of facilitation is to help make an activity or outcome easier to perform or achieve. A moderator can make a

content or procedural intervention without establishing a formal procedure. That is, it is not necessary for discussion groups to be asked to follow a formal decision-making procedure, such as first identify the problem, then examine potential alternatives for solution, and, after such analysis, choose among proposed solutions and ways to implement the decision choice.

One way that procedures are believed to work is by enhancing the quality of thoughtfulness of group members, by *reminding* them of processes that assist a group in analyzing issues and potential remedies, by specifying or asking groups to "discuss this . . .," think about that . . .," "compare and contrast ideas," or "Why do you think this proposal will or will not work?" By asking for individual reactions to problem situations, members are reminded about the functions of group discussion. And all moderator interventions should be expressed in a nonaggressive style with an understanding that a sense of humor and that having fun is a part of the process. Both are important for building group cohesion and solidarity. One prescription for breaking out of conventional wisdom is to be truly devilish by raising new issues in a conventional low-key style, asking such questions as, "Haven't we overlooked . . .?" "Shouldn't we give some thought to . . .?" or "Do we need to spend some additional time analyzing?"—these are some of the techniques that encourage creative thinking.

5. *Preparing to be a Moderator: Responsibilities that Moderators Must Meet: Reframing, Summarizing, and Reminding*: Underlying the concept of *reframing* is that members are encouraged to look at a problem in a nonjudgmental, objective way. If, for example, a question is asked in such a way that the only response is yes or no, then that question will not elicit information that could be important to understanding a person's views. Literally, reframing means restating without value-laden language, without overgeneralized accusations, without the personal attack, but also with a search for some positive value in what the speaker said. As an example: "You're being very inconsiderate—playing that damn music until all hours of the night!" To reframe: "When it is past a certain time at night, I would appreciate peace and quiet."

After the discussion has reached a midpoint, it is a good time to consider *summarizing* what has been accomplished so far. Perhaps it is a timing issue and there is a need to change direction, consider other issues, or get moving to some end point. It is also a reminder of how much has been done and what remains to be done. It encourages prospective "routing statements" and moves a group toward an evaluation of the problem situation and suggested remedies.

The *reminding* function can assist a group both in being analytical and in moving forward. It's a way to introduce questions or statements that indicate a constraint on time, a need to address other issues, or a need to move to some concluding remarks. It can also improve the quality of discussion by reminding group members of certain processes that can lead to a more satisfying discussion. Suggesting such comments as, "Let's think about the issues embedded in this problem" or "Will these facts help us to understand the complexity of the problem?" moves a group to consider or reconsider elements of the problem at hand. It is a technique that allows a continuing examination of the issues.

6. *Problematic Situations Moderators Have Encountered: Barriers that Hinder a Group's Satisfaction:* Every group experiences some group dynamics problems, such as troublesome members, conflict between members, a lack of participation, competitive behavior, a lack of tolerance for other views, group conformity, a fear of opposing a dominant member, or an overly cohesive group. Some of these issues can be identified in your opening statement as the problems that groups have to be prepared to deal with. You can then outline some of the ways that help a group overcome such obstacles. For example, you can discuss the need for turn-taking in a group, how important it is that every contribution gets some type of response. Underlying this suggestion is that group members are encouraged to listen carefully to every comment, to acknowledge the comment in some way, and even to build on a person's idea. You can demonstrate the concepts of reframing and reminding to reinforce that all views are part of a discussion process. You can call on reticent members and pay attention to the reluctant contributors and offer support to the dissenter.

7. *Two Important Factors that Influence Effective Discussion*: (a) the ability to cope with the demands of the task and (b) establishing good working relationships in the group. Another important task is to ask good questions. Broadly speaking, there are two kinds of questions that can be asked: open-ended or focused questions. Open-ended questions allow an expanded response, whereas focused questions limit the response to a specific concern. Another important skill is the follow-up question. Most follow-up questions are variations on the initial question, such as, "Why do you think so?" "Tell me more." Requesting more information is a helpful way to clarify one's thinking. Fundamentally, a good facilitator is a good listener who is naturally curious. As a good listener, you will want to know more about what the participant is saying. You can achieve desirable responses by paraphrasing, generalizing, challenging, and acknowledging each discussion group member. Finally, as with the introduction, you will need to find a way to bring closure to the discussion. It can be a simple statement, such as, "Thank you for your ideas. It certainly has been a stimulating discussion."

But more than anything else, the important rule in facilitating is just to be yourself. Being authentic, even if the discussion does not necessarily go according to your plan, you will find that group members will have respect for your efforts and conclude that what you did was good enough.

REFERENCES

Anderson, J. D. (1985). Working with groups: Little-known facts that challenge well-known myths. *Small Group Behavior, 16*, 276 -283.

Basadur, M., Graen, G. B., & Green, S. G. (1982). Training in creative problem finding and problem solving in an industrial research organization. *Organizational Behavior & Human Performance, 30*, 41-70.

Chilberg, J. C. (1989). A review of group process designs for facilitating communication. *Management Communication Quarterly, 3*, 51-70.

Culbert, S. A. (1972). Accelerating participant learning: A continuing challenge in trainer intervention. In W. G. Dyer (Ed.), *Modern theory and method in group training* (pp. 116-146). New York: Van Nostrand Reinhold.

Fisher, B. A., & Stutman, R. K. (1987). An assessment of group trajectories: Analyzing development breakpoints. *Communication Quarterly, 35*, 105-124.

Gersick, C. J. G. (1988). Time and transitions in work teams: Toward a new model of group development. *Academy of Management Journal, 31*, 9-41.

Gouran, D. S., & Hirokawa, R. Y. (1996). Functional theory and communication in decision-making and problem-solving groups: An expanded view. In R. Y. Hirowawa & M. S. Poole (Eds.), *Communication and group decision making* (2nd ed., pp. 55-80). Thousand Oaks, CA: Sage.

Janis, I. L. (1982). *Groupthink: Psychological studies of policy decisions and fiascoes.* Boston: Houghton Mifflin.

Keltner, J. (1989). The leader-trainer facilitator. *Management Communication Quarterly, 3*, 8-22.

Maier, N. R. F., & Hoffman, L. R. (1960). Quality of first and second solutions in group dynamics. *Journal of Applied Psychology, 44*, 278-283.

Poole, M. S., & Baldwin, C. L. (1996). Developmental processes in group decision making. In R. Y. Hirokawa & M. S. Poole (Eds.), *Communication and group decision making* (2nd ed. pp. 215-241). Thousand Oaks, CA: Sage.

Scheidel, T. M., & Crowell, L. (1964). Idea development in small discussion groups. *Quarterly Journal of Speech, 50*, 140-145.

Schultz, B. (1989). Conflict training programs: Implications for theory and research. *Negotiation Journal, 5*, 301-311.

Schultz, B., & Ketrow, S. (1996). Improving decision quality in the small group: The role of the reminder. In R. S. Cathcart, L. A. Samovar, & L. D. Henman (Eds.), *Small group communication: Theory & practice* (7th ed., pp. 404-410). Dubuque, IA: Brown & Benchmark.

Schwartzman, H. B. (1989). *The meeting: Gatherings in organizations and communities.* New York: Plenum Press.

Shimanoff, S. B. (1992). Group interaction via communication rules. In R. S. Cathcart & L. A. Samovar (Eds.), *Small group communication: Theory and practice* (6th ed., pp. 250-262). Dubuque, IA: Brown & Benchmark.

ABOUT THE EDITOR AND AUTHORS

ABOUT THE EDITOR

Lawrence R. Frey (PhD, University of Kansas, 1979) is a Professor and Associate Chair of the Department of Communication at The University of Colorado at Boulder. He is the author or editor of 12 books, 3 special journal issues, and more than 55 published book chapters and journal articles. He is the recipient of 11 distinguished scholarship awards, including the 2000 Gerald M. Phillips Award for Distinguished Applied Communication Scholarship from the National Communication Association (NCA); the 2004, 2003, and 2000 Ernest Bormann Research Award from NCA's Group Communication Division, for, respectively, the edited texts *Group Communication in Context: Studies of Bona Fide Groups* (2nd ed.), *New Directions in Group Communication,* and *The Handbook of Group Communication Theory and Research* (coedited with Dennis S. Gouran and Marshall Scott Poole); a 1999 Special Recognition Award from NCA's Applied Communication Division for an edited special issue of the *Journal of Applied Communication Research* on "Communication and Social Justice Research"; the 1998 National Jesuit Book Award (Professional Studies Category) and the 1988 Distinguished Book Award from NCA's Applied

Communication Division for his coauthored text (with Mara B. Adelman) *The Fragile Community: Living Together With AIDS*; and the 1995 Gerald R. Miller Award from NCA's Interpersonal and Small Group Interaction Division and the 1994 Distinguished Book Award from NCA's Applied Communication Division for his edited text *Group Communication in Context: Studies of Natural Groups*. He is a past president of the Central States Communication Association and a recipient of the Outstanding Young Teacher Award from that organization, as well as a 2003 Master Teacher Award from the Communication and Instruction Interest Group of the Western States Communication Association.

ABOUT THE AUTHORS

Joseph H. Albeck (MD, Harvard University, 1970) practices at the McLean Hospital and is a Clinical Instructor in Psychiatry at Harvard Medical School. His interests include psychopharmacology and the intergenerational transmission of psychological trauma and resilience. Since the 1970s, he has been a leader of groups for children of Holocaust survivors, has written commemorative poetry and lyrics for choral music, as well as textbook chapters and professional articles on Holocaust-related subjects. He has been active in professional training endeavors, the Harvard Trauma Study Group, has lectured in Europe and North America, and is emeritus chairman for Intergenerational Aspects of Trauma for the International Society for Traumatic Stress Studies. He is also a founder of the New England Holocaust Memorial, and for the past 10 years has been an officer of TRT, Inc., sponsoring participant research encounters between groups in conflict.

Dan Bar-On (PhD, Hebrew University of Jerusalem) was born in 1938 in Haifa to parents of German descent. He was a member of Kibbutz Revivim for 25 years where he served as a farmer, educator, and secretary of the Kibbutz, and worked in its clinic, specializing in therapy and research with families of Holocaust survivors. In 1985, he launched pioneering field research in Germany, studying the psychological and moral after-effects of the Holocaust on the children of the perpetrators. His book *Legacy of Silence: Encounters with Children of the Third Reich* (1989, Harvard University Press) was translated and published in French, German, Japanese, and Hebrew. Bar-On subsequently brought together descendants of survivors and perpetrators for five intensive encounters (the TRT group, shown by the British Broadcasting Corporation on *TimeWatch*, October,

1993), as well as students from the third generation of both sides. His book *Fear and Hope: Three Generations of Holocaust Survivors' Families* was published in Hebrew, English, German, and Chinese and his latest book is *The Indescribable and the Undiscussabe* (1999, Central European University Press). In 1998, Bar-On was the Ida E. King Chair for Holocaust and Genocide Studies at Stockton College of New Jersey and, in 1999, received an Honorary Doctorate from that college. He is permanently a Professor of Psychology in the Department of Behavioral Sciences at Ben-Gurion University, where he served as department chair from 1993-1995 and has assumed that role again for 2003-2005. In 1996, he was awarded the David Lopatie Chair for Post-Holocaust Psychological Studies, and in 2001, he received the Cross of Merit from Germany's President Dr. Johannes Rau. He is currently the Co-Director (with Dr. Sami Adwan, Bethlehem University) of PRIME (Peace Research Institute in the Middle East) near Beit Jala, Palestine National Authority. In June 2001, he and Dr. Adwan received the Alexander Langer Prize in Bolzano, Italy, for their efforts in peace building between Palestinians and Israelis, and in June 2003, he was awarded (with the Palestinian author Mahmud Darwish) the Eric Maria Remarque Peace Prize.

Bernard Brock (PhD, Northwestern University, 1965) is a Professor Emeritus of Communication and Codirector of the Center for Arts and Public Policy at Wayne State University. He teaches contemporary rhetorical theory and criticism with applications to political campaigns and social movements. He has published over 40 professional articles and book chapters and is the author of the texts *Kenneth Burke in the 21st Century* and *Kenneth Burke and Contemporary European Thought: A Rhetoric in Transition*, and a coauthor of the texts *Methods of Rhetorical Criticism: A Twentieth-Century Perspective* (3 editions) and *Public Policy Decision-Making: Systems and Comparative Advantages Debate*. He has been active in political campaigns throughout the Detroit metropolitan area.

Benjamin J. Broome (PhD, University of Kansas, 1980) is a Professor in the Hugh Downs School of Human Communication at Arizona State University, where he teaches intercultural communication, conflict resolution, and group facilitation. His research interests focus on third-party facilitation and interactive design methodologies. Since serving as Senior Fulbright Scholar in Cyprus from 1994-1996, where he offered workshops, seminars, and training in intergroup relations, he has continued to work actively with a number of citizen peace-building groups in the eastern Mediterranean. He also has facilitated design workshops with several Native American Tribes and with numerous government, corporate, and nonprofit organizations. His publications have appeared in leading national and international journals, and his scholarship has been recognized with several awards from the National Communication Association and the International Association of Conflict Management.

Kenneth Brown (PhD, University of Michigan, 2001) is an Assistant Professor at the University of Michigan in the Residential College. He specializes in the history of immigrant movements in the United States. He has been a lead consultant for the National Conference for Community and Justice for over 5 years, specializing in work with public employees and law enforcement personnel.

Donald G. Ellis (PhD, University of Utah, 1976) is a Professor in the School of Communication at the University of Hartford. His research interests are in the area of language and social interaction, with particular emphasis on communicative practices between ethnic groups in conflict. His work seeks to examine the relationship between micro-linguistic and interaction processes and macro-social and communicative categories, such as culture, ethnicity, and dialogue. He is currently involved in research pertaining to dialogue groups between Israeli-Jews and Palestinians. Professor Ellis is the past editor of the journal *Communication Theory* and the author of numerous journal articles. His books include *Contemporary Issues in Discourse Processes*, *Small Group Decision Making*, *From Language to Communication*, and *Crafting Society: Ethnicity, Class, and Communication Theory*. He has lectured widely and been a Summer Institute Fellow at the Asch Center For Ethnopolitical Conflict at the University of Pennsylvania. He also works in his home community with dispute resolution organizations.

Sharon Howell (PhD, Wayne State University, 1983) is a Professor of Communication at Oakland University, where she teaches public argument, multicultural communication, and social movements. She is the author of the text *Reflections of Ourselves: Mass Media and the Evolution of the Female Identity*, has published numerous articles on social movements, and contributes regularly to Detroit-area newspapers. She has been a community organizer for over three decades.

Holly Siebert Kawakami (MA, MBA) is a doctoral candidate in the Department of Communication and Journalism at the University of New Mexico and currently works there in the Center for Health Promotion and Disease Prevention. Her career in intercultural communication spans over 20 years, based in Japan as a U.S. national. She has served as an Associate Professor at the Osaka International Women's University and on the faculty of Kanda University of International Studies and Gakushuin University. Her business-sector work has included intercultural and diversity training and facilitation, and consulting for transnational corporations and Japanese local governments. Fluent in Japanese language and culture, one of her research interests is in the connection of nonverbal and conflict communication to culture, which led to the search for a facilitation methodology—kinesics—for bridging diverse communication styles and building global teams. In recognition of her contributions, she was made an honorary member of SIETAR Japan (Society for Intercultural Education, Training & Research) and the Forum for Corporate Communication (Tokyo). She also has received the International Award from the foundation of former Prime Minister and Nobel Peace Prize recipient Eisaku Sato.

Ifat Maoz (PhD, Haifa University, 1996), a social psychologist, is an Assistant Professor in the Department of Communication and Journalism at the Hebrew University of Jerusalem, where she teaches social psychology and communication and psychological aspects of conflict and intergroup relations. In 2000-2002, she was a director of nationwide evaluation research on Jewish-Arab coexistence activities in Israel, conducted for the Abraham Fund. She was a visiting scholar in the Department of Psychology at Stanford University in Winter/Spring 1996, and during 2002-2003, she was a visiting scholar at the Solomon Asch Center for Ethnopolitical Conflict at the University of Pennsylvania. Her main research interests are cognitive-perceptual mechanisms in conflict and negotiation, evaluation of intergroup contact interventions, peace building and reconciliation through dialogue, and patterns of communication and interaction between groups in conflict.

Beatrice G. Schultz (PhD, University of Michigan, 1969) is a Professor Emerita in the Department of Communication Studies at the University of Rhode Island. She has spent much of the past 30 years conducting research on leadership and the dynamics of group decision-making effectiveness. Her research interests cover various areas of group performance, with a special interest in facilitating group problem solving and decision making. Her research on leadership emergence and decision effectiveness has appeared in *Communication Quarterly*, *Small Group Communication*, *Small Group Behavior*, and *Negotiation Journal*. She is the author of the text *Communication in the Small Group: Theory and Practice* (2nd ed.; Harper Collins, 1996). She currently serves as a trainer in group facilitation and conflict resolution and lives in Santa Fe, New Mexico.

Richard W. Sline (PhD, University of Utah, 1999) is an Assistant Professor of Communication at Weber State University where he teaches organizational communication, advanced small group communication, intercultural communication, and health communication. He also codesigned and teaches an award-winning humanities, general education course on interpersonal and small group communication that is now being offered as a concurrent enrollment course for high school seniors in Northern Utah, as well as at Weber State. His research interests include team and organizational commitment, communication and emotionality, and leadership transition in nonprofit organizations. He has coauthored book chapters on the impact of expressed emotions on work team collaboration and turning points in romantic relationships. He spent the first 20 years of his career as a university administrator before pursuing his doctorate in organizational and small group communication, and he has served as a consultant to for-profit corporations and nonprofit organizations for nearly 20 years.

Shawn Spano (PhD, Indiana University, 1988) is a Professor in the Communication Studies Department at San Jose State University (SJSU), and a senior consultant with the Public Dialogue Consortium. His research interests include dialogic communication theory and practice in public and educational settings. He is the author of *Public Dialogue and Participatory Democracy*, and has published articles in *Political Communication*, *Southern Communication Journal*, *Human Systems*, and the *Basic Communication Course Annual*, among others. He does consulting and communication training workshops for a variety of local government and nonprofit organizations. As the Associate Director for the SJSU Center for Faculty Development and Support, he also conducts teaching workshops and one-on-one teaching consultations, in addition to facilitating focus group meetings and department retreats. He is the recipient of the 1999-2000 Outstanding Professor award at SJSU, and was recently invited to give the Low Lecture at Southeast Missouri State University.

Sunwolf (PhD, University of California, Santa Barbara, 1998; JD, University of Denver College of Law, 1976) is an Associate Professor of Communication at Santa Clara University, where she is also completing post-doctoral studies in counseling psychology. A former trial attorney and Training Director for Colorado's Public Defender Office, Sunwolf regularly facilitates training groups of trial attorneys nationally. She currently serves on the faculties of the National Criminal Defense College at Mercer Law School and Santa Clara University Law School's Death Penalty College, and also teaches at the national Capital Case Defense Seminar of the California Attorneys for Criminal Justice. Her research interests focus on jury deliberations, symbolic processes in groups, and social influence during group decision making. She maintains a commitment to social justice research and is past chair of the National Communication Association's (NCA) Applied Communication Division and serves on the editorial boards of the *Journal of Applied Communication Research* and *Communication Studies*. Her research on real-world jury deliberations (coauthored with David Seibold) received the 2000 Dennis S. Gouran Research Award from NCA's Group Communication Division. Currently, her research examines children's and adolescents' experiences with social exclusion and their communication attempts to penetrate or erect peer group boundaries. She offers workshops to train school administrators, teachers, and children's group leaders in facilitation techniques that promote social inclusion in children's groups.

AUTHOR INDEX

SUBJECT INDEX

Printed in the United States
R3557000001B/R35570PG91981LVX2B/7-18/A